Limited Liability
Companies

FOR

DUMMIES®

2ND EDITION

Limited Liability Companies
FOR
DUMMIES®
2ND EDITION

by Jennifer Reuting

WILEY

Wiley Publishing, Inc.

Limited Liability Companies For Dummies®, 2nd Edition

Published by
Wiley Publishing, Inc.
111 River St.
Hoboken, NJ 07030-5774
www.wiley.com

WILEY

About the Author

Jennifer Reuting is one of the foremost experts on corporate structuring and limited liability companies. She has been entrusted by thousands of companies over the years to address their individual corporate needs. In 2001, she founded InCorp, a registered agent and compliance firm. Now one of the "Big Four" national registered agent companies, InCorp services over 100,000 clients nationwide. InCorp specializes in servicing medium to large businesses, accountancy firms, and law firms.

To service the needs of individuals, upstarts, and small businesses, Jennifer founded MyLLC.com, a company that focuses on offering affordable business entity solutions. Jennifer lends her talents to corporate structuring to the clients at MyLLC.com, providing affordable yet comprehensive solutions for their business needs.

Jennifer's newest venture, DocRun.com, was born out of the need to provide the readers of this book with an easy, affordable way to create operating agreements and other start-up documents.

Dedication

This one's for you, Dad.

Author's Acknowledgments

I'd like to thank Mike Lewis for his time and patience; and Tim Gallan and Caitie Copple for working their magic!

My sincere thanks to my agent, Andy Barzvi, at ICM, whose time and effort has made this opportunity possible. Whoever said agents aren't likeable has obviously never met Andy. Also, I'd like to thank Chris Von Goetz at ICM for being my champion.

A million thanks to my cofounder, Greg Monterrosa — without him, MyLLC. com wouldn't be what it is today — and to Doug Ansell for all of his hard work and dedication to help make this book great.

And last but not least, I'd like to thank Dan Bliss for keeping me smiling, even when I'm buried with work.

Publisher's Acknowledgments

We're proud of this book; please send us your comments through our Dummies online registration form located at http://dummies.custhelp.com. For other comments, please contact our Customer Care Department within the U.S. at 877-762-2974, outside the U.S. at 317-572-3993, or fax 317-572-4002.

Some of the people who helped bring this book to market include the following:

Acquisitions, Editorial, and Media Development

Senior Project Editor: Tim Gallan

Acquisitions Editor: Michael Lewis

Copy Editor: Caitlin Copple

Assistant Editor: David Lutton

Technical Editor: Mark Need

Editorial Manager: Michelle Hacker

Editorial Assistants: Jennette ElNaggar, Rachelle S. Amick

Art Coordinator: Alicia B. South

Cover Photo: © iStockphoto.com/Alex Slobodkin

Cartoons: Rich Tennant (www.the5thwave.com)

Composition Services

Project Coordinator: Sheree Montgomery

Layout and Graphics: Vida Noffsinger

Proofreaders: Laura L. Bowman, John Greenough

Indexer: Broccoli Information Management

Publishing and Editorial for Consumer Dummies

    Diane Graves Steele, Vice President and Publisher, Consumer Dummies

    Kristin Ferguson-Wagstaffe, Product Development Director, Consumer Dummies

    Ensley Eikenburg, Associate Publisher, Travel

    Kelly Regan, Editorial Director, Travel

Publishing for Technology Dummies

    Andy Cummings, Vice President and Publisher, Dummies Technology/General User

Composition Services

    Debbie Stailey, Director of Composition Services

Contents at a Glance

Table of Contents

Introduction

Now more than ever, business owners and individuals alike are realizing the power of the limited liability company (LLC). If you're like many people, you probably understand that LLCs are right for you in one way or another; you just don't know the next steps to take. Maybe you've purchased a piece of real estate and know that it should be protected in some way; you just don't know how to form the LLC and do the transfer. Or, on a whim, you created an LLC for your current business, and now you can't figure out how to transfer assets, what to do at tax time, or how you can take on a partner.

You now hold in your hands the key to some of the most powerful strategies of the rich. This book was written to make your life easier and eliminate the guesswork on forming and owning an LLC. After all, your LLC should work for *you*, not the other way around.

In this book I give you the basics on LLCs and then go into some more-complex strategies. These strategies for protecting your livelihood and assets set this book apart from all the others. The rich have used a lot of these strategies for decades to operate their businesses, protect their assets, and pass on their estates. Now I put the power in your hands. When you find a strategy that may work for you, sit down with your team (your attorney, accountant, and/or corporate consultant) and figure out how to build on it and how to customize it to your specific situation. Use this book as your starting point. Your possibilities are endless, and your asset protection and tax strategies should grow along with you. Now get going on your journey to success and don't look back!

About This Book

Although this book was written in an easy-to-understand, concise manner, I didn't limit it to the basics. You'll find that a lot of other books on LLCs just skim over topics, filling their pages with forms (like the ones you can find on the accompanying CD-ROM) and legal statutes that you can easily access online. They often just cover the basics of filing your articles and creating your operating agreement without delving into the more powerful uses of LLCs or the strategies that can be integrated with LLCs.

Even though this is a *For Dummies* book, you're no idiot. And you don't want to be put to sleep while reading a jargon-laden book on complex strategies that even most attorneys can't understand. You want something that dives deep but keeps it simple, and that's what I strive to give you — well-organized, easy-to-read, and fluff-free information.

Now, even though this book gives you in-depth knowledge on the power of LLCs, it's no substitute for good professional advice. No matter what your situation, you're going to face some unique and complex legal and tax issues. Your attorney, accountant, and corporate consultant should be just a phone call away. Think of this book as a source of knowledge that can lead you to a whole new level of conversations with your team of professionals.

Conventions Used in This Book

I use a few conventions in this book. They're pretty intuitive and easy to understand, but here's the rundown anyway:

- ✔ Any industry terminology that may be new to you appears in *italics,* followed by a clear definition. Some of these terms are also included in the glossary.

- ✔ I **boldface** the action parts of numbered steps and keywords or the main points in bulleted items.

- ✔ Sidebars, which are the gray boxes of text, contain fun stories, examples, or other pieces of information that are great to know but not necessary to read if you're in a time crunch.

- ✔ Nine times out of ten I won't spell out *limited liability company* but will instead use the abbreviation *LLC.* I can't help it — it's just too easy!

- ✔ When this book was printed, some Web addresses may have needed to break across two lines of text. If that happened, rest assured that I haven't put in any extra characters (such as hyphens) to indicate the break. So, when using one of these Web addresses, just type in exactly what you see in this book, pretending as though the line break doesn't exist.

What You're Not to Read

I know, I know — you're busy! You operate on a need-to-know basis and the rest is just gibberish. Therefore, to speed things up a little, feel free to ignore anything with a Technical Stuff icon next to it. The information in those paragraphs isn't really necessary to understand the topic. Also, the sidebars are fun, but they're sort of a bonus for those who aren't time-impaired. Feel free to skip those too.

Foolish Assumptions

In order for this book to cater to a broad audience, I needed to make some foolish assumptions about you, the reader, and your skill level. After all, it's not *Limited Liability Companies For Attorneys* or *Limited Liability Companies For Real Estate Investors*. It's *Limited Liability Companies For Dummies* (in other words, for everyone). I assume that at least one of these shoes fits you:

- ✔ You're a budding (or experienced) entrepreneur, looking for the next leg up.
- ✔ You have a business, and you want to finally get legit and form an entity to protect yourself.
- ✔ You're a real estate investor looking to save some dough and keep your butt out of the courtroom.
- ✔ You're an inventor who wants to protect his patents from a random lawsuit that may be just around the corner.
- ✔ You have intellectual property, and you want to keep it right where it is — in your name.
- ✔ You're old, or young, and are planning your estate.
- ✔ You want to raise money for a project and want an entity that can keep things in order and sweeten the pot for your investors.
- ✔ You were born on a day that ends in the letter *y*.

How This Book Is Organized

Limited Liability Companies For Dummies, 2nd Edition, like all *For Dummies* books, is divided into parts and chapters so you can skip around and easily find what you need. I have organized the text into seven parts, each with three to five chapters that are related to common topics. Here's a breakdown of the parts you'll find.

Part I: The ABCs of LLCs

Part I gives you a complete introduction to LLCs. It goes into the basics of LLCs, including how LLCs came into existence, what they are mainly used for, and some of the terminology that you'll see throughout the book. It also looks at the pros and cons of LLCs and compares them to other entities.

Part II: Your First Steps: Forming Your LLC

Part II covers everything you need to know when forming your LLC. In this part, I go over all the preliminary stuff, such as choosing a name for your LLC (it's harder than it looks!) and then making sure it's available for use. I then help you decide which state to form your LLC in, as well as the pros and cons of forming outside of your home state. After you have all the preliminary stuff out of the way, I show you how to create your articles of organization and file them with your state office. In case you're already operating as a different entity type, I also cover how to convert your current entity into an LLC. And last but not least, I address state and local licensing issues that your LLC will have to deal with.

Part III: Customizing Your LLC

In this part, I explain how to create your operating agreement — which, in my opinion, is the most vital chapter in this book. LLCs are incredibly flexible entities and can be tailored to most business needs, and most of this tailoring happens in the operating agreement. Which is why, without one, you're screwed. But before that, in Chapter 8 I go into the various forms of taxation that an LLC can elect with the IRS and the process to go about making the formal election. And in Chapter 9, I cover membership shares: what they are, how to issue them, and how to transfer them when necessary.

Part IV: Running Your Brand-New LLC

This part is geared toward readers who have an existing (or newly formed) LLC in place. I go over the basics, such as how to maintain company records. I also discuss common precautions and steps you should take to make sure that your contracts are airtight, and you can read about the procedures you need to follow to stay out of court. Then I explain to you the step-by-step process of filing your LLC's taxes. In Chapter 13, I get into the fun stuff: how exactly to raise capital using your LLC. I also discuss how to expand nationally. After all, each state has different requirements for LLCs, and you need to know how to abide by them. Finally, at the end of Part IV I discuss the dissolution process and what to do when you're ready to call it quits.

Part V: LLCs on Steroids: Advanced Strategies

Part V contains some of the more-advanced strategies. I start off by showing you the importance of having an asset protection strategy and how LLCs can be a cheap way for you to gain a pretty powerful defense against creditors and lawsuits. Next up is real estate, the LLC's favorite pastime. I show you how LLCs and real estate go hand in hand, and how to properly structure your properties in an LLC (or two or three). Last but not least is estate planning. I discuss the current estate tax laws and how LLCs can help save your heirs a fortune when you pass away.

Part VI: The Part of Tens

Part VI is for all you type-A personalities out there. It gives you the lowdown on important information, with each chapter segmented into ten bite-size sections. I start off with ten reasons to form an LLC, and I have to say, that chapter was one of the easiest to write. After all, I could have written twenty or even thirty good reasons, but my editors wouldn't let me. Lastly, I go into how to keep intact the liability protection your LLC offers so your LLC doesn't get disregarded by the courts when you need it the most.

Part VII: Appendixes

The appendixes are one of the reasons why, if you are flipping through this book at the bookstore, you need to take it to the register immediately. Here I give all the information that you need to form your entity — for every state! This will cut your research time in half and allow you the extra time to read that fiction book you've been eyeing. I also throw in some info on how to use the CD-ROM.

The CD-ROM

Forms, forms, and more forms! That's what you can expect on the CD-ROM that accompanies this book. Forget the out-of-date forms that you have to tear out of other LLC books (I'm not mentioning any names). All you need to do is simply pop in the CD, open the folder for your state, and grab the form you need. It's that easy! Your partners won't believe how productive you are.

Icons Used in This Book

In this book I use little pictures, called *icons,* to highlight certain types of information. When you see these, make sure to pay close attention — otherwise, you may miss some really good info!

This icon flags helpful tips, tidbits, and secrets that may give you an upper hand on your road to success.

If I mention a topic more than once and/or use this icon, then you should make an effort to remember the information. These concepts are often the most important.

Whenever I use this icon, you should watch out! Obtain advice that is specific to your situation from a professional. Otherwise, legal or financial snares can ensue.

I use this icon to flag some technical stuff that may be a little advanced and difficult to understand for the LLC novices out there. When you encounter one of these icons, don't worry. Just ignore the information or ask a competent professional for advice.

When you see this icon, know that I've got you covered. Any of the forms or documents that are flagged with this icon are on the CD-ROM that accompanies this book.

Where to Go from Here

One of the many great things about a *For Dummies* book is that you don't have to read it from cover to cover to find out what you need to know. If you're a complete novice and are just dipping your toes into the whole LLC concept, you may want to read Chapters 2 and 3 and then skip to whatever topic interests you most. If you have already formed your LLC and are looking for the next step, you may want to skip to Chapter 10 to find out how to create your operating agreement. Only interested in the use of LLCs for estate planning? Skip to Chapter 18. Ready to dissolve your LLC? Feel free to flip to Chapter 15. Wherever you choose to start reading, I make sure you have the info you need so you can immediately put an LLC to work protecting your assets.

Part I
The ABCs of LLCs

The 5th Wave   By Rich Tennant

In this part . . .

If you're currently reading this page, it's a good bet that you've heard somewhere that an LLC may be right for you and your business, but you don't know enough to go out and create one for yourself. Well, you've come to the right place! In this part, I give you a good overview of what LLCs are, what they're used for, and how they compare to other types of business structures.

Chapters 1 and 2 give you a basic knowledge of how LLCs are structured and their different forms and variations. In Chapter 3, I get personal. Because structuring a business has no one-size-fits-all approach, I dive into the different business types and how an LLC can apply to your individual situation.

Chapter 1

What Is an LLC, Really?

*U*nless you've been living under a rock, or in Zimbabwe perhaps, you've most likely heard of limited liability companies, LLCs. And you hear about them all the time for good reason! It's almost as if the corporate gods have smiled down on us and decided to improve on the corporation by creating the LLC. As I like to put it: Where the corporation fails, the LLC prevails.

Think of the LLC as a merger of the partnership and the corporation that has the best of both worlds — all the good qualities of each and none of the bad. It offers full limited-liability protection to all the owners (like the corporation), yet has pass-through tax status (like the partnership). In addition, the LLC has a second layer of liability protection that shields the business from any personal lawsuits that may befall you. And it doesn't stop there! The list of benefits goes on and on. In this chapter, I introduce you to those benefits and other LLC fundamentals while steering you toward the other chapters in the book where you can find out more details.

Understanding How LLCs Work

Compared to the corporation, which has been around for hundreds of years, the LLC is the new kid on the block. Therefore, this new type of entity hasn't been so easy for some old-fashioned folks to accept. However, when you understand how LLCs work, you'll probably see many ways that they can help your business.

Even if you're familiar with corporations — or partnerships, for that matter — LLCs present some new concepts and terminology. The best and most basic way to understand an LLC is to think of it as a regular partnership except all the partners have the huge benefit of full *limited liability protection*. This protection means that the partners (the *members*) aren't personally responsible for the actions or debts of the company. Also, LLCs are more official than regular partnerships because you form them with the state and you can raise financing by selling off pieces of the company (the membership interests). But when all is said and done, LLCs are easy to understand and easy to run. Not to mention, if you make a mistake, the consequences aren't as dire as they would be with a corporation.

LLCs, like most entities, are subject to state oversight. The problem is that not all states are on the same page. So in addition to reading this book, you'll need to do a little bit of research so that you can make sure you're complying with the laws of the state(s) where you transact business. Finding that information won't be too difficult, however, because I have provided each state's information on LLCs in Appendix A as well as loading all state LLC laws onto a public wiki at www.docrun.com/wiki. This book, along with these added resources, will give you everything you need to get started down the right path.

Courts still have a lot to decide about LLCs, unlike corporations, which have hundreds of years of case law backing them up. When operating an LLC, know that some practices are based on assumptions rather than actual legal precedents, and this creates gray areas — and potential problems. After all, you don't want to be the unlucky business owner stuck in the courtroom when everything you thought you knew about LLCs is overturned. The best way to avoid that scenario is to have a great registered agent or corporate attorney who stays abreast of LLC laws for you.

Owners: You gotta have 'em

Although LLCs are separate from their owners in a lot of ways, they still need to have them. An LLC without an owner is like a child without parents: It simply doesn't exist. So until you dole out the ownership in your LLC, it doesn't become its own separate entity.

The owners (see Chapter 9) not only own the entire enterprise and all its assets, but they also generally have the last say. Although they may not manage the business, they do elect the managers. They vote on important issues and ultimately control the company's fate.

The owners in the LLC are called *members.* They have units of ownership called *membership interests* that show what percentage of the company they own and how much influence they have when voting on important company matters. Membership interests in an LLC are comparable to stock in a corporation. However, unlike the S corporation (which is often compared to the LLC), LLCs can have unlimited members of any type. Members can be citizens of other countries or even entities such as corporations, partnerships, or trusts.

The actual term for the members of the LLC and their membership interests varies from one state to another. For instance, in some states, the membership interest is called *ownership interest* or *limited liability company interest.* Just keep in mind that no matter what they're called, the concepts are still the same.

LLCs offer a lot of flexibility in how you issue membership. For instance, your LLC can have many different forms of membership, called *classes,* with whatever rules you want for each class. For instance, one class can have priority on the profit distributions while the other class is second in line. Or one class can have a say in managing the company while another class must remain silent. In Chapter 9, I go into detail on how to issue membership interests in your LLC.

If your LLC has only one member, it's called a *single-member LLC.* Single-member LLCs are treated as sole proprietorships by the IRS for tax purposes. Your state laws, if they even allow single-member LLCs (some don't), may also treat them differently. Single-member LLCs are often disadvantageous, because they don't have the benefit of partnership taxation and aren't guaranteed *charging order protection,* which protects the LLC from lawsuits that may be filed against you personally. (I discuss this concept in depth in Chapter 16.)

Contributions: Where the money comes from

When you buy a share of stock on the stock market, the money you pay is what you are contributing (or *investing*) in return for a percentage of the company's ownership. Well, LLCs are no different. In exchange for their membership interest in the company, members must contribute something of value. This *something* can be in the form of cash, services, hard assets such as equipment, real estate, or even promissory notes (which are allowed in some states). See Chapter 9 for more details on contribution types.

When a member makes a contribution, the other members need to determine the value of that contribution in relation to everyone else's. They then distribute the membership interests proportionally, which is really easy to do when cash is involved. For instance, if Joe, Steve, and Mary each contribute $100,000 in cash, then they each are issued one-third of the company. All the contributions made by each of the members and their corresponding membership interests are listed in the operating agreement.

Most LLCs issue membership certificates that, like stock certificates in a corporation, are evidence of the amount of ownership a member has in the company (see Chapter 9). The membership certificate displays the member's name and the number of membership units the person owns. To determine the member's percentage of ownership in the company, you divide the number of units she owns by the total number of units issued in the company. For instance, if 10,000 membership units are issued to members of the company and you own 100 of those units, then you own 1 percent of the company. If the company doesn't issue membership certificates, then the number of units you own should be listed in the operating agreement next to your contribution amount. (In Chapter 10, I show you how to properly list your members, their contributions, and membership interests in your LLC operating agreement.)

Distributions: Getting what you're due

After the company starts turning a profit, the members will no doubt want to benefit. After all, they didn't invest their hard-earned money into the company for nothing — they want to see a return! At certain points in time — usually at the end of the year, but sometimes at the end of each quarter — the company profit is calculated and doled out to each member, usually in proportion to her percentage of ownership. These payments are called *distributions* and are generally in the form of cash (see Chapters 9 and 10 for more on distributions).

Unlike corporations, LLCs don't have to distribute profits in proportion to the members' percentage of ownership. The members can decide to vary the distributions however they want. The IRS generally allows this variation as long as you pass their tests (mainly to prove that you aren't varying the distributions to avoid taxes). Speak to your accountant if you are interested in doing this.

The birth of the LLC

The LLC didn't come out of nowhere. Business entities with the same characteristics as LLCs have been around for many years. The origin of LLCs can be traced back to 1892, when German law enacted what was called the *Gesellschaft mit beschränkter Haftung* (GmbH) — a modern-day variation of the English private limited company.

Germany's GmbH format was copied throughout Europe and Central and South America. This concept has remained popular in many parts of the world to this day.

In the United States, limited partnership associations actually predated the German concept. These entities were formed in several Midwestern states starting as early as 1874. However, this entity structure fell out of favor soon after. In 1977, the LLC was born in Wyoming and modeled after the German GmbH and the successful Panama variation. LLCs didn't become popular nationally until 1988, when the IRS ruled that LLCs would be taxed as partnerships. And the rest, as they say, is history.

Distributions also occur if your LLC goes out of business, but in this case they're handled differently. The LLC's assets are liquidated, the creditors are paid back (including any members to whom the business owes money), and then the remaining amount is distributed to the members according to their specific ownership percentages. When these final distributions are made, you can't choose how the money is distributed — it must be doled out according to how much of the company each member owns. For instance, if you own 50 percent of the company, you can rest assured that you will receive 50 percent of the remaining cash.

Creating Your Own LLC: It's a Piece of Cake

I'm baffled why so many people go about doing business and owning real estate without the protection of a limited liability company or other entity. They are risking everything! I can only guess that they must be intimidated by the process of forming an LLC and think that it's much more complicated than it really is.

Sure, LLCs don't just think themselves into existence. Someone has to create them, but LLCs aren't complicated at all. Some professionals use them in complicated situations, but when you're dealing with normal, everyday business activities or asset protection strategies, you'll have no trouble forming and operating as an LLC. As you flip through this book, the concepts may seem overwhelming at first, but after getting familiar with a little bit of industry terminology, you'll have enough of a basic understanding of LLCs to get started on your own. And, in the worst-case scenario, if you have a question that isn't answered in this book, feel free to call my office at 888-88MYLLC so that I can make sure you get the correct answer.

To create an LLC, you have to draft a short document and file it with your state. This step is pretty simple to do and, for the most part, won't require an attorney's help. First, though, you need to do some research so you understand some other elements of LLCs and then make some decisions on how you want to structure your company.

Educating yourself

The first thing to do is gain a little bit of an education about LLCs. I know you're busy, so this doesn't have to be too extensive. You just need to know the basics, and the best way to start is by reading this book. Needless to say, you're on the right track!

You can always use professionals to do the work for you. And that's okay. Hey, I'm all for delegation! Just make sure you have a good basic understanding so you can have productive and educated conversations with the people you hire. Not to mention, you'll want to have an idea of whether they really know their stuff.

After you understand the basics, call your attorney or accountant and ask about details that pertain to your situation. You may also want to do some research online and set up some free consultations with corporate consulting companies. You can also find a lot of in-depth information in my syndicated articles, which I put online at www.myllc.com.

Surveying your assets and making a plan

If you have been working hard all your life, you've probably accumulated some valuable assets. Even if you aren't operating a business, creating an estate plan, or investing in real estate, you likely have some things you want to protect from creditors and lawsuits. Some of these assets may include

- ✓ Rental real estate
- ✓ Vacant land
- ✓ Businesses
- ✓ Intellectual property
- ✓ Expensive equipment (business or personal)
- ✓ Vehicles
- ✓ Savings accounts, money market funds, and CDs
- ✓ Stocks and bonds
- ✓ Any appreciating assets

You should consider protecting anything that's of value to you in an LLC. Lawsuits and personal creditors abound in today's society, and by leaving anything in your name, you are virtually handing it over to any attorney who wants it.

When using LLCs, consider forming more than one. After all, you never want to put all your eggs in one basket. For example, if you have multiple rental properties in one LLC and a tenant has an accident on one of your properties, then all the properties will be up for grabs because they are in the same LLC. However, if you separate those properties into multiple LLCs, then only the one property that was sued can be taken.

If you are a procrastinator, watch out. Wasting too much time to put together your plan and act on it can cost you. Lawsuits come out of nowhere, and Murphy's Law states that you will get sued at the worst possible time. After you are faced with a lawsuit or have a creditor after you, your hands are tied. Any attempt to protect your assets at that point is illegal. Not only will you still lose your assets, but you can also end up with some hefty fines or, even worse, jail time.

Deciding who manages

There are two types of LLCs:

- ✔ Member-managed, where the LLC is managed jointly by all its members
- ✔ Manager-managed, where the LLC is managed by a separate manager (who can also be a member)

If you are forming a smaller LLC with only a few partners (members), and each partner will have a say in managing the company, then you may want to choose member-managed. However, if you decide to take on a silent partner and that person will *not* be managing the business, then your LLC needs to be *manager*-managed. Unless *all* members will be managing, you have to be manager-managed.

In most states, you have to list how the LLC is managed in the organizing document that is filed with the state (called the *articles of organization* — see Chapter 6). If your management structure changes, the organizing document may have to be amended. This process involves fees, so be as forward-thinking as possible before you do your initial filings and begin operations.

Choosing your registered agent

Before you can file your articles of organization, you need to choose a *registered agent* (sometimes called a *resident agent, statutory agent,* or *RA*). This person or company is *always* available during business hours, every single day, to accept any formal legal documents for your company in the unfortunate instance that you are sued.

Most registered agents allow you to use their office address for all your mail and other correspondence. A good registered agent should also stay on top of your state filings for you and make sure that you remain in good standing in the state (or states) where you are registered to transact business. If you are registered in many states, this task can be onerous, so you're better off leaving it to the professional service companies or an attorney (a more expensive option). See Chapter 6 for more on using a registered agent.

If your state allows you to serve as your own registered agent, I don't recommend it. Unless you plan on being at your office during business hours every single day, with no exceptions, and you also have a good grasp of all the state filings that need to be done, I suggest you leave it to the pros. Another consideration is that in the event that you're sued, would you really want a process server or sheriff serving you a lawsuit in front of your customers? Eek! Not me!

Bringing your LLC into existence

Your LLC needs to be registered and receive approval in any state where it is transacting business. LLCs don't need to reside in the same state as you — they should reside wherever their headquarters is going to be. In the case of companies that don't have headquarters (like Internet-based companies), they should reside wherever the tax laws are most favorable.

You create your LLC by drawing up a short document called the *articles of organization*. Your articles contain such basic information as the name of the company, how long the company will exist, the initial members or managers, and the name and address of the company's registered agent. In Chapter 6, I show you how to put together your articles of organization. After you are satisfied with your articles, you file them with your local secretary of state's office (or comparable state agency).

Operating Your LLC

Now that you've formed your LLC, you're ready to start business operations, right? Well, not exactly. You still have to create your operating agreement and make some very important decisions.

Operating your LLC is meant to be easy. For the most part, if you forget something or fail to document something in writing, the courts will go easy on you. LLCs aren't like corporations where a single misstep can cost you your limited liability protection. Although this paperwork isn't nitpicked by the state statutes like corporation paperwork is, you can save yourself a lot of time, hassle, and potential legal battles by getting it out of the way and making your agreements as tight as a drum.

Creating your operating agreement

Think of your *operating agreement* as a sort of partnership agreement, except with much more power. Your operating agreement is the blueprint for your company. In it, you state your company's policies on important matters, including

- ✔ How the company will be managed and by whom
- ✔ How important decisions are to be made
- ✔ How profits are to be distributed among the owners
- ✔ The titles and positions of managers and officers of the company
- ✔ The membership information, including who is a member, what that person contributed, and what membership interest they have been assigned

Creating an operating agreement takes some time and planning, but it's vital. With the wealth of information and provisions that I provide for you in Chapter 10, you'll be able to draft an ironclad document. However, you and your partners may take a while to decide what you want to put in it. After all, you are creating an infrastructure that needs to serve you for many, many years to come.

After you create your operating agreement, make sure that all the members and managers of the LLC sign it. Distribute a copy to everyone for their records, and put the original in your company records kit (which brings me to the next point).

Keeping books and records

All companies need to have a records kit. A *company records kit* normally looks like a big, leather binder with the company name emblazoned on the side. The kit can be cheap and low quality — looking like it came from the office-supply aisle of your local supermarket — or it can be made from the finest leather with real gold plating. No matter how simple or extravagant, every kit serves the same purpose: to house your important company records, such as your filed articles of organization and company charter, your operating agreement, resolutions and minutes from any meetings or voting that take place, your membership roll, and your unissued membership certificates. Chapter 11 has more details on how and where to keep your company's records.

When you order your records kit, make sure it comes with a company seal. Think of the company seal as your LLC's signature. You use it to make your company documents and share certificates official.

Paying taxes

One of the most beautiful features of an LLC is that it can elect any form of taxation it wishes (assuming it's not a single-member LLC). This means that your LLC can have partnership taxation, corporation taxation, or S corporation taxation. What flexibility! I dedicate all of Chapter 8 to helping you make this hugely important decision.

The default taxation for LLCs is partnership taxation, so this is what you'll be subject to if you don't elect otherwise. With partnership taxation, the business's profits and losses get passed on to the owners, who report their share on their personal tax returns. These portions of profits and losses that get passed on to the members are called *allocations*. This type of taxation is commonly referred to as *pass-through taxation*.

Because the LLC doesn't actually have to pay taxes itself, the IRS only requires you to file an information statement (IRS Form 1065) that states how the company's profits and losses are allocated among the members. Additionally, the company issues each member an IRS form called a Schedule K-1 that shows the information they need to determine how much tax they must pay on the company's profits.

LLCs aren't required to distribute any cash to the members. However, the members *are* required to pay taxes on the profits, whether or not they received distributions. When the company doesn't distribute the profits to the members, the profit is called *phantom income,* and the members still have to pay taxes on it out of their own pockets.

Chapter 2

LLCs: More Handy Than Duct Tape!

*I*n the first edition of this book, this chapter was broken down into two parts: advantages and disadvantages of LLCs. Funnily enough, with all the new law changes since the first edition, the disadvantages section shrank from five pages to what is now a measly few paragraphs. Hardly worth a mention, if you ask me.

In the past few years, LLCs have gained widespread acceptance, and state governments and the Internal Revenue Service have loosened the restrictions that previously made them unattractive to some business owners. Plus, with these few extra years of case law under the belt to set legal precedents, you no longer have to be the "test dummy" (pun intended) if your LLC gets dragged into court, sparing you the agony over how the case will be decided.

First off in this chapter, I give you the rundown on all the major qualities of limited liability companies — the good *and* the bad. Because everyone's needs differ drastically, I'll let you decide for yourself which facets are benefits and which are drawbacks for your situation. (In the next chapter, I help you explore whether or not an LLC is right for you.) Secondly, I give you an overview of the other types of LLCs that you may hear about while traveling along the road of your endeavors.

Seeing Why LLCs Are Awesome

Everyone seems to be going crazy over LLCs lately, and for good reason. They are one of the most flexible entities — you can choose how to distribute the profits, who manages the business's day-to-day affairs, and how the profits are to be taxed. They also offer a lot in terms of liability protection (hence the name *limited liability* company).

Overall advantages of the LLC include

- ✔ **Personal liability protection:** Any creditors who come knocking or lawsuits filed against your business can't affect you personally. You can rest assured that no matter what happens in the business, your family's assets are safe.

- ✔ **Business liability protection:** An LLC is one of the only entities that prevents personal lawsuits and creditors from liquidating your business to satisfy a judgment.

- ✔ **No ownership restrictions:** You can have as many owners as you need. Even other entities can be owners!

- ✔ **No management restrictions:** Owners can manage and managers can own — you decide.

- ✔ **Flexible tax status:** You can choose from a multitude of ways to be taxed, depending on what works best for your situation.

- ✔ **No separate tax returns:** With a standard LLC, the business's profits and losses are reported on your personal tax returns.

- ✔ **No double taxation:** Unlike some business structures, LLCs can have *pass-through taxation.* This means that the profits won't be taxed at the company level, only at the individual level.

- ✔ **Flexible profit distribution:** *You* decide what percentage of the profits to give to whom — no matter how much of the company the person actually owns.

In the following sections, I provide you with a more detailed overview of these advantages that LLCs offer.

Protecting your personal assets

As the old adage goes: "You aren't in business until you've been sued." As litigious as society is these days, you don't even need to be one of the bad guys to be dragged into court. By simply transacting business with the general public, you open yourself up for myriad potential lawsuits, and no matter how arbitrary the complaint is, the destruction (and legal fees) it leaves in its wake can be crippling.

The states know that if every time entrepreneurs started a new venture they were forced to put their livelihoods at stake, many fewer businesses would be started. Therefore, certain entity types are afforded *limited liability,* which protects the owners and managers of the business from being held personally responsible for the debts, obligations, and misdeeds of the business. Out of all the entities, LLCs offer the most comprehensive form of this protection (hence the name *limited liability* company).

An LLC protects you from the liabilities that you inevitably come across during the normal, everyday course of business. Should your business get sued or go bankrupt, your *personal assets* (home, car, investments, and so on) and other businesses (if they are in different LLCs) *cannot* be taken away. Only the assets included in the LLC that got sued are at risk.

Using an LLC to protect your personal assets must be done in advance, not after you've already been sued. Too many victims of lawsuits have shown up at my office wondering what they can do to get out of them — asking how they can save their home and bank accounts that are about to be taken away. Unfortunately, at this point, it's always too late. If only they had spent some time planning, such as reading this book or working with an advisor, they could have saved everything.

The one exception to the normal protection of LLCs is professional limited liability companies (PLLCs), because personal responsibility is essential to being a licensed professional. I discuss this unique entity type at length later in this chapter.

By establishing your new business or placing your existing business in an LLC, you sign your company up for the most cost-effective, ironclad insurance policy around. A business insurance policy may still have a role in keeping the business itself from having to pay for its own misdeeds. However, they're only effective in lawsuits arising from product or service liability and usually don't pay out to unsatisfied creditors if the company can't meet its debt obligations. Also, whereas insurance companies can be wishy-washy about paying out, the LLC is pretty fail-safe.

Here's the clincher: LLCs are so foolproof that most attorneys often opt to negotiate a settlement, or better yet, avoid the time and cost of suing them in the first place! Now, that's what I call protection!

An LLC's veil of liability protection is not infallible. If you don't take certain measures to establish and maintain that your LLC is not simply an extension of yourself (your *alter ego*), then a court can disregard the LLC and allow the plaintiff or creditor access to your personal assets. This is referred to as *piercing the veil* of liability protection. I discuss this situation — and how to avoid it — in Chapter 11.

Although an LLC shields you from being held personally responsible for minor negligent acts, it will do nothing for egregious criminal acts or willful misconduct. Also, the LLC does offer some protection against certain government creditors, such as the IRS, with one main exception: As a member or manager of an LLC, you can be held *personally* responsible for the failure to pay payroll taxes. Therefore, if you're withholding taxes from your employees' checks and for some reason fail to submit that money to the tax man, you are putting your personal assets at risk.

Taking charge of charging order protection

So now you know that an LLC protects your personal assets if the business gets sued or goes bankrupt. Pretty great, eh? Well, it gets even better. Unlike corporations, LLCs have a dual layer of liability protection called *charging order protection.* Many moons ago when a creditor obtained a judgment against a partner of a partnership, in order to get paid, the creditor could simply take the partner's interest in the business (and, proportionally, all related assets) and liquidate them, often leaving a ravaged business in his wake. Clearly this wasn't fair to the other, innocent partner(s), who was just going about his business when suddenly everything he's worked for is destroyed!

To remedy these unfair acts, the courts amended the laws so that the creditor of a member (the partner) cannot go after that member's individual interest, but only the *economic right* to that interest. Read on to find out how this arrangement works.

Understanding how charging orders work

One day, finally getting a break from the constant demands of the restaurant you started and built, you drive to the supermarket and accidently hit someone with your car. Sure, the woman mindlessly walked in front of your car and you only barely bruised her, but that means nothing when she shows up to court in a neck brace. The jury, sympathetic to the woman's plight, finds in her favor, and you now owe this woman more than your insurance will cover and more than you can afford. After wiping out your family savings, your equity in your home, and your kid's college funds, you still come up short.

But the bad news gets worse. The restaurant you've spent the past four years building is structured as a corporation. Your ownership interest *(stock)* in that corporation is considered a personal asset of yours and the judgment creditor is therefore allowed to foreclose on it. Before you know it, your corporate account's been frozen and you're looking at a fire sale of your kitchen equipment to satisfy the debt. Your company is toast.

Now imagine a different scenario where instead of forming your restaurant as a corporation, you formed it as a limited liability company. This time, when you are sued, the plaintiff can't foreclose on your business, but instead can only obtain a charging order against your LLC. This means that she has no say in the day-to-day operation of the business and can only wait patiently with her hand out, should you decide to issue profit distributions. Which, of course, you don't. (Keep reading to find out how to get away with it!)

Granting economic rights versus other rights

In order to better understand charging order protection, you should know that a member can have two rights in an LLC: *economic rights,* the right to receive profit allocations and distributions from the company, and *other rights,* which include the right to vote on important matters or be involved in the management of the day-to-day business. Charging order protection grants _only_ economic rights to the assignee, unless the operating agreement specifies otherwise. In other words, the creditor has no other choice but to shut his trap and sit back and receive whatever distributions you decide to grant him. You can stop profit distributions altogether and the creditor will have no say in the matter.

This situation is the worst possible for your judgment creditor, because while you are withholding profit distributions from her, she is still required to pay taxes on that allocated share of the profits. This nondistributed share is called _phantom income,_ which I dive into in Chapter 12, and usually isn't a good thing. In this case, however, it works in your favor, allowing you to easily run a trap, forcing your creditor to end up with nothing 'cept the pleasure of paying down your tax bill! It's funny how this arrangement can make even the most bull-headed creditors call up, ready to negotiate an extremely favorable settlement.

Of course, considering that her attorney would know that trying to seize membership interests in an LLC is a losing proposition, she may not even try to sue you at all. But who knows? Maybe that fake neck brace cut off circulation to her brain.

When formed and maintained properly, LLCs always hold up in court. When a creditor sees that you have shielded your assets with an LLC, he very rarely goes through the hassle of taking you to court. And avoiding a lawsuit is always better than winning one — as legendary Chinese strategist Sun Tzu wrote, "The best battle is the battle that is won without being fought."

Enjoying more flexibility than a circus performer

All states offer guidelines that dictate the management and ownership structure of an LLC, and they may seem a bit rigid. Unfortunately, if more people read their state statutes, they would realize how lax these statutes really are. While the default laws can be undesirable, the states allow the majority of them to be overridden with custom rules built into the company's operating agreement, thus (again) making LLCs the most flexible entities around.

No ownership restrictions

Some business structures have severe limitations as to the number and types of owners. For example, S corporations (as described at length in Chapter 3) are limited to having fewer than 76 owners _(shareholders),_ and these owners cannot be other companies or non–U.S. citizens. LLCs, on the other hand, have no such problem. You can issue as many shares as you want to any other entity or individual of any nationality (however, as _individual_ as your pets may be, they don't count!).

LLCs also offer a lot of leeway as to how individual ownership is structured. For instance, each member can be subject to his own buy-sell agreement that dictates the rules and restrictions on his individual membership interest. These rules can vary from member to member if you so choose. I discuss buy-sell agreements in Chapter 9.

No management restrictions

When it comes to the management of the business, an LLC can be managed by one of two groups:

- **Its members:** When you select *member management* for your LLC, all the business's members have an equal say in the day-to-day operations, no matter their ownership percentage (unless you state otherwise in the operating agreement). They all have an equal right to sign contracts and enter into debts on behalf of the business. If you don't want one of your members to have this sort of power, then member management is definitely not for you.

- **Separate managers:** These folks may or may not hold a stake in the company. Most companies that are larger than two or three operating members choose manager management. When you elect manager management, you can have as many of your members be managers as you want; however, not all of them have to be if you don't want them to.

For instance, say you are raising money for your new enterprise and, although you want your investors to profit from the business's success, you don't want them to have a say in the day-to-day operations. To solve this, you form a manager-managed LLC and elect yourself as the only manager. As members without management authority, the investors have limited say in the day-to-day operations of the business.

When establishing your LLC, you state in your articles of organization whether your company will be designated *member-managed* or *manager-managed.* I discuss the ins and outs of selecting the members and managers of your LLC in Chapter 9.

Most states give you heaps of leeway in prescribing exactly how your company is managed. You can create multiple management groups and multiple management roles. You can also restrict some nonmanaging members from voting or having *any* say whatsoever, including who is chosen to manage the company. All these details are up to your discretion and simply need to be laid out in the LLC's operating agreement.

The fact that you can specify separate managers is a trademark quality of LLCs that helps separate them from other entities, such as sole proprietorships and general partnerships. In general partnerships, all members are owners and all are equally (and personally!) liable for the business. In limited partnerships, you can have members who also manage the business; however, they don't have any sort of limited liability protection. I indulge your curiosity on these (in my opinion) inferior entity types in Chapter 3.

The management aspect is one reason why LLCs work well in estate planning. You can place your assets in an LLC with the kids as the full owners *(members)* and yourself as the manager. This way, you still control the company, while your kids can receive profit distributions. Upon your death, the assets will still be in their name, and a new manager will be elected.

LLCs are definitely *not* one-size fits all, and yours needs to be customized to your particular business needs. All this happens in the operating agreement, making it the most important document you'll ever write in regards to your business. I cannot emphasize that enough. If you don't have one, your state's default rules apply, and I promise you they won't give you much more than a headache. But this doesn't mean you should use a shoddy fill-in-the-blank operating agreement you found on the Internet. Those generic forms are mostly antiquated, not state-specific, and most likely won't address all your needs. In Chapter 10, I go into detail on how to create a custom operating agreement for your LLC.

Choosing your own tax status

As the owner of an LLC, you have the unique ability to choose how you want to pay taxes on your business. LLCs can be taxed as partnerships (with pass-through taxation) or as sole proprietorships (if the LLC has only one member); or they can even choose to be taxed as a corporation or an S corporation (which I explain in detail in the next chapter). Although you can't necessarily flip back and forth from one type of taxation to another very easily, this sort of flexibility is unique to LLCs. For instance, corporations can't choose to be taxed like partnerships, and sole proprietorships can only be taxed like sole proprietorships. LLCs have a choice, and in the business world, flexibility and choices can determine success or failure.

Making your selection

The default tax status for LLCs is a partnership tax status. If you wish to elect any other form, you must file a Form 8832: Entity Classification Election with the IRS.

When filing Form 8832, you can retroactively impose the new form of taxation up to 75 days, or up to an entire year if you have yet to file your LLC's first information statement with the IRS (the LLC equivalent of a tax return). Under certain circumstances, the IRS may even allow you to retroactively elect a different taxation for up to about three years prior.

After you file Form 8832 and elect a different form of taxation for your LLC, you are stuck with that chosen method of taxation for five years. In Chapter 12, I discuss potential ways to get around this rule, but because changing may not be possible, I suggest you take some time to choose your form of taxation wisely. Turn to Chapter 8 for assistance in choosing your form of taxation.

Single-member LLCs and the IRS

A single-member LLC (an LLC with only one member) is automatically considered by the IRS to be a *disregarded entity* and is taxed exactly as it would be if it were simply a sole proprietorship. This doesn't affect the basic liability protection of your LLC, but it does change the tax rules. Also, it's important to note that if your LLC is owned by only you and your spouse, then you'll be treated by the IRS as a sole proprietorship. Children and other family members count as legitimate partners.

If you wish to be taxed as a partnership, you can always issue a small percentage of your company to a trusted friend or family member and avoid this situation entirely. Otherwise, you have a few options. You can remain taxed as a sole proprietorship. You can elect to be taxed as a corporation by filing Form 8843 with the IRS, or you can also elect S corporation taxation by filing Form 2553: Election by a Small Business Corporation. Keep in mind that if you elect to be taxed as an S corporation, you'll also be subject to the same membership limitations as S corporations.

You also have the option of forming a corporation, with yourself as the sole shareholder, and making the corporation your partner in the LLC. If you live in a state where forming a corporation is a costly endeavor, you can always form your corporation in a less expensive, tax-free state, such as Nevada. You'll pay about $175 per year in registration fees; however, your LLC will get the benefit of partnership taxation.

Nevada is a great state for forming a partner corporation because of the privacy it offers: Nevada doesn't require you to disclose who the shareholders are of a corporation. This privacy is beneficial if you don't want anyone to know that the partner in your LLC is actually, well, *you*.

If you are a single-member LLC, you are not eligible to elect partnership taxation on Form 8843.

Distributing profits at your whim

With most entities, if a shareholder owns 10 percent of the company, he can only receive 10 percent of the profits that are distributed, no more and no less. With an LLC, you have freedom to choose! You don't have to split the profits in accordance with the percentage of ownership. If all the members agree, you can give 40 percent of the profits to someone who owns 20 percent of the business, or give 10 percent to someone who owns 50 percent.

Say you and John decide to partner together to create a Web design company. You have chosen to partner 50/50, and you alone are putting in the initial $20,000 needed to get the venture started. You'll both be sharing the workload. But do you think splitting the profits 50/50 is fair when you're the only one putting up capital and all else is equal? You know better than that (I hope).

So being the smart cookie that you are, you and John decide to form an LLC. You distribute 50 percent of the company to John and 50 percent to yourself. In the LLC's operating agreement, you both agree that you get first dibs of the profits until $22,000 is reached (giving you an extra 10 percent interest on your initial investment). After you're paid off, you and John will split the profits equally.

Taking a Look at a Few Wrinkles

As I describe in the last several sections, LLCs offer numerous advantages over other business structures. But they're not perfect. Nothing is, after all. You have to be careful about the rules regarding transferring membership, and you have to be aware that the laws governing LLCs can vary from state to state.

Membership can be a bit tricky

Many LLCs restrict the transfer of ownership. Although this restriction used to be a requirement of LLCs, it is now more customary than anything else. Basically, if a member wants to sell or transfer his shares, he can only assign the membership interest, not actually transfer the ownership. So the person purchasing the membership only has rights to the profits that are distributed; he has no voting rights and no control over the business operations.

However, don't fret too much over this limitation — it can be more of a positive than anything else! An *assignee* (the person or company purchasing the membership) can become a full member upon the approval of the majority of the other members. All it takes is a quick vote. But keep in mind that to fully transfer your membership shares, you must be sure that the other members will approve the transfer; otherwise, the assignee may end up as a silent partner with no voting rights or control. (See Chapter 9 for more on transferring ownership.)

Most states allow you to make your own rules regarding the transference of membership interest by stating them in your operating agreement (the über-important document I discuss at length in Chapter 10). But even though you *can,* that doesn't mean you *should.* A lot of the power of charging order protection (which I discuss previously in "Taking charge of charging order protection") stems from the shares not being freely transferable. I can understand if this seems all vague and cryptic to you; if you read Chapter 9, where I dive into all things membership, you'll catch my drift.

If you intend to take your company public, bear in mind that you probably won't be able to do it with an LLC. Ownership is not freely transferable in an LLC, which prohibits the free exchange of membership shares — a must for a public company. This limitation may also create a bit of a disincentive for venture capital groups or larger companies looking to invest in your LLC in exchange for equity. If you were ever to wish to do an initial public offering (IPO), you would need to become a corporation; which could mean a hurricane-sized taxable event. This is why you need to know your exit strategy before choosing your entity type. I guide you through figuring out what entity type is right for you in Chapter 3.

Rules governing LLCs vary among states

Like all business structures, LLCs are governed by the individual states. Some states are progressive and comprehensive in their laws governing LLCs, whereas others haven't updated them since the 1990s. In contrast, corporations have been around for centuries, and after so many years of working out the kinks, the basic structure is pretty much the same no matter where they're domiciled. The disparities in LLC law from one state to another aren't necessarily a drawback, but you must do your homework every step of the way to make sure that you don't inadvertently structure your LLC in a way that your state doesn't allow.

I can't stress enough how important it is to review your state's laws concerning LLCs. You'd be surprised how many attorneys and national formation companies fail to take individual state laws into account. Whatever is in the state's statutes will pervade all aspects of how your company is structured, from what is contained in your articles of organization, to how you can issue membership shares, to what you can and cannot dictate in your operating agreement.

For instance, some states still require that LLCs have a limited life span and establish a dissolution date in their articles! This trails back to an archaic rule that LLCs, as partnerships, couldn't be eternal. (Should you happen to be one of the unlucky few who have to deal with this annoyance, read Chapter 15, where I show you some work-arounds.)

Not only should you know the laws for the state that you wish to form your LLC in, but you should also familiarize yourself with the laws of any state you foresee your LLC registering to transact business in. To make your life a bit easier, I set up a searchable public wiki containing all state laws regarding business entities, real estate, and taxation at www.docrun.com/wiki.

Differentiating between the LLC's Many Variations

With all the hoopla about LLCs, a lot of the more progressive states are hurdling each other to find the newest and greatest form of the LLC. It's as if they have embraced the flexibility of the LLC — especially all the leeway allowed by the IRS — and are amending their laws to fit the business needs of their populace. In some cases, the states are making slight variations to the standard LLC; in others, they're creating whole new entity types.

In this section, I go through all the different forms of LLCs and address whether or not they may be applicable to your situation.

The professional LLC

If you are a licensed professional, your choice in what entity you use to govern your business operations may be more limited than you realize. Rather than forming your practice as a standard limited liability company, you may be required to form a *professional limited liability company* (*professional LLC* or *PLLC,* for short) — that is, if your state even recognizes professional LLCs at all.

The following states *do not* recognize professional LLCs:

Alaska	Illinois	Oregon
California	Indiana	Utah
Delaware	Missouri	Wisconsin
Georgia	New Jersey	Wyoming
Hawaii	Ohio	

If you are a licensed professional in one of these states, then you will have to either operate your practice under a *professional corporation* or a sole proprietorship or general partnership. Unfortunately, if you are a licensed professional, there's a very good chance that you don't have the option of being a regular LLC.

Simply wearing a suit doesn't make you "professional"

So who qualifies as a "licensed professional"? The definition varies widely from state to state but generally involves anyone required to obtain a license from a state agency, the United States patent office, or the Internal Revenue Service. This ranges from such professions as accountants, architects, chiropractors, dentists, doctors, and lawyers to real estate brokers and land surveyors. To give you an idea, here is an excerpt from the Connecticut statute (Sec. 33-182a) governing the definition:

> *"Professional service" means any type of service to the public that requires that members of a profession rendering such service obtain a license or other legal authorization as a condition precedent to the rendition thereof, limited to the professional services rendered by dentists, naturopaths, chiropractors, physicians and surgeons, physician assistants, doctors of dentistry, physical therapists, occupational therapists, podiatrists, optometrists,*

nurses, nurse-midwives, veterinarians, pharmacists, architects, professional engineers, or jointly by architects and professional engineers, landscape architects, real estate brokers, insurance producers, certified public accountants and public accountants, land surveyors, psychologists, attorneys-at-law, licensed marital and family therapists, licensed professional counselors and licensed clinical social workers.

The states differ so widely on which professions are required to be licensed by the state that you could be required to operate as a PLLC in one state while being a standard LLC in another state. Therefore, if you think professional licensing rules may possibly apply to you, be sure to check your state's laws on the issue *before* filing your limited liability company. To make this as easy as possible for you, I aggregated all state laws governing licensed professionals on a public wiki. Check it out at www.docrun.com/wiki/licensed_professionals.

Weaker liability protection

A licensed professional generally has a much bigger impact on his individual clients than, say, the manufacturer of a mundane household product. The effects of an accountant failing to do his job properly are much more profound than the outcome of your bath soap not delivering on its promise. Because personal responsibility is a mainstay of being a licensed professional, the states want to make sure that these professionals don't shirk responsibility for their negligent acts by hiding themselves — and their assets — behind the liability protection of a corporation or LLC.

Regular LLCs protect the members' personal assets in the event the company is sued for an employee's or member's negligent acts, whereas professional LLCs and professional corporations don't. Before you balk, think for a minute: Can you imagine what would happen if an irresponsible doctor or lawyer were able to operate without malpractice insurance without fear of consequences? After all, since the value of his business is him and the LLC is simply an extension of himself, why would he care if it's sued? Assuming he had the forethought to protect his business assets in another entity, there'd be nothing substantial at stake. He'd simply form another entity and continue on his way, leaving damage and hurt consumers in his wake.

In order to protect consumers from these negligent and potentially fatal acts of irresponsible licensed professionals, the states (to various degrees) have significantly reduced or completely removed the liability protection of the entities that these professionals operate under. I'm sure you're not one of the "bad guys" in this scenario, so this restriction may be frustrating for you. Unfortunately, the actions of the few bad seeds have a negative impact on the rest of you straight-shooting folks.

If you're a licensed professional, this sort of liability is a serious concern, so professional liability insurance is a must. Often referred to as *malpractice insurance,* it indemnifies professionals from their mistakes. If you are a licensed professional, you'd be crazy not to have it.

Although the liability protection of professional LLCs is weaker than standard LLCs, you'll still get quite a few benefits by forming and operating under one. For one, charging order protection, the second layer of liability protection unique to LLCs, remains intact. Also, whereas an organization — and the responsible individual and her superiors — is liable for negligent acts, the rest of the partners do not share in this personal liability. Their assets are safe. This separation not only keeps your personal assets safe should your partner accidentally slip and cut someone's ear off during surgery, but it also keeps your malpractice claims separate so your premiums don't go up if your partner screws up. This protection is a huge benefit over operating as a general partnership, in which you are jointly, personally responsible for your partners' mistakes.

Another entity option you may not be familiar with is a limited liability partnership (LLP). Partners operating within an LLP are not held personally responsible for the negligent acts of the other partners. It's an older entity (in a lot of ways the predecessor to the LLC) and for a long time was the default entity choice for professionals such as lawyers and accountants. If your state doesn't allow the formation of a professional limited liability company and you desire the pass-through taxation of a partnership entity, then an LLP may be a good alternative. I discuss LLPs at length in Chapter 3.

Tax treatment

You may have heard that licensed professionals are subject to different tax treatment, and you'd be right . . . if you were talking about corporations. Professional corporations, unlike regular corporations, are subject to a 35 percent flat tax on profits. That's pretty close to the highest tax rate! Luckily, professional LLCs aren't subject to this insanity but are subject to partnership taxation, just as regular LLCs are.

Also like regular LLCs, professional LLCs get to pick their tax treatment (which I discuss earlier in this chapter in "Choosing your own tax status"). Keep in mind, though, that if you elect corporate taxation for your professional LLC, you're subject to the same 35 percent flat tax on profits that professional corporations have. If your company profits over $100,000 per year, then this may be slightly beneficial for you (you may save a few points by avoiding the higher tax brackets). Otherwise, you may just want to consider keeping the partnership tax status or, if you wish to hire yourself and pay yourself a salary, electing S corporation tax status to avoid the hefty self-employment tax that cripples so many highly paid professionals.

If you're a single-member LLC, then you will not get your choice of taxation. Instead, the IRS designates your LLC a *disregarded entity,* and you're treated as a sole proprietorship for tax purposes. Elsewhere in this book I encourage you to avoid this pitfall by bringing on a partner. Unfortunately, with professional LLCs this becomes exceedingly difficult, due to the ownership restrictions I outline in the next section.

Restrictions on ownership

All states have pretty strict restrictions on who can own and operate a professional LLC. Many states restrict membership in professional LLCs to individuals in the licensed profession. For instance, if a legal practice decides to operate as a professional LLC, then non-lawyers cannot hold an interest in that practice. Some states require only a 50 percent majority of licensed professionals. Others allow previously licensed and retired practitioners to be members, and some allow heirs and/or beneficiaries to inherit membership interests upon the death of a licensed practitioner member.

Some states also restrict who can and cannot be managers of a PLLC. Make sure you check your state laws for restrictions pertaining to your business.

Restrictions on business activities

Like the ownership restrictions described in the preceding section, professional LLCs are statutorily confined to only transacting the sort of business or service that the licensed professionals who own it are licensed for. I'm not sure why the states did this. Perhaps they don't want things to get too muddy so the sightline of personal responsibility remains clear.

I, for one, don't like cages. Anything that restricts me drives me crazy. If you're like me, then you're probably thinking, "Nobody's going to tell me what business I can and cannot engage in!" (**Note:** This does not apply to drug-running or clubbing baby seals for a living.) If you're the entrepreneurial sort and, say, want to develop a software solution for your client base, you can't do this through your professional LLC. Luckily, I can offer you an easy solution: Simply form another, nonprofessional, entity to manage your other business objectives.

For your convenience, I posted all state laws pertaining to ownership and business activity restrictions of professional LLCs in a public wiki, accessible at www.docrun.com/wiki/pllc_restrictions. I recommend that you check it out and see where your state stands *before* making the decision to form a professional LLC.

Forming a professional LLC

Forming a professional LLC isn't difficult. The process is roughly the same as forming a standard LLC (which I outline in detail in Chapter 6), with a few major exceptions:

  ✔ You may need to show that you and your other members have been approved by your industry's licensing board before being able to form your professional LLC. In most states, you have to attach to your articles of organization and a copy of the members' professional licenses and/or include in the document the members' license numbers obtained from the licensing board.

✔ One or more of the licensed professionals usually has to sign the articles of organization. Unless you are preparing and filing your articles of organization yourself, getting the articles to a qualified member may cause significant lag time compared to forming a standard LLC, for which a third party can usually file the documents by signing as the organizer.

✔ You have to add a special designation at the end of your business name that identifies your company as a professional LLC. While the options vary somewhat from state to state, the required designation is usually *a Professional Limited Liability Company, a PLLC, P.L.L.C.,* or *PLLC.* Some states also allow such designations as *Limited, Ltd.,* or *Chartered.*

✔ Your name cannot make references to any services other than the services that your PLLC's members are licensed for. In some states, such as Nevada, the law is even more strict: Your name must contain the last name of one or more of the PLLC's current or former members.

In states where the last name of a professionally licensed member is required, you can often still operate under a different name. You simply file a fictitious firm name statement (also called a *DBA*) with your local county clerk. I show you how to do this in Chapter 4.

After you jump through these hoops and finally have your professional LLC filed, the differences don't end there. Throughout this book I advocate the importance of the LLC operating agreement. PLLCs are just as, if not more, in need of a comprehensive and ironclad operating agreement to govern them. Your personal assets may depend on it. Due to the nature of the PLLC, your operating agreement will vary substantially from that of the standard LLC.

The series LLC

In certain states, a limited liability company can be comprised of numerous *series* (or *cells*), each with their own separate veil of liability protection. This asset-protection device is called a *series LLC,* and in some states it saves the formation fees and hassle of creating multiple LLCs for each asset. Think of a *cell* as a protective barrier: Whatever is contained inside of it (usually a valuable asset of some sort) has its very own veil of liability protection. Nothing can touch it. Additionally, you only file one tax return and are only required to deal with the upkeep of one entity, not multiple ones.

Series LLCs were created several years ago under Delaware law for the purpose of simplifying structured financial transactions and collective investments such as mutual funds. Somehow, since that time, series LLCs migrated over to other investments and business ventures, such as real estate. More states started offering them and/or recognizing them, and within a few years, they became the talk of the town. And why not, right? Well, keep reading to find out why it isn't always the perfect fix.

Segregating your assets in a series LLC

I'm a big believer in forming a different entity for each of your assets (real estate, intellectual property, and so on) so you can separate and segregate each asset from the lawsuits and liabilities of the others. For instance, if you own a taxi company, a good practice is to place each vehicle or two into its own limited liability company. That way, if an accident occurs, the liability is confined to the one or two vehicles in that LLC and the rest of the business and its assets remain secure. Same goes for real estate investments: If all your property is in only one LLC, then if a renter sues you and a judgment is awarded, *all* your properties are at risk of seizure.

I get hammered with questions daily from clients who have heard of the series LLC and are interested in using this hot new entity type for their asset protection needs so that they don't have to form a lot of separate LLCs. I'll tell you exactly what I tell them: *New* isn't a good thing when it comes to entity types, and a series LLC is most likely not the vehicle to get you where you want to go. Not yet anyway. Series LLCs lack legal precedent (which means their effectiveness hasn't been tested in a court of law), and although the states that allow for their formation provide for that special barrier of liability protection between the different cells in their statutes, you have no guarantee that other states will agree. And if you form your series LLC in Delaware and register it to transact business in California for the purpose of holding California real estate, then your court case will probably be subject to California law — which, in this case, isn't a good thing!

To make matters worse, some states, such as California, don't offer series LLCs any fee-saving benefits. Whereas in Delaware and some other states you are required to pay an $800 franchise fee per LLC only, now you're required to pay it per series, so your tax bill remains the same as if each series was a separate LLC.

Where allowed, forming a series LLC can definitely save a chunk of change on filing fees in lieu of forming dozens of LLCs. But is saving a few hundred bucks really worth it? Without the liability protection of a series LLC being tried and verified by a court of law, you are signing yourself up to be the test bunny if you're ever dragged into court. The irony is that, in the end, using an entity meant to save you fees may be the very thing that ends up costing you everything!

As of the publishing of this book, series LLCs can be formed in the following states:

Delaware	Nevada	Texas
Illinois	Oklahoma	Utah
Iowa	Tennessee	Wisconsin

Forming a series LLC

Series LLCs are much easier to form than you may realize. The process is very similar to forming a regular LLC. In most states, you simply file the same articles of organization as you would for a regular LLC and add a provision to them which allows for the formation of *series* or *cells* within the company.

From there, the series LLC essentially exists in your company's operating agreement. As you can imagine, series LLCs require much different operating agreements from standard LLCs, and because the rules governing your LLC can vary from cell to cell, the length of your operating agreement will probably closely correspond to the number of cells you have in your LLC. Delaware state law does not cap the number of cells (series) an LLC may have; which means you could potentially have one exorbitantly long operating agreement when you're finished.

Maintaining a series LLC

Series LLCs aren't bad for the businesses they were intended for — structured investments — but relying on liability protection holding up *between* the cells concerns me, especially for high-liability ventures such as real estate. But if you're absolutely intent on using a series LLC for your assets or operating business and are willing to take the risk, this section shows you how to maintain it in order to maximize your chances in court.

First, you need to understand that series LLCs exist primarily in the operating agreement, and, given the flexible nature of the LLC, you have tremendous leeway as to how you structure each cell/series. If you wish to add or remove cells, you do so by simply amending your operating agreement. Your original filing, your articles of organization, remains unchanged.

If your series LLC ever ends up being scrutinized by a court of law, all that will uphold the insular nature of the liability protection among the various cells is whatever you have written in your operating agreement. Therefore, however you choose to structure it, make sure that it's rock solid. In Chapter 10, where I discuss all things operating agreements, I provide you with some sample provisions that can help you.

When you've established that your operating agreement is as comprehensive and cohesive as it possibly can be, you need to simply *be* a series LLC. If the cells of your series LLC are intended to replace separate LLCs, then you need to act in accordance with that. For all intents and purposes, each cell should be treated as a separate entity, complete with a separate set of books, records, and financials; a separate bank account; individual contracts; and so on.

The family LLC

If you've ever heard of the family limited partnership, then you may think you have an idea of what a family limited liability company is all about. Ironically, no such legal entity exists. If you call up your secretary of state and ask how to go about forming one, you'll hear a long pause at the end of the line, followed by laughter. These entities are just regular limited partnerships and limited liability companies that are specifically structured for holding family assets for asset protection and estate planning purposes.

Limited partnerships used to be the entity of choice for estate planning purposes; however, because LLCs are so flexible and have since developed enough case law to make them relatively reliable and predictable should you be taken to court, they're quickly encroaching on the limited partnership's domain.

The strength of the LLC in estate planning purposes is its ability to create a firm separation between the operating members of the business and the silent members. Unlike corporations, an ownership interest in an LLC does not entitle the interest holder (the *member*) to any management of the affairs and day-to-day operations of the company. This allows you to substantially reduce estate taxes by discounting the value of the membership interests in order to increase the amount of the assets allowed to be transferred tax free during your lifetime. I know this may all seem confusing now, but after you read Chapter 18 on estate planning, you'll be a pro, batting technical terms with your attorney while your kids look on wide-eyed.

Most, if not all, states allow you elect whether your entire LLC is treated as a single taxpayer or whether each cell is treated as a separate taxpayer. As an example, here is the statute from Illinois that addresses the topic of taxation:

> *Series of members, managers or limited liability company interests.*
> *(b) . . . A series with limited liability shall be treated as a separate entity to the extent set forth in the articles of organization. Each series with limited liability may, in its own name, contract, hold title to assets, grant security interests, sue and be sued and otherwise conduct business and exercise the powers of a limited liability company under this Act. The limited liability company and any of its series may elect to consolidate their operations as a single taxpayer to the extent permitted under applicable law, elect to work cooperatively, elect to contract jointly or elect to be treated as a single business for purposes of qualification to do business in this or any other state.*

Whether or not this is extended to federal taxation is debatable, because the IRS hasn't yet made any formal rulings on the topic. In the meantime, I advise you to treat each cell separately by obtaining separate tax identification numbers, filing separate Form 1065s, and issuing separate Schedule K-1s to that cell's members at the end of each fiscal year. These steps will help to further establish the segregation of the cells of your series LLC.

The low-profit LLC

The low-profit limited liability company (*L3C* for short), the newest form of LLC, is a hybrid entity that sets out to bridge the gap between the for-profit and nonprofit business structures. L3Cs are a product of the current social-consciousness movement and are still for-profit businesses, with the exception that profit motives take a back seat to the primary objective of public and social benefits. In other words, the first goal of the L3C is to make the world a better place.

Here is the Vermont statute that defines the L3C and its requirements for compliance:

> *(27) "L3C" or "low-profit limited liability company" means a person organized under this chapter that is organized for a business purpose that satisfies and is at all times operated to satisfy each of the following requirements:*
>
> *(A) The company:*
>
> *(i) significantly furthers the accomplishment of one or more charitable or educational purposes within the meaning of Section 170(c)(2)(B) of the Internal Revenue Code of 1986, 26 U.S.C. Section 170(c)(2)(B); and*
>
> *(ii) would not have been formed but for the company's relationship to the accomplishment of charitable or educational purposes.*
>
> *(B) No significant purpose of the company is the production of income or the appreciation of property; provided, however, that the fact that a person produces significant income or capital appreciation shall not, in the absence of other factors, be conclusive evidence of a significant purpose involving the production of income or the appreciation of property.*
>
> *(C) No purpose of the company is to accomplish one or more political or legislative purposes within the meaning of Section 170(c)(2)(D) of the Internal Revenue Code of 1986, 26 U.S.C. Section 170(c)(2)(D).*

The L3C is the first entity to be created with the IRS primarily in mind. The IRS offers tax relief for Program Related Investments, which promote socially conscious efforts, and the L3C was created to help entrepreneurs take advantage of those complex rules. While nonprofit corporations get a heck of a tax break (501(c)(3) organizations pay no tax at all!), limited liability companies offer a lot of financial and limited-liability benefits that nonprofits don't.

Nonprofits are pretty restrictive in nature, but LLCs allow pass-through taxation, flexible membership and management, and freedom in how profits are distributed among the members. The L3C serves to take advantage of these benefits while allowing some of the tax advantages afforded to nonprofits. However, unlike 501(c)(3) nonprofit organizations, investments in L3Cs are not tax deductible. Likewise, L3Cs are not exempt from paying federal and state taxes. They are subject to pass-through taxation, similar to that of a partnership or sole proprietorship, and are *not* allowed to elect a special form of taxation like a regular LLC has the right to do. On a brighter note, the IRS has yet to rule on whether or not the profit allocations of an L3C are subject to less taxation than the allocations from a regular LLC. We can only hope!

To learn more about L3Cs, please check my Web site, www.myllc.com, for updated articles and information. If your questions still aren't answered, feel free to drop me an e-mail and I'll assist you as best I can.

Chapter 3

Determining Whether an LLC Is Right for You

As a consultant, the most common question I get is "which entity is right for me?" That question is also the hardest to answer. With the exception of certain specific professions, such as real estate investors or professional services, the entity type that you should choose depends wholly on your individual circumstances. You have to take into account all aspects of your business, such as the income you anticipate taking in, the number of employees you intend to have, the amount of recordkeeping you're comfortable with, what state(s) you will be operating in, how you intend to obtain financing, your exit strategy, and other personal preferences.

The majority of the time, I can safely refer clients to the limited liability company simply because it's so flexible that it can work for most business needs. However, that's not always the case, and the worst time to find out you chose the wrong business structure is after the fact. As you find out in Chapter 7, where I deal with converting to and from different entity types, rectifying this mistake can result in a monstrous taxable event.

So this chapter is where I help you avoid all that drama and get started in the right direction! Here I compare LLCs with other business structures, and you see how LLCs can help you achieve a variety of different business goals.

Knowing Your Options: Other Business Structures

If you read the previous chapter, you're probably already sold on the limited liability company as the entity type for you — and you're probably right in that assessment! However, a limited liability company simply isn't the right match in a few situations. Before you can know for sure, you need to be aware of all the options. The following sections give you an overview of the different types of entities you have to choose from.

Going it alone: Sole proprietorships

Your kid's school bake sale . . . your stall at the local flea market . . . the consulting job you did where you weren't on the payroll — all perfect examples of sole proprietorships. A *sole proprietorship* automatically exists whenever you are engaging in business by and for yourself, without the protection of an LLC, corporation, or limited partnership. Although it sounds fancy and complicated, forming a sole proprietorship is about as easy as it gets.

Forming a sole-proprietorship

When asked how one goes about forming a sole proprietorship, the simplest answer I can give is: You don't. When you begin transacting business, be it selling crafts at the local art fair or doing Web design work in your spare time, you become a sole proprietor. Your state, city, and/or county may impose some business license requirements and fees on you in order for you to be allowed to do business in your current location, but as far as the federal government is concerned, you're in business.

In order for you to do business under a name other than your own, you can file a fictitious firm name statement (also called a *DBA*) with your county clerk. A DBA allows you to market your services under the name "Super-Duper Fantastic Web Design" rather than simply "<Insert Your Name Here>."

I know this all sounds incredibly easy — and, for the most part, it is — but there are a few drawbacks. Namely, even if you file a DBA, you're still a sole proprietorship. So although you may be operating under a name other than your own, don't get any lofty ideas that your business is anything other than just you. DBAs offer no barrier of legal separation between your business and yourself, and that should scare you. Keep reading to find out more about the considerations you have to take into account before settling on a sole proprietorship.

Shouldering full liability: The buck stops with you

Even though the sole proprietorship is simple to set up, it has many disadvantages. When you are operating as a sole proprietorship, your personal assets are unconditionally at risk of being seized in a lawsuit gone bad or by an angry creditor. There is an old saying, "You aren't in business until you've been sued," and as a sole proprietorship, you are handing over all your hard-earned assets (your home, your car, everything) on a silver platter. So if you're out selling cookies and somebody chokes on the oatmeal specials, you may be cashing out your kid's college fund sooner than you think.

Sole proprietorships are so popular because they are super cheap and easy to form, but if the business you're pondering involves any interaction with the general public, the costs you could find yourself facing can quickly eclipse whatever start-up fees you were trying to avoid in the first place. You won't think sole proprietorships are so "cheap and easy" if you lose everything you own.

Exploring a few other disadvantages

If I haven't scared you away from sole proprietorships yet, here are a few other drawbacks for you to ponder:

- **Limited financing options.** Unlike LLCs, which have membership interests, sole proprietorships don't have interests or any other form of ownership in the company. Your business is *you,* and you can't sell little pieces of yourself. This creates quite the conundrum if you want to raise money for your new venture by selling ownership interests.

- **No separate credit.** As an unincorporated entity, you cannot obtain credit in the name of the business. You're stuck using your own personal credit for things such as business loans and securing leases.

- **Limited life span.** With no legal separation between you and your business, your business is subject to the same limitations that you are; namely, your lack of immortality. In other words, your business dies when you do. After you pass away, instead of carrying on in one piece, your business goes through probate and your business assets get ripped apart; possibly even liquidated.

All these disadvantages don't change the fact that sole proprietorships are *easy.* You don't have to do anything to form them, and you don't have to worry about recordkeeping requirements, keeping separate accounts, or accidently commingling funds like you would with a limited liability company or corporation. In a sole proprietorship, you get the benefit of being autonomous. You *are* the business, and therefore, you answer to nobody. Well, except the customers.

At the end of the day, you need to decide whether or not going through the trouble and expense of forming your business as an LLC is worth your while. I can't give you a set answer to this, because it really depends on your individual situation, taking into account the value of your personal assets and how much exposure your entity has to the general public.

Not too long ago I was teaching a class of MBA students at the University of Southern California, and a woman starting up a T-shirt business asked whether or not she should form an LLC right away. My answer to her was this: When you go into business, you definitely need to be under the protection of an LLC or corporation; however, before undertaking the formation process, operating as a sole proprietor for a bit to test your market is okay. During this trial period, she could print up samples and meet with various retailers to see what sort of reception her T-shirts get. Testing the market allows her to find out whether she has a viable market while risking only what she has paid to the local screen printer.

Losing LLC benefits with disregarded entity taxation

Like the courts, the IRS doesn't consider a sole proprietorship to be separate from its owner, which is why it's treated as a *disregarded entity* by the IRS. Disregarded entities have a form of taxation often referred to as *pass-through taxation,* because the business isn't taxed directly. Instead, the revenues and expenses of the business pass through directly to the owner.

To calculate business profits and losses, the owner adds a Schedule C to his 1040. On one side of the Schedule C, he lists his business revenue; on the other side, he lists his business expenses. Subtract one from the other and voilà! — you get your net profit or net loss. This number gets transferred over to the 1040 and you incorporate the income (or the loss) into your normal tax burden.

Before applying your normal income tax rate to your business profits, you need to factor in a 15.3 percent self-employment tax. This tax serves as a substitute for the Social Security and Medicare taxes that would normally be taken out of your paycheck. Shocked by the amount? Well, you may not realize this, but when you pay the 6.2 percent Social Security tax and the 1.45 percent Medicare tax out of your salary each week, your employer has to match it. Now that you are working for yourself, you get the full burden: 12.4 percent Social Security plus 2.9 percent Medicare equals a whopping 15.3 percent! To ease the burden a bit, the IRS allows you to deduct half of the total amount of the self-employment tax.

Adding a partner: General partnerships

Sole proprietorships, by their very nature, can only be owned by one person, so when a sole proprietor takes on one or more partners, a general partnership is born. Occasionally, partners will create a general partnership agreement, but, like a sole proprietorship, no other paperwork is completed and no filings need to be made for the formation to take place. All you have to do is start transacting business!

Even verbal agreements hold up in most states, so just because you don't have the terms of your partnership in writing doesn't mean you aren't held to them. Unless you want the fate of your business to rest on the hasty decision of a judge (who often is inexperienced), getting any and all agreements in writing is imperative.

Even *non-membership-related agreements,* which take on another individual for services but don't make them a partner, should be executed in writing so that the ownership (or lack thereof) can't be put up for interpretation at a later date.

Doubling the trouble by doubling the partners

As easy as general partnerships are to form, getting into trouble with them is equally easy. In a lot of ways a general partnership is even *more* dangerous than a sole proprietorship. In a business that is organized as a general partnership, all the partners are *jointly* responsible for all the debts, judgments, negligent acts, obligations, and taxes of that business. This means that not only are you held personally responsible for those things that you had a hand in, but you also are personally responsible for the acts of your partners! This holds true even for silent partners who aren't aware of or involved in the day-to-day operation of the business.

All partners in a general partnership are held *jointly and equally liable* for the debts and obligations of the business. For example, say a partner at the deli you own wants to save a buck or two and, without your approval or knowledge, orders the weekly delivery of prosciutto from a shady supplier. A few days later, a customer calls in — his 5-year-old got a severe bout of food poisoning, landing her in the hospital. The angry parent sues your partnership, and he not only has full recourse against the personal assets of the offending partner, but he also can seize your own house, car, and other assets in order to satisfy the judgment.

Finding out other disadvantages

In addition to this added exposure to liability, general partnerships share all the disadvantages that sole proprietorships do. Like a sole proprietorship, a general partnership isn't in any way separate from its owners. This means that your business cannot sell ownership interests in exchange for capital contributions and other forms of investment, making raising any sort of formal financing close to impossible.

Another disadvantage to keep in mind is that the durability of the partnership is only as great as its weakest link. If one of the partners becomes disabled, goes bankrupt, or passes away, then the entire partnership goes with him.

Filing with partnership taxation

General partnerships are subject to *partnership taxation*. This is a form of *pass-through taxation,* where the profits and losses of the business flow through directly to the owners to be claimed on their personal tax returns. The partnership itself is not actually taxed. Instead, the partners are taxed on their share of the partnership income.

At the end of the business's fiscal year, you simply file an information statement (Form 1065, which lists all the income and expenses that the business incurred during that time frame) with the IRS. After you've totaled the amount of profit (or loss) that the partnership has accrued, you then issue each member a Form K-1, which lists their shares of the profits that they must pay taxes on (or losses that they can use to offset income from other ventures). You can generally divide the profits and losses among the partners however you want, as long as all the profit gets allocated. If you're interested in learning more about partnership taxation, I go over it in more detail in Chapter 8.

General partnerships are subject to the same form of taxation that is the default for limited liability companies. However, the similarities end there. A general partnership is not considered an *incorporated entity* and offers zero liability protection for its owners.

Throwing in a little legal protection: Limited partnerships

Think of a *limited partnership* as a general partnership with a little bit of protection against lawsuits thrown in. Whereas a general partnership doesn't protect any of the owners against the business's lawsuits and creditors, a limited partnership protects the silent partners of the business (also called the *limited partners*). Limited partners can receive profit from the company, but they don't manage the business's day-to-day operations. If the business goes south, the limited partners only risk losing the money they have invested in the company, while the managers (called *general partners*) still put all their personal assets at risk.

As far as the general partners are concerned, the business may as well be a general partnership. The general partners are jointly and equally liable to the debts and obligations of the business, even those entered into by the other general partner(s). Also like a general partnership, a limited partnership is subject to partnership taxation.

Limited partnerships can have any number of general and limited partners, as long as they have at least one general partner to take the blame if something goes wrong.

I'm often asked why anyone bothers to use a limited partnership, especially considering that they're somewhat complicated to set up and they lack basic liability protection for the general partners. These reasons alone make the limited partnership a bad choice for business owners; however, because of their limitations on the decision-making power of the limited partners, limited partnerships are still great for use in estate planning (for example, the kids can receive money from, but not manage, the assets of the limited partnership). If estate planning is something you're interested in, I discuss it at greater length in Chapter 18.

Meeting the black sheep of the partnership family: LLPs and LLLPs

Before the limited liability company was born, a few enterprising states decided to create variations on the limited partnership (which I discuss in detail in Chapter 2). The two main variations are the *limited liability partnership* (*LLP* for short) and the *limited liability limited partnership* (or *LLLP*). You probably won't see a lot of these entities in practice nowadays, because the LLC has trumped all their benefits. However, they still have some roles to play in professional partnerships and real estate transactions.

These entity types aren't available in all states. If you're thinking of forming an LLP or LLLP, you should first check your state's laws to see whether or not these entity types are recognized in your jurisdiction.

Limited liability partnership (LLP)

The limited liability partnership is like a limited partnership without any limited partners. LLPs only have general partners who are held personally responsible for the debts and obligations of the business. So how is this different from a general partnership, you ask? Well, LLPs have an added layer of liability protection that insulates the partners of the business from the wrongful acts of the other partners. In other words, if you're a partner in an LLP, then you're only responsible for your own misdeeds, not those of a shady business partner.

LLPs emerged in the early 1990s in response to the real estate crash in the previous years. After a wave of bank failures, there was a rush to recover assets by targeting the accountants and lawyers who had advised the failed banks. LLPs were then created to help shield the personal assets of the innocent lawyers and accountants from the massive claims made on their partnerships. The new partnership structure caught on quickly, and by 1996, more than 40 states had adopted rules on the formation and governance of an LLP entity type.

To this day, LLPs are still used and are a common structure for professionals such as lawyers, accountants, doctors, and architects. This entity makes sense for them because licensed professionals aren't allowed to have the same levels of personal liability protection that are provided by regular LLCs and corporations. Some states — particularly California, Nevada, New York, and Oregon — *only* allow LLPs to be used in this manner.

Limited liability limited partnership (LLLP)

The limited liability limited partnership (try saying that ten times fast!) is sort of a hybrid between the limited partnership and the limited liability partnership. Like the limited partnership, the LLLP has both *limited partners* who have limited liability and only risk losing whatever amount they invested in the business and *general partners* who are personally liable for the debts and obligations of the business. Like in a limited partnership, only the general partners are allowed to engage in the day-to-day management of the business.

From a silent investor's perspective, this sort of arrangement can help keep the general partners honest. After all, they'll be a lot less apt to let the business flounder if their personal assets are at stake. Because of this feature, LLLPs are common in real estate ventures, with the financial backers acting as the silent limited partners.

LLLPs have yet to really catch on and still are only allowed in about half the states. They are usually formed by converting an existing limited partnership.

Separating yourself from your business: Corporations

If this is your first venture, you may think of all corporations as massive multinational conglomerates. Luckily for you, this isn't the case. Corporations have been around for centuries and until recently were the only business structure that allowed entrepreneurs to start ventures without opening themselves up to heaps of personal liability. Contrary to popular belief, they aren't much more difficult to form and maintain than limited liability companies.

You'll notice that the vast majority of the publicly traded companies are structured as corporations. This is because, unlike limited liability companies, corporations have free transferability of ownership interests (called *stock*). They are also backed by hundreds of years of case law that removes any questions as to the outcome of lawsuits. This is especially true in Delaware, where a court of chancery takes lawsuits involving corporations incredibly seriously and has worked hard to develop fair and accurate case law that directly supports and benefits the shareholders of the business. This chancery court is why most publicly traded corporations are Delaware corporations.

Creating a legal "person"

A corporation is different from a sole proprietorship or partnership in that it's considered to be a legal entity unto itself, completely separate from its owners (called *shareholders*). In the eyes of the law, corporations are treated as if they were people with distinct identities. They are able to sue and be sued, and lawsuits have to be brought against the corporation, rather than the individual shareholders. (A limited liability company has a lot of similar characteristics, which is why they are considered hybrid entities.)

Maintaining the separation between you and your business becomes a big concern when you're operating as a corporation. If this legal separation fails, a creditor could *pierce the corporate veil* and go after your personal assets to settle the debts and obligations of the business.

In order to maintain your corporation's liability protection, you must be diligent about your recordkeeping. This includes drafting minutes that document the annual and special meetings of the shareholders and directors. Even if you're the sole shareholder, these formalities still need to be followed, and all major decisions affecting the operation of the business need to be made by formal resolution and properly documented. In addition, you must keep accurate financial records and absolutely refrain from commingling personal funds with those of your business.

These steps to protect yourself may seem like a lot of work, but it will all be worth it in the long run. Limited liability companies have fewer recordkeeping requirements but also less case law that substantiates that recordkeeping *isn't* required. If you decide that a corporation is the route for you, then you'll want to sign up for an online service that automates and stores your company recordkeeping. For a few hundred dollars, you can relax, knowing that your corporate veil will hold up in court. You'll also have fewer intercompany disputes because all major decisions will be made according to procedure and accurately documented.

A corporation also protects its owners from lawsuits and creditors; however, only an LLC also protects *the business* from the liabilities of the owners. So if a shareholder of a corporation is sued for personal reasons, her ownership *(stock)* of the corporation is considered to be a personal asset of hers and can be seized by the judgment creditor. Depending on the level of your personal exposure to liability, the fact that corporations lack this *dual protection* (which is inherent in a limited liability company) may end up being a huge prohibiting factor for you.

Dealing with the blow of double taxation

Like the courts, the Internal Revenue Service also considers corporations to be entities separate from their owners. Corporations are the only entities that are subject to their own taxation. The company's profit (or loss) does not flow through to the owners of the business, but instead remains in the corporation and is subject to corporate income tax.

From there, you can distribute the profits to the shareholders in the form of *dividends*. This is where things can get a bit tricky. After the profit is distributed to the shareholders, it is then taxed again at the shareholder level (usually in the form of capital gains). Because the same profits are taxed twice — both at the corporate level and also at the individual shareholder level — this situation is commonly referred to as *double taxation*.

As scary as it sounds, double taxation doesn't have to be a bad thing. If you pay yourself a salary, then the amount you pay with double-taxation is roughly equitable to the additional amount you would pay anyway in self-employment tax. And if you wish to retain the profits in the company, then you'll actually pay less in taxes than if your business was subject to the pass-through taxation of, say, a partnership or sole proprietorship. In Chapter 8, I go into more detail on ways you can curtail the double-taxation problem.

When a corporation issues dividends to its shareholders, it doesn't have the same flexibility that a limited liability company enjoys. Dividends in a corporation must be issued in proportion to the shareholders' ownership interests.

Unfortunately, the corporation's losses cannot be passed on to the individual shareholders to help offset their other income. While the losses do need to stay in the corporation, this isn't such a bad deal for small businesses that intend to turn a profit any time soon. Corporate losses can be used to offset corporate profits in other years, up to 2 years retroactively and up to 20 years in the future.

As you may have read in Chapter 2, limited liability companies have the option to elect corporate taxation.

The IRS recognizes corporations as separate entities, so unlike in partnerships and sole proprietorships, you can't transfer assets in and out of a corporation without creating a taxable event.

Easing the tax burden: S corporations

All *S corporations* start out their lives as regular corporations. An S corporation is only formed when a regular corporation elects a special small business tax status with the IRS by filing an S Election, Form 2553. This filing is done within a few months of the corporation's formation.

Obtaining pass-through taxation, corporation style

S corporation tax status is a pass-through tax status. This means that, like sole proprietorship or partnership taxation, the revenues and expenses of the business "pass through" to the shareholders' individual tax returns. The similarities end there, however. S corporation tax status requires that the business file its own tax return, the 1120S (instead of the form 1120 return that regular corporations are required to file); however, the company is still required to issue K-1s to the shareholders as it would if it were a partnership.

The main difference between S corporation taxation and that of other entities is that the owners/shareholders can be employed by the business and pay themselves a salary that is subject to the same sort of payroll taxes deducted from all paychecks. If you've been paying attention so far, you're probably wondering what the big deal is — after all, as I mentioned earlier in the chapter, self-employment tax is equal to the Social Security and Medicare tax that gets deducted for each employee. So where are the savings?

Here's the kicker: Any profit allocated to the shareholders above and beyond the "reasonable salary" they've already paid themselves is not subject to the 15.3 percent self-employment tax. If your business generates more than the salary you pay yourself, this can result in substantial savings. What constitutes a "reasonable salary" in the eyes of the IRS? Well, the amount isn't really set in stone, but if you were ever audited, they would want to make sure it is consistent with the standard for a professional with your job title and responsibilities in your industry. If you aren't sure what amount this is, you may want to do a quick search using the Salary Wizard on `www.salary.com`, a site that lists average salaries for various job titles.

Complicating matters with IRS restrictions

The IRS seems to live by the maxim that all roses have thorns, and if a rose doesn't have thorns, gosh darn it, they'll give it some! So the IRS gave the S corporation ownership restrictions. Lots of them. If your corporation (or even your LLC) has elected S corporation tax status, then you are required to abide by these few little rules:

- Your corporation must not have more than 100 shareholders.

- Shareholders can consist only of natural persons, individual trusts (for estate planning purposes), and tax-exempt nonprofit organizations. This specifically excludes any other entity or business structure, such as limited liability companies or corporations.

- Shareholders must be citizens or alien residents of the United States. Sorry, no foreigners allowed!

- The corporation is only allowed to issue one class of stock. You'll have to save the preferred shares for your IPO.

- Banks and insurance companies are barred from being shareholders.

- All shareholders must unanimously consent to the S corporation tax designation. In other words, a majority vote just won't do the trick.

If you're truly a small business, then an S corporation may suit you. Just make sure that you intend to stay small for the time being, because when you elect to be an S corporation, you're stuck with the decision for five years. That's the least amount of time that needs to pass before the IRS will allow you to make another tax election.

Getting Personal: Using an LLC to Achieve Your Goals

I've noticed that a lot of books about LLCs and corporations dive into the advantages and disadvantages of the various entity types but never help you bridge that gap between understanding these business structures and applying them to your real-world situation. It's a tough endeavor, especially because no one's requirements and circumstances are ever exactly alike.

If you haven't already, read Chapter 2 regarding the ins and outs of limited liability companies. The background information there will help you make sense of what I tell you in this section. After skimming Chapter 2, you'll have a pretty good idea of the various entity types you can choose from. And in this section, I show you many of the possible benefits that forming an LLC can bring to not only your business plans but also your personal financial plans.

Keep in mind that if I promote one entity over another, it's not because I'm biased on the matter. The truth is that due to the tremendous amount of flexibility a limited liability company offers, it may very well end up being your entity of choice.

Starting a new venture

The majority of the questions I get from readers are in relation to starting a new venture. My answers depend on whether you're looking to create the next Google or a cure for cancer, or whether you're only interested in putting food on the table and nothing more. If the latter applies to you, then you'll want to skip to the later section "Running a small business." If you want to start a company with the potential to be huge, keep reading.

One of the primary concerns of starting a new venture is acquiring capital. This need can be a game changer when it comes to selecting an entity type for your new business. If you seriously intend to go after private equity (venture capital, institutional investors, and so on) or raise money through an *initial public offering (IPO),* then you may want to form your business as a corporation, rather than as a limited liability company. In this section, I tell you some of the big reasons why.

Your first round of financing is often referred to as your *Series A* round. When you get your first private equity term sheet, one of the things you'll notice is that the venture capital firm or institutional investor isn't issued plain ol' common stock. Instead, it gets *preferred shares,* usually titled Series A, that offer it special privileges, such as

- Liquidity (the shares can be converted to common stock).
- First dibs at dividends and the proceeds of any liquidation that occurs.
- Anti-dilution protection, which allows the investor to maintain its fractional (for example, 15 percent) ownership of the company, even when more stock is issued in the future.
- Mandatory or optional redemption schedules (indicating when the investor can sell out). This keeps the investor in the game until the company's had a chance to prove itself.

> ✔ Special voting rights and preferences giving it special abilities to exercise control over the management.
>
> ✔ A fixed return on investment.

Any future financing rounds are titled Series B, Series C, and so on, with the most recent taking priority and first position. If you want more information on securities issues, such as registrations and exemptions, you can flip to Chapter 13.

Corporation shares were made to be liquid and freely transferable, and although a limited liability company can be structured to have similar flexibility, it isn't designed for it. Also, though the formalities required for corporations may be a drag for the small business owner, sophisticated investors have grown to appreciate them. With the law on their side, they can be sure to get their regular financial statements and know that all corporate decisions are properly documented, which will help avoid intercompany disputes later on. The fixed structure of the shareholders, directors, and officers of a corporation also offer an established set of roles that have been well tried and tested over the years.

Because corporations have been around for so long, a lot of case law has developed around them, which significantly limits any chance of courtroom surprises down the road. This is especially true in Delaware, where a special chancery court handles all business issues and is backed by hundreds of years of case law. LLCs, on the other hand, don't have the benefit of a long history. They are the new kid on the block, and when an investment firm is handing over millions of dollars, the last thing they want is another unknown.

Bracing yourself for phantom income

Now we come to the unpleasant subject of taxes. As the business is expanding, it will undoubtedly be reinvesting its profits for the first few years. Whenever you retain earnings in an entity with pass-through taxation, a phenomenon called *phantom income* occurs. You must *allocate* the profits to the members — this is the number that they carry over to their personal tax returns and pay income tax on — but you don't actually *distribute* the profits to them, thus giving the members no cash to pay the taxes with. No matter how nice your venture capital firm is, I highly doubt it will be keen on paying your company taxes for you.

Phantom income can also cause a hindrance when you're bootstrapping your way to success and issue stock to employees in exchange for reduced salaries. If, at the end of the year, all they get is a fat tax bill with no extra money to pay for it, they'll most likely think twice about working for you.

Seeing when an LLC will work

Small-time angel investors, friends, family members, and other investors who don't require a complex capital structure in order to invest money into your business or idea may actually prefer a limited liability company over a corporation. Most companies don't operate at a profit their first year, and due to the pass-through taxation of LLCs, the company losses flow to the company's owners. These losses can be used as a fat write-off to offset the investor's other income. With all other things being equal, the investor gets to write off the value of his investment immediately.

When you are raising money with your LLC, you must make sure that you have ironclad buy-sell agreements in place. I show you how to draft these in Chapter 9.

Running a small business

Tens of millions of Americans operate small businesses. They range from small, home-based businesses on the side to fully operational companies with many employees. For the most part, these individuals are operating without protection. Granted, they may not take what they do too seriously. They may consider themselves independent contractors or consultants, but in today's litigious society, operating without even a basic level of liability protection is a bad move.

If you are operating as a sole proprietorship, you probably are used to a specific way of being taxed and the liberty of not having to keep any records or officially document any decisions. And, unless you are a full-fledged operation, you may think this freedom is worth the risks. Spending a lot of time and money to form a corporation or limited liability company is overkill for the simple, at-home Web page designer, plumber, or dog walker, right? Well, consider this: What if one of the dogs you're walking bites someone? Or the pipes you installed burst, causing tens of thousands of dollars in water damage? When you're sued, you are at risk to lose everything — not just your business, but all your personal assets as well.

Very few businesses wouldn't benefit from the protection of an LLC or corporation. If you're still operating as a sole proprietor, my guess is that you've been advised to remain so by your accountant or CPA. What a lot of tax professionals don't understand is that even if a particular situation may not derive any tax benefits from forming an LLC or corporation, operating as a sole proprietorship is still a dangerous proposition because of the risk of losing all your personal assets in a lawsuit. In this section, I present the options that small business owners have for protecting their companies and personal assets.

I don't address limited partnerships here because they aren't really suitable for small businesses — they neither limit the liability of the general partners from the debts and obligations of the business nor insulate the owners from the misdeeds of their partners. If you're pondering a limited partnership for your small business, I recommend looking into LLCs instead.

Relying on insurance doesn't cut it

Business liability insurance is a good way to help protect yourself. I happen to be a big proponent of these insurance policies because they add an extra layer of protection . . . the key word being *extra.* Most insurance policies have disclaimers a mile long, and the insurance companies aren't too keen about paying out in a timely manner. Also, having only business liability insurance tends to *encourage* lawsuits rather than deter them, as a limited liability company does. Your best bet is to keep the policy as your second line of defense, rather than your only defense, especially if you're a small-time independent contractor such as a baby sitter or pet sitter.

Following are the only two exceptions to the rule of using an LLC with business liability insurance as a second form of protection:

- ✔ If your company isn't exposed to a lot of liability and is so small that forming a corporation or LLC for your business would be cost prohibitive (like in California, where the fees can be pretty gnarly), then you may want to look into getting a good insurance policy and saving the LLC for later when you're more established and have more dough.

- ✔ If you're a licensed professional and any entity your state would allow you to operate under doesn't offer any liability protection whatsoever, you better have some good malpractice insurance backing you up!

If you don't take your business seriously, neither will your customers. One of the easiest ways to show that you're serious about what you do is to form a corporation or limited liability company. Adding *Inc.* or *LLC* after your name helps reassure your customers that you're official, not some fly-by-night operation. You'd be surprised how beneficial this can be to a small business. So much so that the added business may far exceed the formation costs.

Seeing how S corporations benefit the successful

S corporations have pass-through taxation similar to LLCs, with the difference being that the owner of an S corporation is allowed to hire herself. As long as she pays herself a salary commensurate with those of her peers, all additional profits are *not* subject to self-employment tax.

In a nutshell, this means that if the total income you personally derive from your business each year is more than the average salary of others with a similar job description, then from a tax savings perspective, you should elect to be taxed as an S corporation over any other form of pass-through taxation.

Otherwise, you may want to opt for the pass-through taxation of an LLC, because LLCs are much more flexible entities, have dual liability protection, and aren't subject to the same ownership restrictions as S corporations.

S corporations come with a whole slew of ownership restrictions, which I address earlier in this chapter in "Complicating matters with IRS restrictions." If you aren't prepared to abide by them, you shouldn't elect S corporation taxation. Otherwise, you'll automatically revert to corporation tax status, which can bring about some pretty large tax burdens if you aren't prepared for them.

Taking it to the next level with C corporations

Regular corporations are often referred to as *C corporations* in order to differentiate them from S corporations. C corporations are subject to double taxation of profits, which tends to scare a lot of entrepreneurs away. It shouldn't. Because the corporation is taxed as its own entity, profits are only subject to corporate tax rates which, if under $50,000, are only 15 percent. The tax rate is tiered, and after about $75,000 of profit, the tax rate jumps to the 30+ percent range.

This high rate can seem a bit daunting at first, but keep in mind that most upstarts and growing enterprises operate at a pretty modest profit. This is especially true for corporations, which are allowed to deduct a lot of other business expenses that S corps and LLCs cannot. While the extra paperwork and recordkeeping required for a corporation, as well as the tax structure, may be a bit much for a simple independent contractor trying to feed his family, they're well suited for businesses that place a high priority on growth and want to retain company profits. I discuss corporate taxation in more detail in Chapter 8.

Another scenario in which a corporation is a better option is if your company is operating in multiple states. Multistate taxation is often much more favorable at the corporate tax level than any other form of taxation, especially that of the S corporation. I discuss multistate taxation issues in more detail in Chapter 12.

Combining all the perks in one entity: LLCs

Although in the previous sections I discuss the merits of S corporations and C corporations for small businesses, everything I've said thus far is applicable to LLCs, because they are the only entity type that can choose how they want to be taxed. By default, LLCs are subject to partnership taxation; however, they can also elect corporate taxation or S corporation taxation. When a form of taxation is chosen, you're stuck with it for five years, but this sort of flexibility is one of the reasons LLCs are perfect for almost all small businesses. I devote Chapter 8 to selecting the right form of taxation for your LLC.

LLCs are superior to S corporations and C corporations in so many situations, I could go on all day, but I'll keep this short and sweet: In short, I strongly recommend that you form your small business as a limited liability company if:

- ✔ **You and your partners require varied distributions of profit.** With a corporation, you are required to issue dividends in proportion to the ownership percentages. Not so with LLCs.

- ✔ **You want to allow yourself to grow a bit before electing corporate taxation.** Because LLCs are automatically subject to partnership taxation, you can enjoy the pass-through taxation for a few years until you're ready to elect corporate taxation.

- ✔ **You and your partners have a lot of personal liability.** Remember, LLCs have *dual liability protection,* which protects the integrity of the business if one of your partners *personally* faces bankruptcy, divorce, or the wrath of a judgment creditor.

- ✔ **You want a flexible ownership/management structure.** With LLCs, you have a lot of flexibility on who can and cannot engage in the day-to-day acts of the business, whereas with a corporation, you're stuck with the traditional structure of officers managing day-to-day operations, directors managing the officers, and shareholders managing the directors.

- ✔ **You want pass-through taxation, yet you cannot abide by the restrictions that come with operating as an S corporation.** If you have an institutional investor or a business partner who is not a U.S. citizen, you're automatically put into this category.

- ✔ **You have substantial assets that you want to transfer into (or out of) the business.** Only with LLCs can assets be transferred in and out without creating a taxable event.

- ✔ **Partners of the business will be personally guaranteeing business loans and debts.** Only with an LLC is recourse debt allowed to be calculated as a loss to the responsible member. (This is one reason why LLCs are so popular for holding real estate — so the mortgage interest deduction can be passed on to the guaranteeing member.)

- ✔ **Investors want capital contributions to be immediately deductible.** Should the business not make a profit in that year, the partner will theoretically be able to take whatever he contributed last year as a loss. With an S corporation, that loss can only be taken after the business has folded. With a C corporation, that loss never flows back to the individual and instead remains in the business, allowed to be carried forward up to 20 years.

If you are set on S corporation taxation, your best bet may be to make that tax election through a limited liability company rather than the traditional corporation. LLCs, by statute, require a lot less formal recordkeeping than corporations.

Even if you opt for a corporation, if your business has substantial assets, you should do your best to insulate each asset in its own limited liability company. That way, the asset is safe from the liabilities of the operating business and the liabilities of the individual shareholders. I show you how to do this in Chapter 16.

Flying solo

If you are the sole owner of your LLC, then you're considered to be a single-member LLC by the states. Since LLCs were initially set up to be partnerships, this changes things substantially. First, some states don't even allow single-member LLCs (SLLCs). To see whether or not you're one of the unlucky ones, go to www.docrun.com/wiki/sllcs, where I list each state's laws pertaining to SLLCs.

If you are allowed to form an SLLC, keep in mind the following two main drawbacks:

- ✔ You may not have the dual layer of liability protection — *charging order protection* — that I discuss in Chapter 16. Charging order protection is set up to protect the innocent partners in the LLC, and courts in a few states have decided that because SLLCs have no innocent partners, charging order protection shouldn't apply. So far, in the cases where charging order protection for an SLLC was brought up for question, the courts have *disallowed* this second layer of liability protection for SLLCs. This isn't a good track record for single-member LLCs and definitely packs the odds against you should you ever get dragged into court!

- ✔ When operating as a single-member LLC, in the eyes of the IRS you're a *disregarded entity*. This means that you are taxed exactly as if you were a sole proprietorship. There's no budging with this one; you're stuck with that form of taxation and aren't allowed to elect otherwise. The only instance in which this is desirable is if you're using LLCs to hold real estate. (See Chapter 17 for more on LLCs and real estate.) Otherwise, limiting your taxation options isn't a good thing.

If you're a single-member LLC, I recommend that you find a trusted friend or family member and issue her a small percentage of your membership. Two to three percent should be sufficient. You can even structure your operating agreement in a way that the lucky token partner isn't able to engage in management, vote, or receive profit allocations and distributions. The one caveat to this strategy is that it does not work with your spouse, because an LLC owned by a husband and wife is still considered a *disregarded entity* by the IRS. Kids, siblings, parents, and other family members are okay.

There has yet to be a ruling on whether married, same-sex couples count as one member in the eyes of the IRS. So for now your significant other can technically count as a second partner, but you'll be at the mercy of whatever the courts decide in the future (pray yours isn't the case it's being decided on!).

Handling multiple businesses with multiple options

One of the most common topics I get asked about is how to manage multiple businesses. Sometimes the businesses are so closely related and don't generate enough income to make it practical to insulate each one in its own LLC. In this case, if the ownership structure of each business is the same, then operating them all under one entity should be fine.

On the other hand, if the ownership structure of each business is *different,* then this is one of the few instances in which you may want to form a series LLC. You can place each business in its own *series* with different ownership. In some states, this will help you save on filing fees and other related expenses. Just keep in mind that series LLCs are still unproven entities, so don't count on having a barrier of liability protection between the individual cells. In other words, if one business gets sued, the other businesses in the other cells may be attached to the claim. I address series LLCs in greater detail in Chapter 2.

If your multiple businesses are either substantial enough or different enough in their scope and purpose to justify forming them as individual entities, you have a few options. If the individual entities are each formed as limited liability companies, then nothing else is needed. You can simply hold your membership interests of each LLC in your own name. Too often I see people unnecessarily complicating this arrangement with multiple layers of entities.

However, if your limited liability companies all have the same ownership structure, you may want to form a parent corporation. This structure will insulate all your businesses from each other and also allow the profit of each LLC to flow through to the parent corporation. With this strategy, you can probably get by with only filing one return for the parent corporation, and even having the parent corporation process the payroll for all your entities. In this instance, an extra entity serving as the parent company can *reduce* the paperwork hassle and make your life a bit easier.

If your multiple businesses are either corporations or a mix of corporations and LLCs, then you may want to consider forming an LLC as a *personal holding company.* By having your stock and/or membership in the various entities issued to the name of your personal LLC holding company, you can still benefit from the *dual liability protection* that an LLC offers. This protects the corporate stock (seen by the courts as a personal asset of yours) from seizure, if you get sued personally. And as far as the taxes go, whatever profit the corporation distributes *passes through* your LLC and goes directly to you, with no taxable event taking place. With partnership taxation, when this sort of passive income passes to you, it is taxed as ordinary income and is not subject to self-employment tax.

Do not use a corporation as a holding company for corporate stock. Since profits are taxed at the corporate level and then again at the individual level, these profits that were already subject to double taxation would now be subject to triple and quadruple taxation as they finally get into your hands.

A good rule of thumb for deciding whether to create additional entities as holding companies, subsidiaries, and so on, is to ask yourself why you want to. If you don't have a clear, obvious answer for this, then the extra entities you want to form are probably overkill. And if you're still anxious to throw around the extra dough, feel free to spend it taking me to lunch the next time you're in Los Angeles!

Organizing your professional practice

In Chapter 2, I discuss in detail the restrictions on certain service professionals (such as doctors, lawyers, and accountants) from being allowed to operate as a regular limited liability company. Well, the same goes for corporations. If you are a licensed professional, you may not even be *allowed* to run your business as a corporation. Instead, you may be required to form what is called a *professional corporation* or a *professional service corporation*. If this applies to you, then I suggest you flip back to Chapter 2 and read the section addressing professional limited liability companies.

Professional corporations (also referred to as *personal service corporations*) are taxed differently from regular corporations. Instead of the graduated tax status of a regular corporation, professional corporations are imposed a 35 percent flat tax. So if you're making less than $100k per year, forming your practice as a professional corporation won't be advantageous tax-wise.

You're left with two alternatives:

- ✔ You form your practice as a corporation and elect S corporation tax status by filing a Form 2553 with the IRS soon after your company has been filed. This filing allows all profits to flow to you and your partners, wherein you pay taxes at the personal level.

- ✔ You form your practice as a professional limited liability company (assuming your state even recognizes these) and you're automatically granted pass-through taxation. If your professional LLC has multiple members, it will be taxed as a partnership, and if it only has you as the sole member, it will be treated as a disregarded entity and taxed like a sole proprietorship.

A caveat to these options: Remember, if you operate as an LLC, you're not allowed to hire members (including yourself) as employees of the business and pay a payroll tax on the salaries. Therefore, if you wish to hire yourself, you'll want to go the S corporation route. If you try to hire the members as employees under an LLC and you get audited, you'll have a pretty hefty bill to pay at tax time. However, if your practice builds up substantial assets, a PLLC offers charging order protection that S corporations don't, so it's a trade-off.

No matter what entity you choose, always make sure you have proper liability insurance.

Maximizing real estate investments

First and foremost, I am going to say something that is so important I'm giving it its own line on the page:

Holding investment property in your own name is the worst thing you can do.

Please read that again and again until it is like a mantra that keeps repeating in your head. Of course, this statement is not 100 percent factual. Technically you could do worse things, such as look down a mortar tube after lighting a firework to see why it didn't go off, profess to the IRS that income taxes are not legal and you don't have to pay them, point a gun at the police. . . . However, holding your property in your own name is a really terrible idea. You see, if your tenant slips on the front porch, not only will your property be dust, but also your savings, your other properties, and even your kid's college fund (and possibly even your dog, if he is valuable enough!). If they know you have assets, attorneys and claimants can be vicious beyond belief. Get it? Got it? Good.

So now that you know you need some kind of entity to protect your real estate, the following sections help you compare corporations to LLCs.

Knowing when corps can kill

This section is by far the easiest one to write because the limited liability company has such an acute advantage over all other entities when it comes to holding real estate. With all the characteristics of LLCs — their flexibility, their pass-through taxation, their dual-layer liability protection — it's almost as if they were made for real estate.

If you're using an entity to hold real estate assets, you're most likely looking to gain passive income from the investment. If you were to place that rental property into a corporation, all the passive income you earn would be subject to double taxation — first at the corporate level and then individually when you remove the profits. What's worse is that because assets cannot be freely transferred in and out of a corporation, when you decide to sell, you'll be facing a pretty severe taxable event. Oh yeah, and you'll be facing double taxation on that income as well.

To get around double taxation, real estate investors previously used S corporations for holding properties. If you remember, S corporations are just like regular corporations but have a pass-through tax status. They also come burdened with a whole slew of ownership restrictions. But the big thorn in your side comes when you want to transfer the property out at any point. Unlike an LLC, this cannot be done tax free. This is especially limiting when it comes to estate planning. Unlike a limited liability company, you can't gift ownership of the entity to your heirs without creating a taxable event. Some gift that is — "I got a tax bill for Christmas. Thanks, Gramps!"

You may remember that the one big advantage of S corporations is that profits aren't subject to self-employment tax. Well, that perk doesn't apply here. Because real estate isn't an active trade or business and generally only involves the passive holding of property, the income derived from such isn't subject to self-employment tax anyway. Only regular income tax applies. So, the S corp's one claim to fame doesn't even apply in this scenario. The only time you'd consider using an S corporation with real estate is if you're so active in your real estate endeavors (rehabbing, flipping properties, and so on) that the IRS considers it a business. In this case, you have some number crunching to do before selecting your entity type.

Protecting real estate with LLCs

LLCs, when used to hold passive real estate investments, will rock your tax bill. First, when purchasing the property, it can be transferred into the LLC without creating a taxable event. Second, whatever profits you acquire from the property are considered passive and only subject to regular income tax. Third, because single-member LLCs are considered *disregarded entities* by the IRS and essentially treated as sole proprietorships, they can qualify for such things as mortgage interest deductions and 1031 like-kind exchanges. And fourth, as you get older, your limited liability companies will fit perfectly into your estate planning strategy. I devote all of Chapter 17 to the ins and outs of real estate investing. But I'm warning you, there may be a teeny-weeny bit of proselytizing on the merits of the LLC.

With an LLC, the profits do not need to be allocated and distributed according to the ownership percentages. You can choose to dole them out however you want. For instance, if you only own 10 percent of the limited liability company but want 90 percent of the profits (and the other members are okay with that), then that's what you get. This is just one more advantage that LLCs have over corporations and S corporations. (By the way, if you are lucky enough to find partners that are okay with this arrangement, then please send 'em my way!)

Because the LLC's losses are passed on to the owners, if you own multiple real estate properties, each within its own LLC, and one of the properties encounters a hefty loss, you can deduct that loss at tax time against the income from your other properties. Typically, this sort of loss is only deductible against *passive income,* such as real estate. However, if you work with your accountant or corporate consultant and structure it correctly, you may be able to deduct the loss against *active income* (such as dividends). You can do this by becoming an active real estate investor who spends a certain amount of time each year handling the day-to-day management of the properties.

If you are a silent investor and want your operating partner(s) to add some skin to the game, you may want to check out using a *limited liability limited partnership* to hold your property. Assuming your state allows them, of course (not all states do!). I discuss these entity types earlier in this chapter.

Planning your estate

Note: If you are immortal, you may skip this section.

LLCs are becoming more and more popular in estate planning. Trusts are still king, but now they're generally used in conjunction with LLCs so that your assets are protected while you're still alive. Trusts usually don't provide any asset protection whatsoever, whereas an LLC provides *dual liability protection,* as I discuss in the previous chapter.

With estate taxes as they are, if you have a large estate — more than $1 million — you may want to start gifting your assets to your heirs while you are alive. LLCs are especially useful for this because they allow you to gift small portions of large assets (such as real estate) by gifting the membership shares. They also allow you to maintain control of the assets while you are alive, even if your heir is the majority owner of the LLC. You do this by making yourself a manager of the LLC until your death, at which point your heir will take over.

When you actively plan your estate using trusts and LLCs, you have much more control over what happens to your assets after your passing. An LLC keeps your estate out of probate and avoids the accompanying (often astronomical) *probate fees,* costs that are incurred when the court system has to distribute your estate. (If you aren't familiar with probate, let me just say that if the Spanish Inquisitors had been just a little bit more vicious, they probably would have just subjected their victims to the bureaucratic nightmare that is probate.) In probate, you leave the major decisions up to a judge, and you never know how things could turn out. With an LLC, you can ensure that your assets go to the right people and don't get dwindled away with legal fees until they turn into dust. Turn to Chapter 18 for more help with estate planning.

Protecting your assets

In the "Running a small business" section earlier in this chapter, I go over the importance of segregating business assets out of the operating company and protecting them in their own separate entities. Well, the same applies for individuals. Business aside, if you want to protect certain personal assets from personal lawsuits, then you'll want to follow the same formula.

Without a doubt, the limited liability company is the best entity type for asset protection. Without the *charging order protection* inherent in LLCs, whatever assets you're trying to protect would be open to any personal creditors or lawsuits you may have. In other words, if you place an asset in a corporation and are sued personally, then the judgment creditor would be able to attack your stock in that corporation and seize the underlying asset in order to pay the judgment. If this lack of protection offered by a corporation doesn't automatically disqualify it, then here's something else for you to chew on: You cannot transfer assets in and out of a corporation without inciting a taxable event. Not so with LLCs.

LLCs can protect your assets in myriad ways. If asset protection is your primary goal for your LLC, then flip to Chapter 16 where I discuss these different strategies in detail.

Part II
Your First Steps: Forming Your LLC

The 5th Wave   By Rich Tennant

"So...how did our first stage financing go today?"

In this part . . .

In this part, you find out about the preliminary stuff you need to know to form your LLC, such as what state is best for your LLC and what decisions you and your partners need to make before creating your articles of organization.

Then, in Chapter 6, I show you how to create your articles of organization and file them with your state's secretary of state (or similar governmental organization). If you aren't forming a new company — meaning your company is already operating with the public — I show you in Chapter 7 how to transfer your assets and business operations over to your newly formed LLC.

Chapter 4

Playing — and Winning — the Name Game

In This Chapter

▶ Deciding on a company name

▶ Finding out if the name you want is available

▶ Securing your intellectual property

▶ Switching to a new name if things change

Compared to other decisions you have to make, selecting your company name may seem simple. However, when you get started on the process you may realize that settling on a name can be one of the most agonizing and time-consuming aspects of starting a business. Don't believe me? Well, after a few rare and cherished "ah ha!" moments followed by the discovery that your chosen name is already in use, you'll be able to relate.

Not only should your company name be creative and personal to you and your business, it also needs to be original — so original, in fact, that no one else in your state or industry has recently used a similar name. Like I said, it can be a frustrating process. Unfortunately, you can't move forward with your articles of organization, bank account, or almost anything else until the name is chosen, so putting it off won't do you any good. In this chapter, I help you get started in the hunt for a good (and available!) name and tell you precautions to take so no one else can nab it. I also give you the scoop on changing the name of your LLC, should you ever have the need.

Establishing the Best Name for Your LLC

An inescapable tenet of human nature is that we have an inclination to imitate one another. This collective intelligence is a good thing for all those fashion-challenged folks out there; however, it doesn't do you any good when you're naming your LLC. Without anything to guide you, the "namestorming" sessions you hold may only result in the regurgitation of everyone else's (already considered and rejected) bad ideas. My rule of thumb is to never expect a phenomenal result from an arbitrary process. In other words, you can't expect to pick a great name out of thin air.

So if your LLC happens to be a real-estate development project and you're happy with a name like 543 Winnetaka Street, LLC, you can happily skip this section. Otherwise, check out the following sections for some tips I've managed to pick up over the years of my entrepreneurial journey.

Considering naming guidelines

As vast and varied as the naming possibilities are, you may have already cherry-picked a few brilliant candidates. If this isn't the case, then you're in luck: You don't have to go through the disappointment of finding out the name you like best isn't nearly the best at all.

You may think that having boundless options gives you a better chance of coming up with a great name, but think again. After all, creativity is better served when subject to a few (helpful) restrictions. With unlimited options, the imagination gets sloppy, and, well, the world simply doesn't need another mediocre business name. So before you let the ideas fly, check out a few naming "rules" (which I strongly recommend!):

- ✔ **Be distinct.** Naming your brand-new and improved social media site FaceSpace or MyBook won't give the impression that you are either "new" or "improved." Quite the opposite, actually.

- ✔ **Be memorable.** Avoid acronyms like the plague. I don't care how many public companies are acronyms. Unless you have a huge annual marketing budget to waste, don't attempt to grab anyone's attention with a few letters. If you're serious about shortening your name, condense it into an amalgam, like FedEx for Federal Express, or Nabisco for National Biscuit Company.

  With that being said, contrary to what you may hear elsewhere, long names are often a lot more memorable than short names (think T.G.I. Fridays versus Joe's). So don't worry about restraining yourself with length — especially since you'll have better luck finding a domain name for a longer name than a shorter one.

- ✔ **Be approachable.** Make sure your LLC's name is easy to pronounce. You don't want people to avoid saying the name because they're afraid of mispronouncing it. Try out potential names on a first grader. If he can't pronounce it, ditch it and have him help you find an alternative. Hey, you'd be surprised at what good ideas kids can have!

- ✔ **Be meaningful.** This doesn't mean be descriptive; save the description for your tag lines and slogans. Make your LLC's name evocative and allude to the heart and soul of your business. For instance, Netflix is a great name for an online video rental site, whereas FilmsOnline is not.

- ✔ **Be vivid.** What image and feeling do you want your customers to associate with your brand? Try to paint a picture. For example, the name Stonyfield Farm makes you think of cows in green pastures, which gives the impression of wholesomeness.

- ✔ **Be bold.** With so many names already taken, you can't be afraid of taking risks. As long as your name is evocative, don't worry about being too unusual — just look at Yahoo! and Google.

- ✔ **Be eternal.** LLCs are now made to have a perpetual existence, so why restrict the life of your business with its name? Choose a name that will sound good for decades or even centuries down the road, or you may face the same conundrum as *Twentieth Century* Fox.

- ✔ **Be expansive.** Be careful that your name doesn't restrain your business to a specific location, product, or service. For instance, Los Angeles Rentals would have to spend a pretty penny on rebranding if it ever were to expand to another market. No matter how small you are now, you don't want your name to hold you back or become antiquated as your business moves forward.

- ✔ **Be global.** Make sure your name is internationally friendly. Otherwise, you may be ready to expand abroad one day only to find out that your name has a negative connotation in certain cultures! It's only funny when it happens to other people (like when Chevrolet learned that their Nova translated to *it doesn't go* in Spanish).

  Think this rule doesn't apply to you because you don't intend to go global anytime soon? Take a walking tour of any major city and see how many people speak foreign languages. In order to avoid having entire market demographics laugh at your LLC, get a third-party assessment done to verify that your LLC's name has universal appeal. Catchword (www.catchwordbranding.com) is considered the best company for foreign-language evaluations. Their fee is around $700 per language. If you go with a cheaper company, make sure that whoever does the evaluation is from the country of interest and knows the current slang.

Letting the ideas fly

Now comes the fun part — you get to hold a brainstorming session (otherwise known as a "namestorming" session). Lock yourself away in a quiet room with a pad of paper and write down every name you can think of. Don't judge what you come up with. This is the part where you can let loose. Keep the naming rules in mind while you do this, but don't limit yourself too much. This is a time for creativity; you can be critical later.

Try to come up with 50 or 100 names. Even if you think you've found "the one," don't stop. As a matter of fact, don't leave your namestorming session until you're completely depleted and can't possibly come up with another name. Or until your family calls in a missing persons report, whichever happens first.

After you finish your namestorming session, cross out the names that you don't like. Check that the remaining names comply with the restrictions listed in "Considering naming guidelines," and cross out any that don't. Rewrite the list with the names that make the cut, putting them in order of preference, with the ones you absolutely love at the top of the list. Now you're a big step closer to finding your perfect match, and you're ready to play with the names and see which ones are available.

Not absolutely thrilled with the names you came up with? Don't worry! Either hold another namestorming session tomorrow, when your mind is fresh, or just stick with what you have. Remember, with the right marketing, a good brand (comprised of your name, logo, marketing materials, company values, and so on) transcends its name and inspires an overall feeling that creates a strong and lasting relationship with its customers.

Following naming law: Yes, such a thing exists!

Although you do have autonomy in choosing your business name, the state does have some requirements that you'll have to keep in mind, namely (no pun intended) that you designate your business as a limited liability company. You do this by adding the designator *limited liability company, limited company,* or an abbreviation such as *L.L.C., L.C., LLC,* or *LC* in upper- or lower-case letters to the end of your name.

If the addition of *LLC* at the end of your name isn't catchy, don't fret. You must have the designation at the end of your name when forming your articles of organization, but you can still operate your business without it by filing a fictitious firm name application with your county clerk. I tell you how in "Getting the name you want with a DBA," later in this chapter.

Even if you intend to request corporation or S corporation tax status with the IRS, you still need to add the LLC designation at the end of your name when filing your articles of organization with the secretary of state.

The state also restricts the use of certain words that may imply your business is part of a regulated industry. This policy varies from state to state but typically restricts the use of any words that could give the idea that the LLC is in the banking or insurance industry, such as *bank, credit union, trust,* and *insurance.* To check out a list of all state laws on naming requirements (current at the time of publication), go to www.docrun.com/wiki/naming.

Completing your identity with a logo

Humans aren't just vocal and aural; we're visual, too. So unless your target demographic is of the nonhuman variety (not likely!), you need to take into account the visual element of your brand: your logo.

Logo designs come in four basic forms:

- ✔ **Word mark:** Your name in a specialized typography is your logo. Think of the Coca-Cola logo as an example.

- ✔ **Combination mark:** Partner your stylized name with an icon of some sort, and you have a combination mark. Think of AT&T and its iconic globe.

- ✔ **Symbol:** Some companies are so well known that they can get by with just a symbol. Everyone knows the Nike swish, the McDonald's golden arches, and the Apple . . . well, apple. Usually only extremely well-known brands can pull this off, and even then it can backfire. Remember when Prince changed his name to a symbol? A bad move. Think hard before going down this road.

- ✔ **Emblem:** Some companies go for the more artistic approach and put the company name inside an emblem. Think of the Starbucks round seal or the Porsche coat of arms. This approach can reap big rewards by giving you more creative license to reflect the tone of your brand in the logo.

When deciding what type of logo you want, carefully consider how you want your business to be perceived. I suggest you first take the time to educate yourself by figuring out your complete brand — the image and feeling you want to convey, the demographic you want to convey it to, and the mark of your personal creativity you wish to endow it with. Then draw up a few ideas of what you may want and take them to an experienced logo and/or graphics designer to assist you in creating a final logo.

Before putting too much time and money into your logo, make sure to check to see that the name you want to use and the image you want to convey are available for use. Otherwise, you may go through great expense only to throw it all away and start from scratch. Read on to find out how to determine name availability.

Determining the Availability of a Name

Finding out whether the name you want is available is difficult, mostly due to the level of fortitude it takes to scratch a beloved name or two off your list when you find they're unavailable for use. As difficult as parting with some of your favorites may be, you must do so if they're already in use. Otherwise, not only could you be forced to change your name down the road, after you've gained a considerable following, but you also may have to pay a hefty sum for the error.

Checking names in your state

If the name you choose conflicts with a name already in use in your state, your articles of organization will be rejected by the secretary of state and you'll be required to select a different name before resubmitting. This change can be costly (some states don't return filing fees for rejected filings!) and time consuming.

Most states, when checking to see if a name is conflicting, only allow for entities that are in good standing. For instance, if a corporation or LLC is using the name you want but is in "revoked" status, then you have a very good chance of being able to use the name.

The term "conflicting" is pretty subjective, and the decision whether to allow your name often depends on how conservative the state employee who files your articles is in her evaluations. However, you can still get a relatively good idea of whether or not the name conflicts with others by conducting a name search in your state. Go to the appropriate section of your secretary of state's Web site (you can find the address in the "State Information Listing" document on the accompanying CD) and enter the name you want to use — leaving off all identifiers, such as LLC or limited company. Read through the search results. If any names are very similar to yours, regardless of whether they're LLCs or not, you may have to choose a new name. You can also request a free name search at www.myllc.com/namecheck.aspx. This option is especially valuable if your state doesn't allow you to search company records online.

If the name you want isn't available, you may have a work-around. Assuming the name doesn't conflict with any existing trademarks (which I get into later in this section), you may be able to file the LLC under a different name and then file for a fictitious firm name (a DBA) with your county clerk. Check out the following section for more details.

When conducting your state name search, don't forget to make sure your name is also available in all states where you may someday conduct business. Otherwise, you may find out down the road when you try to register in those states that you're unable to use your own name!

Getting the name you want with a DBA

Also referred to as a *fictitious firm name, trade name,* or *assumed name,* a *DBA* (short for "doing business as") is a name that is secondary to the name your company identified itself as in its articles of organization. A DBA filing is normally done with the clerk's office of the county where your business is located and gives your LLC authorization to transact business under that name, including opening a bank account, advertising to potential customers, entering into lease agreements, taking on debt, and so on. This does not change the name of the business; rather it creates a secondary name that the business is permitted to operate under. Just keep in mind that the official name of your company — the name that's listed on the articles of organization — is the name you put on your tax returns, your membership certifications, and any government or "official" documents.

A business can register an unlimited number of DBAs. Having multiple DBAs can be useful if you're looking to operate certain segments of your business or market certain products under distinct business names while still keeping everything under the same LLC "umbrella."

Keep in mind, though, that a DBA does not give your company exclusive right to use that name. As far as I know, no clerk's office checks DBA filings for conflicting names, which means that the name you want to use could theoretically be used by tens of other companies in your county alone! The only way to obtain exclusivity for a DBA is to file a trademark, which I tell you how to do later in this chapter. Likewise, a DBA doesn't guarantee that someone hasn't already trademarked the name in your particular industry, thereby making it unavailable to use. Therefore, doing a trademark search before committing your company to using this secondary name is imperative. (Check out the following section for info on conducting this search.)

Although DBAs may offer you a separate name for different segments of your business, they do not offer separate liability protection. In other words, if your LLC under one DBA loses a lawsuit, *the entire company* is up for grabs, including the segments that are operating under different DBAs.

DBAs are often required to be filed in-person and over-the-counter, and the fees are usually around $50, depending on the rules of the particular county where the DBA is being filed. Some states require that a notice of the filing be published in a local newspaper, which can add substantially to the cost. If you want to avoid the hassle of obtaining the DBA yourself, many formation companies offer this service. The prices vary, but to give you an idea, MyLLC.com charges $99 per filing.

Conducting a trademark search

When a company wants to protect its name from being used by other companies in similar industries, it obtains a state or federal trademark. A *state trademark* gives the trademark holder exclusive rights to use the name in that particular state. A *federal trademark,* filed at the U.S. Patent and Trademark Office, gives exclusive rights to use the name throughout the entire United

States. This means that, for the most part, the company with that name or set of words trademarked is the only one that has the right to use those words in that business sector.

Before committing to a business name, you must do a comprehensive trademark search for the name that you want to use. You, an experienced law firm, or a trademarking company can do this search. If the name you're interested in is available, I recommend registering it as a trademark immediately, before anyone else does, so you have the exclusive right to use the name. Better safe than sorry.

You can conduct a trademark search online at the U.S. Patents and Trademarks Office's Web site by searching its TESS (Trademark Electronic Search System) database. Go to www.uspto.gov and do a search for Trademarks.

Because trademarks are only exclusive by industry, if you find some trademarked words that are similar to the name you want, you may still be okay. To see if your business and a potentially conflicting trademark are in the same industry, find your company's International Classification (IC) code by searching the USPTO list at http://tess2.uspto.gov/netahtml/tidm.html. Then compare your code to that of the trademarked names that are similar to what you want to use. If their IC codes match yours, then the name you've chosen probably is not available to use.

If you find a conflicting name, the next step is to see whether or not the record is marked as *live* or *dead.* If the record is dead (which means the trademark wasn't completed or maintained over the years), you can still use the name. Otherwise, you'll probably have to cross that one off your list.

For more information on conducting trademark searches, you may want to pick up a copy of *Patents, Copyrights & Trademarks For Dummies,* 2nd Edition, by Henri Charmasson and John Buchaca (Wiley).

Going global

As I discuss in "Considering naming guidelines," you need to do a linguistic assessment of your name to make sure that it doesn't have negative connotations in any other languages, but that's not your only concern when going global. When you're ready to take your business to that next level, you need to make sure that your chosen name is available for use in the countries where you want to operate.

The United States isn't the only country that offers federal trademark protection to businesses. Almost every country has some sort of system in place or is part of an international consortium that provides a legal infrastructure for such matters. Other countries don't care if you have legal authority for your name in the United States. If a conflicting trademark is already filed in their jurisdiction, that trademark prevails and you have to choose a unique name in order to legally operate in that country.

If expanding outside the U.S. borders is a core component of your business's strategy, you need to take foreign trademarks into account immediately; preferably before you file your articles of organization. You may even want to preemptively file trademarks in the countries where you intend to operate. I discuss foreign trademarks in more detail later in this chapter.

Many governmental bodies regulate trademarks, and some overlap in jurisdictions can take place. Before you settle on a name, I suggest you do a quick search of some of the major international organizations to verify that you aren't facing any major conflicts, such as a large, international organization that hasn't penetrated the U.S. market yet. I provide an up-to-date list of the major governmental trademark organizations and the search methods at www.docrun.com/wiki/global_trademark.

Searching online to catch problems early

Before selecting a name, do an Internet search to see if anything out there could interfere with your search engine results. After all, even if a name is available in a certain state and a certain category and you can find a decent domain name to associate with it, you don't want your potential customers to enter your name into a search engine and be flooded with irrelevant results. In this scenario you'd have to buy your way to the top spot, which is an expensive proposition.

For instance, you may want to reconsider naming your new cold-weather clothing company simply Arctic Ice. If you do an Internet search for "Arctic Ice," you see that there are so many search results referencing global warming and glaciers that you'd never be able to compete! If a potential customer wanted to find your site, she'd probably have to use some method other than a search engine.

Don't take potential search-result problems lightly. When trying to reach your target market, you already have many hurdles to overcome. Do you really need another?

Protecting Your Name

Congratulations! If you're reading this section, it must be because you've found a name that not only encapsulates the purpose and essence of your company and brand, but is also so unique that no other business — possibly in even the farthest reaches of the world — is using it. Whew! I know it was hard work, but you probably feel great right now.

You worked hard to get your name, and now all you have to do is keep it. The following sections outline a few tricks of the trade when it comes to keeping and protecting your LLC's name.

Registering your domain

When you finally choose a great, available name, first things first: Register your Internet domain name. And do it immediately. The world of domains is incredibly competitive, and good domains can be snatched away within hours.

If the world is getting smaller (and it is!), it's because the Internet is getting bigger. It doesn't matter if your business is breeding alpacas, hidden away on the plains of Wyoming; you're not in business in the modern world until you register a domain name and set up e-mail and a Web site. These tools are the core of industry nowadays, and making sure that you're marketing your name in the online realm should be at the top of your list of priorities.

Finding a good domain name won't be easy, and, if your business is Internet-based and a short, catchy, relevant domain name is *crucial,* then you may have to pay a premium price to purchase a domain name on the aftermarket. Resale prices can be astronomical, so check first to see if you can get an unregistered variation or comparable domain name for as little as $10. Go to www.GoDaddy.com (or any other domain registrar) and type in the name you wish to register. You'll then find out whether or not the name you want has already been registered by someone else.

If you aren't familiar with registering domains, then you'll probably be shocked to find out how few good domain names are available. You may do 50 searches before you find one you like. If this becomes the case, consider purchasing a premium domain on the aftermarket.

If you do wish to check out some premium domain names, I suggest you go with a domain brokerage firm such as www.sedo.com or www.afternic.com. By going with an established and trustworthy firm, you're assured that the process will run smoothly and nobody will run off with your money.

Double-check how your domain name *looks.* For instance, you may be thrilled that your start-up Therapist Finder has the option to purchase its domain name, only to realize later that that same domain can easily be misconstrued as www.TheRapistFinder.com.

Unless you're willing to register a domain within seconds after seeing it's available, avoid using the search function on a domain registrar's site.

Otherwise, you're giving these companies exclusive information as to what names may be of value to you. Almost all major domain registrars have been cited for *front-running* domain names, which means they find valuable domains you've searched for and register them immediately in order to sell them to you later at a premium. If you search for a domain and go back a few hours later to register it, only to be told that it's no longer available, well . . . you get the picture.

You can make sure your domain search is safe a few different ways. If you use the Firefox Web browser, you can use a free add-on that offers safe domain searches, called *Domain Lookup*. You can download it by going to `addons.mozilla.org` and searching for "Domain Lookup." An alternative is to use a search tool on your computer. Macs come with this function installed, and Windows users can download a program. You can find many free local domain tools by doing an Internet search for "domain search software."

Reserving your name

Imagine this: You go through the painstaking process of selecting a name, checking to see if it's available, and filing a trademark. Then, after the care and expense of preparing and submitting your articles of organization, you get a letter back from the secretary of state that says that your filing has been rejected due to a conflict of name. Someone has taken it in those few weeks between checking the name and submitting your filing! As unbelievable as it seems, this scenario happens more often than you'd think, and it can cause you to start the process all over again, wasting time and money.

The best way to avoid having your name taken is to file a name reservation with your secretary of state, thereby reserving your chosen name while you take the time to prepare your articles of organization. You can do this as soon as you see that the name you want is available.

Unless you have a very popular name or you'll be waiting for some time before filing your articles, you may not need a name reservation. If you'll be filing your articles of organization in only a few days anyway, and the name reservation happens to be costly and/or time consuming in your state, then you may want to consider whether it's worth the hassle.

In most states, you can reserve your company name by going to your secretary of state's Web site (see Appendix A for contact info) and downloading the appropriate form. Complete this form and mail it to the secretary of state. (If you don't want to do this yourself, ask your formation company to do it for you.) Some states allow you to do the name reservation online but may charge more for the convenience. You can usually reserve your name for 60 to 90 days. The process and fees for name reservations vary from state to state.

The person or organization filing your LLC's articles of organization must be the same person who is on the name reservation; otherwise, you may have a problem getting the secretary of state to release the name. For instance, if the name reservation is in your name, but your formation company is filing the articles, the articles probably will be rejected until you sign off on the use of the name.

Each state has its own laws concerning what needs to be in your company name, so before reserving your name, you should double-check to make sure that you're in compliance with all relevant state laws. Otherwise, your articles of organization or name reservation may be rejected, which can be costly.

If you foresee your LLC transacting business and foreign-filing in other states (I discuss multistate operations at length in Chapter 5), you may want to consider doing a *name registration* in each of those states. A name registration is the equivalent of a name reservation but is specifically geared toward a foreign entity (an entity formed in another state) that wishes to reserve its name for later use.

Getting a trademark for your business name

After you register and reserve your LLC name, you need to block anyone who tries to follow in your stead. The only official way to do this is to file a trademark to prevent any competition from mimicking your company or brand elements in order to snatch market share or mislead consumers. A trademark can also prevent foreign companies from importing products or services that may conflict with yours, and it can get deceptive or even simply ambiguous domain names taken down.

When you trademark your company name, logo, and/or brand elements (such as packaging), you create something of inherent value. As you invest in the brand and develop brand loyalty, that value increases. Take the necessary steps to protect this investment for as long as your company is operational.

The different types of trademarks

A trademark, by definition, can be anything — a word, symbol, phrase, shape, color, and so on — that identifies a product with its source. If the mark identifies the source of a service, such as accounting or dry cleaning, it is called a *service mark.* A *design mark* refers to the specific shape or color of product packaging that defines that product. For example, the yellow/ black cover of this book may be protected under a federal trademark so that competitors can't make look-alike products. Another example is the trademarked color Tiffany Blue that designates the Tiffany brand. Design marks can even include architectural details, such as the distinctive red brick–like roof at Pizza Hut.

Much ado about marks

You may want to know about two other federally protected trademarks: *certification marks* and *membership marks.* Certification marks are comprised of an image, usually a seal of some sort, and are used by a national accreditation organization to indicate the quality or standardization of a product or service. The owner of a certification mark cannot use it to create a consumer assurance on his own services, only others'. This is the rare instance in which a mark actually benefits someone other than its owner. A membership mark is used by associations to show that an individual or entity is a member of that association, such as the patch used by the Boy Scouts of America.

The irony of trademark protection is that your business name (also called a *trade name*) is not in itself qualified to be legally protected under federal trademark laws, because it doesn't specifically identify the source of a product or service. After all, trademarks were born to serve products and services, not necessarily the business which owns them. So unless your business name is the same as your product (or service) name, you have to take a few steps if you want to keep it for yourself.

First and foremost, tweak your actual business name a bit in order to make it look less, well, like a "business":

✔ Remove words like *Company, Associates, Group,* and all entity-type identifiers such as *Inc., Incorporated, Limited, Limited Liability Company, LLC,* and so on.

✔ Remove all descriptors, such as *Services.*

✔ Remove identifiers that name the product or service. (For example, Remove *Automotive Repair* from the business name *Red Rock Automotive Repair* and simply register the moniker *Red Rock*).

When you've gotten down to a core name, draft your business name into a fancy logo or "mark." Make your name into an image of some sort, and use a special font and/or a graphic that makes your business name easily identifiable. You are now ready to register your trademark — assuming it's any good, that is. Read on to find out what makes the cut.

Checking out what constitutes a good trademark

So now that you've tossed all the fillers out of your name, what's left? If all you have is something mundane, such as *Vino* for your wine store, you may have problems, because in order for a name to be trademarkable, it must be distinct. Generic words that name your product, such as *lamp,* hold no legal protection at all — after all, can you imagine if the courts allowed people to own parts of the English language? For example, in order for Linens 'n Things to trademark their name, they had to add *'n Things.* Without it, *Linens* is generic and simply describes the products they offer in their stores.

The same goes for names that simply describe the product or services that your company offers. For instance, if this book series was *Easy to Understand Books* instead of *For Dummies,* they'd be unable to acquire legal protection for their name. (Not to mention, you probably wouldn't be reading this now, considering very few people would want to read, much less write, a bland book series called *Easy to Understand Books.*)

The name you are registering also can't be primarily a surname. You can't register *Smith's Bakery* in the baked goods category and block anyone with the surname Smith from using their name in connection with their bakery.

The distinctiveness of a trademark is exactly proportional to how much that trademark will hold up if it is ever challenged in court. Running a business named BookSellers? You'd be laughed out of court trying to defend a trademark like that (assuming you were even granted a trademark in the first place, which is unlikely). However, add *Amazon* to your name and you'd be golden.

Registering your trademark

After you determine that no conflicting names or marks are federally trademarked (refer to "Determining the Availability of a Name" earlier in the chapter), you're ready to file your trademark. Remember, you can't simply file your business name (sans logo or any other type of visual ornament) and be done with it. You must create a logo containing the major elements of your business name and trademark that instead.

You file your trademark with the United States Patent and Trademark Office (the USPTO). You can do so online at www.uspto.gov for a fee of $325 per category of goods or services you wish to register in. This protects your trademark in only those specific categories. You can find your company's IC (International Classification) by searching the USPTO list at http://tess2. uspto.gov/netahtml/tidm.html.

Keep in mind that this $325 fee is nonrefundable and that you'll have to wait approximately four months to find out from the USPTO whether or not your trademark was successfully filed. This lag time makes it imperative that you get your filing right the first time. If you hit any snags on the way or don't feel confident that you know exactly what you're doing, consider hiring an intellectual property law firm or a compliance company that can give you a much better shot at success. Your trademark application is reviewed by a special USPTO trademark attorney who looks at these applications all day long and can probably spot an amateur from a mile away, so help yourself out by getting your filing right.

After you file the online application, in order to finalize the registration you must prove that you've used the trademark *in commerce*. You can submit an *intent-to-use application* for the trademark before you use it in business, thereby blocking any subsequent parties from obtaining the trademark, but you don't actually get it issued until you prove that you've used it in commerce.

When you've got the trademark, you've got it forever — or for as long as you maintain it. You can keep the marketplace from using your name, but now you have to use it and build it into a strong and ubiquitous brand. Just keep in mind that your registration must be renewed every ten years by filing a Section 8 affidavit with the USPTO showing that your mark is still being used in commerce and hasn't been abandoned.

After you register your mark, you need to take action against anyone who infringes upon it. Otherwise, the courts can invalidate your mark. On the flip side, if your mark becomes popular enough to be associated with a particular product class (such as Vaseline for petroleum jelly, or Kleenex for facial tissue), you can lose your trademark protection for being generic (regardless of how distinct the name was to begin with). In other words, Xerox may not like television shows, their competitors, and the majority of Americans referring to copying a document as *xeroxing,* but from a legal standpoint, they can't do anything about it.

If you cannot register your federal trademark for some reason, you may want to consider registering a state trademark in the primary state(s) in which you transact business. This step usually still provides you with some legal protection for your name. The laws pertaining to trademark protection vary from state to state.

Changing Your Name

After you find a good name and go through all the steps to protect it, you probably can't fathom ever wanting to change it. But it does happen, and other than having to go through the processes of vetting and securing the new name that I describe in this chapter, changing your LLC's name isn't usually difficult.

A common misconception is that after you file your articles of organization, you're forever stuck with the name you chose, and the company's name is inextricably linked with the company itself as its sole identifier. Not true. Legally, an LLC can change its name an unlimited number of times. Of course, if this happens too often, your customers may not approve!

Changing the name of your LLC is relatively easy, depending on the state: You simply amend your articles of organization by filing a name-change amendment with the secretary of state in the state where your LLC is domiciled. If you're foreign-filed in multiple states, you also need to contact those particular state agencies with the updated business name.

On the CD, I include most, if not all, of the various forms you need in order to change the name of your LLC with the secretary of state. Otherwise, you can just call your formation company and let them drive out to the county clerk's office to take care of the change.

Chapter 5

Choosing the Best State for Your LLC

Say you've lived in California your entire life, and now you want to create an LLC all the way across the country in Miami. That's where you believe your retirement community real-estate project will have its greatest chance to flourish, but you worry that because you don't live in Florida, you'll have trouble establishing your LLC. Not to fret: Many LLCs have different home states than their owners.

It's a common myth that you need to form your LLC in the state where you live. LLCs are considered *incorporated entities,* which means a layer of separation exists between the business and the owners. Think of them as an individual person that you have full control over. Like an individual, your LLC can live in whatever state benefits it the most. Sandy beaches and nice weather may be the appealing qualities of the state you choose to call home, but your LLC will benefit for other qualities, such as low taxes, privacy, and favorable laws. The state where your LLC is formed is called its *domicile*.

In this chapter, I give you an overview of some of your options when it comes to deciding where to form your LLC. I help clear up some of the confusion that comes with the term *tax haven,* and I also point all you multistate moguls in the right direction when it comes to forming your LLC in a state other than the one where you currently reside.

Domiciling in Your State (or Not)

When choosing a state to live in, your LLC cares little about the weather and even less about the school districts. Your LLC is pretty easy to please: Give it favorable laws, privacy, and low taxes, and you'll have one happy camper! You can choose any state (and maybe even country!) that you want for your LLC — the world is your oyster! But this leads us to the main problem that you're facing — LLCs in different states are not all created equal. Some states have more favorable laws than others. So how do you choose?

LLCs bring with them fantastically flexible options that make them suitable for any industry, for any location, for any dream. If you've read this far, you probably already know that an LLC is right for you. But which LLC? Each state makes its own laws regarding LLCs, and because of this, LLCs tend to look, feel, and act differently depending on where they are formed.

Forming your LLC in a state other than the one where you personally reside may not be right for you. And if it is a viable option, that still leaves you with the question of which state. Before you can answer any of these questions, you first must answer this one: *What's your business?*

In order to know your options, you must have a clear picture of what sort of business you'll be transacting and where you'll be transacting it. You need to know what your future plans are — for instance, do you want to go public or would you prefer to stay small? Is your business ingrained in your community or does it exist in the Internet realm and have no real territory? What are your priorities? Is it important that you save on your tax bill? And what about privacy?

At the end of the day, you can get what you want in an LLC pretty easily. *Knowing* what you want is often the hard part.

Considering another state for your LLC

Some states offer much better conditions for LLCs than others. But if you're lucky enough to live in a state that has low taxes and the privacy you so desire, then why form out of state at all? Before writing off your territory in favor of one of the more popular ones, you need to do a little research. Your state may not be the best, but it may be good enough. For instance, Montana has no sales tax and very low corporate income tax (6.75 percent), and its personal income tax is nominal as well. The state works hard to be pro-business and has created a tax structure that encourages business start-ups and growth by offering millions of dollars in tax credits to certain emerging industries and allowing myriad corporate deductions that many states don't recognize.

Although business-friendly states like Montana aren't commonly referred to as *tax havens,* they do offer very amicable tax climates and corporate laws. If you live in one of these states, then the benefit of doing business close to home is hard to beat! So before you decide to go out of state with your business venture, be sure to check your own state's laws.

If you don't want to go through the hassle of research, feel free to call my office at 1-888-88MYLLC, and we can give you the skinny on your state's qualifications.

Forming your LLC in your home state

An LLC can be formed in any state you wish, but if your LLC conducts business elsewhere, it must register to transact business in those states. This registration is often referred to as *qualifying* or *foreign-filing.* When your LLC registers to transact business in another state, it becomes subject to the laws, taxes, and disclosure requirements of that state. For instance, if you formed your LLC in Nevada in order to keep the ownership of the company completely private and you register to transact business in California, then you'll most likely need to disclose the membership of your LLC. Problems such as these can reduce or eliminate many of the benefits that motivated you to form your LLC out of state in the first place!

When you have a brick-and-mortar business

If you're opening up a brick-and-mortar business that is only operating in one state — for example, a local shop that deals heavily in the community — make it easy on yourself and keep your LLC close to home. Sometimes a business is only viable if it is in close proximity to interested customers, resources, and land, such as your local drycleaners or an oil well. Running this type of hands-on, locally based company means that you have to register to transact business in the state your business (and you!) are residing in and, thereby, abide by its laws. You may as well save on filing fees and paperwork hassles by keeping everything local from the get-go.

The commerce clause in the Tenth Amendment of the U.S. Constitution expressly forbids states from regulating interstate commerce; each state is only allowed to regulate business within it's own borders. Each state has it's own laws governing LLCs and it's own set of case law that furthers the disparity of how LLCs are treated from one state to another. Therefore, if you are transacting business in multiple states (and who *isn't* nowadays?), you must register to transact business in all these states.

So what constitutes "transacting business"? Well, the states purposefully remain vague in their definitions. Case law and attorney general opinions hold a lot of weight, but you can't be expected to sift through all those stacks and stacks of legal history, now can you? To make your life easier, I aggregated all the laws addressing each state's legal definition (if any) of "transacting business" on a public wiki at www.docrun.com/wiki/definition_transacting_business.

Regardless, if you're in any way confused about whether or not your company is considered "transacting business" in a particular state, don't bother calling the secretary of state's office and asking. If the administrator you speak to *does* venture to guess, the answer will almost invariably be yes. Instead, consult with a qualified business attorney. Accountants may be qualified to tell you whether or not tax is due in a particular state, but I recommend that you leave the evaluation of the case law up to attorneys. If your LLC is caught operating in a state that it is not registered to transact business in, your LLC can be denied access to that state's court systems and could also be hit with hefty fines, penalties, and/or taxes.

If your home state doesn't allow the sort of entity you're intent on forming, then you *must* domicile your LLC in another state. For instance, if you reside in one of the few states that don't allow single-member LLCs (and you absolutely *refuse* to take on a partner), then you have to form your LLC in a more progressive state and then simply have that LLC register to transact business in your home state. Same goes for series LLCs, professional LLCs, and any other sort of new form of LLC the states create in the future.

When you want to stick with pass-through taxation

If you want to take advantage of the favorable tax laws of a specific state, you won't be able to do so being taxed as a partnership. With partnership taxation, the revenue and expenses (and the resulting profit or loss) of the business *flow through* to you and the other owners, to be reported on your individual personal tax returns. When this occurs, the owners of the business pay personal income taxes on that profit in whatever state they reside in. This eliminates any tax savings you may get by forming your LLC in a low-tax or no-tax state (often referred to as a *tax haven*). Same goes for other forms of pass-through taxation, such as being taxed as a sole proprietor (referred to by the IRS as a *disregarded entity*) or an S corporation.

A corporation, on the other hand, is considered a legal entity unto itself and is taxed separately. Whatever profit the company makes remains in the corporation, and thus in the state in which that corporation was formed. This profit is subject to any corporate income tax that its home state — its *domicile* — levies on it. In short: Any LLC that is formed in another state for the specific purpose of reducing state income tax must elect corporate taxation in order for the strategy to be feasible.

If you are considering electing corporate taxation for your LLC, then you must speak with a qualified accountant in your state to make sure that you won't face any extraneous tax implications by doing so. You may also want to read Chapter 8, where I discuss at length the differences between the two tax structures and what they mean for you.

If you are a *single-member LLC,* then you are automatically considered a disregarded entity by the IRS and are not afforded the option to elect corporate taxation. If this is the case, you may want to consider giving a friend or family member (other than your spouse) a token share of the membership. This can be as little as 2 percent and will automatically lift the single-member LLC curse from your company name.

Looking for LLCs out of state

If you don't have a brick-and-mortar business — maybe you're running an Internet company or a consulting or service business that isn't restricted to a particular state — and you live in a high-tax state, then you may want to consider forming your LLC in a more business-friendly jurisdiction. Some states have worked very hard to structure their tax and LLC laws for the specific purpose of encouraging businesses to form or move their operations there. Now that's the sort of government action I can stand behind!

The entire idea of forming your LLC in a faraway place can be somewhat daunting at first, but don't let the perceived difficulties overwhelm you. You can go to www.myllc.com/dummies and pull up the "state tax table." Use this to compare the tax structure of the state that you live in to those of the other states. If it looks like you can do much better (eh, Californians?), and forming in another state seems like a feasible option for you, then strongly consider doing so.

Exploring Tax and Privacy Havens

For years, when people heard the term *tax haven* they would think of some shady money-laundering operation in the Caribbean. Thankfully, that's not the case! A tax and/or privacy *haven,* as I define it, is any jurisdiction that has structured its laws in such a way that it attracts businesses and individuals seeking privacy and tax relief.

What most people fail to realize is that, internationally speaking, the largest global tax haven happens to be the United States! Foreign companies form LLCs here in droves, due to our favorable federal tax rates (especially concerning foreign investment) and incredible privacy protection. So you can forget going offshore, because you'll often find what you're looking for right in your own backyard (or a few states over).

That's federal, but what about your individual state? If your state imposes heavy personal and corporate income taxes and forces you to disclose private information about your business, then you lose the benefits of starting a small business in one of the most small business–oriented economies in the world. If this is the case, then read on, because in this section I discuss a few of the major states that are serious about attracting business — *your business* — their way.

Nevada: The small business tax haven

Nevada is notorious for being the ultimate state for small businesses. The number-one reason every entrepreneur and real estate mogul in the state raves about the benefits of Nevada is that the state has no taxes. Yes, you read correctly: no taxes. Zero. Zilch. Nada. No franchise taxes, no corporate taxes, and no personal income taxes. How can Nevada afford to do this? Well, let's just put it this way . . . the next time your buddy loses $200 at a craps table, make sure to thank him!

And if no taxes isn't enough to convince you, how about the privacy? In Nevada, the members of an LLC are not on the public records. This means that you can own an LLC without anyone knowing about it. The managers are listed in public records, so you're only hidden if you're not a manager (check out Chapter 10 for more on managing), but this protection is pretty powerful, nonetheless. If a lawyer doesn't think you own anything, she probably won't want to sue you!

In addition to the powerful benefits already mentioned, Nevada is the *only* state that has consistently refused to enter into an information-sharing agreement with the IRS. Whereas the other states give the IRS information about bank accounts and corporate records, Nevada tells them to butt out. In other words, if the IRS wants to target your Nevada bank accounts in order to settle a debt, they can only get the information via a court order or if you voluntarily let them in the loop. If that's not fighting for small businesses, I don't know what is.

The laws in Nevada governing LLCs are still relatively new and aren't very developed, but they were structured in a way that protects a company's management in the event of a lawsuit. This arrangement is highly desirable for small businesses, in which the owners are often also the managers. These laws are in stark contrast to Delaware, where the laws tend to favor the owners/members more than the guys running the show.

Following are some benefits of forming in Nevada:

- ✔ No personal income taxes
- ✔ No corporate taxes
- ✔ No franchise fees
- ✔ No information-sharing agreement with the IRS
- ✔ Member identities not public record
- ✔ Nominee managers permitted (see Chapter 16 for more information)
- ✔ Relatively low filing fees
- ✔ Trips to Vegas? A business write off!

Wyoming: The birthplace of LLCs

Without the pioneering nature of the state of Wyoming, I wouldn't have written this book. No, I wasn't born there. But LLCs were! Wyoming was the first state to enact laws governing the creation and management of limited liability companies. And you thought Wyoming was just for skiing.

Wyoming, a notoriously pro-business state, has managed to curb the desire to raise taxes and fees on businesses over the years. It's one of the few states that realize that, as tempting as it is to take money from the businesses, tax increases eventually drive them out, leaving the state worse off in the long run. Wyoming offers a lot of the same benefits for LLCs as Nevada, such as no corporate income tax and no personal income tax, but the fees tend to be much lower — about 75 percent less than Nevada's.

Wyoming may be a good choice for you if you want to form your LLC out of state. It's geared heavily toward small businesses, not just big public companies. In the first edition of this book I wasn't a huge fan of Wyoming because at the time they disallowed single-member LLCs. Luckily for all you singletons out there, Wyoming has loosened its restrictions and now allows the formation of small businesses in which only one person holds all management titles.

South Dakota: The newcomer with a serious agenda

I'm not sure who's running things in South Dakota, but the state seems to be on a mission! In all the years I've been working with LLCs, I've never seen a state so serious about attracting small businesses. If you need proof, take a look at your bills sometime and check out the addresses you send payment to. You'll probably find at least one or two billing services operating out of Sioux Falls or Rapid City, South Dakota's two main hubs.

South Dakota ranked #1 on the 2010 State Business Tax Climate Index, an independent report that ranks states by their level of "business friendliness." South Dakota has zero personal income tax and zero corporate income tax. Its fees are minimal, and it offers ample privacy protection. So private, in fact, that only one manager and one organizer are required to be listed on your articles of organization. This means that the members — the owners — of your LLC can remain private.

South Dakota doesn't aim to be simply a tax and privacy haven, though. The state wants your *business*. Yep, the whole thing. The state offers some pretty slick enticements in the form of substantial tax credits (who doesn't love free cash?) and other financial incentives to companies willing to base their entire operations there.

Delaware: The heavy hitter

Do you have great expectations for your venture? Are you designing an LLC that needs room to grow? Then Delaware is the state for you! Delaware is a perfect domicile if you intend to grow really large and do business in several different states.

Most public companies want to be in Delaware because of its chancery court (a special court that makes decisions on business matters) and its long history of case law. Also, the laws (and boy, are there a lot of them!) are geared toward protecting the directors and shareholders — a must for larger businesses. Because of these two qualities, the majority of public companies listed on the stock exchange are domiciled in Delaware. That's a pretty big reputation for such a little state!

Delaware is the only state with a chancery court. Most states' courts are very backlogged, and you may wait years for a judge to hear and decide on a lawsuit. In contrast, Delaware can get cases resolved in weeks. That alone is appealing, but the chancery court goes a step further. When you go to court in other states, you never know how much your judge actually knows about business. ("You mean to tell me that his honor was just promoted from traffic court?") All judges in the chancery court, though, are experts in matters of business and are renowned for their fair and educated decision making. You can rest assured that the person deciding the fate of your company is more fluent in the laws of LLCs than petty larceny.

Another benefit of Delaware is its privacy. The state has earned this reputation by allowing a greater amount of financial secrecy for businesses than any other jurisdiction in the world. Yep, you got it: *in the world*. Delaware is more secretive than jurisdictions in the Caribbean and even Switzerland! Only a registered agent and an authorized signer need to be listed on the articles of organization. Now, that's privacy!

Some of Delaware's benefits include the following perks:

- ✔ The ever-famous chancery court hears business cases.
- ✔ 300 years of business case law has established precedents.
- ✔ Series LLCs are allowed (see Chapter 2).
- ✔ Little disclosure is required, allowing for extensive privacy.
- ✔ Fees are relatively low.
- ✔ LLCs that are formed in Delaware but don't operate there have no state taxes.
- ✔ No company records are required to be kept in the state of Delaware.

Working with a State-Required Registered Agent

"We're suing you, but we can't drag you into court until we serve you in person, so where can we find you?" If this question were posed to most business owners over the phone or e-mail, they'd probably just reply "Mars." For this reason, states require a business to have what is called a *registered agent* — which is interchangeable with the terms *resident agent* and *statutory agent* — in the state where you domicile or "home" your LLC and in every state in which you transact business.

A registered agent's primary duties are to have an address in the state that is not a P.O. box and to be open during business hours in the event that your company is sued and paperwork needs to be served. Fun job, huh? This company or person also accepts government documents, such as correspondence from the secretary of state's office, the clerk's office, and the state tax bureaus, on behalf of your company and then forwards them on to you. In many cases, an agent's office can also serve as your corporate headquarters in the state where your LLC was formed if you don't have an office there.

Why you need a registered agent

In some states you can serve as your own registered agent (provided you have an office address in the state). However, I could fill about five pages with reasons why this isn't ever a good idea. In the following list I touch on the big ones:

- ✔ **You can't ever leave.** Someone must be at the registered agent's office address during all business hours to sign for government papers. If the court service comes to drop off legal documents and you're not around, you could lose the lawsuit by default! Went to lunch? Too bad. Needless to say, that would be one *really* expensive lunch.

- ✔ **You'll look bad in front of employees and customers.** If lawsuits are served at your business address, imagine what your customers (and employees) will think when they see a couple of cops come into your place of business carrying a lawsuit and asking for you. Even if you've done nothing wrong, the talk among your employees and customers can be incalculably damaging.

- ✔ **You lose some of your privacy.** Losing privacy makes you more vulnerable to lawsuits. For example, if you use your own address, someone considering suing you can instantly see online if your home is in an affluent area. This may be the deciding factor for an attorney as to whether he'll take the plaintiff's case without a retainer. By using your registered agent's address on your state filings, you have an additional level of privacy.

✔ **You lose safety.** Imagine if a disgruntled customer wants a refund in the form of your landscaping, or an unlucky day trader comes directly to your home to "discuss" his losses. You're better off avoiding these sorts of scenarios by concealing your personal address and using a registered agent.

What your agent should do for you

Due to the sad truth that a registered agent's primary function is to sit and wait for a lawsuit to arrive, most registered agents now provide extra services. After all, you're a well-behaved citizen and probably aren't getting sued very often, so what's a registered agent to do all day?

A good registered agent warrants its nominal fee by taking on such important tasks as keeping your LLC in compliance with all the state-required filings, forwarding your government mail, and protecting your identity. Because of these extra tasks, registered agents have gone from being legal irritants to becoming important members of LLCs' teams. They have the following responsibilities:

✔ Have a separate business location at a commercial (not residential) address and stay open during all normal business hours to accept lawsuits and filing documents, which they forward immediately to you.

✔ Protect your address by allowing you to use their address as your corporate headquarters.

✔ Forward your state and government mail and/or notices each business day.

✔ Remind you of any state filings that are due and make sure you stay in compliance. Some registered agents even have online "compliance calendars" that keep you up to date with any upcoming filings you may have to make.

✔ File your documents (if necessary) with the requisite state and local bureaus.

✔ Assist you in finding state-specific tax and legal professionals.

✔ Keep copies of your corporate documents in case of theft, loss, or natural disaster. A *lot* of Louisiana businesses were happy they had used a legitimate registered agent after Hurricane Katrina!

How to find an agent

Finding a registered agent isn't too difficult. Finding a legitimate one who can and will do the job for a reasonable price is another story altogether. The best way to find an agent is by calling your secretary of state's office and asking for a recommendation. Some states maintain a list of registered agents on their Web sites, but like the referrals you'll get over the phone, these agents aren't vetted by anyone. In this section, I give you detailed information on how to find and vet a reliable and legitimate agent company in whatever state you wish to form your LLC in.

Calling in the Big Four

I recommend that you retain one of the "Big Four" national registered agent firms. These four big national companies specialize only in registered agent services, for the most part. They're good at what they do, and they're generally more technologically advanced than local companies. Also, as you expand to multiple states, you don't have to deal with a different company in each jurisdiction. Virtually all Fortune 500 companies use one of the Big Four as their registered agent.

Following are the Big Four national registered agent firms:

- ✔ InCorp Services, Inc. (www.incorp.com)
- ✔ CT Corporation (http://ct.wolterskluwer.com)
- ✔ Corporation Service Company (www.cscglobal.com)
- ✔ National Registered Agents, Inc. (www.nrai.com)

Prices for these companies' services vary greatly, so shop around. Registered-agent-information.com, an independent comparison site, has pretty good up-to-date reviews on each company as well as links to sites for the major registered agents doing business in each state (including the Big Four) along with their prices.

Evaluating agents

When interviewing a potential agent, first get a feel for her policies on dealing with lawsuits. You and your registered agent must agree that any legal paperwork she receives on your behalf will be brought to your attention immediately. Perhaps you decide that she will call you and summarize a document's contents and then have it delivered to you overnight. Or maybe she'll e-mail you a copy of the documents and then send the originals to you. Just be sure both of you are clear on what procedure will be followed. The same method should be used for state documents and various tax notices as well. Whatever the delivery method you and your agent agree on, make sure you can track your package.

One characteristic to look for when choosing a registered agent is how long that person or company has been working with the secretary of state's office. If your registered agent has close relationships with the administrators at the secretary of state's office, you have better chances of your filings being completed much faster and issues being resolved easily. Also, it's a good sign of legitimacy. If the administrators at the secretary of state's office have never heard of your registered agent, that person or company probably isn't doing a lot of work there.

If you'll be doing business in multiple states, choose a registered agent who's also located in those states. That way, your filings, your invoices, and your records can be consolidated, and you have one firm that knows the ins and outs of your business and can work for you in multiple jurisdictions. Also make sure that the agent can collect, complete, and file your state and local business licenses and permits for you. (See Chapter 11 for more on business licenses and permit filings.)

Although registered agents don't come free, their services usually cost only a few hundred dollars per year (a pretty fair price for everything they do!). Most fees are billed annually and at the time your LLC was initially created. Think twice about hiring an agent who requests that you sign a multiyear contract with her. A lot of legitimate agents don't require contracts, so why lock yourself in if you don't have to?

Make sure your agent always has your current contact information. If your agent can't find you, she'll have trouble forwarding Uncle Sam's letters to you. I have had numerous clients who used my company as their agent to maintain their privacy, and they were so private that they wouldn't even share their correct contact information with *me!* Needless to say, tracking them down to forward their legal paperwork wasn't always the easiest task.

I suggest choosing an individual within your LLC to maintain regular contact with your registered agent. This helps avoid any unnecessary confusion about who the agent is supposed to contact in the face of a lawsuit. However, all members should feel comfortable contacting the agent at any time.

Attorneys will try to place themselves as your registered agent. Although attorneys are qualified to be agents, be aware that they tend to be much more expensive than commercial registered agents.

Chapter 6

Creating and Filing Your Articles of Organization

In This Chapter

▶ Knowing what you need to include in your articles

▶ Bringing in the right experts to assist

▶ Completing your state filing

*Y*our LLC's most important document is the articles of organization. Why? Because you can't even *be* an LLC until you create and file your articles of organization with your secretary of state's office. And because the filing of this document brings your LLC into existence, it needs to be initiated before you make any other state or federal filings, including business licenses and your application for your tax identification number with the IRS.

The articles of organization describe the basic structure and management of your LLC, such as who your registered agent is and where your company's principal office is located. With so many uses for LLCs and all their flexibility, why on earth would you want your LLC to look and act the same way as someone else's? If you are raising money for a multi-million-dollar real-estate venture and your Uncle Joe is running a paper route, do you really want both companies operating under carbon-copy LLCs? Heck no! You need something that is customized to your specific needs.

Although most of the customization occurs in your operating agreement, which I cover in detail in Part III of this book, some states require you to list some of these specifications in your company's articles of organization in order for them to be valid. In addition, some states may require you to include certain *provisions* (a fancy name for the sections of your articles of organization) in your articles. It can be sort of tricky — all states differ slightly in their requirements, so if you're creating and filing your articles yourself, you definitely need to look up your state's rules. To make this job a bit easier for you, I posted all state laws addressing articles of organization on a public wiki at www.docrun.com/wiki/state_laws_llc_articles.

Making a Few Big Decisions

The articles of organization are what officially make your company an LLC. However, even if you're starting a business from scratch, a lot of important decisions need to be made before you can prepare your articles. For instance, as I cover in Chapters 4 and 5, you need to make some big decisions about your business name and the state your LLC is going to reside in. You also need to lay the groundwork of membership and management, although your operating agreement allows you to customize and modify the players and their roles (see Chapters 9, 10, and 11). At a minimum, you need to answer the following important questions before creating your articles of organization:

- ✔ **What is the name of your LLC? Is the name available for use?** Any particular name may be available for your LLC, but is it available for use in your state? Has it already been trademarked by another company? Trademark infringement can be a time-consuming and costly experience. Even if you have no evil marketing intentions of making money off someone else's name, the courts won't be lenient. Just as with a speeding ticket, ignorance is not a defense (and we've all tried that one before!). In Chapter 4, I go over in detail how to select and verify your LLC name.

- ✔ **What is the purpose of your LLC?** This question is an easy one. Before going into business, you need to know what sort of business you are in! The answer can be as specific or broad as you like. However, I recommend that you keep your company's purpose as broad as legally allowed so you aren't limited by what you put in your articles of organization. I give you some specific examples later in this chapter.

- ✔ **Is your LLC going to be member-managed or manager-managed?** Are all investors going to have a say in the day-to-day business decisions, or will a select few handle everything? Do you want to manage your own LLC, or would you rather step back and let someone else handle it? Most states only require bare-bones information on managers in the articles, so I only touch on this topic briefly in this chapter. However, if your formation is a bit on the complex side, you may want to skip forward to Chapter 10, where I discuss selecting your managers in further detail.

- ✔ **Who will be the initial members?** Some states require you to list your company's initial members in your articles of organization, especially if you select member management. Later in this chapter I address a few ways to get around this requirement, but before forming you should still have an idea of who the initial members of the company will be. You can always change the membership later; however, the process can be time consuming, depending on the process that you lay out in your operating agreement. See Chapter 9 for more on choosing your LLC's members.

- ✔ **In which state(s) are you going to form your LLC?** LLC and tax laws vary from state to state — some states have no taxes, others have less paperwork, and others less disclosure — and you should take these differences into consideration when determining where to form your LLC. Chapter 5 helps you decide which state is the best home for your LLC and also whether you're doing enough business in a particular state to be required to register there.

✔ **Who is going to act as your registered agent?** Every LLC needs to have a registered agent acting on its behalf in *every* state in which it does business. Have you chosen your registered agent for each state you are registering in? Bear in mind that you must rely on this business if your LLC is ever served with a lawsuit. See Chapter 5 for more on registered agents.

Choosing the initial members

LLCs are like children — they need parents! No matter what, your LLC must have at least one owner, and preferably two or more. The owners of the LLC are called the *members*. One of the best characteristics of LLCs (assuming you don't intend on electing to be taxed like an S corporation) is that anyone or anything can be a member. In other words, any person or entity — an individual, other LLCs, corporations, trusts, limited partnerships, and so on — can be a member. Also, you aren't restricted in how many members you can have — you can have 1,000 members or more if you like! This is one of the main reasons why LLCs are becoming popular for raising private capital.

The amount of the business you own is called your *membership interest*. Normally, your membership interest is represented on a piece of paper called a *share certificate* or *membership certificate*. The percentage of your membership interest in relation to all the membership interests that the company has issued is called your *membership percentage* or *ownership percentage*.

The issuance of membership shares doesn't take place in your articles of organization, which is why I don't go into this topic further in this chapter, but instead is executed in either your operating agreement or a separate buy-sell agreement. I recommend you disclose as little as possible about membership in the articles of organization, because that information ends up on public record (and is available to the prying eyes of ambitious litigators).

A really simple way to determine what specific information your state requires to be disclosed about your company in the articles of organization is to check out the default fill-in-the-blank articles the states provide. I don't recommend that you use these forms for your actual filing (unless required) because they don't make it easy to amend the language or add any extra provisions you may wish to include, but they do have some good info on them that can help get you started in the right direction. I provide these forms for each state along with any accompanying instructions on the CD enclosed with this book.

Skirting some of the disclosure rules

If your state is one of the few that require you to list all your members in the articles of organization, feel free to do so. However, if you're adverse to disclosing so much information on public record, you can simply list one or two initial members. Then, when it comes time to draft your company's operating agreement, you can

- ✔ Recognize those members as the initial members of your LLC
- ✔ List additional "initial" members of your LLC

As long as your operating agreement is ironclad and takes all state laws into account, you're golden. I go over how to draft a comprehensive operating agreement in detail in Chapter 10.

If you want to protect your privacy but your company only has one or two members, you can always elect to be manager-managed. In that case, instead of listing your company's initial members, most (if not all) states allow you to list one or more managers. You can then elect a *nominee* — a friend or paid professional to stand in your place on public records, thus allowing you privacy. Then use the operating agreement to direct specifically how the LLC is to be managed.

Be careful of the difference between electing a nominee *manager* and a nominee *member*. Remember, members *own* an interest in your company (nominee or not), whereas managers don't have to. Managers can simply be individuals who manage your company according to the powers afforded to them in the operating agreement. You can strictly limit their involvement this way. Only in rare instances will you want to elect a nominee *member* instead; usually only if your LLC is geared towards asset protection and you want to avoid being a single-member LLC (I go over single-member LLCs in Chapters 3 and 10).

Your state may only require that an *authorized representative* — usually your registered agent or formation company — be listed in your articles of organization. If this is the case, then none of these rules and work-arounds apply to you. You can see what your state specifies on the public wiki at www.docrun.com/wiki/llc_articles_signers.

Considering single-member LLCs

In case you haven't read any of Part I, let me catch you up: LLCs that have only one member are called *single-member LLCs*. And if you're planning on operating as one, you may have a hard road ahead of you.

First and foremost, under federal tax law, an LLC with a single owner isn't considered an entity at all, but instead is taxed as a sole proprietorship or *disregarded entity*. This means that your LLC won't have the option to select a different tax status, and the standard partnership tax status that we all know and love isn't an option for you. Instead, you're stuck being treated as a sole proprietor. Bah. While it's still pass-through taxation, it does differ in a number of ways, which I discuss in Chapter 8.

Another problem with single-member LLCs is that the rockin' dual liability protection that LLCs offer was set up when LLCs were still considered partnerships. Although the LLC has moved away from the partnership designation and into a category of its own, that liability protection is still founded on the premise of needing to protect one partner from the personal liabilities of the other partner. Notice this scenario has at least *two* partners; not *one*. So if the second layer of liability protection — the *charging order protection* that protects your business from your own personal lawsuits — is important to you, then you need to find a partner, stat.

When bringing on this token partner, you only have to issue her a very small percentage of your LLC in order for it to be effective. The amount isn't set, but 2 to 3 percent should do it. Also, you can limit her powers substantially in your operating agreement. Because you need to consider a lot of factors when making arrangements, I recommend using either a qualified small business attorney or other qualified service. When writing this book, I couldn't find any affordable alternatives to recommend to you, so I created the company DocRun (www.docrun.com), which makes forming these sorts of complex operating agreements a snap.

Don't have anyone you can trust enough to give away a small portion of your company? You always have the option of filing as a Nevada or Wyoming corporation (for the privacy those states offer) and then allowing that entity to act as your partner.

Double liability protection doesn't fly for single-member LLCs

For many years, professionals and consultants argued about whether single-member LLCs were allowed the same double liability protection as regular multiple-member LLCs. Finally, in 2003, a case came up (In re: Albright, No. 01-11367, Colorado Bankruptcy Court, April 4, 2003), and the court decided that this double protection (also called *charging order protection*) doesn't apply to single-member LLCs because there are no innocent partners to protect (the reason why the charging order exists in the first place).

Up until this time, many attorneys and financial planners were setting their clients up in single-member LLCs under the assumption that the business liability protections would apply. Needless to say, they're lucky they weren't the debtor in the case in Colorado! Since then, a case in California has reinforced that charging order protection doesn't apply to single-member LLCs.

Deciding how you want your company to be managed

Businesses don't operate themselves — someone needs to manage them! Often, you don't have to immediately decide exactly who will manage and what their specific roles will be (which I go over in detail in Chapter 10), but most states require that you give a basic idea of how your company will be managed in the articles of organization. If your state doesn't require this, then you will most likely have to state it in your operating agreement. So why delay in figuring out how you want to structure your LLC's management? Start now!

An LLC can be managed two ways:

- ✓ **Member-managed:** The LLC's members (the owners) also deal in the business's day-to-day operations. If this option is selected, *all* members are also managers — you can't prevent one member from getting involved while allowing the rest. However, you *can* limit the power of individual member-managers (or groups of member-managers) in the operating agreement.

- ✓ **Manager-managed:** A separate manager (or two or three or ten) handles the business's day-to-day operations. This is a good choice if not all members want to manage and/or an outside person would be a good manager. Some benefits of manager management include flexibility — you can assign certain outside individuals as managers, now or in the future — and alleviating confusion and breaking up the workload.

Just as you're unlimited in the number of members an LLC can have, you also can have an unlimited number of *managers,* but I would choose wisely if I were you. Unless specifically restricted in the operating agreement, managers have absolute authority to obligate the business to contracts, loans, debts, and so on. It only takes one manager to do this, and he can act without the knowledge of the others. Therefore, all the members must absolutely trust whoever is chosen as a manager.

In Minnesota and North Dakota, the managers are called *governors.*

When the members manage

Member management is the most common choice for smaller businesses. This sort of management makes all owners equally responsible for the day-to-day operating of the business. However, you don't have to worry that one of your partners will mismanage the company and land you (personally) in the poorhouse, because all managers of the LLC are exempt from being legally responsible for the debts of the LLC. For instance, if the LLC is sued, the managers can't be held personally liable for the business's actions. They can rest comfortably — anything that they didn't invest in the LLC (like a car, house, or wedding ring) is untouchable by outside sources.

Of course, there's a flip side to this: If you, like most entrepreneurs, put everything you have into your start-up, then a company lawsuit could be devastating. If you're a small business and want to exclude those certain members who have a tendency to make bad decisions, like using company funds for personal, non-business-related exploits and adventures (we all know the type!), then you may want to severely limit that member's management powers in the operating agreement or isolate that member entirely from all management activities by making your LLC manager-managed and not electing that individual as a manager.

Also, if you're a larger company with a lot of members, then you may want to think twice about choosing member management. Think about it — if each member has a say in the day-to-day operations of the business and you have 25 members, it will be a total mess! That's like having 25 CEOs! Not only is it unrealistic, but it will also lack credibility if you are ever taken to court. These members don't need to be managers in order to have basic voting powers over the *big* decisions of the company, and the beauty of the LLC is that you're free to specify what qualifies as a big decision in the operating agreement. I show you how to do this in Chapter 10.

If you choose member management, you may lose the benefit of charging order protection if you don't take a few steps to protect it. If a creditor gets a charging order against your membership interests and those interests come with management rights, that creditor can use his management powers to distribute a good portion of the profits to himself to pay off the claim. See Chapter 10 on how to structure your operating agreement to protect against this.

When separate managers manage

When you select manager management, you must choose at least one manager — even if he or she is also a member. Also, the manager doesn't even have to be a he or a she! You can select an entity (an LLC, corporation, limited partnership, and so on) to manage the LLC. Of course, whoever manages that entity becomes the true manager of the LLC.

Why would you have separate managers manage? Maybe one of the members wants to remain a silent partner. He's willing to risk his money but doesn't want to be bothered with the everyday business decisions that the managers are confronted with. Or, say that none of the members has time to actually manage the business, so they want to hire an outside CEO who can do a better job than they ever could. In a lot of situations, separate managers may make more sense for your LLC.

Manager-managed LLCs are commonly used in estate planning. You can give membership shares in the LLC to your children every year while remaining the only manager of the LLC. While you're alive, your children can't make management decisions regarding the money but can receive profits from it (finally, a gift that truly keeps on giving!). Then when you pass away, they're elected as the new managers and have full rights over and use of the LLC's assets. (For more on LLCs and estate planning, see Chapter 18.)

Managing her LLC means she can have her cake and eat it too

Jill's family and friends have been pressuring her to start a bakery for years now, and Jill finally relents. She is looking forward to the challenge and has even taken business classes to learn how to run the company. She puts together a business plan so she can look for financing. Her credit isn't great, so that leaves her with the option of going to an investor.

Jill's cousin is a very successful lawyer and offers to loan her the money. He trusts Jill's

expertise and is willing to be a silent partner. He lives on the other coast, so he can't be active in the business's day-to-day operations anyway. Considering this, Jill sets up an LLC. She issues 50 percent of the membership interests to herself and 50 percent to her cousin in exchange for the start-up capital. Jill then designates the LLC as manager-managed and names herself as the only manager.

When you have a manager-managed LLC, the Securities and Exchange Commission or your state securities division may determine that you are involved in the sale of securities if your members are investing in an LLC that they have no say in managing. This determination isn't necessarily a bad thing. Just be sure to speak with someone qualified before disallowing any of your investors decision-making power in the company's operations. I go into how to make these sorts of decisions in Chapter 13, where I address raising capital with your LLC.

Bringing in the Big Guns: Finding and Working with Professionals

Building a business is a journey, and the best time to prepare for the future is now, when you're just beginning. In the early years of your business, situations will arise where you need immediate help — be it taxes, lawsuits, human resources, or administrative stuff — and you need a team of professionals ready and waiting to jump in at a moment's notice.

No matter what, you need professionals to handle certain matters as you run your business. For example, you need an accountant to handle tax issues; a bookkeeper to maintain your accounts; a good small-business attorney to handle legal issues; a corporate strategist, a financial planner, a real estate broker, a banker . . . the list goes on and on.

And although you can figure out how to create and file your company's articles of organization yourself, the question remains: Why would you really want to? While I firmly believe that you should have a good, basic knowledge of all aspects of your business, I also believe you should spend your time working on the parts of your business that you do best and entrust tedious, time-consuming tasks outside your area of expertise to the professionals.

Hiring a great attorney

Most of you won't need an attorney to fill out your articles of organization, but you very well may need one for the more complex stuff in the rest of the formation process, such as creating your operating agreement. You'll also need one waiting in the wings when the occasional legal issue crops up. Lawsuits abound, and after the public smells your first sign of success, some people will be looking for any reason possible to sue you. Trust me — you have a very good chance of being served with a lawsuit during the course of business. It's scary, and when it happens, you'll be glad that you've already taken the time to find that perfect lawyer to back you up.

In some cases, you should consult with an attorney and/or qualified CPA prior to the formation process, especially if you're forming a nonstandard LLC, creating multiple LLCs that are intended to work together, or converting your existing business to an LLC and it has assets that need to be transferred. (See more about these types of LLCs in Chapter 2.) You should also consult a securities attorney if you plan to sell a large quantity of ownership shares of your LLC to raise capital.

Getting referrals

Finding a great attorney isn't always an easy task. Despite what some people recommend, contacting your local bar association for a referral is normally pointless. The person you speak with hasn't had any personal experience with the attorney, and she does little to assist you. Usually, she just provides the names of attorneys who have paid the bar association to do so, and some bar associations even charge you for the referral!

The best way, by far, to find the perfect lawyer is to ask around. Talk to everyone you know who has a small business — especially those who have formed LLCs — and ask them about their lawyer. Get them to speak candidly with you — find out what they *truly* think of the person's legal expertise and work.

Don't have a lot of entrepreneur friends? Some Web sites, such as www. perfectbusiness.com and www.startupnation.com, serve as networks and communities among entrepreneurs and small business owners. PerfectBusiness.com actually has a listing of small business attorneys and accountants in each state that other users have vetted and recommended to the community. Because this referral service isn't motivated by profit (in other words, attorneys don't pay to be listed), I find their referrals to be legit. Plus, they also help connect you with investors. Nice!

A slower but equally effective means is to contact your local SBA (Small Business Administration) and attend a few of their mixers. After asking around, you may end up with a few names of qualified locals.

Researching attorneys

Before you call the attorneys to set up an appointment for a consultation, do your homework and find out a little bit about them. Sites that offer good attorney background information include:

- ✔ **www.FindLaw.com:** This site supplies lengthy firm profiles and extensive background information on each attorney.

- ✔ **www.Martindale.com:** At this site you get a firm profile and some background information on each attorney.

When looking at individual lawyers' profiles, I recommend that you focus on attorneys whose area of expertise is limited to small-business issues. If an attorney practices in a wide range of areas, such as business formation and personal injury, count her out. You want an attorney who deals with issues similar to yours on a day-to-day basis, not someone who scours the hospitals looking for her next client. Also, read as much information as you can about the attorney's history and background; does she sound like someone who has focused her career on working with businesses such as yours?

Choosing an attorney

When calling prospective attorneys, let them know right off the bat what you're looking for: a good small-business attorney who can help you help yourself. You are looking for a long-term business relationship. If it's obvious that the attorney isn't for you, disqualify her now — not during a face-to-face meeting where you may not only be wasting your time but also be paying them for the pleasure.

When screening attorneys, evaluate them on two aspects:

- ✔ **A personal basis:** Do you like this person? What do your instincts tell you? Can you trust her? How would you feel working with her for a decade or longer?

  These are tough questions, but also the most pertinent. You're looking to establish rapport and a long-term relationship with this person — even trying to do that is a waste of time if you don't like her.

- ✔ **Her level of aggressiveness:** It should match yours. If she is extremely conservative and risk-averse in her strategies and you are the adventurous type and like to live on the edge of the law, then the relationship should probably end after the phone call. If, however, you're in agreement about how aggressive one should be when using entities to lower taxes and avoid lawsuits, then you should set the appointment.

After you have found one or two lawyers whom you like, set up an appointment with each for a one-hour consultation. You may be charged for this time, but if you come in prepared and full of questions, it will be well worth the money.

Considering formation companies

Don't know exactly what a formation company is? Sure you do! Remember those ads offering to form your LLC for a few hundred dollars? Normally, those ads are placed by *formation companies* — companies whose sole business is forming corporations and LLCs. When I started in the formation business in 2001, there was very little competition, but now it seems these companies are popping up everywhere. With all the advertisements and hoopla, the real question is: Do you really need a formation company? And if so, how do you choose between them?

First things first: Using a formation company to form your LLC makes sense when you

- ✔ **Want to save money:** Attorneys charge upwards of $1,000 for a basic LLC formation, but a good formation company can charge as little as $99. And because these formation companies deal with a much larger quantity of LLCs than individual attorneys, they have the process down to a science. So unless your articles of organization are über-complex, you may want to keep the extra dough and save the legal fees for consulting work.

- ✔ **Want to save time:** When dealing with a large number of filings, formation companies are forced to work out the kinks and get the whole LLC formation process down pat. This avoids any lag time you may encounter when attempting to file on your own. Plus, because they deal with the various secretary of state offices so often, they've developed relationships that can prove useful when you want to get your filing completed in a timely manner. With the right formation company, this nominal fee can save you weeks of tedious research and bureaucratic hassles.

- ✔ **Want to customize your company's articles and operating agreements:** You may want these documents to reflect specifically what you're trying to achieve. If you want to make changes to the standard operating agreement included on the CD that comes with this book but don't know how, a formation company can help you.

- ✔ **Are forming multiple LLCs and want an expert to look over your structure:** Some brick-and-mortar formation companies (the ones that operate outside of the online realm) have consultants who can review your strategy with a skilled eye and set you up in the proper business structure.

> ✔ **Are forming an LLC in a different state than you live:** Different states come with different laws, and a good formation company is well aware of how the various governments in all 50 states operate. It can also serve as your registered agent, hand deliver your filings, and make sure you stay in compliance while you're living hundreds of miles away.

If you decide that a formation company is right for you, make sure you find a quality firm. Screen prospects with the following questions:

> ✔ Do you have an attorney and accountant on staff to advise me on legal and tax issues?
>
> ✔ Will you assign a consultant to work with me on an ongoing basis?
>
> ✔ Are you located in all 50 states? If not, do you have knowledge of and relations in all other states?
>
> ✔ Will you customize the company to my needs?
>
> ✔ Will you customize the articles of organization as opposed to just using state forms?

Shameless plug ahead: As you probably know by now, I'm one of the founders of MyLLC.com, a leading formation company. While I encourage you to do your homework and check out all your options, I think you'll be pretty impressed with the level of service we offer. Plus, I'm offering you a $24.95 discount (the price of this book) on all formations. Just use coupon code **LLCsFD** at checkout.

Preparing Your Articles

Preparing your articles of organization can easily end up being overwhelming — especially if you have your articles rejected by the state a number of times. But keep your chin up. If you stay organized and get any assistance that may be helpful, you should be able to get your articles submitted within a couple of days and be certain that they will be filed without incident. After you submit everything correctly, you can sit back and wait for your approvals to start rolling in.

Meeting your state requirements

The articles of organization are made up of *provisions,* which is just a fancy term for the sections of your document that address particular topics. Some provisions are absolutely required to be in your articles, so I cover those first, and then I give you an overview of other provisions that you may want to (or need to) include.

Each state has different requirements, but I cover the commonly shared provisions in this section. To find out specifically what your state requires, check out the fill-in-the-blank articles of organization that your state provides. This document tells you all the information your state requires and assists you in the planning process.

Provisions that your articles must have

In most states your articles of organization must include the following provisions:

- ✔ **The LLC name:** This is pretty straightforward — your articles need to identify the name of the company they apply to! Keep in mind, though, that this name needs to be unique from any other names registered in your state. I show you how to go about checking for this in Chapter 4.

- ✔ **Company address:** Some states require that you put your company address in the articles of organization. I recommend always using your registered agent's address, but make sure your agent is okay with this and can forward your mail every day. Also be aware that, often, the state won't let you use a P.O. box.

- ✔ **The powers and purpose of the company:** Here you designate what sort of business you'll be engaging in. Although some states require you to be more detailed, most states allow you to be really broad and say that the LLC isn't limited in its purpose and has the power to engage in any activity it wants. I always feel that the broader you make this statement, the less limited you are in the future should you decide to venture into other business areas. Sometimes envisioning where your business will be at its ten-year mark can be an impossible feat, so to be safe, always stick with the idea that "broader is better!"

  An example of a broadly stated provision:

  The purpose for which this Company is organized is to transact any or all lawful business for which Limited Liability Companies may be organized.

- ✔ **Registered agent and office:** Your registered agent can be your greatest asset — especially if you're organized in a state other than the one you live in. First of all, the law requires you to have a registered agent, and secondly, a registered agent can handle much of the paperwork involved in maintaining compliance in your state(s). See Chapter 5 for instructions on how to find and work with a registered agent company.

- ✔ **Member-managed or manager-managed:** As I discuss earlier in this chapter, whether your LLC will be managed by its members or separate managers is a big decision that can really help or hinder your business operations. Carefully consider the implications before making a choice.

- ✔ **Names and addresses of managers and/or members:** Quite a few states require that you give the names and addresses of the managers and/or members in the articles. Because the articles of organization are public record, try to state as little as is legally allowed. As a matter of fact, if your registered agent allows it, try to use his office address in this section.

Some states require that you also state the amount of each member's initial contribution (money, services, equipment, whatever) and the percentage of profits that each member gets. If you don't yet know this information, or don't want to disclose it, you can do one of two things:

- State what you *do* know or are willing to disclose, and then put the remaining information in the company's operating agreement. I show you how to do this in Chapter 10.

- Domicile your LLC in another state that doesn't require this disclosure, and then foreign file in the state where you're operating.

✔ **Organizer:** In most states, only an *organizer* (also sometimes referred to as an *authorized signer* or *authorized party*) is required to sign the articles of organization. This is becoming more and more popular as formation companies do most LLC filings. This person has no true legal responsibility or further obligation to the LLC, so it really can be anybody. This arrangement is great if you're looking for privacy!

The antiquated duration provision

When LLCs first came about, the IRS placed a few restrictions on them in order for them to be eligible for partnership taxation. One of these restrictions was that LLCs can't live forever. The states complied by giving LLCs a limited life span of 30, sometimes 50, years. Though this restriction is long gone, a few states have been slow to adapt and still require a duration to be declared in the articles of organization.

If this is the case, you need to see whether or not your state allows a "perpetual" duration to be listed in the articles. You can quickly assess this by checking the actual state statute addressing the issue, which you can find at www.docrun.com/wiki/llc_duration. If your state statutes allow LLCs to have a perpetual duration, state the following in your articles:

In accordance with all state statutes, the duration of the company shall be perpetual.

If your state does not allow a perpetual duration and lists a maximum duration (usually 30 or 50 years), don't worry — you'll be able to renew your company's existence at the end of that term. You can use this provision to bestow extra powers to your company's operating agreement by stating something like the following:

In accordance with all state statutes, the duration of the company shall be thirty (30) years. However, the Company may still have the option of dissolving during this term.

The Company may, in its Operating Agreement and amendments thereof, confer additional powers upon its managers and members, so as they are not in conflict with the law.

Extra provisions you may want

You're allowed to include whatever extra provisions you want in your articles of organization; however, keep in mind that your articles are public record. Also, in order to amend them, you must go through a costly filing process.

When it comes to customizing your LLC, you get into a lot more specifics in the operating agreement (see Chapter 10) than you do in the articles of organization. If you don't see an important provision discussed in this chapter, that omission is probably because I feel that including it in the operating agreement instead is a better idea because the operating agreement isn't on public record. Privacy is important, especially when it comes to protecting yourself against lawsuits. And if you want to change customized provisions, you don't have to pay a dime to change your operating agreement.

An extra provision that you will likely want to include and *not* want to ever amend is the indemnification of managers and members. When you are *indemnified,* you can't be held personally responsible for the acts of the company or even for your acts on behalf of the company. This provision is normally provided in state law, but it's always good to publicly state in your articles of organization that each member is permitted the maximum indemnification available to them.

Following is a sample provision:

Article IX: Indemnification of Managers and Members

> A. *Under the current law, including any amendments hereafter, each manager shall be entitled to the fullest indemnification available to them.*
>
> B. *Each manager shall be liable to the Company for the following actions:*
>
>> 1. *The breach of the manager's or member's loyalty to the Company, or its members.*
>>
>> 2. *To be liable hereunder the manager in question must have acted in a malicious or grossly negligent manner, as defined by law.*
>>
>> 3. *A transaction in which the manager benefits to the detriment of the Company or its members.*
>>
>> 4. *An action for which there is no indemnification provided by law.*
>
> C. *This indemnification shall not deter or cancel out other rights to which the manager or member is entitled.*

Provisions for professional LLCs

In most states, if you are a licensed professional you must have a special provision in your articles of organization designating you as a *professional LLC* (or PLLC, for short). As I explain in Chapter 2, a PLLC is very similar to a standard LLC; however, professionals can't be exempt from personal responsibility and malpractice, so they have less liability protection. The PLLC's formation is the same, but the articles are slightly different, and the filing fee may be slightly higher, depending on the state.

If you are a licensed professional, before creating your articles of organization, read Chapter 2 and make sure you're well aware of your state's laws in regards to professional LLCs (and whether your state even allows them to be formed). Also, keep in mind the following points:

- ✔ Typically, you have to abide by name restrictions. You must add the word *Professional* or the letter *P* to the designator. In some states, the name of the LLC must contain the professional's name. For instance, if you're a doctor and your name is Jane Goodman, then your professional limited liability company can be called *Jane Goodman, MD, P.L.L.C.*

- ✔ You can't state a broad purpose; it must be specific to the service you provide. You must use a purpose provision stating something like the following:

  The purpose for which the Company is organized is to engage in the professional service of:_____.

- ✔ In some states, you may need to have your licensing board approve your articles of organization and sign them before the secretary of state will accept them for filing. Contact MyLLC.com at 1-888-88MYLLC or your local secretary of state to see if this is required. If it is, you may need a good dose of patience — these things can take time!

- ✔ The fees may be slightly higher when forming a professional LLC. Also, if you are using the generic, state-provided articles of organization, you must check to see if you need to use a different one for PLLCs.

Putting it all together

After you figure out what provisions you're going to include in your articles of organization, you need to wrap everything up into a professional-looking document. One option is to just amend the state's generic form with your extra provisions, but do you really want to walk into a bank, ask for a million-dollar business loan, and then hand them articles that look like a patchwork quilt of legalese? Not likely.

If your state allows it (most states do), retype the articles into your own document so it looks more professional. A lot of people who can make important decisions that affect your LLC likely will be looking at these articles — bankers determining your eligibility for a business loan, investors looking to buy in, and so on. You want to demonstrate that you take pride in your company documents.

Different states require different formats, so contact your secretary of state's office to make sure that it doesn't have any special requirements as to how the articles of organization are laid out. However, most states have the basics in common, and with that in mind, here are a few tips:

- ✔ Always print your articles of organization on regular 8½-x-11-inch white paper. Use black ink and only print on one side of the paper (no double-sided copies). Make sure that the articles are clean and legible.

- ✔ Spell your company name exactly as you want it to look on your checks, letterhead, and other official documents.

- ✔ Structure the document into articles, sections, and subsections. This makes referencing different provisions a breeze. For example, Article A, Section 4, or Article II, Section B, Subsection 4. You can see this structure by looking at any professionally drafted contract.

Articles of organization are pretty simple, and for the most part, you can draft them yourself. However, your time may be better used doing other important things, so if you don't feel like researching laws and typing out provisions, consider going to a formation company. These companies are generally well versed in creating articles of organization (after all, they do it every day!) and charge a heck of a lot less than an attorney.

Choosing who signs

So you put all this work into forming your articles of organization and now you need to sign it, right? Probably not. Believe it or not, in most states, a manager or member doesn't even need to sign the articles before filing them.

Most states assume that when an LLC is organized, it hasn't had its first member meeting. At that meeting, managers are traditionally elected. If the LLC doesn't have any managers, they can't sign the articles. Most states also assume that you're forming your LLC through an attorney or formation service, and to make it easy for everyone, states allow someone at the law firm or formation company to sign the articles, rather than the client. That is why most states allow an *organizer* to sign and file the articles of organization.

The organizer doesn't have to be associated with your company, and she isn't a manager or member (unless you want her to be). She is simply the person who creates the LLC. After the LLC is formed and the managers and members are assigned, the organizer fades away — she has no future position of power in the company.

Although most states allow an organizer to sign the articles of organization, some states require a manager and/or member to sign. Also, some states require the articles to be notarized. A quick way to determine who must sign the articles of organization in your state is to look at the filing form for your state (which is included on the CD with this book).

Getting the necessary signature sounds fairly simple, but there's a catch. In most states, the LLC's registered agent is required to sign the articles of organization before it can be filed. The agent normally signs an acceptance of appointment document that is appended to the articles. Getting this signature can be a little bit of a headache for most people, especially if you live in a different state than the one you're filing in. In that case, I recommend that you make sure your formation company and the registered agent for your entity are one and the same.

Filing Your Articles

Filing your articles of organization with the secretary of state can be an exciting process. Especially when you receive your file-stamped articles in the mail! After that you can *finally* get to the important stuff you need to do to get your business up and running: opening bank accounts, printing marketing materials, hiring employees, renting office space, and so on.

If you're interested in the how-tos of filing, then you've probably created your articles of organization by now, and there's no point in waiting to do the filing. After all, your LLC can't come into existence until it's been approved by the secretary of state. Think of the date that your articles of organization are stamped as your company's official birth date. If you're ever asked what your date of organization is, you'll refer to this date (called the *formation date*) — not the date that you drafted the articles, nor the date that you received the filed articles in the mail. Along with your filed articles, you'll receive a company charter that shows the date of formation.

In the following sections, I go over the step-by-step process of filing your articles of organization.

Dotting your i's and crossing your t's

Before you file your articles of organization, *please* take the time to do a bit of research to make sure you file your articles properly. When you follow the filing steps to the letter, you save yourself a lot of time and headaches later because your filing won't be rejected. From my personal experience working with secretary of state's offices, I can tell you that they often have to reject filings for silly reasons: The fee amount is incorrect, the organizer only sent in one copy, and so on.

To file your articles, the first thing you need to do is to go to your secretary of state's Web site (I provide the Web addresses for each state in Appendix A) and determine a few things, such as

- ✔ What fees are required?
- ✔ To whom do you make out the check?

> ✔ Can you pay with a credit card?
>
> ✔ Are you allowed to fax the copies?
>
> ✔ How many copies are required?
>
> ✔ To where do you mail the documents?
>
> ✔ Are any cover sheets required to be submitted with the articles?

After you answer these questions and double-check your filing against the state's filing procedures, make a copy of the articles (for your own files), put a copy of the articles and anything else the state requires in an envelope (don't forget to include the fee; see Appendix A), and mail them. I recommend sending your filing packet by a service that requires the recipient to sign for the package.

Another alternative now available in most states is the option to file your articles of organization online. You may not end up with the prettiest corporate documents at the end of the day, but the sheer amount of time saved may be worth it. Most states offer an easy step-by-step process, and any mistakes that you make in the filing process can be immediately corrected online, whereas with a paper filing you may have to wait weeks to receive a rejection notice in your mailbox.

Sending it off

You're eager to put your business plan into action. Your first official day of work with your new company is planned out in your head. And of course, the one thing holding you up is the need for some file-stamped articles that prove to the world your company is in existence.

After you send in your articles and payment, the secretary of state's office can generally take as long as it wants to file your articles of organization. Don't be alarmed if six weeks later you still haven't heard back. Some states, such as California, can take up to three months if you file by snail mail!

 In some cases, you can file the articles of organization in person and get moved much further ahead in line. If you can't file personally because you're in a different state, you can always have your registered agent do it for you. (See Chapter 5 for details about registered agents.) For other ways to speed up the approval process, see the following section.

After the secretary of state's office approves your articles, you receive your file-stamped articles back in the mail. Attached to your filed articles, you normally receive a *company charter.* This one-page document shows the all-important date of formation. The charter and the file-stamped articles of organization are your proof that your business is formed as an LLC in your state.

When you don't want to hurry up and wait: Fast-forwarding your filing

Some states will — for a fee — actually put your filing at the top of the pile! Depending on the state, you may be able to expedite the processing of your articles of organization. Some states give you the option of getting your articles back within 48 hours, 24 hours, or even the same day.

When submitting expedited articles, label the outside of the envelope *Expedited Handling Required.* Also putting a sticky note on your document that says the same thing is a good idea.

Although this seems like a perfect scenario, beware that the fee for this quick turnaround can range from an extra $10 to hundreds of dollars. Call your secretary of state's office or visit its Web site (listed in Appendix A) to find out the exact cost. Also, keep in mind that if your articles of organization aren't perfect and are rejected as a result, you're still required to pay the expedited processing fee.

Dealing with a rejected filing

If you receive a large envelope from the secretary of state's office and open it, expecting to see your filed articles but instead seeing a rejection-of-filing notice, your heart will sink. It's a bummer when your articles are rejected — especially when you can't wait to get your business up and rolling.

The worst part of a rejection is that a small error can be time consuming to fix because you may need to wait at the end of the line. For instance, if your documents took three weeks to be reviewed by a clerk the first time, after you resubmit them they may go to the bottom of the pile, and you'll have to wait another three weeks to get them looked at. (Of course, you can always take the expedited route if your state offers it. See the sidebar "When you don't want to hurry up and wait: Fast-forwarding your filing" for the skinny on expedition.)

The secretary of state may reject a filing for any number of reasons. Here are a few mistakes applicants make and how you can avoid them:

- ✔ **The name you want to use conflicts with another LLC (or other entity) that is formed in that state or a name that has been reserved.** In this case, you just need to choose a new name. If you don't want to do that, you can contact the competing firm and try to get a letter from them giving you permission to use their name, but this is usually a long shot.

✔ **The name is considered misleading.** The name may have forbidden words, such as *banking, financial,* and so on. In this situation, you can do one of the following things:

  • Go to the department in your state that regulates that industry and get approval for the wording from them (probably requiring you to jump through a lot of hoops)

  • Change your company's name

✔ **Your filing fees may be incorrect.** In this case, just write a check for the additional filing fees and resubmit your documents. Or, if the state returned your old check to you, void it and send a new one for the correct amount.

✔ **You may not have specified a registered agent.** This error is common. When individuals form an LLC, often they don't know what a registered agent is or does, so they leave this section blank. But you won't have this problem, because you can read Chapter 5 for more information on these folks and then fill in the appropriate section on the form.

✔ **A provision is missing.** In this case, you most likely prepared the documents yourself and missed a *provision* (a section of the document that deals with a particular topic) that is legally required to be in the articles of organization. In this case, just add the provision to your articles (you can create a fresh draft so they look nice) and resubmit them.

✔ **You are missing a cover sheet.** Some states require cover sheets to be submitted with the articles. In this case, obtain the cover sheet from the secretary of state's Web site, fill it out, and resubmit your articles with the cover sheet.

Although a rejection is a setback, don't get too down about it. Nothing bad will happen. You just need to fix the problem indicated in the rejection notice and resubmit your documents. If the notice isn't specific enough, call the number listed on the form for your secretary of state's office and ask them for more information. Or better yet, consider using a formation company to set up your LLC. If you use a reputable company that deals with these sorts of formations all the time, they probably won't mess up in the first place.

Chapter 7

Converting Your Current Business into an LLC

Chances are, if you're considering forming an LLC, you're not starting from scratch. LLCs are relatively new entities, and if you've been in business for a long time, you're probably operating your business or maintaining your assets as a sole proprietor, partnership, or corporation. You likely know the benefits of operating under an LLC, but you may not know how to convert your existing business into one.

When you're in the throes of a bustling enterprise, the last thing you want to do is cause any more chaos by changing your infrastructure and switching to a completely different type of entity. In most cases you have to navigate a tax minefield and spend a lot of time changing contracts, business loans, and even marketing materials over to your new name. Although the conversion to an LLC can be hairy, the protection, freedom, and tax benefits offered by LLCs make it well worth it in the long run.

In this chapter, I show you how to convert your current business structure into an LLC, no matter what entity type you're currently using. I also show you how to avoid most of the fees and taxes that pop up and how to avoid unknowingly falling into a tax trap that you can't get out of. Although this process may seem complicated on the surface, the situation isn't as dire as it first appears. With proper planning and the help of a qualified accountant, you can be operating under your new LLC in no time!

Considering Conversion to an LLC

Life is good: Your business is flourishing. But you know that as you operate more and more with the public, your chances of being sued increase tenfold, so you've decided that you need the reassurance of liability protection. Or, you may want to take on investors or acquire loans to help you grow. For your business to have the best protection and advantages, you need a powerful and flexible entity, and, as I'm sure you're aware, the LLC is your best bet.

In Chapters 2 and 3, I give you an overview of LLCs and all the other major forms of business — sole proprietorships, partnerships, and corporations. If you haven't read those chapters yet, I suggest that you stop here and backtrack to discover the benefits and drawbacks of an LLC compared to whatever entity structure you are currently operating under. After you understand all your options, call your attorney or formation company consultant to discuss what is right for your specific situation. If you don't already have a trusted advisor on this topic, you can call my office at 888-88-MYLLC (888-886-9552) and speak with a specialist.

When I use the term *conversion,* I'm not only talking about converting a corporation, limited partnership, or other *incorporated entity* (an entity that needs to be filed with the state to exist); I'm also referring to *nonincorporated* business structures, such as sole proprietorships and general partnerships. You may be surprised to know that even if you're simply operating under your own name, converting to an LLC can be just as complicated as converting from a corporation. Of course, a few factors play into this, which I discuss further along in the chapter.

I can't possibly list all the reasons why you may want to convert your business to an LLC, but the following example situations give you a taste of why a conversion can be an incredibly powerful step on your path to success:

- You're operating as a sole proprietorship or general partnership and are afraid of being sued by a customer or employee.

- You're operating as a corporation and you're afraid that you may be sued personally, or may someday face bankruptcy or divorce, and your ownership of the business will be taken away from you.

- Your company — which is currently a corporation — is becoming more and more profitable, and your corporate tax is up to almost 35 percent. You want to minimize this tax burden by electing partnership taxation.

- You just purchased real estate in your own name, and you want to protect the property from lawsuits, so you know that transferring your property into an LLC is your best bet. Luckily, unlike a corporation, you can transfer assets in and out of an LLC tax free!

- You're currently operating as a sole proprietorship or general partnership and want to raise financing to get the business off the ground.

✔ Your business was formed as an S corporation and you've outgrown the ownership limitations imposed on you (for instance, you want to take on a non–U.S. resident as an investor). By converting to an LLC, you can remove any ownership restrictions while also maintaining pass-through taxation (see Chapter 8 for details on the differences between the two types of taxation).

✔ You're operating as a corporation and you will be investing a substantial amount of additional capital. You prefer the partnership taxation of the LLC so that you can immediately write off that contribution as a loss on your personal tax return (thereby offsetting other income).

The question often isn't whether or not a conversion is right for you — if you have gotten this far into the book, then you've probably already determined that an LLC *is* right for you. Instead, the question is how to make the conversion work. Depending on your current entity structure, a conversion may seem a bit daunting, especially if a conversion looks like it will bring a lot of tax consequences. But don't fret — if you've got the will, I can show you the way!

Navigating the Tax Minefield

Any drawbacks encountered while converting your business into an LLC are likely to be tax traps of some sort, but being informed can help you navigate the best path. LLCs can trick you! Because you can transfer money and property into them without creating a taxable event, you may think any transactions you want to perform while converting to an LLC are good to go. Unfortunately, you need to take into account any taxes or fees you may encounter with your old entity (corporations are the worst when it comes to this!) and taxes incurred by changes in debt structure or ownership interest. Also, if you aren't on the lookout, you may be hit with a bunch of local and state taxes, such as sales tax, use tax, transfer tax, and so on.

Although you can elect an alternative form of taxation for your new LLC, in this section I assume that you intend to go with the default form of LLC taxation, partnership taxation. After all, it is the most flexible and least restrictive of all forms of taxation. (If you aren't sure of your options, turn to Chapter 8 to find out which form of taxation is right for you.) Be aware that electing some other form of taxation for your brand-new LLC (such as corporation or S corporation taxation) is a game-changer. The strategies and information in the rest of this chapter may not apply. The same goes for single-member LLCs, which are considered *disregarded entities* by the IRS and are taxed as if they were sole proprietorships.

If you think you may be straying from the norm, you'll definitely want to get the advice of a qualified accountant before executing the conversion. Don't make assumptions when it comes to LLC taxation and conversions; way too much is at stake.

Converting from a sole proprietorship

Considering that the most common, albeit dangerous, method of operating a business is as a sole proprietorship, you may well be running a sole proprietorship currently. Although sole proprietorships are easy and cheap to start, they offer zero liability protection, and they give your customers and employees little confidence in your business acumen. Plus, due to the fact that sole proprietorships don't have shares you can sell, you'll never be able to even think about raising capital or finding investors.

If you're currently operating as a sole proprietorship, I strongly recommend that you form an LLC immediately. Luckily, converting from a sole proprietorship to an LLC can be a pretty effortless, tax-free process. Your business assets are currently in your name, so transferring them is easy. You simply contribute the business's assets to the LLC in exchange for your ownership interest.

Considering a single-member LLC

You may face a few hurdles when converting your sole proprietorship to an LLC; namely that you must make sure your state allows the formation of a single-member LLC. A quick glance at Appendix A is all you need to figure this out. If your state is one of the few that doesn't allow them, you may need to take on a partner.

(***Note:*** Before throwing this book across the room, be sure the trajectory is clear of all living beings.)

I'm well aware that if you haven't taken on a partner at this point, then it's probably because you have absolutely no desire or need for one, and I understand that. But when LLCs came into existence, they were intended to be partnerships. Therefore, by operating an LLC with only one member, you miss out on a lot of the benefits that probably inspired you to convert to an LLC in the first place. (Turn to Chapter 2 if you need a reminder of the benefits.)

So even if your state *does* allow the formation of a single-member LLC, I encourage you to take on a minority partner. This step can be as easy as issuing a trusted friend or family member (other than your spouse) just 2 to 3 percent of your membership interests. Depending on how much you like that person, you can even structure the partnership so that even though he owns a portion of your company, he doesn't receive any profit distributions.

Avoiding a few common tax traps

If you convert your sole proprietorship to a single-member LLC simply by contributing your business assets to the LLC in exchange for membership interests — in other words, you use your business assets as the currency to purchase ownership in the new entity — then no taxable event occurs. Yep, it's all tax free.

However, you face one potential tax pitfall, a *deemed cash distribution*. In a business, the two kinds of debt are *recourse debt,* debt that one or more of the members is personally responsible for should the business default on the loan, and *nonrecourse debt,* debt that's only secured by the business and in which the owners have no personal stake. A deemed cash distribution occurs when a member reduces his share of the business's recourse debt.

The IRS treats any reduction in a member's share of recourse liability as a cash distribution, and, like a cash distribution, the member must pay taxes on any of this amount that goes over his *tax basis* (I discuss tax bases in Chapter 8). Luckily for LLCs, being the most flexible entities around, allocations and distributions of profit can be amended and handed out disproportionately (as long as a majority of the members agree).

Frankly, getting around the deemed cash distribution problem isn't too difficult if you have a qualified accountant to help you. If your company has substantial business loans and liabilities and you're bringing on a partner, speak with an accountant who has extensive experience with partnership taxation. If you don't currently have anyone onboard, try to find other businesses with structures like yours and get a referral. Try hitting up the mixers at your local Small Business Administration (SBA) or check out the entrepreneur referral section on www.perfectbusiness.com. The ins and outs of deemed cash distributions can get pretty complex, and you need to have a clear map through any potential tax minefield. A neighborhood bookkeeper simply won't cut it.

You know that old adage, "Don't change horses midstream"? Remember it if you're considering changing your accounting method. When you convert to an LLC from a sole proprietorship, keep your accounting method the same. For instance, if you are on a cash-based system, don't switch to an accrual-based system. In the IRS's eyes, this switch could "accelerate the income," which means taxes, taxes, and more taxes! If you really want to change your accounting method, wait until the conversion has been completed and then have your tax advisor assist you.

Converting from a general or limited partnership

The conversion to an LLC from a general or limited partnership is probably as straightforward a switch as you can get. No matter if you're a general partnership, a limited partnership, or a limited liability company (electing partnership taxation), you're all the same in the eyes of the IRS. The different entity types may be treated differently by the states, especially when it comes to liability protection; however, they are all subject to partnership taxation.

Keep in mind that before you can convert your general partnership operation to an LLC, all the partners must unanimously agree to the decision. You can't convert without them knowing it! All the partners usually have to sign off on it in the company's operating agreement.

The big nontaxable event

Assuming everything is straightforward, a conversion from a general partnership or limited partnership to an LLC is a *nontaxable event,* so you won't get hit with a big tax bill at year's end. All you have to do is contribute the assets of your current business to the new LLC in exchange for membership shares. Most of this is done in your operating agreement, which I show you how to draft in Chapter 10.

This easy step makes converting from a general partnership or a limited partnership to an LLC a relatively pain-free process. You simply execute the conversion with the state (I describe exactly how to do this later in the chapter). As long as nothing changes in regards to ownership percentages or business debt, nothing changes with the IRS. You can have the same tax year-end and you can continue to be taxed as a partnership with the same year-end filings due as before.

It gets even better: Under Section 721 of the Internal Revenue Code, you're even allowed a friendly little exemption for any appreciation that your business property may have accrued. For instance, if your limited partnership purchased a piece of property five years ago for $100,000 and it is now worth $150,000, when you convert the limited partnership to an LLC, you don't have to recognize the new fair-market value of the property ($150,000) or pay taxes on the $50,000 appreciation your property accrued in the past five years. The IRS allows you to put that burden off for later years, when you legitimately sell the property. To learn more about this and other partnership tax tricks, you may want to check out Chapter 12, where I discuss taxation at length.

The usual partnership tax trap

The entire conversion is absolutely, 100 percent tax free? It sounds too good to be true! Well, that's because it is. As with sole proprietors who may be looking to bring on another partner, if your business adds or removes members or changes any percentage of ownership during the conversion process, you may inadvertently end up with some pretty gnarly tax consequences.

The same problem occurs if you change who underwrites the business debt. If an owner personally guarantees a business loan, that loan is considered *recourse debt* and the owner can use it as a deduction of sorts against any income he derives from the partnership. If, when converting to an LLC, this partner changes the amount of debt he personally guarantees or writes it off entirely, the IRS likely will consider it to be income to the partner (because he's no longer responsible for the debt), and the total amount offloaded may end up being treated as if it were a cash distribution from the company. This means that, depending on the member's tax basis in the company (which I discuss in detail in Chapters 8 and 12), he may be taxed on this amount as if he were being paid in cash. Although this tax trap can occur in sole proprietorships, it's much more common with partnerships. After all, more hands in the pot usually means more issues popping up.

To illustrate this tax trap with an example: You own a piece of property worth $200,000, with a mortgage on it for $150,000. You've been a good customer, so your bank decides to release you from having to personally guarantee the $150,000 loan and instead just puts it in the name of the business. At that point, depending on where your capital account stands, with previous deductions and so on, you may need to pay tax on $150,000, simply because you're no longer responsible for the debt. Bet it ain't lookin' so bad on your credit report now, eh?

Keeping the ownership and distribution percentages the same is the only way to avoid a taxable event when changing an existing partnership into an LLC.

Converting from a corporation

If you're currently operating as a corporation, converting to a limited liability company is a clear good move, unless you plan on going public or raising venture capital. The double taxation inherent in corporations is rarely helpful for a growing business. Unfortunately, as good a move as the conversion to an LLC is, especially where taxes are concerned, it can also be a pretty hairy process . . . again, especially where taxes are concerned.

The upside is that under Section 721 of the Internal Revenue Code, you (or in this case, your corporation) can contribute property to a limited liability company in exchange for membership interests without having to recognize any gain or loss. Your corporation then owns all the membership of the LLC, thus the total management and control of the LLC passes through to the corporation, which retains the original shareholders and directors. Therefore, you won't have to pay any tax on the appreciation of any of your corporation's assets when they're transferred. As far as the IRS is concerned, the assets retain the value they had when first purchased, rather than being reset to the fair-market value that they're worth today (and thus forcing you to recognize and pay tax on any appreciation that occurred).

With this provision, a good accountant, and some in-depth brainstorming sessions, you can find multiple ways to accomplish your conversion with very little tax burden.

Navigating state taxes

Transferring assets from a corporation to a limited liability company without the help of a qualified accountant is akin to crossing the freeway wearing a blindfold. If you somehow manage to make it across the IRS obstacle course, you still need to take into account state and local taxes as well. First, know your enemy: Find out what sales tax and transfer tax your state may hit you with. In high-tax states such as California, they can be crippling, so you need to be aware of the worst-case scenario.

Knowing your many options

When you have an idea of what you're dealing with, you and your accountant can structure the conversion in a way that minimizes (or even eliminates!) these taxes. If your state allows *statutory conversions* (converting your corporation into an LLC instead of dissolving the corporation and starting a new LLC), then this could be a viable option. (See "Executing the Conversion" later in this chapter for more on statutory conversions.) Or maybe you'd be better off doing a merger, with your LLC remaining as the surviving entity. Or perhaps your state provides a tax exemption that allows you to go the conventional route of forming a new LLC and transferring the business assets in exchange for membership interests.

If, after looking with your accountant at all the routes available to you, you still can't find a work-around, consider leaving your assets in your corporation. After all, no law says a business's assets need to be maintained in its operating company. Actually, I always think *not* having your business assets in your operating company is better. Not only is isolating your assets from potential lawsuits a good asset-protection strategy, but it can also help you *save* taxes in the long run.

Converting smoothly with a merger

You may be able to save taxes when converting a corporation to an LLC by forming a brand-new LLC and doing a standard merger with it and your corporation. A *merger* is the combination of two existing entities into a single surviving one, and merging your corporation into an LLC is a great way to avoid sales and transfer taxes that are associated with moving assets from one entity to another.

All states have laws regarding mergers, so you have to research whether the laws of your state allow two different entity types (a corporation and an LLC) to merge into one with the LLC being the surviving entity. Some states provide no guidance at all, and in this case, your attorney is the best person to direct you through the proper procedures.

Keeping the corporation

Sometimes the best thing to do is nothing at all. A *dual-entity strategy* is an arrangement in which a newly formed LLC serves as your operating company and leases assets from your corporation. I discuss this strategy at length in Chapter 16, but I give you a quick rundown here.

If your business assets are located in a corporation, separate from your operating company (in this case, a newly formed LLC), then you can lease those business assets to the operating company (the LLC) for a certain sum commiserate with the going rate in your industry. When your LLC operating company makes those lease payments (a fully deductible expense) to your corporation, that income (which would otherwise be deemed profit) is then shielded from whatever hefty state taxes would otherwise be imposed on them.

For example, if you own a local pizza company and you want to convert your corporation into an LLC, you set up your new LLC, transfer your contracts to the LLC, and convert your business operations over to it. However, you leave your stoves and other equipment in the ownership of the corporation. Your corporation becomes a leasing company and leases the equipment to your operating LLC. This arrangement has two benefits:

- ✔ If one of your customers gets food poisoning and sues your company (your LLC), your assets are protected in your old corporation.

- ✔ If you want to retain profits without having to pay personal income tax and self-employment tax on them, you have a legitimate way of transferring them to a corporation (thereby only subjecting them to corporate income tax — usually a much lower amount — until you use them).

A dual-entity strategy is only effective at saving you some tax dough if your corporation is in a low-tax state such as Nevada, Wyoming, South Dakota, or Alaska. If it isn't, you can always relocate it (called *redomiciling*), but check first with your accountant that this step doesn't inadvertently create a taxable event on either the federal or state level.

Creating a leasing arrangement between an existing corporation and a new LLC may be overkill for you if you aren't too concerned with avoiding state taxes. If this is the case, then don't worry so much about the state that the corporation is in or transferring profit, but do take into consideration the fact that leaving your assets in your corporation often is cheaper than transferring them out, and you better protect your company by isolating your business assets from whatever entity is handling your company's day-to-day operations and is most likely to be sued.

If your corporation is in a tax-free state, such as Nevada or Wyoming, you may want to lease the assets to your operating LLC at a standard lease rate (so the lease is legitimate and you don't raise red flags). This way, that profit won't be distributed to you at the end of the year and be subject to your personal income and self-employment taxes; it will be safely sitting in a corporate bank account free from hefty state corporate taxes and franchise fees. What a great way to save up to buy more assets and equipment! I discuss using a tax-haven for the dual-corporation strategy in more detail in Chapter 16.

Executing the Conversion

Before you begin to convert your business to an LLC, be sure to do the following:

- ✔ Carefully consider whether converting your current entity to an LLC is the right thing to do, and decide yes
- ✔ Scope out any tax issues that may arise
- ✔ Sit down with your accountant and work out a plan

When you've done your homework and are ready to move forward, you need to decide what type of conversion you will do. When I say *conversion,* you probably think of one of two things: Actually transforming your old entity into a limited liability company by changing its structure (often referred to as a *statutory conversion*), or what I call the *form and liquidate process,* which I discuss later in this section. These two methods are the most popular ways of executing a conversion, but other possible conversions, such as a merger or an acquisition, may end up being the best bet for what your situation requires. These advanced strategies are used in complex situations and are best handled by a qualified tax attorney and/or CPA. At the end of the day, all you really care about is getting assets from Point A to Point B without major tax ramifications and with as little legal paperwork as possible.

If your state allows statutory conversion

If your state is one of the few that allow what is called a *statutory conversion,* consider yourself lucky! A statutory conversion is a means for entities such as corporations and partnerships to change their entity type by simply filing a certificate of conversion, along with the articles of organization of the new LLC, with their secretary of state.

Statutory conversions are only available for *incorporated* entity types, which means they don't apply to sole proprietorships and general partnerships. I show you how to convert from a sole proprietorship or general partnership later in this section.

Note that statutory conversions don't result in the dissolution of your old company and the formation of a new one. Instead, your company is simply *converted* to a new entity type. If done properly, the conversion qualifies as a reorganization under Section 368(a)(1)(F) of the Internal Revenue Code, which offers much more favorable tax treatment than simply transferring assets to a new LLC. A qualified CPA or tax attorney can further inform you on whether or not this conversion is the best option for your particular situation.

With a statutory conversion, you keep your same tax-identification number (you simply contact the IRS to change the entity type associated with that tax ID), and most states' conversion laws automatically transfer over the rights of creditors and liens on property. Neither of these little tidbits may seem so important, but they can save you a world of hassle when you go about emending your contracts with your lenders, creditors, and vendors with your new name with *LLC* at the end.

When executing a statutory conversion, keeping the structure of the company — including percentages owned, voting rights, and so on — the same is important for tax purposes. And regardless of tax implications, most states actually require that no significant changes in this regard take place in order to complete a statutory conversion. Depending on the laws of your state, you may even be required to structure the management in a similar manner.

Knowing what your state requires

Some states, such as Alaska, simply require articles of conversion that declare the name of the entity before the conversion, the name of the entity after the conversion, and the date that the conversion is to be effective. However, other states require a *lot* more detail. For instance, California requires a plan of conversion that rivals the page count of *War and Peace.* Most states also require that an *operating agreement* for the LLC be completed prior to the conversion taking place (which I address in detail in Chapter 10).

I can't overstate how dramatically the states' laws on conversions differ, so doing some research to learn exactly what your state law requires is very important. The easiest way to do this is to read the actual law. At www.doc run.com/wiki/llc_conversion, you can find a list I put together of the state laws that address converting to a limited liability.

Here are a few documents that your state may require from you in order to execute a statutory conversion to a limited liability company:

- ✔ **Articles of conversion:** By far the simplest document of the bunch, the articles of conversion are normally just one or two pages containing some basic information, such as the name and entity type of the old and new entities, any updated company addresses, and the date that the conversion is to be effective. Usually your secretary of state provides a basic fill-in-the-blank document for you online.

- ✔ **Articles of organization:** All states (that allow statutory conversions) require you to file articles of organization for your new limited liability company. I give you details on how to create articles of organization for your LLC in Chapter 6, but when converting, you may want to do things a little differently and give the date the company was first formed as the "effective date" of the LLC. Again, look to your state's laws for direction on this.

✔ **Plan of conversion:** Not all states require this document, and, for the ones that do, the specifications can vary dramatically. In a nutshell, this document lays out exactly how everything will be moved from one entity to another, what the new articles of organization are going to say, how the new entity is going to be structured, and so on.

Keep in mind that your plan of conversion can be a tool for you and your partners that helps keep everyone on the same page. The information and decisions that you lay out in it don't necessarily have to be limited to what the state requires. As a matter of fact, even if your state *doesn't* require you to file a plan of conversion, I think creating one anyway for your company's own internal use is a good idea. As I'm sure you know, business can get chaotic, and a plan of conversion keeps everything on track so the conversion runs smoothly and without a glitch, or even worse — a day of missed work!

All the possible required filings are relatively simple and intuitive to fill out, but the plan of conversion requires a great amount of detail. To give you a taste of what you may be in for, following are some items that California requires you to address in the plan of conversion:

✔ The terms and conditions of the conversion

✔ The jurisdiction of the original entity, the jurisdiction of the new entity, and the name of the new entity

✔ How shares will be converted into ownership of the new entity

✔ How the new entity will be run, including partnership agreement, articles of organization, and operating agreement

✔ Any other details required by law or that the entity wishes to include

As you can see, this state requires a lot of information, yet doesn't give you a lot of guidance on how to format it, what decisions to make, and so on. This is where the help of a qualified business attorney comes in handy, so be sure to talk with someone who can help you with the details.

Documenting approval for the conversion

Some states require the plan of conversion to be approved by a specific majority or unanimous vote of the shareholders or partners of the original entity as well as the board of directors (if a corporation) or managers or general partners (if a partnership). Regardless of whether or not your state requires this proof, make sure you wrap up your old entity type properly and document *everything*.

If your company is a corporation, this requirement means you need to file a resolution of the board of directors and also of the shareholders that records the plan of conversion and the approval of all members. Just because you are converting to a limited liability company that requires a lot less recordkeeping and fewer formalities doesn't mean you shouldn't respect your current entity type before the conversion takes place.

Filing the conversion

Normally, all the necessary documents are filed with the secretary of state at the same time in one complete package. As complex as organizing all these pieces may sound, these filings shouldn't be too expensive — probably the cost of filing the articles of organization (which is listed by state in Appendix A) plus a couple hundred dollars. That's probably even less than the cost of forming a new entity and dissolving your old one!

After the filing is approved by the secretary of state, some states require that you report the filing in a local newspaper or publication. Be sure to check for this requirement, because failing to meet it can potentially leave you in a bad standing with the state.

If your state doesn't allow statutory conversions

If your state doesn't allow statutory conversions, then you'll probably want to opt for what I call the *form and liquidate process,* which entails forming a new limited liability company, transferring business assets from the old entity to the new LLC in exchange for an ownership interest in the new LLC, and finally, dissolving your old entity.

You may face tax implications by doing a conversion this way, so clear things with a qualified accountant before proceeding. If you're currently *unincorporated*, namely operating as a sole proprietor or a general partnership, then you want to follow this same process with the exception of the *liquidate* part. After all, you need to first *have* an official entity before you can dissolve, or *liquidate,* it.

Following is a broad view of the steps you need to take to convert your business to a limited liability company:

1. **Form a brand-new LLC.** When you form your LLC, you need to do it just as I describe in Chapter 6. Nothing fancy required.

2. **Check all your loans for a *due on sale* clause that may become effective upon the conversion.** If you see this clause, you may be required to pay your entire loan if you transfer it. This requirement could force you to refinance, and, if the interest rates aren't good, can cost you a lot of money in the long run. You can normally work with your bank to avoid this scenario.

3. **Revise any contracts that your current entity is party to so the contracts reflect your new entity name.** In this case, you may want to work with your attorney, because some of the people you are in contractual arrangements with may see this as an opportunity to get you to renegotiate the contract before transferring it.

4. **If you are currently operating as a sole proprietorship or general partnership, check whether your business name is available for use.** If it's taken, you may have to form your LLC under another name and then file a *fictitious firm name statement* (or *DBA,* which stands for "doing business as") at your county clerk's office. I go over these naming issues in Chapter 4.

5. **If you have any current fictitious firm names, transfer them to your new entity.** The same goes for other intellectual property, such as trademarks, copyrights, and patents.

6. **Check to see if your insurance carrier requires a new premium after the conversion takes place.** Often, insurance isn't transferable from one entity to another, so you may run into some snags if you don't find out ahead of time.

7. **Dissolve your old entity.** I go into the basics of dissolving your old entity later in this chapter and also show you how to do a formal dissolution in Chapter 15. If you are a sole proprietorship or general partnership, you don't have an "official" entity to dissolve, so this step doesn't apply to you.

8. **Check to see whether you must publish a notice of dissolution or conversion in the local newspaper.** Some states require that you give notice to the public when you do a conversion; contact your secretary of state's office or registered agent to find out whether this step is needed in your state.

If you have a sizeable number of contracts and/or agreements (such as mortgages, employment contracts, lease agreements, loan documents, and license agreements) that your business is a party to, collect them all and take them to your attorney. She can review each document, determine whether any dire consequences will result from a conversion, and, if necessary, renegotiate any contracts that need to be transferred to your new entity. (A word of caution: You may want to work out a flat fee in advance because having your lawyer do this work can easily become relatively costly.)

Wrapping Up Loose Ends after the Conversion

It's official: Your business is a limited liability company. Congrats! So now what happens? First, you must amend all your official documents — your licenses, permits, and registrations — with your new name and entity type. Even if you're using the same name as before, you must be careful never to refer to your company without having *LLC, L.L.C.,* or *Limited Liability Company* after the name. Most states legally require it anyway; however, if you're ever taken to court, the proper name ensures you'll be able to prove that you were operating as an LLC when transacting business.

Following are some of the common licenses and permits that you'll need to update or even refile (especially if you've gone the liquidate-and-form route):

- ✔ Your tax identification number
- ✔ Your state business registration/license
- ✔ Your sales tax permit
- ✔ Your DBA (fictitious firm name) filings
- ✔ Your city and/or county business license
- ✔ Any professional licenses or permits

Also, don't forget that you're now an LLC, which means you need a comprehensive operating agreement that governs the structure, ownership, management, and day-to-day operations of your business. Limited liability companies are much different — and much more flexible! — than all other entity types, so this document is *absolutely imperative* to have. You can adapt your corporate bylaws or your current partnership agreement for your operating agreement, but you need a document that's specifically tailored to your brand-new LLC, so these documents can't be used as they are. Go through the steps in Chapter 10 to create your custom operating agreement.

Getting around the contractual stuff

At this point in the process, you've managed to sort out the tax stuff and arrange your conversion so that you don't have to dish out too much dough. You do the conversion and . . . ouch! You get served with a lawsuit from one of your vendors stating that you voided your contractual obligation and owe it a lot of money. And unless you did a statutory conversion, the vendor is probably right.

If you look at the fine print on the contracts that your company has signed over the years, some of them say that the contracts can't be assigned or that that they'll be terminated upon the termination of the company that entered into the contract. This stipulation means that after you convert and terminate your old business structure, you may have some problems with the people or companies you were contractually obligated to.

The following common contracts may be affected:

- ✔ Lease agreements for office space
- ✔ Equipment lease agreements
- ✔ Bank loans

> ✔ Personal loans
>
> ✔ Contracts with vendors
>
> ✔ Employee agreements

In some cases, you need to renegotiate the contract or buy your way out of the legal trouble, which can cost you a lot of money. Speak with an attorney before starting any negotiations. I've found that the money spent on attorneys in these cases is money well spent.

If you can't get out of the contract, you may want to consider just leaving your old company active so the contract doesn't have to be terminated. Whether this can be done depends on the contract, the type of business entity you are currently using, and your attorney's opinion on the matter.

Transferring your assets

After the LLC is set up, the next step is transferring the assets, which can be an expensive proposition in some cases — especially if you're transferring assets from a corporation, in which case you may have to pay some pretty hefty taxes on them when you take them into your possession. This entire process can be taxing (literally!). Before transferring assets to your new entity, be sure to read "Navigating the Tax Minefield" earlier in this chapter, where I go into some ways that you can alleviate the tax burden.

If the assets are currently held in your own hands, or if you are a sole proprietorship or general partnership, you can simply invest those assets into the new LLC in exchange for membership shares. LLCs make this process pretty easy because contributing assets to an LLC is, for the most part, a tax-free event. Just be sure that if you and/or your partners have personally guaranteed any debt for the business, nothing changes in that regard. Otherwise, as I discuss in "Converting from a sole proprietorship," you can get hit with a *deemed cash distribution* that you must pay tax on.

While you're going through the process of transferring assets and moving operations from one entity to another, work closely with your tax advisor and small-business attorney. Although I can provide useful suggestions in this book, you need to coordinate the actual execution of the conversion with a professional who knows your business.

Dissolving your old entity

After your new LLC is set up and all the assets and contracts have been transferred, you can begin winding up the affairs and dissolving your old business structure. Again, this is assuming that you are *not* currently operating as a sole proprietorship or general partnership and you have not executed a statutory conversion, which simply transforms your current entity into a limited liability company, eliminating the need to dissolve the old entity.

If your previous business structure was a sole proprietorship or general partnership, then you don't need to complete any special filings. You just need to make sure that you don't accidentally revert to your old ways and put contracts, notes, correspondence, and debts in your own name. You also need to make sure that you avoid combining personal funds with those of your business.

In some states, before a partnership can be terminated it must publish a *notice of termination* in a local newspaper. This public notice may even be required before the conversion can be effective. To find out whether this is the case in your state, call your secretary of state's office. I put a list of contact information for every state in Appendix A.

If your old entity was a limited partnership or corporation, then you must file a *certificate of dissolution* (also called a *certificate of cancellation*) with the secretary of state's office. It terminates your old entity in the eyes of the state and keeps old ghosts, such as company creditors, from haunting you. An officer, director, or member of the company must sign off on it, and it can only be filed after all the company's owners approve. To make sure the dissolution is legal and thorough, be sure to hold a meeting, document the meeting minutes, and have all owners sign the company resolution to dissolve. In Chapter 11, I tell you how to properly hold meetings and prepare meeting minutes.

If your entity has been registered to transact business in states other than the one you initially formed in, then you'll need to *withdraw* from those states before filing for a dissolution in your home state. Withdrawal is usually accomplished by filing a *notice of withdrawal* with the secretary of state of each state you're registered in, along with the requisite filing fee.

Before you can file a dissolution with the state or withdraw from a state you're foreign-filed in, you must make sure that the company is in good standing with the secretary of state's office and that no fees are due. You must also make sure that the company has paid its taxes. If the entity isn't in good standing, the certificate of dissolution probably will be rejected.

Although the dissolution of an LLC has key differences from other entities, you may want to read Chapter 15 to get an overview before contacting your local secretary of state to obtain more information on how to dissolve your particular entity type. An alternative to doing this yourself is to have a formation company handle the dissolution for you. Because all the assets and contracts are being transferred to the new entity, filing the paperwork with the state is the last step in completing the dissolution. A good formation company handles dissolutions all the time, so it can make sure you have all your bases covered. You still have to pay the state filing fees, but the fee that formation companies charge for this is usually pretty nominal. For instance, MyLLC.com charges $99 for dissolutions or withdrawals, regardless of the state.

Part III
Customizing Your LLC

The 5th Wave   By Rich Tennant

"Well, apparently our liability wasn't as limited as I thought."

In this part . . .

After your articles of organization have been filed with the state, you still need to customize your LLC. In this part, I show you how.

For starters, in Chapter 8, you find out how to choose your LLC's tax treatment with the IRS. Then I get into the real meat-and-potatoes stuff: In Chapter 9, you discover how to claim ownership of your company — called *membership*. Before you know it, you'll be printing off membership certificates, assigning voting rights, and arranging hostile takeovers. (I was just kidding about that last one!)

After all that, you'll be ready to create an operating agreement, which I show you how to do in Chapter 10. Your operating agreement is the backbone of your business, so this is easily the most important chapter in the book.

Chapter 8

Tell Uncle Sam How It Is! Choosing How You Want to Be Taxed

*I*n 1997 the United States Treasury instituted the current entity classification laws (which you may hear referred to as the *check-the-box regulations,* because the corresponding IRS form is comprised of a series of check boxes). This profound move established LLCs as one of the few entity types whose owners can dictate to the IRS how they want their company to be treated for tax purposes. LLCs can be taxed in four main ways — partnership taxation, disregarded entity taxation, corporation taxation, and S corporation taxation — and in this chapter, I discuss them at length.

The chosen taxation has no bearing on the actual integrity and structure of the LLC; for instance, an LLC that elects to be taxed as a corporation is still considered an LLC by state law in every sense of the word. The key benefits of an LLC — dual liability protection, flexible management and ownership, and flexible allocations and distributions of profits and loss — are all still in full effect. The LLC simply pays taxes like a corporation does.

The default taxation for LLCs is *partnership taxation*. If you file no Form 8832: Entity Classification Election with the IRS, you'll be subject to partnership taxation at the end of the year. This policy applies to all LLCs, except those with only one member (commonly referred to as *single-member LLCs*). I go into all this in the following sections.

Before you get too excited about how simple this arrangement can be, however, know that the IRS isn't as forgiving as they first seem. After you make a taxation election, you're stuck with it for about 60 months. This strict rule has a few work-arounds, but they aren't easy. So whatever decision you make, it better be a good one! Don't worry; by the end of this chapter you'll have enough information to go out and make an informed decision about the type of taxation that is right for your circumstances.

Getting to Know the Tax Types

The IRS really only recognizes four entity types, which each have a corresponding *tax type*:

- ✔ Partnership
- ✔ Disregarded entity
- ✔ Corporation
- ✔ S corporation

Assuming you aren't a single-member limited liability company (an *SLLC,* for short), you have the option of being taxed like any of these entities. Make sure you fully understand all your options and make an educated choice on which form of taxation to choose. The following sections detail each of these four taxation types.

Partnership taxation

All LLCs are created with a default tax status. It's like hair color — you're born with one color, but as you get older you can choose to change it if you want. If your LLC has at least two partners (not including your spouse) and you don't make any tax classification election with the IRS, then you stick with the default, which is *partnership taxation* — a favorable form of *pass-through taxation* — and it's actually a pretty good deal.

All forms of taxation that I address in this chapter, with the exception of corporation taxation, are forms of pass-through taxation. The various forms have some differences, but the premise remains the same: The business itself doesn't pay federal income taxes; instead, the profits and losses of the business *pass through* to the owners to be reported on their individual income tax returns. The individual owners then pay regular personal income tax and, in most cases, self-employment tax on this amount.

Corporations can elect to have a form of pass-through taxation (creating what is called an *S corporation*), but it's not the same as the default partnership taxation of an LLC. Partnership and S corporation taxation differ dramatically from one another, and the regulations on structuring are different (for example, S corporations have more restrictions on who can and can't be an owner), so don't make the amateur mistake of forming a corporation and electing pass-through S corporation tax status, thinking it's the same as the partnership taxation of an LLC. You can check out the later section "S corporation taxation" for more detail.

If you are a single-member LLC and wish to elect partnership taxation, then you absolutely, unequivocally must bring on a partner. Your spouse doesn't count in the eyes of the IRS; however, issuing a small percentage of the company to a child, parent, sibling, or even a friend may be all that you need to make the change. If you don't have someone whom you trust, then you can always form a corporation (preferably a Nevada or Wyoming corporation, for privacy purposes) and bring on that entity as your partner.

Taking advantage of flexible allocations and distributions

To understand partnership taxation, you need to understand two concepts: *allocations* and *distributions.* At the end of the year, your company generates either a profit or a loss, which passes through to the members on their personal tax returns. This number is referred to as the *allocation,* and each owner pays individual taxes on this amount. A *distribution,* on the other hand, is the actual cash you get from your LLC. It's what you are able to deposit into your personal bank account and spend as you please.

More often than not, the amount of profit you're allocated at the end of the year and pay taxes on isn't the amount of hard cash that drops into your pocket. Why not? Well, you'll most likely decide at some point that you want to retain some money in the company to pay for growth or to keep as a buffer. Or perhaps you or your partners will knowingly or unknowingly make a company expense that isn't deductible. When this happens, you have to pay taxes on these profits, yet you don't actually get to cash the check and go hit up Vegas for a nice little shopping spree.

Allocations and distributions are inherent in all forms of pass-through taxation; however, one very pertinent difference applies to limited liability companies taxed as partnerships: The amount of profit that's allocated and/or distributed to a particular member doesn't need to be in proportion to his percentage of ownership in the company. Corporations (including S corporations) cannot even get close to this sort of awesome flexibility. Disregarded entities (sole proprietorships and single-member LLCs) by their very nature can't do anything like this.

Here's an example of how you can use varied allocations and distributions to your advantage: Say you really need some last-minute capital to grow your business. You're even willing to give up a 30 percent stake in your LLC to accomplish this. As an enticement for an investor to give you an infusion of capital, you offer to structure the deal so that she receives 100 percent of all company profits until she is paid back. After that point the profits will be distributed according to ownership percentage, with the investor receiving 30 percent and you receiving the remaining 70 percent. This is just one of thousands of ways you can use this flexibility to your advantage. Don't underestimate how powerful this concept is!

Getting a nice "thank you" for cosigning on business loans

Another aspect of partnership taxation that sets it apart from other forms of pass-through taxation is that you can essentially deduct the amount of any form of company debt that you're personally guaranteeing at any one time. To understand how personally guaranteeing your LLC's debt can equal money in your pocket, you need to know some background information on *tax bases.*

All forms of property have a fluctuating value called a *basis.* It's used for tax purposes and creates a point at which you can formulate capital gains or losses on that asset. For instance, if you sell an asset with a tax basis of $20,000 for $100,000, then you have $80,000 (the difference) in capital gains, which you're required to pay taxes on.

LLCs electing partnership taxation have two forms of tax bases:

- **Inside basis:** The LLC's basis in regards to its own assets

- **Outside basis:** An individual member's basis in his membership interests, which usually consists of the amount of money and property he's contributed to the LLC (called his *capital account*) and his share of the LLC's liabilities that he's personally responsible for. You often hear these liabilities referred to as *recourse debt,* because guess who gets to be the recourse should the business fail. You got it — you!

Only partnership taxation allows you to calculate recourse debt into your tax basis. Think of your tax basis as one big, fat tax deduction you can apply to any profit allocations your LLC throws at you. And as all deductions go, bigger is definitely better.

For instance, say you contributed $100,000 into your LLC in exchange for 50 percent of the membership interests. This sets your tax basis at $100,000. Business takes off in the first year and you get allocated (and distributed) $200,000 in profit! Woo hoo! But wait — even though you only have to pay taxes on the amount of profit you've been allocated that goes over your tax basis, this is still $100,000. Apply personal income tax and self-employment taxes and you're pushing $40,000 that you need to hand over to the IRS. Yikes.

On the other hand, your business partner, Dan, did something a little different. Like you, he contributed $100,000 for 50 percent of the company and was issued the same amount of profit at the end of the first year, but he also cosigned and personally guaranteed a $250,000 business loan for the LLC. Because this guarantee is considered recourse debt, that amount can be added to his tax basis, pushing it up to $350,000! Dan was allocated (and distributed) $200,000 just like you, but because he did the LLC a favor by cosigning on a company loan, he gets a big fat deduction that you don't get. The bottom line? Dan pays zero in taxes this year, and even gets to carry over the remaining $150,000 to apply to next year's profits.

After your company pays down the loan, Dan has to make up for his earlier tax savings. The tax basis is reduced in direct proportion to the reduction of the recourse debt. And when the tax basis hits zero, the burden doesn't stop there; any further reduction in the tax basis is deemed a *cash distribution.* So what does this mean for Dan? If the following year you two decide to pay down the $300,000 business loan to $150,000 instead of taking profits for yourselves, Dan's recourse debt has a $200,000 reduction.

Dan only had $150,000 left in his tax basis, carried over from the preceding year. When the $200,000 reduction in debt is applied to his tax basis, it leaves him with a zero tax basis and a $50,000 overage that the IRS considers to be cash in his pocket. Hopefully he saved a bit of his good fortune from the previous year, because he now has to pay taxes on that $50,000 and he's not even getting any hard cash to do it with.

This situation can be pretty stressful if unplanned for, but don't let that dissuade you. If you make sure you don't offload the debt before you're ready for the tax consequences, recourse debt can be a pretty powerful way to save some dough. After all, until your recourse debt is paid, the money you would've spent in taxes right out of the gate gets to grow tax free, instead. It's like a free loan from the IRS. You don't see those every day!

Deducting LLC losses from your other income

If you have sources of income other than your LLC, you may be able to deduct your LLC's losses from that other income to pay less in taxes. The IRS recognizes three types of income:

- ✔ **Portfolio income:** Such as dividends from stocks held.
- ✔ **Active income:** Wages and 1099 compensation.
- ✔ **Passive income:** Income from a business or rental property in which you are not an *active participant* — in other words, you don't make the day-to-day operational decisions for the business, and you don't work very many hours in the business.

Assuming your LLC has elected partnership taxation, you can use your share of the business's losses to offset any additional passive income that you may have received from other sources.

If you aren't an active participant in your LLC, you can't deduct your LLC's regular business losses from your personal portfolio or active income, such as the income from your day job. In other words, under the passive income rule, if you're not active in the business and your LLC passes on $50,000 in losses to you, you *cannot* use it to offset the $50,000 you made when you made a good trade on Wall Street (portfolio income). So you can sound like a smarty-pants when talking to your accountant, this is called a *passive loss limitation.*

All forms of pass-through taxation — not just partnership taxation — are subject to the passive loss limitation. However, as a member of an LLC that's elected partnership taxation, you get a wicked bonus those other guys with S corporations and sole proprietorships don't get. Say you've shunned the slacker lifestyle and are continuously engaged in the day-to-day operations of the LLC, making you an *active participant* in the eyes of the IRS. Never underestimate the value (literally!) of hard work, because you now get to deduct your portion of the LLC's losses from *all* other income, including wages and stock dividends, without limitation. Starting a small business and not yet ready to quit your day job? This incredible tax deduction is reason alone to form an LLC and elect partnership taxation.

If your LLC holds rental property, to be considered an active participant you have to be so actively engaged in the managing of the property that you qualify as an active real-estate professional. Otherwise, your involvement in the LLC holding is deemed not active (you're *passive*), and if the LLC distributes losses to you, they are subject to the passive loss limitation rules. Personally, I don't think you'll ever have better incentive to learn how to fix toilets. . . .

To help clarify the ins and outs of what partnership taxation allows you to do, check out Table 8-1.

Table 8-1	Offsets Allowed by Partnership Taxation		
	Can Offset Portfolio Income with LLC Losses	*Can Offset Active Income with LLC Losses*	*Can Offset Passive Income with LLC Losses*
Active in LLC	Yes	Yes	Yes
Passive in LLC	No	No	Yes

Avoiding self-employment taxes

If you elect partnership taxation, you're assessed a 15.3 percent self-employment tax in addition to the personal income taxes you are required to pay on the profit that's allocated to you. In addition, even if you're an active member of your LLC, you are not allowed to hire yourself and use payroll taxes as a way to get around the hefty self-employment tax bill each year. This is one of the only drawbacks of LLCs when compared to S corporations, which only assess self-employment taxes on the amount of salary that's above the norm for your industry.

A caveat, however, lands this rule in the LLCs favor. Although you may not be able to officially hire yourself (and thereby avoid self-employment tax), you can slack off a bit, to the point where you're no longer considered an *active participant,* but instead a *passive participant.* In the case of an LLC electing partnership taxation, only active participants are required to pay self-employment tax, whereas inactive participants aren't. The income itself is considered *passive,* which, as far as income goes, is about as favorable as the IRS gets.

Disregarded entity taxation

If you're the only member in your limited liability company, you're what is referred to as a single-member LLC. Even if your state permits you to form and operate a single-member LLC (some states don't), that business form still doesn't fly with the IRS. To them, you're deemed a *disregarded* entity — no better off than a sole proprietorship — and this is one case where being disregarded by the IRS probably isn't a good thing, because you don't get the option of electing partnership taxation.

Single-member LLCs cannot elect partnership taxation, and contrarily, if your LLC has more than one member, you can't elect to be taxed as a disregarded entity (although with the exception of a real estate transaction, which I discuss later, I'm not really sure why you'd ever want to). Like partnership taxation, disregarded entity tax status is a form of pass-through taxation, and in this case the sole member pays personal income taxes and self-employment taxes on the company's profits and/or losses on his personal tax return. However, unlike partnership taxation, a disregarded entity is pretty limited in its deductions and flexibility.

Just because you're a single-member LLC doesn't mean you don't have choices. You can still make a tax election — you just can't elect partnership taxation. If you want to be subject to corporate taxation instead of disregarded entity taxation, simply file IRS Form 8832, Entity Classification Election, within 75 days of your formation date. From there, you can either pay tax as a corporation or take things a step further and elect S corporation taxation. I discuss these two types of taxation later in this chapter.

Even if you remain a disregarded entity in the eyes of the IRS, with the same tax regulations as an individual, your LLC can still have the limited liability protections that the state offers. If your LLC owns real estate, this arrangement can be very beneficial. Because the property is owned by a disregarded entity, you still can engage the property in a like-kind, tax-free 1031 exchange (I discuss tax-free exchanges in further detail in Chapter 17). If this is something you're doing, speak with a tax-free exchange professional.

If you're currently operating as a sole proprietorship, general partnership, or limited partnership, you're already familiar with a pass-through form of taxation. It's pretty basic — all the business's profits and losses flow through to you (the owner) and get reported on your personal tax return. You pay personal income tax and, in most cases, self-employment tax on whatever profit passes through to you.

Corporation taxation

No matter whether you're a single-member LLC or you have multiple members, you can always elect to be taxed like a corporation. Corporate taxation is completely different than partnership taxation. First and foremost, a corporation (or an LLC electing corporation tax status) is considered by the IRS to be an entity completely separate from its owners and is treated as if it were an individual. Instead of passing through profits and losses to the members, it files its own tax returns. All that a member must report on his personal tax return is the actual cash the company decides to distribute to him, which is referred to as *dividends*. The member cannot report losses and therefore can't deduct them against other personal income. You don't have to worry about allocations, tax bases, phantom income, and deemed cash distributions, because they aren't relevant when it comes to corporations.

Although corporations are taxed as completely separate entities and are treated as individuals in the eyes of the IRS, they do receive a few benefits you and I don't get. Individuals are required to pay federal income tax on all income. Granted, a good chunk can be deducted, but those deductions usually aren't so "adequate" at the end of the year, because they rarely add up to the amount of money you're forced to fork over. Corporations, on the other hand, only pay federal tax on the profits that remain in the company at the end of the year. This may not seem like a very significant point, but as someone who's operated both entity types over the years, I can tell you I always end up paying less tax with the corporation tax structure.

When it comes to the corporation tax structure, many people worry about something called *double taxation*. It's understandable — who *wouldn't* balk at a term that implies paying double the amount of tax? Double taxation occurs when the owners of the corporation take the profit out of the company and the profits are taxed on the individual owner level. This means that the same profits are taxed once at the corporate level, and then taxed again at your (the member's) level when they're paid out. As horrific as this sounds in theory, it's usually not so bad in practice. Check out the following section to find out why.

Knowing when to choose corporation taxation

To explain why corporation taxation may result in less tax than any of the forms of pass-through taxation (such as sole proprietorship, partnership, and S corporation taxation), I'll use an example from my own life. As an entrepreneur, I often make use of loans from my established businesses to help cover the cost of establishing new businesses (rather than paying double taxation by taking the money as personal income before investing it into the new business). All my companies are owned by me, so approval for these loans doesn't present much of a problem.

After the company is established, I may pay myself a salary; however, I rarely issue dividends. Instead of taking a lot of money from the business, I reinvest it and use it to help propel growth, which is the only way a business can achieve exponential growth. If you reinvest those profits into further building your company — a tax-free endeavor — instead of just buying yourself a fancy car, you're compounding your resources, and the results you can achieve are much greater.

By following this plan you manage to grow your company while maintaining a nominal — almost *nonexistent* — tax burden. And when the company reaches its peak, you can sell it. I keep my stock for over two years, so any income from the sale of my ownership of the company is considered long-term capital gains, which are only subjected to a 15 percent long-term capital gains tax. The government is happy because creating new companies creates new jobs and helps stimulate the economy, and you're happy because now you can get the fancy car you've been wanting!

With an LLC, you don't have to make this tax election right away. If you're going to be putting a lot of money into the company and want to be able to deduct the losses of your initial, formative years, you can maintain default partnership taxation for a few years, and then make the tax election to switch to corporation tax status. However, this change may have other tax implications that aren't obvious at first glance, so run any strategies like this by a qualified accountant before committing.

Until you are *profiting* more than $75,000 per year, you may want to elect corporate tax status. Generally, until you start profiting more, the corporate tax rates are lower than the individual tax rates of the members who will be paying taxes on the LLC's income.

Seeing how corporation taxation can be the death of you

In a few instances, you should *never* elect corporation taxation for your LLC; namely if your LLC holds real estate. Using an LLC to hold real estate is a good move, but you're going to find yourself in a world of hurt at tax time if you elect corporate taxation.

Corporations were born for business. They are the perfect vehicle for building and growing a business to mammoth proportions. Hundreds of years ago, when corporations came about, everyone held his own assets in his own name. In today's litigious America, the idea of putting your personal assets in another name to protect them is a generally accepted practice. But which entity is best suited for holding passive investments, such as real estate? Not corporations, and not an LLC with corporate taxation. An LLC with partnership taxation really does the trick, but avoid corporate taxation at all costs.

If you hold a piece of investment property in a corporation or an LLC electing corporation taxation, you're subject to double taxation on all the income that property receives, such as the rent it collects. Also, you're going to face a problem when you want to offload the property, because removing the property from the entity is a taxable event. Switching back to partnership tax status before selling the property won't do you much good, either. You'll still be forced to calculate the appreciation that occurred during the corporation tax election and pay a BIG tax on that amount. Literally! *BIG* is an acronym for *built-in gain,* and it's well suited to the tax term, considering the rate is currently hovering around 35 percent! When you make the corporation tax election, you're stuck with it for five years, so this can be a pretty hefty chunk of change.

In addition, myriad other tax problems can pop up if you subject your rental property to corporation taxation. You can spend time and money getting a second opinion from a CPA, but I think you'll find it's a universally accepted rule: *Never* elect corporation tax status for an LLC that's being used to hold passive investments, such as real estate.

S corporation taxation

S corporation taxation is the corporation's answer to a pass-through tax status. Just like a corporation can elect S corporation tax status, so can a limited liability company that has elected corporation taxation. You may think this is a waste of time considering LLCs already have a pass-through tax status by default, but S corporation taxation differs from partnership taxation on some pretty big issues; namely in what taxes you pay when you take money out of the company.

If you're a single-member LLC and therefore not allowed to choose partnership taxation, you're allowed to elect corporation taxation and then elect to be taxed as an S corporation. This method provides favorable pass-through taxation without the need to take on a partner. Just be aware that S corporation taxation differs substantially from partnership taxation and, should you take on a partner sometime in the future, you may be restricted in your ability to change back.

Reducing your taxes

S corporations get a pretty big advantage when it comes to taxation, though at first glance the situation looks comparable to partnership taxation status. If you're a member of an LLC electing partnership taxation, you are required to pay personal income tax on all company profits that are allocated to you. In addition to personal income tax, you're also required to pay a 15.3 percent self-employment tax, which is simply both the employer's and employee's shares of Social Security and Medicare taxes. But with an S corporation, you're allowed to pay yourself a salary, which is a deductible expense for the company, and any amount over that is *not* subject to self-employment tax. You simply pay personal income tax on those profits and nothing more once they are distributed to you. This differs substantially from LLCs, because *all* profits you derive from the company are subject to the 15.3 percent self-employment tax.

In other words, if you are taxed as an S corporation, the amount of Medicare and Social Security that you pay is limited to the amount you take as a salary. As long as your salary is commensurate with others in your position and your industry, then any profits taken above that amount are *not* subject to extra taxes.

In a nutshell, you save 15.3 percent in taxes on all profits above an appropriate salary. So if you have a business from which you intend to remove a substantial amount of profits — more than the commensurate salary you are taking — then you'll probably see some pretty hefty tax savings by electing S corporation taxation.

Dealing with the restrictions

Unfortunately, even if S corporation status is the best choice for you, you may not be able to elect it. When the IRS created the S corporation election, they wanted to make sure that it was employed by genuinely small businesses and not exploited by large enterprises strictly as a tax-saving strategy. Therefore, you must meet quite a few restrictions in order to take advantage of S corporation taxation:

- ✔ Your corporation must not have more than 100 shareholders.

- ✔ Shareholders can only consist of natural persons, individual trusts (for estate-planning purposes), and tax-exempt nonprofit organizations. This specifically excludes any other entity or business structure, such as limited liability companies or corporations.

- ✔ Shareholders must be citizens or alien residents of the United States.

- ✔ The corporation is only allowed to issue one class of stock. You'll have to save the preferred shares for your IPO.

- ✔ Banks and insurance companies are barred from being shareholders.

- ✔ All shareholders must unanimously consent to the S corporation tax designation. In other words, a majority vote just won't do the trick.

In addition to these ownership restrictions, you may want to take into consideration a few other downsides before committing:

- ✔ **There is no step-up in basis on assets after you die.** When your heirs inherit your assets in an S corporation, they'll have to pay capital gains tax on the appreciation from the date you first purchased the asset, instead of just from the date that you passed it on to your heirs. I discuss this snag in more detail in Chapter 18.

- ✔ **You can't add debt to your tax basis.** Earlier in this chapter, I discuss how LLCs allow you to deduct from your distributions the amount of debt the company has that you can be held personally responsible for. With S corporation tax status, you receive no tax benefits for being personally responsible for the company's debt.

This rule makes S corporations a bad choice for holding real estate. Even though S corporation status lets you get around the double-taxation nightmare that comes with a regular corporation, you're still limiting yourself by not being able to personally deduct the mortgage.

Check to see how your state taxes LLCs that elect S corporation taxation. Most states conform with the IRS on this, but about a half dozen states tax S corporations as corporations. Don't underestimate state taxes! If you're holding real estate or are in another form of business in which double taxation can kill you, you may be in trouble. Make sure to speak with your local accountant or do some research on state law before making this election.

Notifying the IRS of Your Election

Making a tax election for your LLC is as simple as filling out a single form: IRS Form 8832, one of the simplest tax forms you'll ever complete. They don't call them *check-the-box regulations* for nothing — all you have to do is check a box! In this section, I walk you through the process of making your tax election, starting with the necessary background work.

Applying for your Tax ID Number

All businesses must obtain an *employer identification number* (*EIN* for short, but also called a *tax identification number* or *tax ID*) from the Internal Revenue Service. The IRS uses this number to identify your LLC when it pays its taxes. Over the years, the EIN has become an important number for the government, financial institutions, and other businesses to identify different entities. After all, an LLC in Georgia can have the same name as your LLC in California — how would Uncle Sam be able to tell them apart? Think of it as a Social Security number for your enterprise.

Obtaining credit, paying taxes, and even opening a bank account are virtually impossible without a tax identification number, so don't delay! Some attorneys, accountants, and formation companies may charge you an arm and a leg to obtain this number for you, but you're smarter than that. With a few little tips, you can have your tax ID within an hour.

You can obtain a tax ID immediately online at www.irs.gov. On line 8a, check yes and subsequently complete lines 8b and 8c. Here's the tricky part: On line 9a, check the box that best describes the tax classification you want to elect for your LLC:

- ✔ If you're a single-member LLC electing the default disregarded entity tax status, check the box next to Sole proprietorship.

- ✔ If you're a multimember LLC electing partnership tax status, you'll want to check the box next to Partnership.

- ✔ If you're electing corporation tax status for a single- or multimember LLC, check the box next to Corporation, and in the following field, enter the form number "1120."

- ✔ If you're a single- or multimember LLC electing S corporation tax status, check the box next to Corporation, and in the following field, enter the form number "1120S."

By far the easiest and fastest way to file your Form SS-4 is online, and you receive your new tax identification number instantaneously. You can also call the IRS at 1-800-829-4933 (215-516-6999 if outside the U.S.) and complete the application over the phone. I recommend that you fill out the paper version first so you have all your answers prepared. You can also fax the application to 859-669-5760. If you fax it, you'll probably receive approval with your tax ID by fax within one to two business days.

When you receive your tax identification number, this number stays with your company no matter whether you change owners, do a statutory conversion to another entity type (see Chapter 7), redomicile your LLC to another state (see Chapter 5 and Chapter 14), or change your tax status.

Making the tax election: Filing Form 8832

The best time to file Form 8832: Entity Classification Election is when you form your LLC; otherwise, you're automatically assigned your default tax status (disregarded entity taxation if you're a single-member LLC or partnership taxation if your LLC has more than one member). After you file Form 8832, you don't need to continue to file it each year; the taxation election automatically lasts until you file another Form 8832, electing a different form of taxation.

Note that this entity classification is for income tax purposes only and has no bearing on how you're treated by the state, especially for liability purposes. For instance, if your LLC elects corporation taxation, you still have the protection of the dual-layer liability protection that's unique to LLCs.

Completing the form

Form 8832 itself is pretty straightforward. I provide a current one with instructions at www.myllc.com/dummies. The first section (lines 1 to 3) asks you a series of questions to determine your eligibility.

When you choose a tax classification, you're stuck with it for 60 months (five years). The IRS does this to keep you honest. They figure that in order for a business process to work, it needs a few years to work the kinks out. They don't want shady tax avoiders to exploit the classifications for their personal benefit.

This rule has an exception: If you elect a taxation classification within the first 12 months of formation and on Form 8832 specify the "effective date" as your LLC's date of formation, then your LLC is allowed to switch to another form of taxation at any time. From that point forward, however, any additional switch will be subject to the 60-month rule.

Under line 6 of Form 8832, you're required to select your type of entity. If your LLC is formed within the continental United States (and I'm assuming it is), only the first three options apply to you. You notice that none of these options allow for S corporation taxation, and that's because you need another form, 2553, to make that election. Select Corporation taxation on Form 8832; then attach a completed Form 2553 and file them both together.

In order to make a tax election for your limited liability company, all members must agree and sign. If for some reason you and your partners don't wish to be listed on this form, you can stipulate otherwise in the articles of organization by putting this decision-making power in the hands of the manager(s).

Your LLC's tax election should also be indicated in your LLC's operating agreement. Your operating agreement is an internal document and isn't publicly accessible, so by recognizing the tax classification in the operating agreement, you show that all members agree on it. You should also document any tax classification changes by special resolution of the members of the LLC (I show you how to draft resolutions in Chapter 11).

Most states, but not all, comply with the federal tax election you make on Form 8832. Before making any assumptions, consult with a qualified accountant in your state.

Using a tax termination to change your status

If you're stuck with an election of partnership taxation and don't want to wait 60 months before you can change your election, you may have an easy way out. If you are an LLC subject to partnership taxation and more than 50 percent of your membership is transferred within a 12-month period, the IRS considers your partnership to be dissolved and a new one formed. It's not as scary as it sounds, trust me. A tax termination has no bearing on your actual LLC that you registered with the state (it's still alive and kicking, just as before!), doesn't affect your tax identification number, and has little or no effect on your taxes, except it may cause you and your partners to realize a gain or loss that you may have to pay taxes on. (I discuss tax terminations in more detail in Chapter 15.)

One consequence of a tax termination that can actually work in your favor is that it causes all tax elections to be disregarded, so your LLC is reset to its default tax status (disregarded entity for single-member LLCs; partnership taxation for multimember LLCs). After this tax election has been disregarded and your tax status reset, you can file another tax election at your whim.

If you think you may need to ditch your election by way of a tax termination, then you'll have to structure your LLC accordingly. Unless, of course, you want to keep transferring 50 percent of your company's membership interest to random friends. (Yeah . . . didn't think so.) An easy way around this little conundrum is to form a corporation to hold 50 percent of the membership of your LLC. When you want to instigate a tax termination, you can simply form another corporation and transfer the membership from the first corporation to the second one. Voilà! (But remember, a corporation cannot be a member of an S corporation.)

Chapter 9

The Power Source: Issuing and Transferring Membership

In This Chapter

▶ Understanding LLC membership

▶ Determining the rules of membership in your LLC

▶ Issuing, transferring, and canceling membership shares

*I*n the eyes of the law, your LLC is a separate entity — almost like a separate person. But because it's not alive and can't think or act on its own, someone must do so on its behalf. In this case, the owners — that is to say, *you* — will make sure the business stays alive.

The LLC's members are the company's major decision makers. For the most part, the business's success falls on their shoulders. Even if they don't manage the day-to-day affairs, they still control *who does*. As far as I'm concerned, until membership in your LLC has been issued — in other words, until the LLC is actually *owned* by someone — the business doesn't really exist.

In this chapter, I outline all you need to know about membership and ownership of your LLC, showing you how to take ownership of your LLC by issuing membership interests to yourself and your partners. Then I go into detail on how to sell and transfer membership shares and deal with sticky situations such as the death or divorce of a member.

Interpreting the Terminology: Members, Interests, and Certificates

The legal term for the owners of an LLC is *members*. Some states have a specific definition for what a member is, while other states have no definition at all. Don't let this throw you off.

Think of the ownership of the LLC as a big pie made up of *membership units* (otherwise referred to as *membership interests*). Each owner gets a piece of the pie, and each piece is made of a certain number of membership units. When pieces are assigned to members, they represent *membership interests* or *ownership percentage* (different states tend to use slightly different terminology, but they all mean the same thing). When you issue membership interests, the entire pie must be consumed, so to speak.

For instance, if the company has a total of 100 membership units and you have 35 membership units, then you own 35 percent of the company. In other words, you have a 35 percent *membership interest* in the LLC. An easy way to calculate your membership interest is to divide your membership units by total number of membership units the company has issued.

The piece of paper that proves your ownership of the LLC is called your *membership certificate*. A membership certificate includes the name of the member, the date that the certificate was issued, the amount of membership interests, and the signature of one or two members and/or managers.

The reality of membership shares

Childhood friends Ed, Sal, and Greg have dreamed forever of opening up their own motorcycle shop. Although they all work odd jobs, they soon realize that together they could finally make this mere vision a reality. Ed owns an excess of equipment for building custom bikes, including the paint and specialty tools. Sal has full access to, but doesn't own, an old vacant warehouse, and Greg has saved $50,000 in his successful entrepreneurship. Together, they possess all the pieces to build their own custom bike shop, ESG Motorbikes.

They form an LLC and divvy out their membership shares. Although Greg is fronting the capital to get the business afloat (providing the largest set of funds), Sal and Ed aren't letting Greg overlook the value of their contributions, so after some persuasion, Greg finally relents and agrees to spread the shares out evenly at 33.3 percent. The LLC protects the members from losses that can't exceed what they invest into the company, but it seems Greg has much more at risk and may deserve a bigger piece of the pie.

A couple years down the road, when the going isn't great, a private investor offers to purchase ESG Motorbikes for $100,000. Greg, having invested the most money, isn't too happy about this, but Sal and Ed out-vote him and decide to sell. Sal and Ed make a quick profit, but unfortunately for him, Greg's membership certificate states that he owns one-third of the company. Because no special provision has been made for him in the operating agreement stating otherwise, he is only entitled to one-third of the proceeds from the sale of the business, and because he never took any profit from the company, this means he only gets a $33,300 return on his $50,000 while his friends make out fat and happy. Greg's risk in the venture exceeded his reward, while his buddies gained probably more than they should have.

It's a strange thought — you can invest thousands of dollars into an enterprise, and all you get is a simple piece of paper! But that piece of paper gives you the most important thing in business — control. Without that certificate, you have no say in how the LLC is run, how the money is spent, or how the company is structured. The business could be terminated tomorrow, and you would get nothing. That little certificate means everything in the world of business, so make sure you have one!

Believe it or not, in most states, membership certificates aren't actually required by law to be distributed to the members — the ownership breakdown can just be stated in the operating agreement. However, just because it isn't required doesn't mean you shouldn't do it anyway. I recommend that all members get a membership certificate as proof of their ownership.

Before putting anything in writing, do a quick review of your state's laws regarding LLC ownership to figure out what terminology the state uses. You can peruse various state laws applicable to LLCs at www.docrun.com/wiki/.

Setting Up and Managing Your Membership

After you file your articles of organization (discussed in Chapter 6), you then have to create your operating agreement (which I show you how to do in the next chapter). It is here, in the operating agreement, that you take ownership of the LLC by issuing membership shares to yourself and your partners. The percentage of the LLC that a member owns should be relatively proportional to the amount that he initially invests, be it money, equipment, or services. All this is reflected in the operating agreement, possibly a buy-sell agreement (if you want to create special terms for specific members), and the membership certificates that each member receives.

In this section, I explain most of the basic rules of membership shares. After you've got that down and you know what your limitations are, I show you how to issue membership shares for the first time.

Instituting some membership rules

LLCs are really flexible entities where members are concerned. The laws give you a lot of freedom in how you can structure your LLC. Some examples of an LLC's flexibility are:

- ✔ **Most states allow members to make contributions in the form of services in exchange for membership interests.** *Services* are defined as time that the member puts into the organization. This allowance means that someone who has a talent you need can invest his time and skill instead of money. Just make sure that if you allow services as a type of contribution, you specifically state so in the operating agreement.

✔ **Distributions can be varied from member to member.** In other words, assuming you have a valid non-tax-evading reason for it, you can change the company's allocation and distribution of profits and losses to be different from the percentage of ownership. For example, if you and your partners choose, and you meet IRS criteria, you can own 10 percent of the company and get 50 percent of the profits and 0 percent of the losses.

✔ **The number of members is unlimited.** Unlike an S corporation, you can have hundreds of thousands of members (owners) if you want! This is a huge plus if you are looking to raise capital for your business. An added benefit: All members get two levels of ironclad liability protection (see Chapter 16).

Keep in mind, especially if you're a really small business, that you may want to set your own limit for the number of members you bring on. Even if your LLC is managed by separate managers who aren't involved in the business's day-to-day operations, you'll still need the members to vote on important issues, such as selecting the managers and taking on sizeable debt. If your members are not easily accessible or you have too many, making a quorum or getting a majority of the members to vote can be an issue. Not to mention the fact that the more people who are involved in the decision-making process, the harder it is to reach a consensus.

✔ **The members can be non-U.S. citizens and even be other entities such as corporations, trusts, limited partnerships, and LLCs.** Making another entity a member in your LLC is a huge benefit if you're trying to set up an asset protection plan where the LLC needs to be a subsidiary of another company. Also, if you are the only member in the LLC and you don't want to share any control, you can form another entity to be your second member. This way you'll keep all the power but avoid having to deal with the hassles of being a single-member LLC.

✔ **You can have different types (*classes*) of membership.** For instance, you can issue a Class A membership, where the members can participate in the management of the LLC, and a Class B membership, where the members are only silent partners with no participation in the day-to-day operations. In most states, you can structure these classes however you want; just put the details in the operating agreement. (I go into more detail on this in the next section.)

✔ **You can decide how members will transfer their membership shares.** Members can be restricted to transferring only the economic interest (the distributions), or they can transfer their full membership (voting rights, economic interests, and all) but only on a vote of the majority of the other members. This ensures that you won't end up with some stranger as a business partner, telling you how to run your business.

As you can see from this list, the amazing flexibility of LLCs allows owners to run many different types of businesses, from raising financing for a real estate deal to producing a film to running a small business. Also, keep in mind that with an LLC, the members don't have to manage the company. Instead, separate managers can be selected. These managers can be owners or non-owners. LLCs are gaining popularity as an entity to raise capital with because you can fully manage the entity yourself while your investors remain silent in the business's day-to-day activities.

If a person in the organization isn't given membership, then he isn't an owner. If he manages the LLC, he has a say in the day-to-day operations, but his position isn't necessarily permanent. The members decide who manages the LLC, and the manager's involvement depends solely on the members' approval. In other words, a manager who isn't a member is little more than a glorified employee.

Establishing membership classes

The LLC is the most flexible entity around, allowing you to tailor it completely to your needs, and it definitely lives up to its reputation when it comes to the ownership: You can choose to set up different classes of membership in your LLC. *Membership classes* designate certain rights and rules for different groups of members. Often, these different classes are marked with a letter (Class A membership, Class B membership, and so on). You create these various classes by specifying the details of each class in your company's operating agreement. I show you how to do this in Chapter 10.

Now, when you have these different classes at your disposal, what can you do with 'em? Anything! The state laws are pretty lax on the whole thing — as long as the attributes of the classes are fair and are clearly listed in the company's operating agreement, you can go to town! With membership classes, you can give some of your partners more voting rights than others. Or the rules regarding the transfer of the membership shares can be different among members. You decide. Hey, no one said life is fair, and your LLC needn't be, either.

To establish membership classes, you create one set of rules and procedures for the Class A membership and another set for the Class B membership. For instance, you can create different classes of membership for the operating partners, the investors, and the employees. Their control in the company can be limited according to their respective positions. You can also use membership classes as an incentive for investors to contribute more money to the business. After all, the investors who contribute the most money should have more influence in the company than those who barely invest at all.

After you decide what you want your different membership classes to be and include the details in your operating agreement (which I show you how to do in the next chapter), you also include the information on your membership certificates. You usually do this by putting the class (such as *Class A, Class B,* and so on) on the front of the certificate. Then you put a *legend* — a paragraph stating the class restrictions — on the back of the certificate.

When creating classes, if you want to allow some but not all of your members to manage, then you need to make sure your LLC is designated as manager-managed. In most states, if you designate your LLC as member-managed, then all members are equal managers in the business, regardless of the classes set forth in your operating agreement. For more information on manager-managed versus member-managed LLCs, see Chapter 6.

Creating a buy-sell agreement

A *buy-sell agreement* outlines the rules that govern how members voluntarily or involuntarily transfer their membership. It also explains what the members should do when a member retires, goes bankrupt, becomes incapacitated, or passes away. Normally, if your buy-sell agreement covers all members in the company, then you just include these provisions in your operating agreement. But with LLCs, you don't have to hold everyone to the same standard. If you want, you can have individual buy-sell agreements for each of your members, each containing different rules and restrictions.

A buy-sell agreement prevents situations like the following two:

- Your best friend and long-term business partner dies in a skiing accident. You are devastated. When you think it couldn't get worse, his nephew, his only heir, decides that he has the right to step in and take control of the business. Legally, you and your partner had no agreement in place that provided for a situation such as this one. When you show up at court to provide your defense, you are empty-handed. Meanwhile, the little scamp is acting like a tyrant and undoing all your years of hard work.

- You and your brother start a pet shop and put it in a member-managed LLC. When the two of you get into a quarrel, he finds the only person in the world who doesn't like puppies and sells her his membership shares. The next day, Cruella DeVille, your new partner, shows up for work and starts making changes. She fires your best employees and spends the company money like there's no tomorrow.

A buy-sell agreement must cover

- How much money a member's membership shares are worth
- Who controls the member's shares if she leaves the LLC for any reason
- The reasons why someone may be admitted as a member and issued membership shares

✔ What happens to a member's shares when the member departs or withdraws. For example:

- The LLC or the other members can purchase the shares
- The shares can be sold to the general public

✔ The process of transferring membership shares

✔ What happens if a member declares bankruptcy or divorces

In situations where all members have to follow the same rules and regulations, the buy-sell agreement is usually a component of the operating agreement. However, you don't have to put your buy-sell agreement in your operating agreement. If different members are subject to different rules and regulations (for instance, a certain set of members can't transfer their shares, but the rest can), then you need a separate buy-sell agreement for those members. In this case, you have individual buy-sell agreements instead of a company-wide one that resides in your operating agreement.

When you issue your membership shares, you must create a buy-sell agreement at the same time. Otherwise, a buy-sell agreement that you create after issuing membership shares may not be retroactive and cover all members and any future transferees. If you've already issued your membership shares and now want to create a buy-sell agreement, make sure that

✔ All your members vote on it

✔ The agreement specifically states that it covers all *current* LLC members

Like operating agreements, buy-sell agreements can vary substantially, and what is contained in them is very particular to your state's individual laws on what's allowed and what's not. With that in mind, patching together an agreement from various fill-in-the-blank forms you find on the Internet (I know you've done it!) can be a dangerous proposition in this case. Rather, you should bite the bullet and hire a qualified attorney. To help you save some cash, I created a pre-attorney drafting service that can create a comprehensive operating agreement at a fraction of the price. Go to www.docrun.com for more information.

Determining profit and loss distributions

At the end of every year, whatever income (profit) the company generated during its operation passes on (or is distributed) to the owners' personal tax returns, almost as if it were their personal income. The owners report these profit distributions on a Schedule K that they attach to the Form 1040 that they file every year. The same goes with the company's expenses and losses — they are also passed on to the LLC's owners.

Normally, the amount of profits and losses that are passed on is determined by the amount of the company they own. For instance, if you own 20 percent of the company, then you will be allocated 20 percent of the company's profits and 20 percent of the company's losses. When you don't distribute the profits and losses according to the percentage of the company that a person owns, it's called a *special allocation* of the profits and losses. This may all seem complicated, but don't fret — I go over it in detail in Chapter 12.

But it's not just a free-for-all out there regarding company profits. To prevent fraud, the IRS doesn't let you decide how to allocate profits however you want. If it did, members with the most personal income would make sure they received all the LLC's losses to offset the income they made from other ventures. For instance, unless you have a good reason, one partner can't receive 100 percent of the losses, while another takes 100 percent of the profits. You have to be able to substantiate your decision. In other words — you can't play with the profit distributions for tax-evasion purposes — you must have a real reason behind it. (See the sidebar "When special allocations make sense" for an example of legitimate reasons.)

Want to be guaranteed that you can change your distributions of profits and losses at a moment's notice without getting nailed by the IRS? Well, there is a way. The IRS provides guidelines for determining whether special allocations are okay. You can put certain language in your operating agreement and do some simple things to protect yourself from any tax troubles. Here are a couple of ways to make sure you're covered:

- ✔ **The partners' *capital accounts* (how much *interest* each partner has in the partnership) should be tracked by you or your accountant according to the IRS regulations.** Don't worry — this isn't as difficult as it seems and is nothing out of the ordinary. For more information on this, speak with your tax professional or read the regulations regarding capital accounts under Section 704 of the Internal Revenue Code.

- ✔ **The operating agreement must specify that upon termination and liquidation of the LLC, the members will receive the profits according to their capital accounts.** If a member's capital account is in the negative (that is, she owes money to the company), then that money must be paid back when the company ceases operations or before the member sells her membership shares. Look at your equity as a loan that must be paid back if the investment isn't profitable.

As your company distributes profits and losses, accepts contributions, and the assets appreciate and depreciate through the year, you'll need to adjust each members' individual capital account. Because this is a complex process unless you're well educated in accounting, you should work with your company accountant so he can adjust each member's capital account. You'll also want to reissue the membership so it properly reflects each member's new percentage of the company.

When special allocations make sense

Eric decides to partner up with his best friends Martin and Adam. They have been thinking about setting up a film production company since they were kids and have decided that now is the time to jump in. Martin and Adam will be putting in the upstart capital ($30,000 each), and the three of them will be sharing equally in the work.

Eric, knowing that it wouldn't be fair for them to split the profits equally, works out a deal with Martin and Adam. Each partner will own one-third of the company, so they all have equal voting power and control over the company, but Martin and Adam will receive all company profits until they have been paid back their initial investment plus 20 percent. Martin and Adam agree and they decide to form an LLC — the only entity that allows them to distribute the profits and any deductions from company losses not according to the percentage of ownership each member has.

Setting up a single-member LLC

If you're planning on being the only member of your LLC, watch out! Your LLC will be designated as a *single-member LLC.* LLCs were designed to be *partnerships.* Therefore, the IRS only agreed to accept LLCs if they follow some simple partnership rules — the main one being that you have an actual *partner.* And no, it can't be your cat or your dearly deceased Aunt Peggy.

Several states' courts have ruled that single-member LLCs (SLLCs) don't offer the dual-layer of liability protection, called *charging order protection,* that regular LLCs offer, and, unless you are completely diligent in your recordkeeping and dot every *i* and cross every *t,* SLLCs can also lack the basic liability protection that an LLC offers. And this protection is one of the LLC's fundamental benefits. The IRS doesn't even consider an SLLC a partnership (after all, there aren't any partners!). SLLCs are taxed as sole proprietorships, and you pay the company taxes on a Schedule C, Profit or Loss From Business, attached to your personal tax return.

In IRS terms, an SLLC is a *disregarded entity.* And disregard it you should. Without the basic limited liability, why even go through the hassle of forming an LLC in the first place?

Some states don't even *allow* single-member LLCs. If you are unfortunate enough to be located in one of these fussy states, you can just file your LLC in another state, such as Nevada or Wyoming, then register to transact business in your home state (see Chapter 5 for more on choosing a state to file your LLC in).

If, as a single-member LLC, you claim a home-office deduction (IRS Form 8829, Expenses for Business Use of Your Home), your home *could* theoretically be considered a business asset and could be seized if you lose a lawsuit.

Although the law doesn't automatically offer it to single-member LLCs, you can still demand the basic liability protection that an LLC or corporation offers — that which protects your personal assets should the company get sued. This isn't easy, though, because you must be rigorous in making sure that everything is filed correctly, and you have to go above and beyond to treat your entity as though it were truly separate from yourself.

To keep the liability protection in your SLLC, do the following:

- ✔ **Be diligent about keeping your business assets and cash flow** *completely* **separate from your personal assets and cash flow.** You must have documentation to this effect.

- ✔ **Sign all your filings as owner, on behalf of your LLC.** Never sign any business documents without this designation.

- ✔ **Add your federal EIN number and your LLC's filing number (provided by the secretary of state) to your Schedule C.** Adding your LLC's file number makes your LLC look much more legitimate and can deter anyone looking for a lawsuit.

- ✔ **Act like a corporation.** Comply with all corporate formalities, such as meetings of the members and managers, keeping extensive minutes, and passing resolutions. Just because only one person is involved in your entity, don't think you can get out of these tasks. It may seem silly to have a meeting with yourself, but documenting all decision-making affecting the company is necessary.

- ✔ **Elect corporate tax treatment on IRS Form 8832, Entity Classification Election.** When electing corporate tax treatment, you are automatically saved from being considered a proprietorship, and none of the above rules need to be followed.

Do you still want to be the only owner of the LLC, but are afraid of the risk of operating as a single-member LLC? Don't worry, you have some other options.

- ✔ You can form another entity to act as a second member of the LLC.
- ✔ You can choose someone whom you trust to act as a secondary partner.

The person or corporation that you select as the second member doesn't have to own that much interest in the LLC — you only need to issue another party a small percentage of membership to avoid being considered a single-member LLC.

Partners in life don't always make the best partners in business. A husband and wife who are the only members of an LLC are considered one unit; therefore, the LLC is a single-member LLC. Not good! So far this hasn't been extended to same-sex partners; however, I'd bet that if it ever were to be questioned in a court of law, you and your partner would be subject to the same drawbacks that other married couples face. So play it safe and elect a close friend or other family member to be your partner in the LLC.

If the thought of having a friend involved in your business makes you cringe, or if you don't have anyone whom you can trust, you have the first option: form another entity to act as the second member. You can form a corporation and make it your partner in the LLC. This may seem like a lot of work, but you can use the corporation to protect your assets even further. If you are serious about flying solo and protecting your assets, this move may be the best one.

Adding and Withdrawing Members

When you're jumping headfirst into business and then working flawlessly with your partner, you may think that discussing the prospect of a change in ownership is silly. After all, you and your partner work incredibly well together, and everything is moving forward seamlessly — there's no way the ownership will ever change!

Listen, I know that you may think coming up with a contingency plan when things are running so smoothly is bad luck or too touchy to bring up, but when else are you going to do it? When the you-know-what hits the fan? Not a good plan! Not to mention that a change in ownership doesn't necessarily have to be the result of some argument or other sort of falling out. A change in ownership can occur for myriad other reasons, good and bad.

Transferring an LLC's membership units is somewhat more difficult than you may expect, for the following reasons:

- An LLC is considered a *partnership* by the IRS, and one of the primary things that sets a partnership apart from a corporation is that the ownership isn't freely transferable.

- Your state believes in the importance of protecting the partners in a business from showing up for work one day and finding out they have a new partner who they now have to find a way to work with.

Ultimately, the laws are designed to protect *you,* and these little guidelines make LLCs the phenomenally superior entities that they are. For instance, the fact that ownership isn't freely transferable really works for you when you lose a lawsuit and the plaintiff is about to seize your ownership of the LLC. Because the LLC's shares aren't easily transferred, the plaintiff can't seize the actual shares. He can only seize the profits (and losses!) that you receive from your interest in the company. You can use this little rule to your advantage to stay out of lawsuits. I go over this in detail in Chapter 2, but for now, keep in mind that these rules work *for* you more often than they work against you.

All the rules regarding adding and withdrawing members can be laid out in your operating agreement. You want to make sure that the required provisions are there, because if your operating agreement or buy-sell agreement doesn't address an issue, then state law decides. If you require a vote of the members before a membership share can be issued or transferred, then your operating agreement or buy-sell agreement should state what percentage of members must approve the transfer. Will you require a unanimous decision among members, or will a simple majority do? You and your partner(s) decide.

Doing the membership shuffle

No one should be stuck in an investment that isn't working out for them, just like no owners should be stuck with partners whom they don't like or agree with. You may need to remove (technically called *withdraw*) a person from your LLC team in the following situations:

- ✔ A member passes away
- ✔ A member retires
- ✔ A member becomes severely ill or incapacitated
- ✔ A member goes through a divorce
- ✔ A member goes bankrupt
- ✔ The other members are unhappy with one member
- ✔ A member needs cash and wants to sell his membership
- ✔ A member wants to gift his membership to someone close to him
- ✔ A member has his membership units seized
- ✔ The owners want to bring on an additional partner

Sometimes you may want to add members after your LLC is already established. Following are some reasons why:

- ✔ You want to raise additional capital to take your LLC to the next level. In exchange for someone's investment, you want to offer him a piece of the pie.
- ✔ You have a member-managed LLC, and the workflow is becoming too great. You want to bring on another owner who can contribute her experience and expertise to help your business grow.
- ✔ Your employees have worked hard for your company over the years. As a way of repaying them, you want to issue them a small percentage of ownership.

Make sure that all actions on behalf of the members of the company, especially those concerning adding and withdrawing members, are clearly documented in the company minutes. Recording these changes shows a history of the company procedures and will be invaluable if any actions are contested or if the company is taken to court.

Giving new members their share

When a new member joins your LLC, how do the profit distributions work? If you are distributing the profits according to the ownership percentages, you would pay her a percentage of the profits based on her ownership shares and how long she has been a member during the current fiscal year.

For example, if a new member, owning 10 percent of the LLC, is admitted to the LLC on July 1, does she get 10 percent of the profits at the end of the year? Of course not! Your accountant can assist you in your exact calculations, but in this case, if the total profits distributed are $100,000, then the new member will receive 50 percent (for the half of the year she was a member) of the 10 percent (her ownership share) for a grand total of $5,000. After that distribution has been made, the remaining $95,000 can be distributed according to the other members' percentages.

Make sure that you outline this provision on prorated distributions in your buy-sell agreement, especially if you allow members to come and go. Can you imagine the outcome if a member were to buy in on December 20, take a huge chunk of the distributions for that year, then sell out on January 2? Trust me, it's happened, and the only way to prevent that situation is to make sure your operating agreement or buy-sell agreement clearly states that distributions are calculated according to the number of days of the year that the member has been admitted to the entity.

If a member is contributing a piece of property or equipment in exchange for membership shares, her tax basis may change (especially if the item carries a mortgage or other debt). As you find out in Chapter 12, recourse loans are deductible to the members who personally guarantee them. This is called a *return of capital* in IRS terms and can be a great thing in the long run. The member should hire a qualified small-business accountant or CPA to keep track of her tax basis.

Speaking of taxes, whenever a new member contributes money, property, equipment, or any other type of asset, the IRS doesn't consider any gain or loss taking place by the member or the LLC itself. It is considered an *equal-value exchange* in IRS terms. This means it's a tax-free transaction; even though you report the transfer on your tax return, the IRS takes no money out of your pocket.

Moving on when a member wants to leave

When a member withdraws, two things can happen to the person's membership shares:

- ✔ The withdrawing member will want the LLC to buy her interest back from her.
- ✔ The withdrawing member will sell her interest to another member or a third party.

When the LLC buys back the membership interest

The first option you should attempt is for the LLC to purchase the membership interest itself. After this has been done and the member has relinquished her shares to the LLC, the other members can reconfigure their ownership percentages. For instance, if three members each owned 33 percent of the company and one member decides to sell her shares back to the LLC, then the remaining two members will each own 50 percent of the company.

Make sure you outline the purchase amount and specifics of the sale in your operating agreement or a buy-sell agreement. If you don't do this, in some states, the state will decide the sale amount for you, and the LLC may have to pay the member the value of his initial contribution or the book value of the membership shares he wants to get rid of. Even if this is the price you wish to buy back the shares at, documenting the transaction in as much detail as you can allows you to keep control over it.

In other states, the complete opposite may happen, and the withdrawing member may have to pay damages to the LLC to cover the losses that the LLC incurred by her withdrawal. As you can see, the laws vary widely, and the best way to control what happens in the event of a member withdrawal is to state what you want in your operating agreement or buy-sell agreement.

If the member wants to sell her shares, the most common way to handle this situation is to give the other members *right of first refusal.* This means that the other members have the option of purchasing the membership shares at their *current value* (the total value of the LLC divided by the percentage of membership shares being sold). If no members purchase the shares, then the withdrawing member is off the hook (woo hoo!) and then has the right to sell them to the general public.

When the LLC doesn't buy back the membership interest

If someone who is not a member buys the shares, the incoming member won't have full rights in the LLC; she'll only have *economic rights,* which means she gets the profit and loss distributions but has no right to vote or manage the LLC. However, the other members can vote to allow the incoming member the rights that were previously denied her. At that point, she becomes a full member.

When you just gotta say goodbye!

Say you gave membership to an employee, and six months later, you catch him stealing from the till. You and your partners are furious, and you decide that the only option is to fire him. Unfortunately, he still has the membership that was given to him. Considering that you and your members want to cut ties with the thief, you consult your buy-sell agreement.

Luckily, you see that you were smart and included a provision that allows for the expulsion of a member. You and your members take a vote and send a letter to the excommunicated employee letting him know that he is being expelled as a member of the LLC and will receive the value of his shares in a structured payment plan that suits the company. This is all in accordance with the buy-sell agreement that he signed and received a copy of when he was issued his shares.

If a member withdraws during the fiscal year, it's usually up to the withdrawing member and the incoming (new) member to determine how to work the distributions. In most cases, I advise you to pay the distributions to the new member and let him then pass on the profits and/or losses that are due to the old member. If you want to be nice, you can calculate the distributions on a per-day basis and pay the old and new members their individual shares.

When it comes to hiring, firing, and retiring managers, state law is usually silent on the issue. So you need to have provisions in your operating agreement that discuss how managers will be retained and replaced. If the LLC is manager-managed, the operating agreement should state that the members get to vote every year on whether to replace the current manager. The members should also be able to take a special vote to expel the manager at any time, if need be. Managers should also be admitted in much the same way — with a vote of the members. As for the manager withdrawing, you have to choose whether to allow it; if you do not allow it, you have to decide what penalties will be assessed for the damages incurred by his withdrawal. These terms should also be placed in the operating agreement.

Dealing with the death of a member

Although you can decide on your own how your LLC behaves in the event of a member's death, the law always protects the remaining members' interests, especially from the passing member's heirs. Because membership shares of LLCs are considered personal property, those shares will go through estate and probate much the same as the other assets of the deceased. The membership shares will be distributed according to his will or estate plan. Therefore, you can easily end up with a new partner.

The plus side is that, if your operating agreement is worded correctly, the beneficiary of the LLC membership interests has no real power in the company, only an economic interest. So the beneficiary can only receive the portion of profits and losses that his membership shares entitle him to. When it comes to voting, he has no say. When it comes to managing, he must remain silent. He can only become a full partner if the other partners take a vote and agree.

Different states may handle these situations in other ways, so to avoid having to follow these default laws, make sure you add a provision in your operating agreement that outlines what happens if one of the members dies. You may also want to add a provision that states that the LLC has the right to buy back the shares within a certain time frame.

Transferring membership shares

You normally can't automatically transfer your membership shares like you can when you own stock in a corporation. You must first assign them, which means that whomever you assign the shares to doesn't have voting and/or management rights. She can only receive the distributions. Upon a vote and agreement among the majority (or whatever you set in your operating agreement) of the members, the member then can be transferred the shares in full, meaning she will no longer have any restrictions to her membership.

When approving a transfer of membership, most state laws don't require a unanimous vote — just a majority. You can put whatever you want in your operating agreement as long as a majority vote is required.

Not all states make a distinction between transferring membership shares to members and transferring to nonmembers. However, the IRS doesn't require that all members consent when it comes to transferring to other members. Make sure to have a provision in your operating agreement that goes over this.

When the transfer is complete, don't forget to reissue the membership shares of the LLC to reflect the transfer and, just as important, collect and cancel the old certificates.

Although you can set up your operating agreement to allow membership interests to be freely transferred (like stock), I don't recommend that you do so. By allowing the ownership of your company to be freely transferable, you become less like an LLC in the eyes of the law and more like a corporation. This can be a big issue if someone sues you and you ask for charging order protection (see Chapter 16), a benefit that is exclusive to partnerships such as LLCs.

Regardless of whether you want your membership to be freely transferable, the feds may not like that idea. In their opinion, any membership shares that were purchased under a registration exemption will be considered *restricted securities,* which means that they can't be offered or resold without the resale taking place under an available exemption. Otherwise, you may have to register the shares as securities with the Securities and Exchange Commission (SEC). If you think this may apply to you, flip to Chapter 13, where I address raising capital with your LLC.

If you or your partners really want to transfer your membership shares and have obtained approval from the other members, then all you have to do is transfer the membership in accordance with one of the exemptions that I detail in Chapter 13. Also, make sure that the state laws allow for the same exemption; otherwise, you risk getting in trouble with the local authorities.

Chapter 10

Make It Official! Creating Your Operating Agreement

- -

In This Chapter

▶ Knowing the ins and outs of the operating agreement

▶ Customizing your operating agreement

▶ Creating the finished product

▶ Changing the operating agreement when necessary

- -

Your *operating agreement* is the backbone of your business. It governs how you decide your company's important issues and how you manage your business's internal affairs. Should a cataclysmic event happen, such as the passing of one of your partners, you (and the courts!) will look to your operating agreement for guidance.

Like partnership agreements or corporate bylaws, your operating agreement is your organization's blueprint. Just think of your business as a house and your operating agreement as the framing. It is a governing constitution, of sorts, for your LLC. It puts all the managers and members on the same page in regard to how the company is to operate. The document itself doesn't have to be too long or drawn out — it simply delineates the relationships between the LLC and its members, managers, and the public (its customers).

You can easily customize your operating agreement by choosing different provisions that fit your business and wrapping them all up in the format I provide for you in this chapter.

Defining an Operating Agreement

Ever want to make up your own laws? Just disregard the ones that the government imposes on you and decide how you want to behave? I know it sounds too good to be true, but believe it or not, LLCs make that wish a real possibility. You may never have gone to law school, but now you can single-handedly operate as the legislative branch of your own LLC. You see, LLCs are often allowed to use their operating agreement to "replace" state LLC law. For the most part, if you place something in your operating agreement that contradicts your state's LLC statutes, your operating agreement will almost always win in the event of a lawsuit or disagreement among members.

Although the articles of organization can be created pretty easily on your own (see Chapter 6), I encourage you to involve your small-business attorney in the process of creating your operating agreement. I provide most of the *provisions* (various sections of the agreement that deal with specific topics) in this chapter and even show you how to put your operating agreement together, but you may need some legal guidance regarding which provisions to include and how to structure your LLC. If nothing else, an attorney can provide a sounding board in your negotiations with your partners and, with his opinion, may make the process easier and less argumentative. Just make sure that your attorney is well versed in LLC state and case law and that he doesn't make the document so complicated and dense that you and your partners can't easily understand it.

What the operating agreement governs

Operating agreements generally don't get into specific issues such as minor employment matters and the day-to-day business operations (with the exception of major decisions and/or purchases). You won't look at your operating agreement to see what sort of commission structure you should impose on your new sales reps. Nor should you look at your operating agreement to tell you what credit terms or payment plans you can give to your clients.

Your operating agreement covers the bigger issues, such as large purchases, the decisions to take on debt, profit and loss distributions, selling membership shares, and assignment of duties. It paints the big picture as to how your entity is to operate. If you are a small business, creating an operating agreement may seem like overkill now, but it's necessary. As you grow, you'll need guidance, and you should be able to turn to your operating agreement. If you and your partners negotiate and decide on everything in the beginning, then you'll most likely experience less chaos and fewer disagreements when your company hangs in the balance.

Assigning manager titles and duties

Regardless of whether your LLC is manager-managed or member-managed, some managers will still need guidance. Forming your operating agreement is the perfect time for you and your partners to sit down and delineate all the specific roles and titles that each manager will take on. For instance, one manager may be great at numbers and will take on the role of chief financial officer, whereas another manager may have a solid vision of the company and is the person to lead the others on the path to success — this person can be named president or chief executive officer.

Keep in mind that while managers are legally called *managers* by the state, they can have whatever titles they want. So don't think you're missing out on the title of president or CEO if you're forming an LLC!

Outlining members' rights

After you have laid down the law as far as managers are concerned, what about the members? Members have responsibilities also, and your operating agreement needs to specify their roles in the company. With LLCs, you can create your own rules, and, if you choose, you can limit or expand your members' powers.

LLCs can have different classes of membership, so all members don't have to be treated the same. Some members can get voting rights while other members have to remain silent on all issues. Some members can also be managers and take charge of the company's day-to-day issues while others can only watch from afar.

Also, don't forget that members have certain powers that are inherent to owning the company, such as deciding who manages the LLC and whether to accept new members. You can also make the issuance of membership shares to a certain member contingent upon the member fulfilling his duties.

Why you need an operating agreement

Although an operating agreement is optional and not required by law, you should never run your company without one. With all the paperwork you already have to deal with, I know you may be tempted to write off this task, but don't. If you ever go to court, all your documentation will be revealed, and the judge will likely look to your company's operating agreement for guidance in the event of a dispute. If you don't have an operating agreement, you leave yourself open to being judged by your state's statutes — which you have no control over — and you probably won't like the outcome. You want your LLC to be governed by *your* rules, not those created by a state legislator who has no interest in your business or, most likely, business in general.

The easiest way for me to convince you of the necessity of an operating agreement is to describe what you may face without one. Here are a couple of scenarios of what could happen if you face problems in your business sans The Agreement:

- ✔ One of your members passes away, and his family wants to step in and take control of your business. Without an operating agreement with a provision protecting the surviving partners, you could end up losing everything that you have worked so hard for to a partner's relative who knows nothing about your industry.

✔ You and your partner, each owning half of the company, decide to give your partner's assistant 2 percent of the company for her loyalty and service. One day you come back from vacation to find that the company has been liquidated and dissolved in your absence. When you go to your attorney to see what can be done, you find out that because your LLC had no operating agreement that stated that all members need to agree for dissolution to occur, state law prevailed. Unfortunately for you, your state law says that a company can be dissolved with only a majority of the members agreeing. Your partner and his assistant outvoted you while you were away.

Although oral agreements may technically be valid in most states, you should never rely on them in lieu of a written operating agreement. Oral agreements are not only subject to different interpretations by the members, but are often taken with a grain of salt by the court system. In other words, if two members disagree, the so-called agreement can be completely disregarded in the event of a lawsuit.

How single-member LLCs rely on operating agreements

Is your LLC a single-member LLC owned only by you? Although it may go against common logic that you need an operating agreement — after all, why would you need to create your own rules just for yourself? — it's even more imperative that you, the single-member LLC owner, have one. If you are ever taken to court, your operating agreement will ensure that your personal veil of limited liability remains intact. (See Chapter 16 for more on the veil of limited liability.)

You see, a one-person LLC looks a lot like a sole proprietorship; therefore, anything you can do to look and act like an LLC (or even a corporation, for that matter) will prevent the courts from deciding that you are liable for the lawsuit as a sole proprietor would be. In other words, you want every piece of proof you can get that establishes your LLC as a completely separate entity.

Establishing Your Provisions

You pretty much have all the freedom in the world when creating your LLC; you just have to state what you want in the operating agreement. Your operating agreement is composed of different parts, which are called *provisions*. Each provision deals with a different topic relating to your company, such as how it is managed or how new members are admitted.

Unfortunately, people are often intimidated by all the legalese, so they don't create the agreement for fear of saying something wrong or using incorrect terminology. If you feel this way, just remember that something is better than nothing. The agreement doesn't have to be perfect — just do your best. And, don't forget, you can always ask your small-business attorney for guidance.

To make things easy for you, this section includes some provisions that you can use when creating your operating agreement. For the most part, you can pick and choose which ones you want. First, I give you a good outline for the operating agreement, and then I follow with sections containing some details about parts of the outline. Put together your document by choosing and modifying the provisions so they apply to your business.

Note: I couldn't possibly list all the variations of the provisions here, especially if your LLC has special needs such as varying allocations or creating membership classes. This is why you'll want to have an attorney review or even assist in the creation of your LLC's operating agreement.

Here's a sample outline of a basic operating agreement:

    I. Organization

        A. Formation and Qualification

        B. Name

        C. Principal Office

        D. Governing Law

        E. Term

        F. Registered Agent and Office

        G. Purpose of the Company

    II. Membership Interests

        A. Initial Members of the Company

        B. Percentage of Ownership

        C. Membership Classifications

        D. Management by Managers (if Manager-Managed)

        E. New Members

        F. Capital Accounts

        G. Liability of Members

        H. Transfer and Assignment of Interests

   III. Allocations and Profit Distributions

        A. Allocations of Profits and Losses

        B. Distributions

1. Organization

You may as well just copy and paste the text from your articles of organization (see Chapter 6) in this section of your operating agreement because, for the most part, that's all it is. The Organization section just reviews the items you already decided on in the articles of organization. Your articles may have been signed and submitted by an organizer who, for the most part, has no actual involvement in your business. By placing this information in your operating agreement, you tell the world that all members and managers of the LLC are in full agreement with the terms outlined in the articles of organization that were filed with the state.

In this section, you should include such provisions as the name of your LLC (under the subheading "Name"), your LLC's main office address (under the subheading "Principal Office"), the state in which your LLC was formed in and whose laws your LLC will abide by (under the subheading "Governing Law"), how long your LLC is to remain in existence (under the subheading "Term"), the name and address of your registered agent in all states your LLC is transacting business in (under the subheading "Registered Agent and Office"), and, lastly, the purposes for which your LLC was formed (under the subheading "Purpose of the Company"). Of course, all operating agreements are different and these subheadings are interchangeable, so feel free to arrange your information however you like — as long as it's there!

11. Membership Interests

Your LLC must have one or more *members,* owners of the company. Your members are usually the ones who invested their money or time in the business in the first place because they believed in the idea. When a lot of people have a lot at stake, emotions are bound to get involved, and people tend to act irrationally. That's why you need to create some guidelines from the get-go that clearly delineate what each member's responsibilities are and what they can and cannot do.

Also, many situations come up that can be fatal to the business if they aren't dealt with properly. These also need to be addressed in the operating agreement so that you have a contingency plan that allows the business not only to stay afloat but also to prosper. A few questions that need to be addressed in the subsections of this section are

- How can a member sell or transfer his membership shares?
- What happens when a member gets divorced, passes away, or goes bankrupt?
- What happens when a member wants to retire?
- How can the company take on more members, if needed?
- How can the company expel members?
- What sorts of contributions are allowed?
- Are there different classifications of members?

If not all members have to abide by the same rules and restrictions, then you should create a *buy-sell agreement* for each member. That way you can have many different rules and provisions for many different members, such as who can transfer membership shares and how. Buy-sell agreements will use a lot of these same provisions relating to membership interests and can range from 2 to 50 pages, depending on the size and scope of your LLC and the investment being made.

Initial Members of the Company

Unlike corporations, where the shares are completely transferable and the shareholders change often, LLCs generally keep the same members that they have from the start. Because of this, you can list the initial member information in the operating agreement. If your LLC has a lot of members, you may want to list them on a separate piece of paper and refer to it as *Addendum A.*

Here's the information you should include for all members:

- ✔ Their full names
- ✔ Their home addresses
- ✔ The type of contributions they made (cash, equipment, services, and so on) and their values
- ✔ Membership shares or percentage of the company that was issued to each of them
- ✔ What class of membership shares they were issued (if your operating agreement allows for multiple classes, as described in the "Membership Classifications" section)

You may also want to have each member sign next to her name. This shows that they all concur with the information stated in the operating agreement.

Percentage of Ownership

When discussing how much of an LLC you own, you generally specify what percentage of the company your shares represent. For instance, if you have 10 shares and the sum of all the members' shares (including yours) is 100, then you can safely say that you own 10 percent of the company. Even if your shares are nonvoting and everyone else's are voting (see the next section), you still own 10 percent. Here's a sample provision you can use:

> *A member's ownership of the Company is the total of his Voting Shares and Nonvoting Shares, together with all the rights that arise from the ownership of such shares. The Percentage of Ownership ("Ownership Percentage") shall be calculated by adding together that Member's membership shares (Voting and Nonvoting) and then dividing this sum by the total of all the Members' membership shares (Voting and Nonvoting).*

Membership Classifications

LLCs give you the flexibility of giving your members as few or as many powers and responsibilities as you want. And all members don't have to be equal! You can classify membership shares by the powers and responsibilities associated with them. One common method is to have one classification of shares for voting and one classification for nonvoting. If you only intend to issue one type in the beginning, but you want the option of issuing the other type of shares in the future, then you can specify this by using the different phrases "The company *shall* issue . . ." and "The company *may* issue. . . ."

Here are a few sample provisions you can use:

> *The Company shall issue Class A Voting Membership Shares ("Voting Shares") to the members who vote (the "Voting Members"). The Voting Members shall have the right to vote on all company matters, as outlined in this Agreement.*

The Company may issue Class B Nonvoting Membership Shares ("Nonvoting Shares"). Nonvoting Shares hold no voting rights whatsoever, and members who only own Nonvoting Shares will have no right to vote on any matters. Members may hold both Voting Shares and Nonvoting Shares.

Management by Managers

Some businesses have two kinds of partners: operating partners, who manage the day-to-day affairs, and silent partners, who keep their noses out of the daily goings-on. If this is how you've structured your LLC, with only one group of your members doing the managing, do you really want your silent, nonvoting members to be muddling in your daily operations? Not likely.

First, you need to make sure that your LLC is manager-managed (not member-managed, because not all members will have an equal say in the management), and then set up two classes of shares. Remember, you can set this up however you want. For this example, I've used voting and nonvoting classes. Then you state that one class shall have full management rights and shall be managers, while the other class has no management rights at all. Here's an example of some provisions that you can draw from:

The Voting Members shall manage the Company. In their capacity as Managers, they shall have the right to make decisions and vote upon all matters as specified in this Agreement, in proportion to their respective Ownership Percentage of the Company. Voting Members need not identify whether or not they are acting as a Member or a Manager when they take action.

Nonvoting Members have no right to participate in the management of the Company, nor vote on any matters of the Company. No Nonvoting Member shall take any action or enter into any contract or obligation on behalf of the Company without the prior written consent of all the Voting Members. Likewise, no Nonvoting Member shall perform any act that is in any way pertaining to the Company or its assets.

New Members

As your company grows, you may want to take on new partners. When and how you add these folks is an important element of the operating agreement that you should decide on at the LLC's conception. This section doesn't have to be lengthy, but the provision's wording will be determined by what you and your partners decide.

You may want to consider the following points when drafting this section of your operating agreement:

- ✔ Will new members have to make a contribution of any sort? If so, what types of contributions are acceptable?

- ✔ How do you determine the value of the shares of the company? This is important to figure out, considering that your company's value may have appreciated since inception. If your company is worth, say, $2 million, you don't want to take on a 50 percent partner with only a $100,000 contribution.

✔ Will the new member be required to sign a copy of the current operating agreement, wherein she agrees to be bound by its terms?

✔ Does the current members' vote have to be unanimous to admit a new member with full voting privileges, or is a majority vote enough?

Here's a sample provision you can use:

The Voting Members may issue additional Voting Capital or Nonvoting Capital and thereby admit a new Member or Members, as the case may be, to the Company, only if such new Member (a) is approved unanimously by the Voting Members; (b) delivers to the Company his required capital contribution; and (c) agrees in writing to be bound by the terms of this Agreement by becoming a party hereto.

Upon the admission of a new Member to the Company, the capital accounts of all Members, and the calculations that are based on the capital accounts, shall be adjusted appropriately.

Liability of Members

Although state law normally provides a default liability protection for the LLC's members, it's always good to throw in a provision that calls for it anyway. It doesn't have to be anything too lengthy. Here's an example of a limited liability provision that you can use:

No Member shall be personally responsible for any debts, liabilities, or obligations of the Company solely by reason of being a Member. All debts, obligations, and liabilities of the Company, whether by contract or not, shall belong solely to the Company.

Transfer and Assignment of Interests

By default, most LLCs don't allow membership shares to be freely transferred. However, they can be *assigned*. This means that I can give my membership shares over to my brother, but he won't actually own them along with all the voting rights and other perks. He will only receive any distributions of the profits and losses that the membership shares get. Operating agreements often state that membership interests can be transferred upon the approval of all or the majority of the other members.

You can structure this section however you want. However, I wouldn't allow your membership shares to be freely transferred like corporate stock is. Here's why — one of the three things that set LLCs apart from corporations is that the stock can't be easily traded. If you sidestep this little rule and look and feel too much like a corporation, you can lose your *charging order protection* (the idea that the LLC is protected from the members' debts and obligations; see Chapter 16 for a complete explanation). Instead, I recommend that you require all the members to vote on whether to allow the shares to be transferred.

In the Transfer and Assignment of Interests section, you deal with a lot of pertinent issues that need to be sorted out before you proceed with business. You probably will want to sit down with your attorney and have her help you and your partners decide how you want your company to run in the future. Some important subjects that you will want to address in this section of your operating agreement are

- ✔ When and how can a member resign?
- ✔ If someone resigns, does he get his contribution or capital back?
- ✔ What happens when a member passes away?
- ✔ What happens when a member retires?
- ✔ What happens if a member goes bankrupt?
- ✔ Can a member be expelled?
- ✔ How are membership shares transferred?

Also, you should add a provision that states what happens if a creditor successfully obtains a charging order against a member. A good trick of the trade is to include a paragraph in your operating agreement that states that, should a *charging order* (a court order that takes any profits that would be distributed to a member and gives them to the creditor instead until the debt is paid; see Chapter 16 for more details) be obtained on a member, the remaining members have first right of refusal on purchasing the member's shares at a portion of their fair market value.

First, you want to uphold the charging order protections:

> *If a creditor obtains a lien or a charging order against any Member's membership interest, or in the event of a Member's bankruptcy or other involuntary transfer of interest, this act shall constitute a material breach of this Agreement by such Member. The creditor or claimant shall only be considered an Assignee and will be limited to the rights of such. The creditor or claimant shall have no right to become a Member or have rights to management participation nor have the right to participate as a Member or Manager in any regard to the affairs of the Company. Said creditor or claimant shall only be entitled to receive the share of profit and losses, or the return of capital, to which the Member would otherwise have been entitled.*

Then you want to state that the partners have the option of purchasing the membership shares at a discount:

> *The Members may unanimously elect to purchase all or any part of the membership shares that are subject to the charging order, bankruptcy, lien, or other involuntary transfer at a discounted price. The price shall be equal to one-half of the fair market value of such shares. Written notice of such purchase shall be provided to the creditor or claimant.*

111. Allocations and Profit Distributions

Considering that all the LLC's members have contributed a portion of the upstart capital — whether in the form of cash, equipment, or services — everyone should be due a portion of the business's profits. Generally, this amount should be proportionate to their ownership percentage or their *capital account*. After all, the more you invest into the company, the more you should profit, right?

One of the great benefits of operating as an LLC is that you don't necessarily have to distribute the company's profits and losses according to the members' percentage of ownership. You can vary the distributions however you like, as long as you make sure you can give the IRS a good reason for doing so (which doesn't include tax avoidance. You didn't think they'd let you get away with that now, did you?).

Allocations of Profits and Losses

An *allocation* is the amount of company profit and loss that is passed on to each member for him to report on his personal tax returns. How much is allocated to a member has no bearing on how much cash is actually distributed to a member. This can cause what is called *phantom income,* in which case you'll be forced to pay taxes on company profits even when cash was never distributed to you.

The IRS allows allocations to vary from member to member — and not just according to their ownership percentage. Of course, it's customary to allocate profits and losses to each member in accordance with how much they actually own, but if you want to change it up, you can — provided that you follow the IRS's stringent rules. Make sure that you work with your accountant before doing this so she can help you avoid potential tax pitfalls.

For instance, some members may want to be allocated more losses than other members. Why? Well, they may have a lot of passive income from real estate properties and such that they want to offset. In this case, they can deduct the passive losses (from the LLC) from their passive income (from their real estate endeavors). The remaining amount is what they are taxed on. You just have to make sure that if you're going to be messing with the allocations this way, you have some reasoning behind it that isn't simply to avoid taxes, such as you invested a lion's share of the start-up capital, or you took on more risk than the other partners.

Here's a standard provision that you can include in your operating agreement that allows you to vary the allocations whenever you and your partners choose:

> *The profits and losses of the Company shall be allocated to the Members in proportion with their individual ownership percentages. Should the Company wish to make special allocations, they must comply with Section 704 of the Internal Revenue Code and the corresponding regulations.*

Distributions

When the cash actually hits your pocket, it becomes a *distribution*. Although all company profits have to be allocated to the members (for them to pay taxes on it), not all company profit has to be distributed — you can leave some in the business. And you can schedule your distributions whenever you want; they don't necessarily have to be once a year. You can make the payouts quarterly or even monthly if you like.

You should also specify in your operating agreement the *kind* of distribution that can be made. For the most part, you'll only be distributing cash to the members. If the company doesn't have the money to pay a member, then that member can't demand an asset in lieu of the cash. He'll just have to wait until the LLC has the money or the entity is dissolved.

Here is a sample provision that you can use:

> *Subject to applicable law and limitations elsewhere in this Agreement, the members may elect to make a distribution of assets at any time that would not be prohibited by law or under this Agreement. The amount and timing of all distributions of cash, or other assets, shall be determined by a unanimous vote of the Voting Members. All such Distributions shall be made to those Members who, according to the books and records of the Company, were the holders of record of Membership Interests on the date of Distribution.*
>
> *The Voting Members may base a determination that a distribution of cash may be made on a balance sheet, profit and loss statement, cash flow statement of the Company, or other relevant information. Neither the Company nor any Members shall be liable for the making of any Distributions in accordance with the provisions of this section.*
>
> *No Member has the right to demand and receive any distribution from the Company in any form other than money. No Member may be compelled to accept from the Company a distribution of any asset in kind in lieu of a proportionate distribution of money being made to other Members except on the dissolution and winding up of the Company.*

Make sure that your operating agreement contains a contingency plan for members who come and go in the middle of a fiscal year. Normally, the distribution that they receive is calculated according to the number of days that they held membership. You can create whatever formula you think works best for your situation.

IV. Meetings and Voting

Chapter 11 has a lot of information about holding meetings, taking votes, and keeping records. In the meantime, you need to figure out how and when you'll hold meetings, and what issues need to be approved by a majority of the members.

A few of the issues that you should make sure to touch upon in this section of your operating agreement are

- ✔ When holding a meeting, what sort of notice needs to be given to the members?

- ✔ What sorts of decisions require a meeting of the members and a vote to take place?

- ✔ How many members need to be at the meeting in order for a vote to be taken (that is to say, what's the quorum)?

- ✔ How are voting interests calculated? For instance, does every membership share get one vote, or do all members have an equal vote, regardless of their percentage of ownership?

- ✔ If a member is unable to make it to the meeting, will you allow her to vote by proxy?

Notice of Meetings

Before having a meeting, you gotta give notice! After all, how will everyone know when and where you'll be meeting? Notice is required for LLC meetings, not just because it's polite and considerate, but also because it keeps the members from purposefully withholding meeting time and location information from certain members to prevent them from showing up at the meeting and voting against their proposals. Here's a sample provision you can use:

> *If any action on the part of the Members is to be proposed at the meeting, then written notice of the meeting must be provided to each Member entitled to vote not less than ten (10) days or more than sixty (60) days prior to the meeting. Notice may be given in person, by fax, by first-class mail, or by any other written communication, charges prepaid, at the Members' address listed in Exhibit A, attached. The notice shall contain the date, time, and place of the meeting and a statement of the general nature of this business to be transacted there.*

Quorum

Exactly what percentage of members it takes to hold a meeting is called a *quorum*. Quorums can be unanimous, a simple majority, or a set percent of the members. It's entirely up to you. If you don't have the requisite number of voters at the meeting, whether in person or by proxy, then no voting can take place. A new meeting time and place must be scheduled, and you can then try again to get the members there. I know that getting members to a member meeting can often be like herding cats — especially when you have a lot of members. If this is the case, then you may want to make the quorum a simple majority. That way, it only takes about half of your members to be on the ball to make things happen. Here's a sample provision:

> *Members holding at least fifty-one percent (51%) of the Voting Membership Interests in the Company represented in person, by telephone, or by proxy shall constitute a quorum at any meeting of Voting Members. In the absence of a quorum at any such meeting, the Voting Members may adjourn the meeting for a period not to exceed sixty days.*

When drafting your operating agreement, you need to determine whether any decision or issues, regardless of quorum, require a unanimous consent of members. The minority shareholders often get the short end of the stick when it comes to voting on business affairs. To combat this, you can set up your LLC so that pertinent issues need to be approved by *all* members before they can be put through. This includes such issues as selling the business, offloading major business assets, acquiring a large amount of debt, or settling major litigation claims.

Voting

Not only do you have to determine what specific issues require a vote of the members, but you also have to determine how members get to vote (usually called their *voting interests*). You can structure voting interests two ways:

- **Allow each membership share to have one vote.** That means that if your membership shares represent 55 percent of the company, then you have 55 percent of the vote. This is the most common way to structure voting interests.

- **Give one vote per member.** This means that if you have 55 percent of the company, you will have one vote, which is equal to the member who owns only 1 percent of the company.

You also have to take into account that you may have different types of membership shares: voting and nonvoting (see the earlier section, "Management by Managers"). If this is the case, then only the voting shares receive votes — no matter how you structure it.

Here's a sample provision you can use:

Except as expressly set forth elsewhere in this Agreement or otherwise required by law, all actions requiring the vote of the Members may be authorized upon the vote of those Members collectively holding a majority of the Membership Interests in the Company. The following actions require the unanimous vote of all Members, who are not the transferors of a Membership Interest:

  i. Making an Amendment to the Articles of Organization or this Agreement;

  ii. Absolving any Member from the obligation of making a capital contribution or returning money or property that was distributed to such Member in violation of law or this Agreement;

  iii. Approving the sale, transfer, assignment, or exchange of a Member's interest in the Company and the admission of the transferee as a Member with full rights therein;

  iv. Purchasing, by the Company or its nominee, the Membership Interest of a transferor Member.

You may want to calculate each member's voting interest from the get-go and place it in the operating agreement where you state their names, addresses, and initial capital contributions. This way, when a vote takes place, the voting interests are already calculated, and the members have already approved and signed off on their individual voting interests.

Proxies

Say that you can't make the meeting but still want to vote on the issues that are being addressed. A common solution is to do a *proxy vote,* which means that you assign another person to vote in your place. If you have ever held shares of a publicly traded company, you may be familiar with proxy voting. You tell your proxy how you want him to vote, and he submits the vote for you. Otherwise, every time a Fortune 500 company that you own a share or two of holds a meeting, you'd be required to fly around the country to cast your vote.

If you want to allow your members to vote by proxy, you need to say so in the operating agreement. You can state whatever terms you like; however, a common provision is as follows:

Proxies are only valid when signed by the Member entitled to the vote and must be filed with the secretary of the meeting prior to the commencement of voting on the matter in which the proxy is being elected to vote upon. Proxies shall become invalid after 11 months from the date of their execution unless otherwise stated in the proxy. Additionally, the proxy may be terminated at will by the voting member. The termination of such proxy must be submitted to the Company prior to the termination being effective.

V. Management and Duties

This section is especially important for manager-managed LLCs. If your LLC is managed by the members, as opposed to a separate manager or two, then all members have equal say in the management of the company. On the contrary, if your LLC is manager-managed, then you have the option of bringing in an outside person (or group of people) who may not even be associated with the business. They don't even have to own a percentage of the company.

The *manager* is the person who runs the company. His actions determine whether the business succeeds or fails. He is a pertinent player in the game, and, for this reason, the members must choose wisely. The members must also retain control of the manager. If the manager screws up, the members need to have the power and authority to replace him on a dime. If you are a manager-managed LLC, this is probably the most critical part of the operating agreement.

Unless you plan on changing your managers out often, you'll probably want to place the names of the initial managers in the operating agreement. If there are more than a few, you can attach a separate piece of paper with the names and refer to it as *Addendum A* or *B*.

If you have multiple managers, you'll want to state in this section who is the Big Boss. You'll probably want to give the Big Boss a more official title like CEO, president, operating manager, chief yahoo, or whatever you want. If you have other positions that you can place managers in, feel free to list them here. You may want to list positions such as chief financial officer, treasurer, vice president of yada yada yada. . . . Make up whatever you want; just make sure to include what that position entails, such as the limits of responsibility and the day-to-day duties.

Election

If you are in business for a while, you'll probably see a lot of people come and go. You see it happen with Fortune 500 companies all the time — they recycle leaders on what seems like a weekly basis. If you're like most people investing in a business, you'll want to make sure that if the people you put in charge aren't cutting it, you can kick them to the curb and find someone who can do the job better. Hey — it's your hard-earned money you're talking about. You wouldn't entrust it to some yackahoo, now would you?

I didn't think so. That's why you need to sit down with your partners at the beginning and decide how you're going to manage your managers. If you want to give your managers some job security, you may want to state in this section that the managers stay in power for a one-year term; then the members have to vote to reinstate them. At this point, the members can choose someone more qualified if they want to.

If you're a little more cutthroat, you may want to write the provision so that the manager can be replaced at any time by a vote of the majority of the members. At that point, the members will elect a new manager or select someone to serve in the interim.

Here's a sample provision you can use:

> *The Company shall be managed by one or more appointed Managers. The name and address of the Managers of the Company can be found in Exhibit B, attached. The Members, by a majority vote, shall elect and appoint as many Managers as the Members determine shall be in the best interest of the Company, though no less than one.*
>
> *One manager shall be elected to take the position of Chief Operating Manager. The Chief Operating Manager shall be held responsible for managing the operations of the Company and shall carry out the decisions of the Managers.*
>
> *Members shall serve until they resign or their successors are duly elected and appointed by the Members.*

Delegation of Powers

This question will come up: "What can and can't we do as managers?" Although managers must use common sense to avoid overstepping their boundaries and making important decisions without consulting the members, the operating agreement must have a section that gives them guidance. This section tells them what decisions they can make on their own and what decisions require a resolution of the members. Here's a sample provision you can use:

> *The Managers are authorized on the Company's behalf to bind the Company to contracts and obligations, and to do or cause all acts to be done deemed necessary or appropriate to carry out or further the business of the Company. All decisions and actions of the Managers shall be made by majority vote of the Managers as provided in this Agreement. The Managers have in their power to authorize or decide the following:*
>
> > *i. The employment of persons or institutions for the operation and management of the company affairs.*
> >
> > *ii. The execution of all checks, drafts, and money orders for the payment of company funds.*
> >
> > *iii. The delivery and execution of promissory notes, loans, or security agreements.*
> >
> > *iv. The purchase or acquisition of company assets.*
> >
> > *v. The sale, lease, or other disposition of company assets.*
> >
> > *vi. The granting of security interests in the company assets in exchange for capital.*

vii. The prepayment or refinancing of any loan secured by the company assets.

viii. The execution and delivery of all contracts, franchise agreements, licensing agreements, assignments, leases, and subleases that affect the company assets.

For the most part, your managers can bind the LLC to contracts and other obligations. You can limit their powers in this section of the operating agreement. However, even if they act out of their authority, it doesn't necessarily void any contracts that they entered into. Ultimately, it's up to a judge to decide.

You may want to include a paragraph that states that any expenditure over a certain amount (say, $5,000) requires an additional authority. This can mean that a vote of the members is required. Or perhaps more than one manager or member has to sign off on the expense.

Compensation

The managers' compensation isn't something normally decided by the managers — for good reason. Generally, most LLCs are structured so that before any high compensation or bonuses can be doled out, the members must take a vote, and the majority must approve. This is a great provision which can really keep company costs from spiraling out of control. It maintains a checks-and-balances system and is a great way to keep payroll in check.

You can also throw in a sentence or two that states that the company is required to reimburse the manager for all expenses she incurred on behalf of the company. Here's a sample provision that addresses reimbursement of expenses:

> *Any Manager who renders services to the Company shall be entitled to compensation in direct proportion to the value of such services. Additionally, the Company shall reimburse all direct out-of-pocket expenses incurred by the Managers while managing the Company.*

VI. Miscellaneous

As you now know, you can put anything you want in your operating agreement. You can make it as detailed or as basic as you like. I have laid out a basic format for your operating agreement, but you don't have to stick to it. You can organize your provisions however you want. Then you can put all your leftover provisions — the ones that don't easily fit into the categories — in a Miscellaneous section.

Financial Records and Reporting

This section gives members the right to inspect all the business's financial records. It should tell them where the financial records are held and what sort of financial reporting they can expect as members. After all, as a member, wouldn't you want to know what's going on with your investment?

Following are a few specific things you should include in this section:

- ✔ **Books and Records:** Here you should state that all company records shall be held in a corporate kit (see Chapter 11). Also state where the corporate kit is to be maintained — whether at the registered agent's office, the company's headquarters, or at the company's attorney's office. Here's a sample provision you can use:

    The Members shall maintain at the Company's principal place of business the following books and records: a current list of the full name and last-known business or residence address of each Member, together with their capital contribution and membership interest; a copy of the Articles and all amendments thereto; copies of the Company's federal, state, and local income tax or information returns and reports, if any, for the six (6) most recent taxable years and a copy of this Agreement and any amendments to it.

- ✔ **Accounting and the Company's Fiscal Year:** This provision states when the company's year-end is and also who the company bookkeeper or accountant is. You can choose whether to include this in your operating agreement. It's not vital, but may be nice to have, depending on your situation.

- ✔ **Financial Reporting:** Many businesses require the company manager to provide regular financial reports to the members. The type of financial reports (balance statements, profit and loss statements, and so on) and the frequency of distribution should be noted here. Here's a sample provision you can use:

    The complete and accurate accounting and financial records of the Company shall be held by the Managers at the Company's principal place of business. Such records shall be kept on such method of accounting as the Managers shall select. The Company's accounting period shall be the calendar year.

    The Managers shall close the accounting records at the close of each calendar year, and shall prepare and send to each member a statement of such Member's distributive share of income and expense — in the form of a Schedule K-1 — for income tax reporting purposes.

Who is responsible for maintaining the company books and records? Will one person be in charge of this? If you have a larger company, everyone will most likely go about their daily business and not give a care in the world about dealing with the random recordkeeping tasks that come up. You may want to assign one person to handle everything; that way, someone is responsible for the job and can be held accountable if it isn't completed.

Indemnification Clause

Although all managers and members are provided a basic level of *indemnification* (a fancy word for limited liability), it's always good to restate it in your operating agreement. Essentially, you're telling the world that all the LLC's managers, members, and employees are free from and are not responsible for the obligations and debts of the company. Like I said, this provision isn't required, but hey — it can't hurt! Here's a sample provision you can use:

> *The Company shall indemnify any person, to the fullest extent permitted by law, who is a party defendant or is threatened to be made a party defendant, pending or completed action, suit, or proceeding, whether civil, criminal, administrative, or investigative (other than an action by or in the right of the Company) by reason of the fact that he is or was a Member of the Company, Manager, employee, or agent of the Company, or is or was serving at the request of the Company, so long as the person did not behave in violation of law or this Agreement, for instant expenses (including attorney's fees), judgments, fines, and amounts paid in settlement actually and reasonably incurred in connection with such action, suit, or proceeding.*

Dispute Resolution

Whenever a lot of people get together and work on a project for an extended period of time, disputes are bound to come up. Often, they come out of nowhere, blindsiding you at the worst times. Unless dealt with properly, they can seriously harm your business, and resolving them can take time and precious resources that your business needs to grow and prosper. To prevent these situations from occurring, you and your partners should be forward-thinking enough to add guidelines on how to effectively deal with disputes when they come up.

First, you should specify the state in which the disputes are to be dealt with. Handling lawsuits and disputes in states other than where your company is headquartered can be incredibly expensive. Therefore, a great policy is to require that all members take legal action only in the state where your company is located.

Second, you'll want to keep your disputes out of the courtroom. Lawsuits can be costly and, at times, debilitating. You should provide your members with a means to get their disputes handled in a friendlier, laid-back way. Specifically, you'll want to bind them to *mediation and arbitration* (a diplomatic way to handle disputes in which a third party hears both sides of the disagreement and then makes a decision about the outcome).

Here's a sample provision you can use:

> *The Members agree that in the event of any dispute or disagreement solely between or among any of them arising out of, relating to, or in connection with this Agreement or the Company or its organization, formation, business, or management, the Members shall use their best efforts to resolve*

any dispute arising out of or in connection with this Agreement by good-faith negotiation and mutual agreement. The Members shall meet at a mutually convenient time and place to attempt to resolve any such dispute.

However, in the event that a member dispute cannot be resolved, such parties shall first attempt to settle such dispute through a nonbinding mediation proceeding. In the event any party to such mediation proceeding is not satisfied with the results thereof, then any unresolved disputes shall be finally settled in accordance with an arbitration proceeding. In no event shall the results of any mediation proceeding be admissible in any arbitration or judicial proceeding.

Dissolution

The dissolution provision is an incredibly important one that you definitely should include in your operating agreement. Just because it's in the Miscellaneous section doesn't mean that it should be taken lightly or disregarded altogether. All good things come to an end, and chances are that your LLC will be no different. Eventually, you'll have to go through the dissolution process. If you are in a short-term project, then this provision is especially imperative because it specifies how the profits and losses are divvied up among the members.

You'll want to make this section as detailed as possible. First, outline what scenarios or actions will cause the company to dissolve. (For more information on the actions that can trigger a dissolution, read Chapter 15.) You also need to specify what percentage of members it takes to approve a voluntary dissolution. It's common to require a unanimous consent from all members — that way, no members can come back and dispute the dissolution, saying that they never approved it.

You should also outline the process for winding up the company's affairs. After the company is liquidated, what is the order in which people are paid? By law, you generally have to pay the company creditors first, but then what? You should check your state laws to see how much leeway you have. In most states, you are legally obliged to distribute profits according to the member's ownership percentages.

Putting It All Together

How you put your operating agreement together isn't nearly as important as what it contains. However, if you're going to take the time to create it in the first place, why not make sure it's organized and easily readable? It isn't hard to make your document look like a million bucks — or at least like the million bucks it probably would have cost to have an attorney draft it from scratch.

Achieving A+ form and structure

The operating agreement is laid out similarly to the articles of organization (see Chapter 6) in that that there are articles, sections, and subsections, all designated with letters, numbers, and/or Roman numerals. If you use a lot of legalese or industry terminology, you may want to consider making the first article a "Defined Terms" article with a list of definitions so the reader understands what certain words mean as he reads through the document. After all, if he is binding himself to the contract, he needs to understand it fully.

Signing and ratifying

With an LLC, all your managers and members should sign the operating agreement (if you are used to running a corporation, this part may throw you off a bit). As attorney David LeGrand has told me over and over again, "Some of the worst client problems I have seen arose because not every member had signed the operating agreement, resulting in thousands of dollars of legal fees and lost time from disputes."

To protect against this, not only should each member (and manager, if manager-managed) sign off on the operating agreement, but they also should sign off on their capital contribution, membership interest, and distributive shares that are listed in the agreement. If your LLC has a lot of members, then you can include a signature page as a separate piece of paper.

You should also make sure that you hold a meeting of the members (and managers, if you like) and take a vote to approve the completed operating agreement. You should draft minutes of this meeting to further document that all the members got together and approved the document. This way, if the document is ever contested in court, you can prove that the contesting member was there when the document was up for a vote and could have disputed the document at the time. This is why it's a good idea to have *all* the members approve the operating agreement as opposed to a simple majority.

Sharing the copies and storing the original

You may want to give copies of the operating agreement to each of the members and managers. This ensures that everyone is on the same page and each person is familiar with company policies and procedures. You will want to keep the original safely tucked away in your company kit (see Chapter 11).

Before putting your operating agreement away, run it by your company attorney to make sure that you aren't missing any pertinent information that is applicable to your company or industry.

Amending the Agreement

As companies grow and change, so should their infrastructure. If you are in business for the long term, then you'll probably reach a point in time when the operating agreement needs to be amended. How you amend your operating agreement is largely determined by the laws of the state that your LLC is domiciled in. All in all, you need to check your state laws.

When amending your operating agreement, you go through the same process that you use for amending your articles of organization (see Chapter 6). You hold a meeting of the members (see Chapter 11), present the amendment for a vote, and then draft a resolution stating that all (or a majority) of the members resolved to amend the operating agreement. Draft meeting minutes to this effect and keep the minutes and resolutions in your corporate kit. Having this proof that all members agreed on changing the operating agreement is vital, because if a member ever takes you to court over something in the operating agreement, you can prove that he voted and signed off on the amendment.

Unlike when you amend your articles of organization, you don't need to file the amendments to your operating agreement with the state or local jurisdictions because your operating agreement isn't a public record. Your operating agreement is a private contract between the members (and managers) of the LLC. This means that your amendment is valid as soon as it has been voted on.

Part IV
Running Your Brand-New LLC

The 5th Wave   By Rich Tennant

"Our profit statement shows a 13 percent increase in the good, a 4 percent decrease in the bad, but a whole lot of ugly left in inventory."

In this part . . .

As important as setting up your LLC right is, the fun
begins when you start actually running it! This part
shows you the ropes of how to operate your LLC, including how to keep your company records so your LLC stays
in good standing with your members, the government,
and your customers.

In Chapter 12, I dive into all things tax-related and give
you an overview of what tax filings to expect, no matter
what form of taxation you've chosen for your LLC. I also
warn you of the major tax traps you're liable to fall into
and how to avoid them.

Then, in Chapters 13 and 14, I address the topics of
growth and expansion of your business: going national,
expanding globally, and raising capital. And finally, in
Chapter 15, I address the sad eventuality that nothing
gold stays and explain what to do when you have to close
up shop and dissolve your LLC.

Chapter 11

Maintaining Your Records (And Your Sanity)

In This Chapter
▶ Filing your initial report
▶ Acquiring the necessary business licenses
▶ Keeping your company's records properly

I'm sure by now you're hankering to jump right into building your business, but not so fast! You didn't think you could simply file some articles of organization and the government would let you go scot-free, did you? Well, nope. You still need to take care of removing some red tape.

Although the amount of red tape varies depending on what industry you're in, it usually isn't too much of a hassle if you know how to stay under the radar. First and foremost, you need to file an *annual report* with your local secretary of state or franchise tax board. Each state refers to this report by a different name, and the requirements also differ substantially depending on where your company is domiciled. I show you how to file your report in the next section. Then I discuss the necessary business licenses you need to obtain and the regular recordkeeping that you'll need to do in order to protect your business's limited liability. With these details arranged, your LLC will be legit and protected, and you'll be free to begin transacting business.

Filing Your Initial Report

When creating your LLC, you created and filed your articles of organization (as discussed in Chapter 6) and also drafted a complete, customized operating agreement for your LLC (see Chapter 10). When you drafted the operating agreement, you made certain decisions about how the company is managed and who the managers are, among other things. Well, if you remember correctly, one of the major benefits of an LLC is *privacy.* A lot of the decisions you make regarding your company remain in your operating agreement, which isn't public record. In a perfect world, you'd just be able to leave it at that. In *our* world, however, a few of those decisions that you made must be revealed to the government and, subsequently, to the public eye.

The amount of disclosure that is required varies substantially from state to state. As I talk about in Chapter 5, these disclosure requirements can be a big incentive (or disincentive) to form your LLC in a particular state. The first and most important document that you may be forced to disclose is your company's *initial report,* which is usually filed within a month or two after the formation of your company and reveals the managers and/or members of your LLC.

Getting to know your state requirements

Each state is different in what they require to be contained in the initial report. For the most part, the initial report lists information such as:

- ✔ The names of your managers and their addresses
- ✔ The name of your registered agent and your registered office address
- ✔ The members who own the LLC

Keep in mind that whatever you include on your initial report is *public record,* which means that anyone in the world can see it.

The name and the filing processes also vary substantially from state to state. Some states refer to this initial report as an *initial list of managers or members* or an *information statement.* Or, because the report is required to be filed annually or biannually in most states, the initial report may be lumped into those other reports, which are collectively referred to as *annual reports.*

The fees for the initial reports can be hefty — sometimes as much as the fee for filing the articles of organization — and depending on the state, can be due either annually or biennially. Also, unlike the articles of organization, which can be submitted by a separate *organizer* (a person who files your articles but otherwise has nothing else to do with your company), a manager or member of the LLC needs to sign the initial report.

Keeping your company current

Although this detail may seem trivial, if you don't file your initial report (or subsequently, your annual reports) in a timely manner, you'll not only face some pretty hefty penalties and fees, but your LLC may go into *revoked status* relatively quickly. After all, when it comes to the life of your LLC, the state giveth and the state can sure as heck taketh away!

Often in these cases, the state doesn't even tell you that your company has been revoked; you may not find out until you've been sued and realize that you don't have the LLC protection that you thought you had. When your LLC is in revoked status, it's considered an *administrative dissolution* and you may very well lose all liability protection, which was a key component to why you created an LLC in the first place.

Luckily, you're usually not required to go through the expense of filing an updated report every time your information changes. In most states, you're only required to file the report on its due date (normally on the anniversary of the LLC's filing date). Not only does this save fees, but — in case you haven't caught on to this already — it may also be a good way to get yourself and your LLC a little bit of privacy: If you only have to list the names of the members of the LLC *when you file the report,* this gives you an entire 11 to 23 months (depending on how often an updated report is due) to allow whoever you darn well please to own the company.

Filing public announcements in Arizona and New York

Two states — Arizona and New York — require you to file a public announcement of your articles of organization in a newspaper or other daily or weekly publication.

If you're setting up an LLC in Arizona, follow these steps to file the public announcement:

1. **After filing your articles of organization with the Arizona Corporation Commission, publish the entire text of your articles in a newspaper of your choice (as long as the periodical is published at least weekly and has at least 5,000 or so subscribers) for three consecutive days within 60 days of your filing date.**

2. **File your** *affidavit of publication,* **given to you by the newspaper, with the commission within 60 days of filing your articles of organization.**

    The affidavit of publication tells the state that you submitted your articles for print.

Your LLC goes into effect only after the affidavit of publication has been filed.

If you're setting up an LLC in New York, follow these steps for the public announcement:

1. **After filing your articles of organization with the New York Department of State, publish your articles in two separate newspapers once per week for six consecutive weeks.**

    Your county clerk's office chooses the newspapers in which your articles will be published.

2. **File the affidavit of publication, given to you by the newspaper, with the department of state within 120 days of the LLC's filing date. Until this publication has been filed, your LLC is not in full legal compliance with the state of New York.**

If you are really looking for a foolproof method of privacy, you can form a corporation in Nevada, where the shareholders aren't on public record, and use that to hold your interests in the LLC. Just make sure that, if you expect to take a lot of profit from the company (outside of a normal salary), you don't cause yourself any tax issues by using this privacy strategy. A good accountant can point you in the right direction.

Paying to Play: Business Licenses

After you file your initial report with the secretary of state, you need to get yourself a business license (or two, or three!). Unless you're in the business of mass weaponry, drug development, or peddling junk bonds, the federal government usually keeps its distance and leaves business licensing to the state and local governments. It's sort of like "pay to play," and the last thing you should ever do is open up shop without first forking over some cash for official government approval. Avoiding this step is the fastest way to get shut down. (Yes, the U.S. *does* have a free market, but you didn't think that means it's *actually free*, did you?)

Acquiring state, city, and possibly county business licenses

Most states require that all businesses apply for a standard *business license,* the "letter of approval," so to speak, that you need to legally conduct business within the state. The state tax board uses the licenses to keep track of all enterprises that are responsible for paying state and sales or use taxes.

In addition to the state license, you may also be required to file for a city and/or county license, depending on where you live. If your business is located within city limits, you need to obtain a license from the city; if outside, you must obtain your license from the county. Depending on where you live, you should contact your county clerk's office or the city's business license department and ask which local licenses and permits you need to obtain. Keep in mind that you'll most likely be required to pay an annual fee for each license.

When applying for business licenses, each state requires different details. Normally, you can expect a business license to request the following information:

- Business name, physical location, and mailing address
- Type of business and formation date
- Prospective business activities and expected income

- Federal tax identification number (see Chapter 8)
- Names and addresses of managers/members and possibly percentages of ownership

To find out where to obtain the business license application and where your application must be filed, check the secretary of state's Web site for the state you filed in.

If the ownership of your business changes, most states require that the new owners apply for a new business license under their names, even if the business name stays the same. Moving your business to a new address also usually requires a new business license application. Essentially, you just refile the form with the updated information. If a change doesn't significantly alter the structure of the business (such as adding or dropping a member who only owns a small percentage of the LLC), you normally don't have to file a new application. However, some states require you to submit a letter to the business license department describing the change that took place. The department uses the information to update your business license.

Applying for a sales and use tax permit

If you're selling tangible goods, then you're required to collect sales tax from your customers and pay the government. What is a *tangible good?* Although the definition may vary slightly between states, you can pretty much classify a tangible good as being any item that may be seen, weighed, measured, felt, or touched, or is in any other manner perceptible to the senses. Real estate is excluded.

To collect sales tax on the products you sell to your customers, you need a *sales and use tax permit.* What's the difference between sales tax and use tax? I'll explain:

- **Sales tax** is imposed on all retailers (anyone who sells tangible goods — not services — in the state). Retailers are required to pay and report sales taxes to the board of equalization, and they have the option of collecting sales tax reimbursement from their customers at the time of the sale.

- **Use tax** is imposed on you when you purchase something from out-of-state vendors and use, consume, or store the item in the state. Use tax also applies if you lease the item. Ha! And you thought you were avoiding tax when you bought that fancy TV off eBay.

You are normally imposed a statewide sales tax and a local sales tax that differs from city to city. If your business isn't located in an incorporated city, then you're required to pay the county at its local tax rate. By combining the state and local tax rates, you come up with the amount of sales tax you can charge your customers.

What if you aren't selling tangible goods? What if you run a dry-cleaning service or a dog-grooming facility? Aren't you in the clear? Well, in some states, you are. Unfortunately, in many states, you likely are still required to go through the application process. State governments prefer that individuals aren't the ones deciding whether they are liable for paying sales and use tax. The government prefers that a seasoned tax collector make that determination.

But although this may seem like a hassle, this application is a process you *want* to go through. The alternative is going through the harrowing experience of having a state tax auditor set up shop in your office for two (or more!) weeks and proceed to pore over each and every income and expenditure record, tallying up use tax on sticky notes you bought online and sales tax on small thank-you items you shipped to your clients. Not only will the auditor pull every single penny of unpaid taxes out of the woodwork, but the state will impose hefty fines on top of it all. Needless to say, this process isn't fun.

Most states call the department that collects the state taxes the *board of equalization.* (I have no idea what that means or why they decided to use such a dumb name — I suspect they decided that "the board of tax collectors" didn't sound so friendly.) A lot of people pay this department a hefty chunk of dough every quarter.

Following special licensing requirements

If you are one of the lucky ones who decided to set up shop in a heavily regulated industry, such as healthcare, gambling, auto repair, or the law, then you're probably going to be required to obtain special licensing. If you own your own building, you have to comply with building codes and obtain special permits. If you deal with any sort of food products, then health-code regulations come into play. Now that I think about it . . . if you're in business at all, you should read this section. I'm sure you'll find one thing or another that applies to you!

In this section, I go over some common special licenses that you may have to obtain. All states are different, though, and I can't possibly list every single license requirement in every single state! To make sure you have everything covered, give your state's licensing bureau a call before starting business operations.

In most states, because you'll be filing so many documents with so many different state and local agencies, you'll be assigned a nine-digit *UBI* (Universal Business Identifier) *number* upon filing your state business license. You use this number on all your state and local filings so that all state and local agencies can easily identify you. A UBI number is sometimes called a *tax registration number,* a *business registration number,* or a *business license number.*

State-issued licenses

In addition to the basic licenses required for most businesses, you may be required to file for other licenses, depending on your state. Here are a few that you may be required to apply for:

- ✔ **Licenses based on type of product sold:** Most states require you to obtain a license if you're selling certain products, such as liquor, tobacco, lottery tickets, gasoline, and firearms. These licenses can be hard to obtain and are often heavily regulated.

- ✔ **Professional/occupational licenses:** If you (and/or your employees) will be offering services in a specialized area that requires certain skills or training, then you, personally, and each of your employees performing that service are required to obtain a specific license before opening shop. Some occupations that often require licensing are

  - Medical care — doctors, dentists, and so on

  - Auto repair

  - Real estate sales

  - Contractors

  - Cosmetology

  - Tax services

  - Legal representation/attorneys

- ✔ **Licenses for other regulated businesses:** Every state has industries they like to control. These industries vary widely from state to state (which is why you need to do your research), and they may include jewelry manufacturing and sales, furniture sales, automobile repairs, carnival operation, tree trimming, motorcycle sales, auto towing, dating services, swimming pool services, janitorial services, taxicabs, movie and television productions, dance clubs, and adult entertainment-related businesses.

Locally issued permits

Some licenses aren't regulated by the state but instead are issued by the local government, such as your city or your county. Here are a few licenses to be on the lookout for:

- ✔ **Fire department permits:** For those businesses that attract a large number of customers, such as nightclubs, bars, and restaurants, the fire department must conclude that the location is clear of any fire and safety hazards.

- ✔ **Health department permits:** These permits are most often required for businesses that prepare and/or sell food or for any other business where the health of the general public is a primary concern.

✔ **Property use permits:** If you start a business that involves manufacturing, or if you decide to operate a retail-type business out of your home, depending on your location, you may need to obtain a *land-use permit* from your city or county's zoning department that says you can use the land for something other than residential purposes.

✔ **Building permits:** If you're constructing a new building or expanding or renovating an existing building, you need to obtain a *building permit* from the city or county. Getting a building permit can take years, and you probably will have to submit a detailed set of plans to the department and work with your builder to gain approval.

✔ **Zoning permit:** Some cities require that all new businesses get a *zoning compliance permit* before they open. This permit proves that you aren't operating a business out of a location that is zoned for residential use only. Some locales are even more complicated. For instance, you may only be able to operate a retail store out of a property that is zoned specifically for retail.

✔ **Home occupation permit:** If your business is home-based, you may be required to obtain this permit when you file for your business license. It allows the state to keep track of which employees are working in what type of environment and whether your family members are involved in the business.

✔ **Use and occupancy permit:** In most states, when you apply for your business license, you must also apply for a *use and occupancy permit* from the building department (or equivalent in your state). This application normally results in the building inspector (and possibly the fire inspector) visiting your business location to get an idea of what sort of conditions employees will be working under. The inspector looks out for the interests of the people working at the location and checks for things such as fire hazards, life safety issues, code compliance, building permits, zoning issues, and so on.

Federally issued licenses

If you are in a heavily regulated industry, then a federal license in your area of expertise may be required. This lets the public know that not only do you know your stuff, but you are also a reputable company operating under the watchful eye of the government. Here are some industries that are required to operate under special federal-issued licenses:

✔ **Selling securities or providing investment advice:** You are required to be licensed by the U.S. Securities and Exchange Commission (www. sec.gov). If you are only selling *securities* (your membership shares in exchange for capital investment) and are looking for a small number of investors, you may be exempt. See Chapter 13 for more information on registration exemptions.

- ✓ **Interstate trucking or any other form of interstate transportation:** You are required to be licensed by the U.S. Department of Transportation (www.dot.gov).

- ✓ **Preparing meat products or other foodstuffs:** You are required to be licensed by the U.S. Food and Drug Administration (www.fda.gov).

- ✓ **Manufacturing of tobacco, alcohol, or firearms, or the selling of firearms:** You are required to be licensed by the U.S. Bureau of Alcohol, Tobacco, and Firearms (www.atf.gov).

- ✓ **Radio or television broadcasting:** You are required to be licensed by the Federal Communications Commission (www.fcc.gov).

- ✓ **Manufacturing, testing, and/or selling of drugs:** You are required to be licensed by the U.S. Food and Drug Administration (www.fda.gov).

If you require federal licensing before being allowed to open your business, consider having your small-business attorney guide you through the application process. The applications can often be lengthy, and you'll want to make sure you do everything correctly because whether you are approved or not can make or break your business.

Meeting Other Pertinent Requirements

You thought you were finished? You're dealing with the government here, remember? Between the federal, state, city, and county requirements, the paperwork is never-ending. Regardless, all businesses *must* handle two more things. The first is your federal tax identification number — you won't get very far without it! Second is your workers' compensation insurance — don't even *think* about hiring employees until this is taken care of.

Federal tax identification number

In Chapter 8, I go into detail on how to obtain your LLCs tax identification number *(tax ID* for short; also called an *employer identification number* or *EIN)*. If you haven't done this yet, be sure to flip back to that section and *do it now.*

If you're reading this sentence sans tax ID number, then you're in trouble! No, not with me, but with everyone else you intend to do business with. As a matter of fact, I don't think you can even make any of the filings I address in this chapter without having that annoying number. You can't file for business licenses or professional licenses, hire employees, or even open a bank account without one. I'd be surprised if you don't know your company's tax ID number by heart by the time you finish this book.

Workers' compensation insurance

All businesses that have employees are required to carry workers' compensation insurance to protect employees in the event that they get injured on the job and can't work or have medical expenses that need to be paid. This insurance is provided by private insurance companies but is required by law for each employee who works for you.

(Record) Keeping Your Liability Protection

As you may have read in Chapter 2, limited liability companies offer two forms of liability protection:

- ✔ That which protects your personal assets from the liabilities of the business
- ✔ That which protects the business from your personal lawsuits and creditors

This second form of liability protection is, for the most part, unique to LLCs and is commonly referred to as *charging order protection.*

The best way to understand basic liability is to think of it as a piece of fabric — a *veil* — that protects you and your personal assets from your business's litigious predators. The term *corporate veil* specifically refers to the protection that the LLC provides your personal assets if a lawsuit is filed against the business.

Whenever this veil of protection is breached by a creditor of the LLC and your personal assets are seized, this is called *piercing the veil.* In short, the limited liability, perhaps the most important attribute of an LLC, has been lost.

The one and only way to keep your veil of limited liability intact is to keep perfect records in accordance with your state's laws. You must keep a close eye on your company's recordkeeping practices. Not only is properly keeping records a practical solution for keeping all members on the same page, but it shows the courts that you are a serious business and it motivates them to treat you like one.

To pierce your veil, the creditor has to add you, as an individual, to the lawsuit against your company. In the complaint, she will seek to impose personal liability on you, the owner, for the business's debts or wrongdoing (in other words, she'll plead the court to pierce the veil of limited liability). Then the creditor has to prove to the court that the veil of limited liability should be pierced. If the creditor proves that the veil should be pierced, the court will make you personally responsible for the judgment. This means that the creditor can seize and liquidate your personal assets to settle the claim.

In Chapter 20, I list ten important steps you must take to keep your liability intact; however, here I address the most important one: recordkeeping. In this context, recordkeeping entails the following:

✔ Holding regular meetings of the members and recording clear minutes of those meetings

✔ Drafting comprehensive resolutions that document important decisions as they are made

✔ Storing your records in a special customized company kit or online in a secure recordkeeping storage site

✔ Maintaining an updated membership roll

✔ Keeping all tax and financial records organized

Piercing the veil of limited liability is one of the most frequently litigated issues involving small businesses. If you get a creditor persistent enough to sue your LLC, you can be confident that she'll attempt to pierce your veil. After all, it costs nothing for her to add you to the lawsuit. So you must make sure all your ducks are in a row *before* you ever hit the courtroom.

If you're doing business in a particular state and haven't registered to transact business there or aren't in good standing, don't worry too much — your limited liability is still intact. Your status in the state that you originally filed in (your *domicile*) is what matters. However, make sure that you catch up on your filings before heading into court.

Staying in touch: Holding regular meetings

What would a business be without meetings? You know — those boring snooze fests where the only thing accomplished is a mutual sense of frustration? Yeah, those. But at least you can skip out on them from time to time (which really means every time). After all, it isn't like they are legally required, right? Wrong. The government has managed to make everyone's least favorite pastime an actual legal requirement. Luckily, the government is pretty lax when it comes to LLCs (as opposed to corporations), and therefore, meetings only need to take place once a year and before making important decisions that affect the fate of your company.

Another plus is that the law doesn't state *where* the meeting must take place. And you can deduct the travel expense from wherever it does take place. Hawaii, anyone? Tahiti, perhaps? Aruba? It doesn't matter if it's just you and your business partner. Or, if a corporation that you own is the only other partner, then it'll be a relaxing party of one on the island.

The most important aspect of the meeting is the meeting minutes. *Minutes* are the detailed records of what took place at the meeting. Larger companies have secretaries who record the discussions as meeting minutes while the meeting takes place. The minutes of smaller companies just record any issues that were brought up in the meeting and any decisions that were made (called *resolutions*). Minutes serve as a record that all partners in the business got together to discuss the issues at hand and that all major decisions were approved by a majority of the partners.

Deciding when to meet

Corporations are required to meet annually to go over corporate business. However, LLCs aren't obligated to have set meetings unless the LLC's operating agreement requires them. I recommend that you provide for yearly meetings in the operating agreement, because getting all the members together with the sole purpose of discussing infrastructure and business affairs is important. LLC members also typically reelect the managers at these annual meetings.

In addition to the annual meeting, you should call a meeting if

- A legal or tax issue needs to be addressed, approved, and recorded
- Membership shares are to be issued or transferred
- The LLC is purchasing the membership shares of a withdrawing member
- There is a change in management or managers need to be elected
- Assets need to be sold
- The company's tax election is to be changed
- Major purchases need to be made
- Leases or other debts need to be incurred
- The company is to be dissolved
- The company's name changes
- The company's articles of organization are to be amended
- The company's operating agreement is to be amended
- The company is altering profit/loss allocations and/or distributions
- Any other pertinent decisions need to be made that require the consent of all the members

Assembling the members for the meeting

In order for it to be worth your while to hold a meeting in the first place, you have to assemble what is called a *quorum*. A quorum is the number of members it takes to pass a vote and should be stated in your operating agreement. If it's not stated there, the state law prevails. Some states require a simple majority of the members (51 percent); other states require three-quarters. Without the proper number of members at the meeting, a vote can't take place.

For instance, if your LLC's operating agreement states that the quorum is a majority of the members, and four of your ten members show up, then a quorum is not present. You need to have six members for a quorum. Otherwise, nothing can be resolved by a vote.

If getting all your members together for a meeting is like herding cats, then you may want to allow your members to vote by proxy. A *proxy vote* is cast by a person (a *proxy*) on behalf of a member who can't attend the meeting. The member will tell the proxy in advance how they want their votes represented. Proxy votes count toward meeting a quorum.

Like most non–Fortune 500 companies, you most likely can't afford to hire an expensive professional proxy-voting service. However, you have a cheap alternative that works just as well: If you wish to allow your members to vote by proxy, you can send out cards or a sheet of paper that describes the issues up for debate and allows the member to check how they want to vote. After they have marked their response, they send in their card to the proxy, who represents their vote at the meeting.

Is it hard for you to get all your members in one place? You can have your meetings in cyberspace! Online meetings can be held through a lot of different software solutions. Some Web sites that facilitate meetings are www.goto meeting.com and www.webex.com.

Holding the meeting and recording minutes

As much as you dread the idea, you know you have to call a meeting. I'm sure you've spent more hours than you'd care to count attending seemingly pointless meetings called by your colleagues. You want your meetings to be a valuable use of time, and you want everyone to leave the meeting feeling as if something worthwhile was accomplished. You can do this.

Say your Uncle Joe wants to get involved with your business and is even willing to make a sizeable investment in exchange for some membership. You approach two of your five partners, and they agree that it's a good idea. It's time to call a meeting.

Here are the steps that you take to conduct an efficient, effective meeting:

1. **Loosely gather information from your partners on what would be a good date and time for the meeting. Then prepare a notice of meeting and send it to all partners.**

2. **Prepare a meeting agenda with all the items that you would like to resolve. Make a copy of the agenda for all partners in attendance.**

    In this case, you include an agenda item to discuss whether your Uncle Joe should become an investor.

3. **When you assemble for the meeting, appoint a chairperson to conduct the meeting and a secretary to document the votes and the resulting decisions that are made.**

4. **The chairperson calls the meeting to order and the meeting begins.**

5. **The secretary determines whether a quorum is present.**

    See the "Assembling the members for the meeting" section for an explanation of a quorum.

6. **If any unfinished business was tabled at the last meeting and needs to be addressed at this meeting, the secretary reads the minutes of the last meeting, and any issues being carried over are addressed first.**

7. **The managers present their reports on how the company is operating.**

    This step is not required, but a lot of your silent partners will appreciate it.

8. **Go over the agenda items one by one and discuss them. Then take a vote of the members on each issue. Make sure to write down what was discussed!**

    The notes you take during the discussions and the votes become the minutes.

9. **Have all members sign the minutes.**

    If there are too many members for this step to be practical, the secretary can sign the minutes himself.

10. **Adjourn the meeting.**

Saving time by drafting resolutions

In some situations where a major decision needs to be made and properly documented by the members, you can save time and avoid a formal meeting by drafting a *resolution,* a documented decision of the members of the LLC. This is an option if you meet all three of the following requirements:

✔ You only have one issue at hand.

✔ Your operating agreement doesn't require all members to be present for a vote.

✔ The decision doesn't directly affect the members themselves and their stake in the company.

When you create your operating agreement, you specify what percentage of approval is required to make major company decisions, as well as what constitutes a "major decision" in the first place. (It could range from things like taking on a new building lease to taking on an investor.) If you and your partnership specified in the operating agreement that a simple majority of membership interests is all that's needed to approve a decision, and you are a majority stakeholder, then you are the only member who needs to agree to and sign the resolution.

Because drafting a resolution is such an easy process, you should use this method to document as many company decisions (that don't require a formal meeting) as possible. Some common decisions you may want to make by way of a resolution include:

✔ Allowing the treasurer to open and use LLC bank accounts along with a designation of authorized signers

✔ Adopting a fictitious firm name (a *DBA*)

✔ Approving a contract

✔ Leasing of property by the LLC

✔ Acquiring an independent audit of the LLC's tax and financial records

✔ Changing the LLC's fiscal tax year

✔ Approving salaries and bonuses of key employees

Completing the company kit

All limited liability companies need to have a company kit, whether it be in the physical form, such as a binder, or in the digital realm. Your company kit will keep all your important documents organized for you and cover your butt if you end up in court. With every physical kit comes a *company seal,* which in most states is required by law. Your company seal is a little device that imprints your company name and formation date onto paper. Think of it as a signature of sorts — it's often used to show that a document is a true and original copy that was verified by the company.

The kit is not very complicated. Normally it's a nice binder that is closed by either a zipper or a slipcase. The kit allows you to easily carry your corporate records from place to place. If you intend on meeting with banks or private investors for capital, you will definitely want a corporate kit. It's the only truly accepted method of presenting your company documents in an organized and professional manner.

Don't order your corporate kit through your attorney or formation service — you will pay a premium price. Instead, order it online from a corporate kit supplier. My company uses CorpTech Supply (www.corptechsupply.com), where for about $60 you can get a customized kit shipped the same day you order.

When ordering from a kit supplier, your company kit should come with the following:

- ✔ A professional binder that either zips closed or is enclosed in a matching slipcase and is customized with your LLC's name on the spine
- ✔ A seal customized with your LLC information
- ✔ Custom-made, numbered membership certificates printed with your company name
- ✔ A complete set of index divider tabs including at least *articles of organization, operating agreement,* and *membership certificates*
- ✔ Some blank template documents including a sample operating agreement, some sample meeting minutes, and a sample membership issuance agreement
- ✔ A blank membership roll
- ✔ Perhaps some business licensing information that is applicable for your state

Because LLCs are so customizable, a one-size-fits-all approach doesn't work. Therefore, I strongly suggest you avoid (like the plague!) most of the fill-in-the-blank forms that come with your company kit. Most of these forms aren't even tailored to your state's specific laws governing LLCs. Instead, you may want to consider using a service like www.docrun.com (a company I started in order to make these sorts of complex agreements affordable for small businesses) or a qualified attorney in your state to draft the corporate documents.

When you receive your kit, collect the following documents to place in it:

- ✔ Your state-filed articles of organization and company charter
- ✔ Your operating agreement
- ✔ Your company meeting minutes and resolutions
- ✔ Your membership roll

- ✔ Any cancelled membership certificates
- ✔ Your federal tax ID number and filing
- ✔ Your business licenses and state filings
- ✔ Any foreign filings that you have made in other states
- ✔ Your company's registered agent information for each state

Important: After you have your kit completed, always keep it in a safe place and keep backup copies just in case the originals are lost.

If your attorney is forming your entity, he should supply you with a corporate kit. This is the standard practice and is the only professional thing to do. Some attorneys try to save money and make their own corporate kits out of plastic binders that they buy at the local office supply store. Those attorneys also don't often supply their clients with company seals. If your attorney cuts corners like this, consider where else he may be shorting you on value.

Creating and maintaining a membership roll

Creating a membership roll is very simple. You just take the blank form that you received in your company kit and fill in each member's name and address. Next to this information, put the amount of membership shares each person has. Make sure to update the roll every time your LLC's membership changes. Some states even require that you supply your registered agent with an updated copy of your membership roll. That way, if members want to view the membership roll, they can arrange to do so with your registered agent.

Tracking tax filings and financial information

Your tax returns and financial reports show the backbone of your business. These records undeniably prove that your LLC is an operational business. Because they are backed up by bank statements and receipts, they are taken very seriously by the courts as testimony to the intricacies of your business.

You need to hang on to your pertinent tax records and financial statements for seven years. These tax records show the courts that your company is, financially, a separate entity than the owners — in other words, you and your LLC don't share a bank account. Your financial information proves that you have been actively engaging in business and not using the entity as an extension of yourself (also called an *alter ego*).

Your operating agreement (see Chapter 10) should designate what sort of financial reports the members have access to and how they can go about viewing the records. Tax returns, balance sheets, and profit-and-loss statements should be kept at your corporate office in case one of the partners wants to view this information. Also, in the event of a lawsuit, you will most likely be required to hand over copies of this information to the plaintiff.

Chapter 12

Making Cents of Taxes

*J*ust the thought of taxes probably makes you want to throw this book across the room, but don't do it. This isn't the most entertaining chapter you're going to read, but it's quick and painless, I promise. Although taxes can be a pain in the butt, by educating yourself about them you gain the upper hand and end up paying less. Just think, after reading this chapter, you'll be able to stride into your accountant's office with your head held high, with no problem discussing the tax basis of assets, tax reporting requirements for LLCs, and how you can avoid sending a chunk of change to the IRS.

LLCs can be taxed a multitude of ways, but most LLCs just stick with the default pass-through taxation. And why not? It's a great way to be taxed! In Chapter 8, I go through all the various forms of taxation that you can choose. At this point you have already elected your tax structure and are now ready to deal with the ins and outs of managing your company's tax structure — maintaining books, filing your federal returns, and so on — and avoiding any potential hiccups you may encounter along the way. Although I touch on all types of taxation in this chapter, I spend the most time discussing partnership taxation because it's the most common to LLCs and, in my opinion, the least understood form of taxation.

If you're like most people, you get confused by tax information at times. Don't get discouraged. You don't need to know everything — just enough for planning purposes and to have an informed conversation with your accountant. After all, an accountant spends his days poring over tax law and dealing with the IRS, so take advantage of his experience. Although having a basic understanding of the tax information I cover in this book is helpful, use an accountant for the important stuff, such as distributing money to the members and filing the end-of-year tax forms.

Reviewing the Tax Types

Because LLCs are allowed to elect pretty much any tax status that suits them, the federal returns, information statements, and/or notices they are required to file each year vary accordingly. To review, an LLC can choose disregarded entity, partnership, corporation, or S corporation taxation.

Disregarded entity taxation

Disregarded entity isn't so much an election as a default tax status for single-member LLCs. Single-member LLCs don't qualify for partnership taxation because no partners exist, so they're automatically subject to this form of taxation unless they elect corporation or S corporation tax status.

This form of taxation can actually be beneficial for some real estate and investment transactions. When considered a disregarded entity by the IRS, your company is treated as if it doesn't exist and you're taxed simply as an individual (or as a sole proprietorship, to be exact). This arrangement can be beneficial when executing tax credits, deductions, and strategies that only apply to individuals, such as mortgage interest deductions and special exception rules in a 1031 exchange of real estate (see Chapter 17).

Partnership taxation

Partnership taxation is the default tax status for limited liability companies with more than one member. It's a form of pass-through taxation. The primary benefit of partnership taxation over other forms of pass-through taxation is that you can vary the profit and loss allocations to the partners. Additionally, recourse loans are, for the most part, deductible to the member(s) who guarantees them.

Corporation taxation

The corporate tax status differs dramatically from all others. It's the only non-pass-through form of taxation an LLC can elect. The revenues and expenses, and thus the profits and losses, of the company do not pass through to the members, but instead are retained in the company and taxed at the applicable corporate income tax rate. Because the corporation tax rate is generally lower than what an individual pays, this status can often be beneficial.

Additionally, when a member sells his interests in the company, the profit from that sale is subject to a very favorable long-term capital gains rate. This can result in substantial tax savings. The major drawback of corporate taxation, though, occurs when ordinary profits (called *dividends*) are removed by the members, causing a double-taxation scenario.

S corporation taxation

The corporation's answer to pass-through taxation, S corporation tax status came about when small, closely held businesses (such as independent contractors) needed the ability to operate under the liability protection of a corporation but without the heavy tax and regulatory burden that comes with the standard corporation. Note that *S corporation* is not an entity type, but instead simply a tax election that can be made by either a corporation or an LLC.

The S corporation's claim to fame is the members' ability to hire themselves and pay themselves a salary. Although the resulting tax burden is ultimately equal to the income tax and self-employment tax they would pay with partnership taxation, the members only pay income tax on amounts over the salary they pay themselves, as opposed to members subject to partnership taxation who have to pay income tax *and self-employment tax* on all profits over their salary. Obviously, you can't just pay yourself $1 and be done with it. The IRS stipulates that your salary must be consistent with others in your industry and your position.

Filing Your Federal Returns

Although you'll most likely delegate the filing of your federal tax returns to a competent accountant, I still recommend that you have a good, basic knowledge about what your LLC needs to do at tax time. You'll have much more educated conversations with your accountant and also be able to review his work. After all, you sign those filings — don't you want to know exactly what you're signing?

Sucking it up with sole-proprietorship status

If you have a single-member LLC, the IRS classifies it as a disregarded entity by default and taxes it as a sole proprietorship. This means that the company doesn't have to file an information statement with the IRS like an LLC does and you don't have to issue yourself a K-1. You simply report your company's income and expenses on a Schedule C: Profit or Loss from a Business and attach it to your personal income tax return (your Form 1040) like you do for any other side income you have. If you have rental property, the profit and loss information is instead listed on a Schedule E: Supplemental Income and Loss.

Keep in mind that as a sole proprietor, you can't pay yourself a salary. Therefore, all your income is subject to self-employment tax, which you report on a Schedule SE, Self-Employment Tax, that you attach to your Form 1040. You can, however, deduct other employees' salaries as an allowable business expense.

If you have less than $5,000 in expenses for the year, you should be allowed to file the short form of the Schedule C, the Schedule C-EZ. Double-check with your accountant to make sure that this is the case.

Ponying up with partnership taxation

With partnership taxation, you don't file an actual tax return for your LLC. Instead, you only file an information statement — IRS Form 1065: U.S. Return of Partnership Income. On this statement, you report the company's income, deductions, gains, losses, and the allocations that are being made to the partners. After this statement has been filed, the company then issues a Schedule K-1 to each member that shows what income and deductions have been allocated to her. The member then reports the allocations made to her (individually) on Part II of a Schedule E, which she attaches to her personal tax return.

Before you can file your IRS Form 1065, or any return for that matter, you need to obtain a tax identification number for your LLC. You can do that by submitting a Form SS-4: Application for Employer Identification Number, to the Internal Revenue Service or applying online at www.irs.gov. I recommend that you apply online so that you can get your number immediately.

Preparing Form 1065

All partnerships, including LLCs, are required to file a Form 1065 by April 15th of each year. The 1065 isn't a tax return; it's a summary and information statement that lets the IRS know who is responsible for paying which percentage of the company's tax burden for the year. It is four pages long and contains six different schedules. (About ten other schedules can be filed with the 1065 if your accountant deems them necessary.)

The company also must make some tax decisions called *elections*. Elections can include decisions concerning the research credit, for example, and also depreciation of assets. These decisions can affect all the members and can have huge tax consequences. Therefore, whoever is preparing and filing the Form 1065 must look to the operating agreement for guidance on how tax elections are to be decided. If the operating agreement doesn't address them, then all members should come together for a vote.

After Form 1065 is completed, only one member needs to review and sign it; however, that member must answer to all the other members if they have a question or problem with the filing.

Taking your accounting system into account

On Form 1065, you indicate the accounting method that your company uses. If you have a bookkeeping service or an accountant, you can just ask them. If not, you have to choose one yourself.

Cash-based accounting is the simplest method of accounting and is generally used by smaller companies that do their bookkeeping themselves. With cash-based accounting, you classify income only when you actually receive it, and you classify expenses only when the checks you wrote have posted to your bank account. If your register matches your bank statement, with no other debits or credits showing, then you're probably on a cash-based accounting system. If your income is over $1 million, however, I recommend that you ditch

this accounting method and go with *accrual-based accounting* instead.

Accrual-based accounting is a little bit more difficult to track, but it offers the most tax benefits. It is a standard for most professional bookkeepers because it provides a more accurate picture of how the business is actually doing. Essentially, with accrual-based accounting, you record income when the sale occurs, not when you actually receive the money. You also record expenses when the invoice is received, not when your check is cashed by the vendor. With this type of accounting, spending more money than you have is virtually impossible. Also, at the end of the year, you'll show less profit that you'll need to allocate and pay taxes on.

 If you are operating as a single-member LLC, you don't need to file Form 1065, because the IRS treats you as a disregarded entity and you are taxed as a sole proprietorship. I go over what filings are required for single-member LLCs in the "Sucking it up with sole-proprietorship status" section.

 Form 1065 asks for the tax year of the LLC. It's customary to make this a calendar year. LLCs are required to have the same tax reporting period as their majority members, and majority members are normally U.S. citizens who pay taxes on a calendar-year schedule.

Distributing K-1s to the members

After your accountant fills in the Form 1065 for your LLC, she creates a Schedule K-1 for each member of the LLC. The K-1 contains the allocation information for each partner, including how much and what type of company income the member has been allocated and what sort of deductions he can write off. It also provides an updated analysis of each partner's tax basis.

 The operating agreement tells you what percentage of profits and losses each member is allocated, but unfortunately, filling out the K-1 isn't always as simple as just writing in the portion of each member's profits and losses. The schedule calls for different types of income to be reported separately, such as short-term capital gains, long-term capital gains, charitable contributions, royalties, interest income, and rental real estate income, among others. Having to calculate percentages of different types of income for a multitude of members can be a *huge* headache, so I recommend you leave it to the professionals.

Remember that one of the benefits of an LLC is that the company's profits and losses don't have to be allocated to the members according to their ownership percentages. LLCs allow for *special allocations,* which means that you can own 10 percent of the company and feasibly receive 100 percent of the profits and losses for a specific year. Granted, you can't make these decisions without having a good reason (that doesn't include tax purposes); however, special allocations are common and easy to do. You just have to prove that you have the LLC's business goals in mind and that you aren't making special allocations to avoid tax liability.

When your accountant creates the Schedule K-1s, she files the originals, along with Form 1065, with the IRS. You'll get a photocopy of your Schedule K-1 that you can use when filing your individual tax return.

The amount of profit that's reported on your K-1 isn't necessarily the profit that was distributed to you. In other words, you may have to pay taxes at the end of the year on the company's profits when you haven't even seen a penny of a cash distribution. Remember — what the LLC *allocates* to you and what it *distributes* to you are not necessarily the same thing. Allocations are the profits and losses that you have to report on your personal tax return and pay taxes on. Distributions are your cash portion of the profit that you actually receive.

Paying the actual taxes

If you're a United States citizen, you pay your personal taxes on IRS Form 1040. But your 1040 tax return doesn't include a line that specifies LLC income. If you take a look at Form 1040, you see that line 17 mentions business income. So here, you list the total income stated on your Schedule E, Supplemental Income and Loss, which you submit with your Form 1040.

You use a Schedule E to report all income and losses from business activities that don't constitute your primary source of income. If you're managing the day-to-day business of the LLC, then you should be on the company payroll, and your regular paycheck is what's considered your primary source of income. The allocations that the company makes on a yearly basis are considered secondary income. In other words, if all you do is sit at home and collect profits from businesses that you don't actually operate, and you don't have any "job" per se, that income is still reflected on a Schedule E.

If you're a single-member LLC and you're an operational manager of the company, then this doesn't apply to you and you don't list your business income and deductions on a Schedule E. Later in this chapter, I go into single-member LLCs in more depth.

When filling out your Schedule E, you report all the business income and deductions in Part II.

Because the Schedule E isn't as simple as copying and pasting the information from your K-1 (a few other schedules are involved), I recommend leaving the preparation of this form to your accountant. I include the basic how-to here only so you can familiarize yourself with it. Armed with this information, you can check your accountant's accuracy and have intelligent discussions with your accountant about the documents that she prepares.

If you are actively engaging in the business, you're required to pay self-employment tax on your percentage of the company profit. You must calculate your self-employment tax on the Schedule SE: Self-Employment Tax, which you file with your Form 1040.

Coughing up cash with corporation tax status

When you decide to be taxed as a corporation, you are subject to the same type of taxation that corporations are — with no exceptions. If you aren't used to corporate taxation, just think of your company in terms of being an official person that's separate from yourself. You don't pay taxes on behalf of your company. All taxes are paid *by the corporation* on the profits that are left in the business at the end of the year.

You report all your business's income and deductions on IRS Form 1120: U.S. Corporation Income Tax Return — a separate tax return. (You send a signed copy of Form 8832: Entity Classification Election to the IRS with your corporate tax return.) Your profits are subject to the federal corporate tax rate, which averages around 15 percent. Then, if you distribute them to the members, those same profits will be taxed again as capital gains income to the members. This is called double taxation.

Licensed professionals get a bad deal

If you are a Professional LLC, you may be subject to a special form of taxation unique to professional LLCs and professional corporations. This form of taxation is governed by special rules by the IRS and can change your tax outlook drastically. For instance, professional LLCs are subject to a 35 percent flat tax (one of the highest rates of corporate taxation) and also get a smaller exemption to the accumulated earnings tax, which means they get to keep less money in their corporation without being forced to pay an extra 15 percent penalty tax. If you're a licensed professional, it's imperative that you find an accountant who has experience with this sort of taxation and can guide you through the process of operating your company under these strict limitations.

Shelling it out with S corporation tax status

If you elect to be taxed as an S corporation, you file an IRS Form 1120S: U.S. Income Tax Return for an S Corporation, instead of the traditional partnership returns. The 1120S is more of an information statement than anything else, because S corporations don't really pay taxes; they just pass the profits on to the owners for them to handle the burden.

When filing a Form 1120S, you prepare a Schedule K-1 for each member (called *shareholders* in this case), give a copy of the K-1 to each member (so he can use the information when preparing his personal tax returns), and submit one copy to the IRS with your Form 1120S. With the K-1, you must also send to each member a copy of the Form 1065 tax classification election and Form 2553: S-Corporation Tax Election. Not only is this a requirement by the IRS, but it also explains to your fellow members why their LLC is filing taxes as an S corporation. For someone who isn't hip on all the tax flexibility inherent in LLCs, getting a K-1 for an S corporation can be pretty confusing without an explanation attached.

You're required to file Form 1120S by March 15 of the following year, or if you're on a fiscal year, then the 15th day of the third month after the close of the fiscal year. Depending on your state, you may also have to send a copy of Form 1120S and the corresponding K-1s to your state tax board. Or, they may have a similar form that you need to file. Your accountant can assist you in pulling together all the required filings for your LLC.

Avoiding LLC Tax Traps

Business is business, and the unwary can easily fall into quagmires. Every entity has its tax traps, and LLCs are no different. You just have to make sure that you plan around them and you'll be fine. Oh, and a great accountant helps, too!

Transferring assets into your LLC

For the most part, when your LLC elects partnership taxation, transferring assets into your company in exchange for membership is a *nontaxable event*. This means that, for income tax purposes, no gain or loss is recognized. Problems only arise when debt or liability is involved.

LLCs have a tax pitfall known as a *deemed cash distribution*. It only occurs when one of the members reduces the amount of his liability. The IRS

Triggering gains on securities LLCs

Although a securities LLC — an LLC created for the sole purpose of holding securities — can be a great way to diversify and protect your investments at the same time, it can also be subject to a pretty serious tax trap. A securities LLC may be subject to the investment company rules that state that the transfer of appreciated securities into the LLC triggers capital gains. This means that after you transfer your securities into your LLC, you have to pay taxes on the capital gains that you realized from the date you purchased the securities to the date you transferred them to the LLC.

These rules only apply if

✔ You are classified as an investment company (which means that more than 80 percent of your LLC's assets are in the form of publicly traded securities).

✔ The securities that you have transferred are not already in diversified portfolios, and the transfer results in the diversification of your securities.

If both of these stipulations are the case, then the tax basis is *reset,* which means that all your appreciation thus far is subject to capital gains taxes.

considers the reduction in liability to be a cash distribution, and like a cash distribution, the member must pay taxes on any of this amount that goes over his tax basis. (I describe tax bases in greater detail in Chapter 8.)

A good example of a deemed cash distribution is a member who transfers a piece of property into the LLC. Say that the property has a mortgage on it for $80,000. When the property is transferred into the LLC, the two members decide to refinance the property to include the other member as a personal guarantor. Unfortunately, the partner who transferred the property didn't realize that by refinancing it he was reducing his debt by $40,000 and that the IRS would consider that $40,000 a cash distribution. This means that at the end of the year, the contributing member has to pay taxes on $40,000 that he never actually received.

Had the members talked to a professional earlier in the game and, instead of refinancing the property, chosen to obligate the member in some other way, the contributing member could have avoided a big tax surprise.

Dealing with phantom income

When a partner is allocated a sizeable company profit that she has to pay tax on but is not actually distributed any profits, this is called *phantom income.* Phantom income can be dangerous because a partner in the LLC can end up with a pretty hefty tax bill but no profits to pay it with.

Members often experience some phantom income — especially in your LLC's beginning stages when you need to keep the profits in the business to help it grow. However, you can feel pinched in the pocket if the business doesn't even distribute enough cash to the members to help cover the tax burden. You'll have to scrounge up the dough on your own. Garage sale anyone?

Phantom income has a good side and a bad side. The bad side is that it can happen to you. The good side is that you can force it upon a creditor who obtains a *charging order* on a member's interest. A charging order is all that a creditor can go after if a member is liable personally, and it only gives a creditor access to the allocations and distributions that a membership interest can receive. If you only allocate profits to the members (which includes the creditor with a charging order) and don't give any cash distributions to pay the taxes on those profits, how happy do you think the creditor will be? Needless to say, he'll be running for the hills and eager to settle the lawsuit in the member's favor. (Chapter 16 covers charging orders in more depth.)

You can add a provision to your operating agreement that can force the company to distribute enough cash for the members to be able to pay the taxes on their allocations. You can figure out a percentage that works for all members and also includes a percentage for state taxes. However, by doing this, you completely undermine the strategy outlined above that gets rid of creditors who have obtained charging orders.

Minimizing self-employment taxes

Even though LLCs aren't imposed with the same double layer of taxation on profits like corporations are, if you aren't careful, you can still end up paying more in taxes. And aren't you supposed to be saving on taxes, not paying more?

The IRS hits LLCs and sole proprietorships the hardest with self-employment taxes. Self-employment taxes are Social Security and Medicare taxes, and they're imposed in addition to the federal income taxes that you have to pay. These taxes amount to about 15.3 percent of the total income allocated to you. About 12.4 percent goes to Social Security, which will be paid out to you when you reach retirement (I hope), and 2.9 percent goes to Medicare, which is a form of hospital insurance. You use Schedule SE: Self-Employment Taxes to determine the self-employment tax that's owed and file it with your personal Form 1040 tax return.

You have to pay self-employment taxes if

- Your LLC offers licensed services to the public, including accounting, actuarial science, architecture, consulting, engineering, health, and law.

- Your LLC is actively engaged in business. If your LLC only engages in passive activities, such as holding rental properties, with the rent being the only profit distributed to the members, then it's passive income and not subject to self-employment taxes.

✔ You work more than 501 hours during the LLC's tax year. That is, on average, about ten hours per week.

✔ You have the authority to execute contracts on behalf of your LLC.

If you are an investor or partner in the business, you aren't required to pay self-employment tax on the money you earn.

Luckily, a cap limits the amount of earnings subject to self-employment taxes per year. Unluckily, that amount is $94,200, which is way over the national average — and that only applies to Social Security. Anything over that amount is still subject to the 2.9 percent Medicare tax.

Currently, you can only deduct half of what you paid in self-employment tax when calculating your *adjusted gross income* — the amount that you have to pay income tax on.

Becoming a silent partner

Not everyone is required to pay self-employment tax. SE tax is for wage earners, not necessarily big fish. So if you're a silent partner who doesn't deal with the day-to-day matters of the business, you may be able to find a way around the mandatory self-employment tax.

First, make sure that your LLC is manager-managed. If it's member-managed, it's hard to attest that you, as a member, aren't doing any managing of the day-to-day affairs! Then find someone trustworthy who can act as manager and will be able to enter into contracts with your and the company's best interests in mind. Finally, make sure that you work no more than 500 hours per year for that particular company.

Obviously, this work-around isn't possible if you're one of the operating partners. But if you're simply an investor, you may be able to eliminate the required self-employment taxes and keep a hefty chunk of change in return.

Choosing to be taxed as an S corporation

Unlike owners of partnerships, the owners of S corporations can hire themselves. In fact, they are expected to hire themselves — an S corporation without any owners on the payroll is a sure path to an audit. The main benefit of hiring yourself is that you're paid as a regular employee, as you would be if you had any regular job. This means that the regular salaried income you receive isn't subject to self-employment taxes. You still have to pay regular payroll taxes, but this is often much less.

Of course, you must hire yourself for a wage that's standard in your industry. If your company hits a windfall, you can't necessarily take all the cash out as a bonus, because you're limited to having a salary that is believable for an executive of your rank, in a company your size, in your industry. For instance, if everyone else in similar positions is pulling around $100 thousand per year, you can't take home a million bucks and not expect to get audited.

After you take your maximum salary, any other cash you take out of the business must be taken as a distribution. You have to pay tax on it (including self-employment tax!) as you would if you were a regular partner and not an employee of the company.

Keep in mind that if you are an owner who is active in the business's day-to-day operations, the IRS considers you to be an employee. Therefore, you need to include yourself on the company payroll and pay payroll taxes on that income. Make sure to take enough of a salary that it's in line with the standard for your position in your industry. After that, the remaining income you take is classified as company profit, which you don't have to pay self-employment taxes on. You are only subject to personal income tax on this profit. That's a 15.3 percent savings!

Chapter 13

Raising Capital with Your LLC

In This Chapter

▶ Issuing membership in exchange for cash

▶ Getting around securities laws with registration exemptions

▶ Navigating tricky state laws

*I*f you're an entrepreneur, one of the most fundamental tasks when starting a company is seeking out and acquiring capital to fund your start-up. This fund-raising can be as simple as asking friends and family members to pull up their couch cushions and donate some extra change or as complex as raising millions in private equity or venture capital. Regardless of your methods or the amount you're raising, you have to contend with some hurdles. Namely, the Securities and Exchange Commission (SEC) — a government agency endowed with the task of keeping the little guys from being swindled out of their life savings.

Luckily, when you know the federal and state securities laws you're contending with and can navigate them with ease, raising financing should be a breeze. Well, aside from the talking people out of their money part; that's sometimes easier said than done! Thankfully, you were smart enough to form an LLC for your fundraising activities, and with the flexibility in membership rules, management, and profit distributions, you have the freedom to come up with some pretty creative incentives that make the prospect of investing with you much more attractive than, say, with a stiff, old corporation.

Structuring Your LLC to Attract Investors

More often than not, upstart capital for budding enterprises comes from the founders and people willing to finance it for a piece of the action (otherwise known as *investors*), which is why raising capital is a vital aspect of any up-and-coming business. Unlike sole proprietorships or general partnerships, LLCs can actually sell portions of the ownership, the membership shares. Membership shares are normally given to investors in return for cash, property, or other assets. You can also give them to employees or contractors in exchange for their services, which is a great tactic to use if you're just starting out and don't have a lot of money to pay employees.

In some states you can give *promissory notes* for future money, property, or services that someone intends to contribute. That way, you can issue the shares first, and then the person can make his contribution later. Promissory notes can be a big incentive for investors to get on board, but be careful! Make sure the investor does in fact have the money to invest and is committed to living up to his end of the agreement. As a precaution, make sure to note in your operating agreement that if the individual doesn't live up to his promises, his shares are confiscated.

One of the reasons LLCs are quickly becoming the entity of choice for raising money is because they provide unmatched limited liability protection for everyone involved in the business. Not only are the members protected from the liabilities of the business, but LLCs also get the benefit of *charging order protection* — a second layer of liability protection that protects the business from the liabilities of the owners. (See Chapter 16 for more on limited liability protection.)

Although you aren't legally required to do so, when setting up your LLC and creating your operating agreement (a process I walk you through in Chapter 10), make sure to list all the members, their membership interests, and all the contributions received from them. When membership changes, you'll have to update your operating agreement, and all new and existing members will have to reconfirm their agreement on the policies outlined in the operating agreement, which keeps everyone on the same page.

If you have many members, having everyone reconfirm the operating agreement isn't very practical. In that case, I recommend you use a *membership role,* a separate document that maintains an updated record of the members, their membership interests, and their ownership percentages.

Membership certificates aren't a requirement, but I always recommend them. They add legitimacy to the investment, and investors like to have them. If your operating agreement includes restrictions about transferring the membership, then you should print a notice of these restrictions on the actual certificate. This notice is commonly called a *legend*.

In the following sections, I go over federal and state laws regarding investments. Then I show you ways that you can get around the detailed process of registering your offering with the federal and state securities commissions. These tactics are called *registration exemptions*. Remember that term, because these exemptions are your lifeline when navigating the securities law minefield.

Skirting the SEC with an LLC

You know that an LLC is the best entity to use when raising capital. Now the question is whether you legally can. After all the hard work of finding investors, you're nearing the finish line and just need to cut a deal, right? Unfortunately, you may not be able to just take their money. Special *securities laws* protect the innocent from bad investments, and you must comply with these laws before legally raising financing. I know it seems like a pain in the neck — and it is — but trust me when I say that you do *not* want to mess with securities laws. The penalties for noncompliance are steep and include huge fines and jail time.

Most people think of securities laws and the SEC as only applying to large public corporations trading on exchanges like NASDAQ and NYSE. Not so! If you sell shares of your small business or real estate property to the general public, then securities laws apply to you.

The federal government considers anything to be a *security* if an individual or entity invests cash, property, services, or other assets into a business and isn't involved in the business's management decisions. This means that whenever you accept any form of contribution in exchange for your membership shares, you are dealing in securities.

Two major pieces of legislation control all U.S. securities: the United States Securities Act of 1933 and the Securities and Exchange Act of 1934. Both pieces of legislation have their own sets of rules and regulations and have been amended numerous times over the years. These acts were set up to protect investors, but complying with them is difficult for most small businesses. First of all, the process of registering your securities with the Securities and Exchange Commission is not only a lengthy one but also comes with some enormous expenses, including registration fees, CPA fees, attorney fees, underwriting fees . . . the list goes on and on.

So what's a small business to do if it can't afford the huge costs of raising just a little bit of money? Well, the feds got smart, and they now allow registration exemptions for businesses that want to raise a limited amount of money and don't mind playing by some pretty strict rules. I get into these exemptions in more detail later in this chapter, in "Exploring securities registration exemptions."

Seeing how the laws apply to you

One of the first ways to legally get around securities laws is to make sure that when you raise capital, the membership shares you offer aren't considered securities in the first place. The best way to determine whether securities laws apply to your organization is to take a good look at how the management will be structured after you raise the financing.

- ✔ If the investors have a full and equal say in the management of the company, then the securities laws do *not* apply.

- ✔ If the LLC is managed by separate managers or the investors have limited managerial powers, then the securities laws *do* apply.

I generalize the stipulations of the laws into a few loose rules to determine whether you will be selling securities. If any one of these rules applies to your LLC, then you are automatically required to comply with securities regulations:

- ✔ Your LLC is manager-managed.

- ✔ Your LLC is member-managed, but some or all of the investors are junior managers and don't have a full say in the business's day-to-day operations.

- ✔ Your LLC has hundreds of members. Even if they all have a say in the company's management, there are too many to realistically manage the day-to-day operations.

- ✔ You're widely advertising the investment and looking for multiple investors.

These guidelines are loose and based on federal interpretations of the law. When it comes to states, the laws and the interpretations of what a security is differ greatly. For instance, New Mexico, Ohio, Vermont, and Alaska consider *all* membership shares to be securities, whether the LLC is manager-managed or not. I discuss state security registrations in "Navigating State Securities Laws (Blue Sky Laws)," later in the chapter.

If you're just looking to raise a little bit of money, I suggest that you find an investor or two who may have good input in the business operations. This way, you can avoid a lot of the securities laws, but your investor can also be an asset in terms of knowledge and experience.

When you want to create a member-managed LLC, make sure that the articles of organization and the operating agreement both specify that each member is equally responsible for the operations and success of the LLC. Unlike corporations, your LLC should have no centralized management in which the shareholders elect directors who then elect the officers who manage the LLC. Avoid that structure and instead get used to managing as a team. All members collectively must be in charge of the major decision making and have the power to select or remove key employees. (See Chapter 6 for how to form a member-managed LLC.)

If you transfer your membership shares to someone, such as a family member, as a gift, the securities laws do not apply. However, this gift can only happen once — you may not make multiple gifts of unrestricted membership shares.

Exploring securities registration exemptions

If you review the rules in the preceding section and find that securities laws apply to your situation, you may still want to sell membership shares as securities if you don't want your investors to have control over the operation of the business. As a matter of fact, because the federal government knows how difficult, costly, and time consuming it can be to register your securities with the SEC, it provides some exemptions that mostly apply to small businesses or projects that are looking to raise a small amount of capital.

The exemptions that I discuss here only apply federally. You still need to look at the laws for each and every state in which you intend to sell your securities and determine whether you meet the criteria for an exemption from registration.

To help navigate the laws, I recommend working with an attorney who specializes in securities law and is familiar with conducting searches on securities laws in multiple states (a regular business attorney won't cut it). To save money, you may be able to work out an agreement with the attorney in which you take on some of the workload yourself.

In the following sections, I outline the federal exemptions available to small businesses. *Note:* Rules 504, 505, and 506 are called *Regulation D exemptions,* and they all belong to Sections 3 and 4 of the Securities Act. If you're using a Rule 504, 505, or 506 offering exemption, you must read and follow some corresponding general rules, Rules 501, 502, 503, 507, and 508. You can find them at www.docrun.com/wiki/regulation_d.

Intrastate exemption

The *intrastate exemption* requires that you find investors or members only in the one state that your LLC operates. This exemption sounds better than it is, because it has the following problems:

- ✔ All the members of the LLC must be in the same state where the LLC has its business operations.

- ✔ The LLC can't advertise for investors in any state other than the one where it has its business operations.

- ✔ The LLC can only operate in this one state. This rule is the worst of all and where most people get disqualified. Nothing related to your business can be done in any state other than your home state. You can't market to people out of state, and you can't have customers in or purchase supplies from other states.

The world is getting smaller every year, and most companies find raising money under this exemption increasingly impossible. However, if you're a small mom-and-pop business that only operates locally, this exemption may work for you — just make sure that you don't do any business out of state. Also, keep in mind that you'll still be required to file the SEC Form D (which you can find at www.myllc.com/dummies) with your state securities commission. Just make sure to clear everything with a qualified securities attorney before doing so.

Rule 504 exemption

If you're looking to raise less than $1 million, you're automatically exempt from having to register your securities with the SEC. This is the *Rule 504 exemption.* In general, you can't advertise the investment opportunity, and you aren't required to make any specific disclosures about the investment. However, the money must be raised within a 12-month period. After that time, you must register the securities with the SEC or find another exemption.

After you first sell some of your securities, you have to file a Form D with your state securities commission. The form includes some basic information about the company, such as the names and addresses of its owners and stock promoters. You can download a Form D from www.myllc.com/dummies.

You can only use this exemption if your LLC isn't selling any other securities that are registered with the SEC. For instance, if your LLC has another class of membership that is being offered for $50 million and is registered with the SEC, the same LLC can't use this exemption to raise under $1 million.

The Rule 504 exemption is by far the most popular of all securities exemptions. Not only does it directly apply to most small businesses looking to legitimately raise financing, but if your company is selling its securities using a Rule 504 offering (an offering using the Rule 504 exemption), then your LLC isn't required to bear the burden of state qualifications. Rather, it simply needs to abide by the exemption rules and make the requisite state securities filings for each state it's selling its securities in. I show you how to do this in "Finding an exemption in each state," later in the chapter.

Rule 505 exemption

If you plan to raise less than $5 million, you may be able to use the *Rule 505 exemption.* It has a few more limitations than the Rule 504 exemption (but that isn't surprising, considering you're raising more money):

- ✔ You can't use *general advertising* (any advertising that is targeted to the public at large, such as newspaper ads, TV ads, and so on) to sell your securities.

- ✔ Like the Rule 504 exemption, you can't take longer than 12 months to raise your funds.

- ✔ Your LLC's financial statements must be certified by a CPA to assure prospective investors that the profit/loss and assets/liabilities you state on your financial statement are factual.

- ✔ You can only have a maximum of 35 regular-Joe investors.

- ✔ When selling to the regular Joes — *nonaccredited investors* — you must adhere to the SEC rules regarding investment disclosures. These disclosures must be completely forthright in outlining the risks inherent in the investment. Your attorney can help you write disclosure statements that comply with both federal and state laws.

Although you're limited in the number of nonaccredited investors, you can have as many accredited investors as you like. What's an *accredited investor?* It's a person or institution that meets certain financial criteria. These investors are well-off enough to suffer the financial hit of a bad investment. They normally have a net worth of more than $1 million. Generally they are more educated about investing and can make better decisions on where to place their money than the average person.

Rule 506 exemption

Rule 506 is the golden rule that most companies use to raise funds over $5 million. When offering securities under the *Rule 506 exemption,* you are doing what is called a *private placement,* and you can generally raise as many funds as you like. The guidelines for Rule 506 are very similar to Rule 505:

- ✔ You're also limited to 35 Joe-schmo investors (but you can still sell to an unlimited number of accredited investors).

- ✔ If you sell any securities to nonaccredited investors (Joe-schmos), you must make very specific and comprehensive disclosure statements regarding the investment to all investors.

- ✔ You can't do any general advertisement of the investment.

To streamline the process of a Rule 506 offering, many companies issue what is called a *private placement memorandum* (or PPM, for short), which adheres to the SEC guidelines on what needs to be disclosed regarding the investment. If you ever come across investment opportunities that aren't listed on the stock exchange, you will most likely see them in this format. Or you may see what is called an *executive summary,* which is just a summary of the PPM that teases your interest in the investment. After the company has your interest, they give you the full PPM.

A PPM is normally a complete business plan, 30 to 50 pages long, put into a special format that includes certain disclosures, such as who is involved in the business and the risks that are inherent to the investment. I encourage you to be completely forthright when drafting your PPM. Most smart investors will look for these disclosures and, believe it or not, will be a lot more confident in the investment when they see that the company is being very open and honest about the risks involved.

You can purchase a template for a private placement memorandum online. However, you may want to have your attorney draft it for you, even though the cost may be in the thousands. Most templates only comply with federal laws, and your attorney will have to make sure that your PPM and your financing plan comply with the blue sky laws (state securities laws) as well. Not to mention, your presentation will end up looking much more professional to prospective investors.

Regulation A exemption

If you plan to raise less than $5 million, you may want to consider offering your securities under the *Regulation A exemption*, rather than some of the Regulation D exemptions I discussed previously.

With a Regulation A offering, you aren't limited to the number of investors you bring on board. You will still need to do a *private placement* (a long-winded form that is comprised of your basic business plan and some hefty disclosures about the investment); however, Regulation A allows you to advertise the investment in more ways than a Rule 505 or 506 exemption does. For instance, you can use radio or mass mailing to advertise your investment. Also, when registering under a Regulation A exemption, you can advertise your investment before having prepared a private placement memorandum, so long as you don't take in any money. This allows you to test your response rate before incurring the cost of creating all your disclosure and financial statements.

As part of the disclosure, you must show financial statements; however, they can be unaudited if no audited statements are available.

If Regulation A offers fewer restrictions and downsides than Regulation D, why is Regulation A so rarely used? For one reason: Unlike with Regulation D offerings, companies taking advantage of the Regulation A exemption must file an *offering statement* with the SEC — a circular for investors regarding the company's business details, the risk factors of the investment, the management of the company, financial details, and other pertinent details. The offering statement not only results in public disclosure of your company's private details, but also is expensive to produce.

In addition, Regulation A offerings are more difficult than Regulation D offerings to coordinate with state securities laws (often referred to as *blue sky laws,* which I discuss in the next section). As with many things, the Regulation A exemption is great in theory, yet doesn't work so well in practice.

Navigating State Securities Laws (Blue Sky Laws)

Think the federal security laws are a hassle? Well, the ride ain't over! Not only do you have to comply with federal laws, which are regulated by the SEC, but you also have to follow state laws — *in every state in which you are prospectively looking for money.* Just hope the investor you're targeting doesn't live in a backward, complicated state with expensive filing fees!

State laws are referred to as *blue sky laws.* The term *blue sky* originated from a judge who said that a certain stock being advertised had "about the same value as an area of blue sky."

Registering your securities

If you want to advertise your investment nationally or find investors from all over the United States, then you have a long road ahead. It isn't as simple as just registering your securities with the state that your LLC was formed in; you have to register your securities in every state that you seek and/or find investors in. Because the laws differ from state to state, registering your securities in multiple states can be very time consuming and very expensive — especially if you have a securities attorney doing all the research and filing.

Finding an exemption in each state

You can get around the arduous and costly process of registering your offering with every applicable state securities commission, but it still takes some good old-fashioned research on your part. You can use the registration exemption offered by certain states, after you find out which states offer it.

Registration exemptions started when the federal government decided to cut small businesses a break and let them raise money without too much red tape. However, even when companies could navigate the federal securities laws, they were still getting hung up by state securities commissions. So to help out the small businesses and real estate transactions that don't raise a large amount of financing (between $1 million and $5 million), the Uniform Commission of State Laws, with the blessing of the SEC, tried not only to put all the states on the same page, but also to offer registration exemptions that matched those of the federal government.

The result was a set of provisions titled the *Uniform Limited Offering Exemption* (or ULOE), and the federal government offered it to the states on a silver platter, begging them to copy and paste that set of securities laws into their own state statutes. The idea was that if a company complied with the federal registration exemptions, then they'd be in compliance with the state securities laws. Some states agreed, but others copied only part of the code. Therefore, you and your attorney must go through each state's code to see whether that registration exemption is available in your state, and, if so, what the specific rules are.

Basically, the ULOE took the federal registration exemptions 505 and 506, made a few simple variations, and then handed them over to the states, ready for the taking. If you want to file under the ULOE, you can get the SEC Form D document at www.myllc.com/dummies. *Remember:* Run things by a qualified securities attorney before filing!

Most states offer some variation of the Rule 505 and 506 exemptions. You should check the laws yourself or contact a securities attorney who can check for you. Unless you can find an exemption in the individual state's laws, you are required to register in that state if you advertise your investment there or take investment from it.

Chapter 14

Expanding Your Empire: Going National!

*W*ith technology advancing at a blinding pace, the world is getting smaller by the hour. Throw up a Web site, and all of a sudden you're transacting business with customers all over the globe! The world is yours for the taking. Just keep in mind when you're wheeling and dealing all over the place that the various countries and U.S. states you touch down on in the process are going to want a piece of the action. The implications of having physical operations in multiple countries can get very complicated and are beyond the scope of this book, but before you even consider going global, you may very well be looking to take your LLC *national.* And that in itself can be a quagmire if you don't have a road map to guide you.

If you're simply selling to customers in a particular state, then you aren't beholden to that state in any way. However, when you get into hiring employees and owning property, the line starts to blur a bit. You need to know whether or not, according to the laws of the state in question, you are considered to be *transacting business* there. The definition is usually left vague and open-ended . . . and most often ends up in the state's favor. So if you think you may be transacting business in a particular state, you need to know how to formally take your company to the national level.

With proper planning and the right help, the process of going national can be as exciting as it gets. So have fun with it, big shot!

Registering Your LLC in Multiple States

Say you have a restaurant in Florida, your home state, but want to expand to Georgia and North Carolina. After you open your locations in those states, you are *doing business* there. By law, if you're doing business in other states, you must register in those states (called *foreign filing*). The foreign-filing process is similar to the actual formation process, but it's always in addition to the initial formation. Your *domicile* (the state where your LLC is formed) won't change; you'll just be legally allowed to transact business in the other states you've registered in.

Not foreign filed anywhere? Doing business only in the state where your LLC is formed? Then you're simply called a *domestic LLC.*

Defining "doing business"

The term *doing business* is important in LLC law because it creates the guidelines under which you may or may not be required to foreign file. Of course, you'll want to foreign file in as few states as necessary. With each additional state comes additional laws to learn and red tape to follow, as well as some pretty hefty fees. Unfortunately, as you find out in the next section, foreign filing is sometimes necessary.

Determining whether you're actually "doing business" in another state can be hard. What if you shipped your product across the country to a single customer, yet most of your business is accomplished in your LLC's home state? Which state's laws must you follow? Remember, each state's laws are different. Here are a few questions to point you in the right direction:

- ✔ Does your LLC operate out of a physical office or retail store in the state?

- ✔ Are you physically there, meeting with customers (instead of just speaking with them over the phone or by e-mail)?

- ✔ Does a large portion of your LLC's revenue come from that state?

- ✔ Do any of your employees physically work in the state? Do you pay state payroll taxes?

If you answered yes to any of these questions, then you are probably doing business in the state and are required to foreign file your LLC there.

Even though you may be making money from customers in a particular state, it doesn't necessarily mean that you're transacting business there, as far as the law is concerned.

Knowing you are *not* doing business in a state

The Revised Model Business Corporation Act (RMBCA) gives criteria for when an entity is *not* transacting business in a state. Although it was written for corporations, the act also applies to LLCs.

Not sure if you are technically "doing business" in a particular state? If you are doing only one or two of the things listed below, you're probably not, but if you're doing three or more, you will likely have to foreign file. Talk to a corporate consultant in that state to double-check.

✔ Maintaining, defending, or settling any proceeding (that is, being involved in a lawsuit)

✔ Holding meetings of the board of directors or shareholders or carrying on other activities concerning internal corporate affairs

✔ Maintaining bank accounts

✔ Maintaining offices or agencies for the transfer, exchange, and registration of the corporation's own securities or maintaining trustees or depositaries with respect to those securities

✔ Selling through independent contractors

✔ Soliciting or obtaining orders, whether by mail, through employees, through agents, or otherwise, if the orders require acceptance outside the state before they become contracts

✔ Creating or acquiring debts, mortgages, and security interests in real or personal property

✔ Securing or collecting debts or enforcing mortgages and security interests in property securing the debts

✔ Owning real estate or other forms of property

✔ Conducting an isolated transaction that is completed within 30 days and that is not done in the course of repeated transactions of a like nature

✔ Transacting business in interstate commerce

Foreign filing to do business in multiple states

Yes, foreign filing is a necessary evil, but with the help of your registered agent and perhaps a good advisor, it can be a breeze. Just be aware that if you're planning on doing business in numerous states, the filing fees can get pretty hefty, especially considering that a lot of states charge more for filing foreign LLCs than they do for domestic ones. Unfortunately, you can't get out of the fees, but you can at least try to incorporate this cost into your budget.

Preparing and filing the paperwork

Registering (also called *qualifying*) your business in another state is remarkably similar to the formation process. This stuff should almost be second nature after creating your original LLC. (I cover those steps in Chapter 6.) Registering is relatively easy, and generally, foreign entities have less paperwork to deal with in terms of certain licenses and permits after the registration is completed. Whew . . . something to look forward to!

When you register, you submit an application for a certificate of authority. You can normally download the basic form off the Web site for the secretary of state in the state you are attempting to register in, or you can have a formation company create the application for you.

When filling out the application, you'll most likely have to provide the following information:

- ✔ **The name of your foreign LLC:** List the name as it appears on the articles of organization in your home state.

- ✔ **The name of your foreign LLC in the state you are registering in:** If your name isn't available in the state you're registering your LLC in, you may have to select an alternate name to do business under.

- ✔ **Entity domicile:** List the date of formation and the state where the LLC was formed.

- ✔ **Registered agent name and address:** Give the name and address of your LLC's registered agent in the state you are registering to do business in.

- ✔ **Your principal office address:** You may want to list your registered agent's address here as your principal office in the state. However, you can also list your corporate office address, if you have one.

- ✔ **Name and address of each manager and/or member:** The information that is required here varies from state to state. Contact your formation company if you have any questions.

- ✔ **Signature of a manager or member:** One manager or member's signature is required to file the registration.

- ✔ **Signature of registered agent:** Your registered agent is required to sign the application stating that he has agreed to be your registered agent.

For a nominal fee, you can have a multistate registered agent company serve as your agent in all the states where you're doing business. If you're registering to transact business in multiple states, keeping all your paperwork in order and staying on top of your filing dates while obtaining the necessary signatures can be difficult, and having a single agent simplifies your work. Running a company is hard enough without all the tedious paperwork involved in maintaining your LLC's compliance in a zillion jurisdictions. The company can assist you with the filings, stay on top of your paperwork, and even let you know when your filings are due!

Haven't foreign filed? Tsk, tsk . . .

So, you've been doing business in a state and haven't registered there . . . what do you do? First, call your attorney. Second, drive immediately to the police station and turn yourself in. Don't worry — just kidding!

The reality is that nothing major will happen to you. If your LLC is sued, you should be able to defend it in the local courts. You may simply have to get legit and foreign file first. However, if you decide that you want to sue someone in that state, you definitely need to register there first.

As for penalties, some states are stricter than others. You may have to pay the fees and taxes that should have been paid, plus possible fines and interest. However, if your tax burden wasn't huge, most states are just happy to have the business and will waive the fines and fees just to get you in compliance. In other words, it's not such a big deal. Just make sure you register ASAP.

In some states, before you can file your application, you must show a proof of good standing in the state where your LLC was formed. This proof is often called a *certificate of good standing* or *certificate of existence.* To make it more difficult, some states also require that you provide a certified copy of your articles of organization. You can contact the secretary of state's office in your home state to obtain these documents, or you can have your formation company do it for you. After you have obtained your certificate of good standing (and your certified copy of your articles, if required), send it in with your application.

Maintaining Your Multistate LLC

Although saying you're a nationwide company may sound sexy, every state you register in to transact business brings a pile of paperwork and loads of fees. Some of your annual or biannual filings may include

- ✔ Annual report of members and managers
- ✔ Annual publication in a local newspaper
- ✔ Franchise tax reports
- ✔ Income tax reports
- ✔ Business licenses

Depending on the state, many other filings may also be required.

When you're operating in multiple states, you'll probably be required to go through a similar filing process for each and every state you are doing business in. If you don't have a physical location in that state, some filings (such as building permits) may not be required; however, others, such as initial reports and business licenses, are still necessary. If you aren't sure about these basic filing requirements, you should contact the secretary of state's office (I provide contact information in Appendix A) or your registered agent in that particular state.

Because of the multitude of filings that are required for every state you are transacting business in, you may want to consider hiring a formation company to handle everything for you. That way, you maintain compliance and can spend your time running your business rather than struggling with strange filings for states you aren't familiar with. Many of the Big Four registered agents (Incorp, CSC, CT Corporation, and NRAI) offer services tailored to each state. For instance, for $99 per state, Incorp offers a Company Compliance & Resident Agent Service that tracks your filings, filing dates, mail forwarding, and so on. It also has an online system where you can view all your filing dates, your filings, and your corporate documents. This organization system, which is comparable to offerings by the other three big agencies, is a huge help because your filing dates vary from state to state and you'll pay hefty late fees if you miss filings.

Submitting several initial reports

In all states in which you *foreign file* (register to do business in states besides the one in which your LLC was formed), you need to file an initial report. This report is usually exactly the same as the initial report you file when forming a new LLC, which I show you how to do in Chapter 11. You need to make sure that the information you submit in one state on your initial report is the same information that you submit in another state. When you're doing so many filings in other states, you may start to forget that your LLC is still only one entity with one set of members and one federal tax identification number!

Obtaining multiple business licenses

If you are foreign filed in multiple states, you need to apply for your state and local business licenses, just as you would if you were forming your LLC in that state in the first place. Determine what your local jurisdiction is (your city or county) by whatever your corporate office address is in that state. If you're using your registered agent's address as your corporate office address, then you'll use that zip code to find what local agency you'll need to register with. Your registered agent should have this information for you.

In addition to the general state and local business licenses, your LLC may need to obtain other special permits, depending on the type of business it's engaged in. For instance, if you're operating a physical office in that state, then you may have to obtain a use and occupancy permit. If you're engaged in a heavily regulated industry such as that involving alcohol, then you may need to obtain special alcohol permits. In Chapter 11, I show you how to file for and obtain the requisite business licenses for your LLC.

Paying taxes in multiple states

If you determine that you are, in fact, doing business in multiple states, the tax man in each state will want a piece of the action. How much will he want? Well, that depends. Each state handles taxes differently. In general, each state will require you to allocate a percentage of your sales according to an *apportionment* formula, which is necessary because sales alone don't give a complete picture of how much business you are doing in each state. For example, you may have your headquarters and manufacturing operations based in Rhode Island but make most of your sales in other states. The formula will entitle Rhode Island to a larger share of your income.

Fortunately, most states use a common formula using three factors of your business: property, payroll, and sales. The property factor is the average value of your *in-state property* (furniture, equipment, buildings, inventory, and so on that's stored or used in that state) divided by your *total property* (the furniture, equipment, and so on that you own everywhere). The payroll factor divides your *in-state payroll* by *total payroll*. Your sales factor equals your *in-state sales* divided by *total sales*. **Note:** Some states give sales a double weight because it's the most important factor. These three factors are averaged to determine how much "business" you are doing in that state.

Because a particular state may use a different formula than the rest, you may end up paying taxes on more or less than 100 percent of your actual income. Your accountant can verify the formula in each state.

If you're selling tangible goods and will be paying sales tax, you definitely need to open up a separate bank account for that state. Keep your sales receipts for each state separate so you know which state to pay sales tax to.

Withdrawing from a state

What happens when you're no longer doing business in a particular state and don't want to keep up with the paperwork of being registered there? Withdrawing (or *canceling*) your LLC is very easy — you just file a *certificate of cancellation* with the secretary of state's office in the state you want to withdraw from.

Want to change your home state?

When Bart opened Bart's Bikes, he was a different man. He lived on Venice Beach and was a California boy at heart. But as the company grew, so did he. Soon, he was doing business in Oregon, too, and little did he know that Oregon was a bike lover's paradise. Within months, Bart's Bikes took off. Bart, getting older and wanting to trade in his surfboard for some hiking boots, decided that a move to Oregon was in order.

Within a year, all of Bart's business was in Oregon, and he decided to close up shop in Venice Beach, leaving that life behind for good. Now Bart faced a predicament. Bart's Bikes, LLC, was formed in California and foreign filed in Oregon, but he wanted to change his company's domicile to Oregon. After all, why should anyone put up with California's high taxes and exorbitant fees if he doesn't have to?

Bart heard about a process called *domestication,* in which he could file some forms with the secretary of state where he wanted to move to make that state the LLC's new domicile. Unfortunately, Bart discovered that Oregon is one of the states that does not provide for domestication. In this case, he had his attorney assist him in withdrawing and dissolving his California-based LLC and transferring the assets to a new, Oregon-based LLC.

The certificate of cancellation is a pretty standard form and contains some basic information, such as

- ✓ The name of the LLC as stated on its articles of organization
- ✓ The name of the LLC as it is doing business in that state, if different
- ✓ The effective date of the cancellation, if different from the filing date
- ✓ Any other information that the manager or member filing the certificate of cancellation feels is relevant

You can normally just download this form off the secretary of state's Web site and mail it in with the filing fee. You don't really need an attorney to file the certificate of cancellation. However, you should seek legal advice if the entity you are withdrawing has assets or physical locations in that state.

Chapter 15

Dissolutions: Every Beginning Has an End

*A*ll things eventually come to an end to make room for new beginnings, and your LLC is no different. Sometimes, business simply doesn't go as planned and you're left with no option but to close up shop. Other times, legal or tax technicalities get in the way and force the demise of your business.

Whatever the reason, you need to make sure you do things by the book. If you don't cover all your bases before and after the dissolution, you may be asking for a fiasco later on. So before dissolving your LLC, I urge you to thoroughly review this chapter, get together with your fellow members, and create a detailed plan for dissolution.

After you create the dissolution plan, make sure your accountant reviews it thoroughly and clears you of any gnarly tax traps you may be inadvertently walking into.

Getting Clear on the Context

Listen up, 'cause this is important: Just because your LLC dissolves doesn't mean that it's gone for good. The term *dissolution* is used in so many varying contexts and so often changes meaning from state to state that it'll make your head spin. So to keep you from developing a migraine, I lay out the basic terminology for you in this section.

The most important thing to know is the difference between a *dissolution* and a *termination*. When your LLC faces what's often referred to as a *dissolution* (an event that forces your LLC to reorganize), your LLC doesn't necessarily need to wind up its affairs and terminate all business activities. In many cases, you and your partners have the option of continuing business, just under slightly different circumstances. If your LLC faces a *termination,* though, your whole operation is at the oh-so-irreversible end.

The one exception to the difference between a dissolution and a termination is a *tax termination.* Just when you were getting pretty clear on the terminology, leave it to the IRS to come in and muddy things up, right? Here's the skinny: A tax termination is not fatal and generally doesn't affect your LLC (unless you want it to); it only results in the termination of your tax status. I go into this topic in the later section "Tax terminations."

It's Melting! Examining the Reasons Your LLC May Dissolve

The following sections list and explain the common reasons why your LLC may dissolve.

Voluntary dissolutions

Business is hard. Really hard. If you're tired of struggling and have decided to move on to greener pastures, don't beat yourself up about it. You aren't alone: One in ten businesses don't make it past their first year. All great entrepreneurs have had to call it quits on something at one point or another, and because you had the foresight to set up your businesses as an LLC, closing up shop is relatively painless. Well, aside from the unending slew of questions from your non-business-owner friends and relatives, of course.

Voluntary dissolutions aren't always cause for mourning. If an LLC is used for a short-term project, such as film financing or a real-estate deal, the members understand that the LLC will be dissolved when the project has run its course, thus allowing the members to dissolve the operation and split the cash, simple as pie.

A voluntary dissolution is relatively simple to perform. If all the members are onboard and no legal proceedings are looming, terminating the LLC is pretty straightforward: You wind up the affairs of the company and file articles of dissolution with the secretary of state. I cover the process in the "Undergoing the Dissolution Process" section later in this chapter.

If your LLC isn't up to date with state filings or has outstanding tax liabilities, your articles of dissolution may very well be rejected, and you won't be allowed to formally dissolve until you handle those burdens and pay up. Ironically, if you neglect these responsibilities long enough, the state dissolves your LLC for you, which I discuss in the next section.

Administrative dissolution

When I was little and would disobey, my mother always used to threaten (jokingly, of course), "Jennifer Leigh Reuting, I brought you into this world and I can take you out." Well, the secretary of state shares that credo, except in this case, there's no kidding around. If your LLC "misbehaves" — doesn't file its required disclosure statements or doesn't pay its state taxes — the secretary of state automatically dissolves your LLC, often referred to as an *administrative dissolution.*

Luckily, should you be faced with an administrative dissolution, most states have an option for *reinstatement* (also called a *revival*). In order for this to happen, you'll likely have to file an updated disclosure statement and pay all back taxes and fees, along with pretty hefty penalties. Upon reinstatement, the default is fully remedied, and it is as if no dissolution had ever occurred. Even the state forgives you fully: At the end of the day, they're just happy they got the extra money out of you!

Reinstatements must be completed within a set period of time from the date of dissolution; often two years, depending on state law. So don't dawdle!

Only the state in which your LLC is domiciled has the authority to dissolve your LLC, even if it's registered to transact business in multiple states.

Judicial dissolutions

In rare cases, the court of law has the authority to dissolve and/or terminate the existence of your LLC with what is called a *judicial dissolution*. It may also be referred to as an *involuntary dissolution,* because, well, if it happens to your LLC, you can probably bet that the majority of your members weren't rooting for it to happen (to say the least).

Generally, judicial dissolutions are only done at the request of the state attorney general, one or more members of the LLC, or an unsatisfied creditor. Because of the irrevocable nature of this sort of dissolution, judges often consider it a method of last resort.

Courts are only granted the authority to perform a judicial dissolution if your state's laws have a specific statute allowing it. To understand how your LLC may be at risk, review your state's laws in regards to this. A list of state laws on dissolutions can be found at www.docrun.com/wiki/llc_dissolution.

Action by the attorney general

If you or any of your members are in the habit of performing criminal acts in the name of your LLC, you'll definitely want to plan for a sudden dissolution by mandate of the state attorney general.

What are "criminal acts," you ask? The term is pretty loose, but it generally refers to forming your LLC under fraudulent circumstances and/or engaging in illegal conduct, gross negligence, or fraud. Let's just say, if your business involves running a sweatshop or swindling elderly folks out of their pensions, you can pretty much assume you qualify.

Luckily for the consumers of the world, LLCs that have been dissolved by mandate of the courts often cannot be reinstated. Of all dissolutions, a judicial dissolution directed by the attorney general for criminal acts has the greatest chance of resulting in a permanent termination of the business.

Action by one or more members

Judges love operating agreements. Why? Because if every LLC had a well-planned and executed operating agreement in place, the judge could actually make his afternoon tee time instead of suffering through *another* case involving member disputes.

Most member-dispute cases arise from situations that could have been avoided from the get-go with a well-written operating agreement, such as a voting deadlock among members, or a disenfranchised minority member that feels her investment is being wasted. If, upon formation of the LLC, all rules and expectations were laid out in the operating agreement, then there would be a guiding framework in place to mediate any disputes or misunderstandings as they arise. Instead, the judge has the right to mediate by imposing a judicial dissolution that may fully terminate an operating company, all because of a simple disagreement.

If you happen to be the minority member with the bone to pick, a judicial dissolution can work in your favor. The law allows for LLCs to be dissolved at the request of a member for acts of misconduct or negligence by the other member(s) or for breach of the operating agreement. When this happens, your LLC is forced to terminate and liquidate.

If the judicial dissolution wasn't ordered for reasons of criminal acts or negligence, your state statutes may provide for the ability of the remaining members to continue on with the business should they choose to do so. In some states, even a *minority* of the members has the option to continue! It simply needs to be allowed for in the organizational documents (the articles of organization) of the LLC. In this case, a formal dissolution takes place, thereby distributing the share of the company's assets to the disgruntled member, and then the remaining members can decide to not take their share of the distributed assets and instead continue the existence of the company on their own.

The courts have more important jobs to do than referee disagreements among members, not to mention that the legal fees of using the court system make it incredibly cost prohibitive. The best thing you can do is sit down with your partners as soon as possible (*before* any disagreements arise) and devise an operating agreement containing a detailed procedure for dealing with disputes. I show you how to do this in Chapter 10.

Action by an unsatisfied creditor

If a creditor obtains a judgment for a claim against your LLC, or your company has acknowledged in writing that a claim is owed, he can drag your LLC into court and request a judicial dissolution. This step is usually taken on the grounds that the LLC is insolvent and will not have the ability to pay the debt at any point in the near future. Creditors must be paid first from the sale of assets in the event of a dissolution and liquidation, so forcing that sale may be the only way they can recoup their losses. In some states, if you've provided for it in your organizational documents (your articles of organization), then you and your members may choose to patch the company back together after the creditor has been paid, and continue on with business.

In the case of a judicial dissolution and subsequent liquidation, the court will appoint a *receiver* (or *liquidator*) to receive the LLC's assets and distribute them to the creditors and then to the members.

Tax terminations

What most people fail to realize is that even if your LLC elects to be taxed like a corporation or even a sole proprietorship, the IRS still considers you to be a partnership. Not a "special LLC partnership," either; as far as the IRS is concerned, you're no different from two wiseguys off the street who wrote a partnership agreement on a napkin and didn't remember to file a DBA ("Doing Business As," also referred to as a *fictitious firm name*). And, as with partnerships, if one of you wiseguys leaves, the partnership is null, kaput, deader than a donut. Terminated. As in "tax terminated." (Get it?)

If your LLC transfers 50 percent or more of its membership within a 12-month period, the IRS considers your partnership to be terminated and, assuming the remaining partners want to continue the business, a new one to be formed. This dissolution can happen easier than you realize — for instance, an equal or majority partner retires or passes away, or you decide to take on a sizeable investor.

Now, before you freak out, with the exception of this event possibly causing a fictional dissolution (which I address in the following section), your LLC inherently remains unchanged. You don't need to make any filings with the secretary of state. You don't need to notify your vendors, creditors, or employees. You don't even need to obtain a new tax identification number! It doesn't sound like much of a termination at all, does it?

Well, I *am* talking about the IRS here, so there's a downside. First, any existing tax elections that your LLC made (see Chapter 8 for more info on tax elections) are terminated, and you must make new ones. Second, although tax terminations are generally nontaxable events, they can force the existing members to recognize a gain or a loss on their personal tax returns, so you definitely want to plan for any possible tax traps before transferring membership.

If you think you may have cause for a tax termination at any point in the near future, flip back to Chapter 12 where I go over the whole muddle in more gritty detail.

Fictional dissolution

When LLCs first came around, the IRS had a bit of a fit. A few rogue states created this new entity — a sort of hybrid between a partnership and a corporation — and the IRS had no idea how to tax it. They finally decided that LLCs were subject to partnership taxation, but in order to qualify, the LLCs must be substantially differentiated from corporations.

To make a long story short, the IRS mandated that LLCs were forbidden from taking on two of the four main corporate characteristics: They couldn't have a *perpetual duration* (an unlimited life span) and they couldn't have free transferability of ownership. To comply with the first restriction, the states ruled that a maximum duration (often 50 years) needed to be specified in the articles of organization upon forming the LLC.

As for the second restriction, well it's a bit more complicated. The states created their own version of the *tax termination* (see the previous section), mandating that any transference of 50 percent or more of the membership results in a *dissolution event.* This means that unless the remaining members get together (often within 90 days of the dissolution event) in a formal and documented fashion and unanimously decide to continue the partnership, then the LLC is dissolved. Because a dissolution event is so easily remedied by a vote of the members, a dissolution of this sort is often referred to as a *fictional dissolution.*

Luckily, in the years since LLCs came on the scene, the IRS has seen the light (albeit slowly) and now no longer imposes the rudimentary partnership characteristics on LLCs. The limited-duration rule was the first to go, and most, if not all, states now consider LLCs to be entities with unlimited life spans. As for the free transferability of ownership, the states have been much slower to adapt to accommodate the new freedom allowed by the IRS. For the most part, the IRS allows free transferability of ownership interests as long as the portion of membership being transferred doesn't exceed 50 percent. In this case, a *tax termination* may occur, which I discuss earlier in this chapter in the section "Tax terminations."

If you look at all the state laws on the issue, you see that they're varied. The more progressive states now automatically allow free transferability of ownership — in other words, no more silly *dissolution event* business — unless the members specify otherwise in the operating agreement. Other states reverse that policy, keeping the fictional dissolution limitation as the default law while allowing the members the power to do away with it in their operating agreement. And some states haven't updated their laws at all.

The moral of the story is that depending on the laws of your state, the fictional dissolution may be a very real problem for your LLC. To make your life as easy as possible, I used a wiki to organize a list of all the state statutes that address the fictional dissolution so you can easily check to see what does or doesn't apply to you. You can view it at `www.docrun.com/wiki/llc_dissolution`.

Considering the Future

Sometimes a dissolution isn't simply a dissolution, as in the case of administrative dissolutions, tax terminations, and the other types in which your business can continue to operate. If you and your partners are voluntarily dissolving the company, then that decision will undoubtedly lead to the termination and liquidation of your LLC. Winding up the affairs of a business can be super-simple or complex and troublesome depending on the circumstances. However, all terminations share one characteristic: They're pretty darn *final.*

In other words, usually you can't take it back. So you owe it to yourselves and the business you've created to do some preliminary work before closing that chapter for good. Read on to find out what steps you should take before termination.

Keeping your LLC on life support

First, you and your partners need to determine whether or not dissolution is even the right move for your business. I know that when the going gets tough, you may have trouble seeing any alternatives. And you're all probably looking forward to when you can completely resign the failed business to the past and move forward with a clean slate. I, like any entrepreneur, have been there before.

However, if there is any possible way you can avoid formally liquidating and terminating your LLC, do it.

The beauty of LLCs is that they come with more durable liability protection than any other entity. The caveat is that the LLC actually has to be *in existence* in order to offer this sort of impenetrable stronghold. A dissolution substantially weakens your LLC's liability protection. In California, for instance, creditors of the LLC can go after the members *personally* for the debts of the company within four years after the date of dissolution or until the statute of limitations has expired on the cause for action, whichever is sooner (see California Corporations Code Section 17355). Dissolving your LLC may give a greedy plaintiff complete access to your personal assets.

If your LLC has substantial debt, your best bet is to wind up the affairs as much as possible without formally dissolving the LLC with the secretary of state. In other words, keep your LLC on life support as long as you can. Or, at least, until the *statute of limitations* (the length of time after an act occurs that the law will allow you to be held responsible for it) runs out.

Keeping your LLC on life support does have drawbacks. You'll have to continue paying state fees and maybe even franchise taxes. In high-tax states such as California, which has a minimum $800 annual franchise tax, the best move financially may be to take the liability risk and wind up your company.

All in favor? Taking the vote

If you've made it to this point, you're probably aware that LLCs are ridiculously flexible entities. You can generally structure your LLC however you want by placing certain restrictions and allowances in your operating agreement. A common restriction is forcing certain members into a sort of silent partnership by issuing them *nonvoting* membership interests. However, in the event of a termination of the company, most states are quick to override this restriction. Even if the operating agreement specifies that a certain class of membership isn't allowed *any* voting privileges whatsoever, most states still give those members a say in whether or not the LLC can be dissolved.

Unless you and your partners have already unanimously agreed to terminate the company, you need to check your state's laws and see where you stand when it comes to the voting rights. Some states require a unanimous vote, other states require a majority, and other states allow each LLC's members to decide for themselves by placing a special provision in the articles of organization. To make the arduous task of terminating your company a wee bit easier for you, I aggregated all state laws regarding this topic on a wiki page at www.docrun.com/wiki/llc_dissolution.

When you're finally ready to take the vote for dissolution, make sure to hold a proper meeting, keep meeting minutes, and create a formal, written resolution that all members sign. I go into detail on how to do this in Chapter 11. This way, the other members have no recourse if they change their minds afterward, and they can't claim that you did it without their permission.

If your LLC is managed by separate managers, your state laws likely require that the dissolution of the company be approved by a majority of the managers (in addition to approval of the members).

Planning for the future

When you decide that the end is imminent, you and your partners need to sit down and work out a few things. Going into this meeting, all members should have a pretty good idea of what they want to do with their lives after this chapter is closed. Your future plans often play a big role in the negotiations, and things can get pretty sticky when two or more of the members are interested in continuing on in the same industry, whether they intend on starting new companies or going to work for competitors.

When creating — and often, negotiating — a plan for the future, you and your members may want to address the following questions:

- ✔ Are any of the partners going to remain in the same industry? If so, are any of those partners restricted from contacting the defunct company's customers, suppliers, and/or previous staff members?

- ✔ Do any members have the right to use the business's intellectual property? If so, under what conditions? You may have spent a small fortune building your brand, and you may want to protect it.

- ✔ Who will handle the dissolution process? The members need to agree on which of them will spearhead the process of dissolving, as described in the next section.

- ✔ Who is responsible for maintaining the company records so that they can be accessed if any issues arise in the future?

Undergoing the Dissolution Process

With all the steps to dissolve an LLC, it almost seems harder than forming one in the first place! After years in business, your LLC may have a lot of baggage. In the end, dissolving your company is something akin to a divorce — the longer you have been married, the more you have to sort out. In this section, I take you through the dissolution steps so you can file your one or two-page dissolution form with the secretary of state, knowing that you're completely protected from anything coming up in the future and biting you in the ass(ets).

Everyone must go through the following three-step process when dissolving an LLC:

1. **Acknowledge the end is here.**
2. **Wind up the affairs.**
3. **Terminate the company.**

In the following sections, I go over some of the more important steps in greater detail.

Settling your debts: Paying creditors

When your LLC is formally dissolved, your liability protection diminishes substantially. Therefore you need to be as meticulous as possible in dealing with any current and possibly future creditors and claims.

The laws that dictate how an LLC manages its creditors vary from state to state, so you have to research your state's laws on the issue before taking any action. I collected all the state laws (current at the time of publication) regarding the notification of creditors and posted them here: www.docrun. com/wiki/llc_dissolution. Generally, most states recognize the distinction between creditors and claims that the LLC knows about *(known claims)* and those that it doesn't *(unknown claims)*.

Dealing with known claims

Any money that your LLC currently owes and any judgments that have been filed against your LLC generally fall into this category of *known claims*. All known claims must be dealt with properly before the company can be dissolved. You may even be required to include an affidavit to this effect in your articles of dissolution you file with the secretary of state.

Your state laws provide a specific process for you to deal with known claims. This procedure varies widely from state to state, but is probably a variation of this: You must notify the creditor in writing that your company will be dissolving and request that he submit his claim within a certain time frame. Generally, the deadline for a creditor to submit claims can be no less than 120 days.

Include the following information in the notification letter:

- A statement that you intend to dissolve, including an approximate dissolution date, if you have one
- What information you want the creditor to give when they send in the claim (invoice numbers, dates, and so on)

> ✔ The deadline by which claims should be submitted (check state statutes for the minimum time frame you can allow)
>
> ✔ A paragraph stating that any claims received after the deadline won't be honored
>
> ✔ The person and mailing address to which the creditor must send the claim (normally your registered agent's address)

Send all notification letters via certified mail. You need to have receipts proving you sent each letter.

The good news is that if a creditor fails to submit his claim(s) prior to the cut-off date, his claim no longer has merit and will not be honored, even by the courts. This means that when it comes time to distribute the proceeds from liquidating the assets, the money that would have gone to that creditor can instead go to other obligations, or even be distributed to the members!

If you are dissolving and don't want to give your hard-earned cash away to creditors, you may be tempted to transfer the assets into a safe place before dissolving, thereby preventing the claimants access to it. Unfortunately, as simple as this remedy sounds, it's also very illegal. It's called *fraudulent conveyance* of assets and is a very serious offense that the courts will undoubtedly not take lightly.

Accepting or rejecting claims

After you receive a claim, you have the option of either accepting it or rejecting it. If you choose to accept it, keep in mind that everything is negotiable. You can often settle a claim for less than the total amount. Just make sure that after you settle a claim with a creditor, you pay it.

If you choose to reject a claim — usually because you don't think it is valid — you have to use your discretion to consider whether the creditor will seek recourse. If you think the creditor may be a problem, talk to your attorney to prepare for any actions the creditor may take after the company has been dissolved. When you reject a claim, you should write a letter to the creditor stating that you are rejecting it. If possible, and if your attorney thinks it's a good idea, give a brief explanation as to why you are refusing the claim. This way the rejection will hold extra weight if it is ever brought for questioning in a court of law.

Dealing with unknown claims

While your LLC was in business, it likely left some sort of mark on the world. Even if the operating business has been dissolved, your products are still out in the world and/or your services have still made an impact, therefore your LLC is still going to have residual liability. Any claims that could arise in the future from things like negligence or product liability fall under the category of unknown claims.

Because you can't notify these claimants in writing — after all, you don't know who's going to come out of the woodwork later on — the state provides a remedy: Publish a notice of dissolution in a local newspaper. With the advent of the Internet, it's a rather arcane remedy . . . but hey, it works in your favor! After all, who reads those notices, anyway?

Again, you have to check your state's laws for the details, but the publication should be published in the county where your business is located and should contain a description of the LLC and its business and specify that claims against the LLC must be filed within a certain period of time, say, five years, or the claim will be no longer enforceable. The publication should also clearly state the method that claims are to be filed.

If the claim is filed within the set time period, or prior to the statute of limitations, whichever is sooner, the creditors have the right to go after the members personally for the judgment to the extent of the amount of money that was distributed to the member upon the liquidation and termination of the company. Because of these sorts of unknown claims, I encourage you to rethink formally dissolving your company, and instead allow the statute of limitations to run out. (See "Keeping your LLC on life support," earlier in the chapter).

If you are registered in multiple states, publish the notice of dissolution in every state that your LLC conducts business in. This step can be time consuming, so I recommend that you get your multistate registered agent to help you.

The LLC can provide for unknown claims by obtaining insurance and/or setting aside some of its assets instead of distributing that portion of the proceeds to the members. This may be a good idea if your company has substantial liabilities and you just want to sleep better at night.

Giving each his due: Paying members

After the proceeds of the sale of your LLC's assets have gone to settle its debts (as discussed in the preceding section), you can now focus on distributing whatever is left (if anything) to the members. The Internal Revenue Code of the IRS directs a specific order in which the members are to be paid; however, this order can be overwritten in the operating agreement.

Generally, the first to be paid are the members who are owed distributions. For instance, if the LLC recognized a profit but for some reason didn't distribute that money to a member (the cash was needed for something else), then that member is first paid what he is owed. Also, if a member has made a loan to the company, then that member is paid back first.

After the members have been paid what they are owed, the remaining money is used to refund the members for their initial contributions. This may seem strange, but the money that you invested is returned to you before receiving any share of the actual profit. If there isn't enough money to return the member's initial contributions, then whatever profit is distributed is split into relevant proportions. However, this isn't set in stone, and how members are reimbursed upon dissolution can be structured whichever way you like in your LLC's operating agreement, which usually requires the consent of at least a majority of the members. Check your state laws for clarification.

After the initial contributions have been returned to the members, any remaining cash is usually distributed to the members according to their percentage of ownership. If a member owns 30 percent of the company, then she gets 30 percent of the remaining cash. If you and the other members of your LLC want to vary this arrangement, you have to amend your operating agreement or create a formal resolution showing that all members are on board. You also need to check that your plans are in line with your state's laws.

Wrapping up the government affairs

After the creditors have been paid and the members have been reimbursed — and perhaps even given some extra dough — you need to deal with taxes. In most cases, you have federal, state, and local tax forms to file.

To file your final federal return, you just file a normal return (or information statement, depending on how your LLC is taxed) and check the box at the top that indicates that this is a final return. If your state requires you to file a special LLC tax return, then you also need to file a final version of this return as well.

The numerous tax returns and addendums that you're required to file vary widely depending on the type of taxation your LLC has elected, so make sure to clear everything with your accountant before formally dissolving your entity with the state. I discuss tax returns in more detail in Chapter 12.

Only after you are in *good standing* — all filings are up to date and all taxes have been paid — in each state where your LLC transacts business can you start the withdrawal and dissolution process. Your registered agent should be able to provide you with your status in each state and tell you whatever steps you may need to take to get back into the state's good graces. Sadly, if you have failed to file your annual returns in many states, this can be a costly endeavor.

Making it official: Filing the dissolution

After your affairs have been completely wrapped up, you officially dissolve your LLC by filing articles of dissolution with your secretary of state (also referred to as a *cancellation*). When these articles have been formally filed, your company's record doesn't disappear altogether; instead, its public status is shown as *dissolved* or *terminated*.

If your LLC is registered to transact business in multiple states, you need to *withdraw* (often referred to as a "withdrawal" or "cancellation," depending on the state) from all other states before you can *dissolve* your company in your home state. The withdrawal process is similar to the dissolution process and usually requires a nominal fee. Just keep in mind that you don't file articles of dissolution to withdraw from a state. States have separate forms for this purpose. After you've withdrawn from all states where you are foreign filed, you can formally dissolve your LLC in your home state.

If you have a multistate registered agent, you may benefit by letting him handle the entire withdrawal and dissolution process for you. Coordinating with many state agencies at one time can be a big hassle, especially because they all have different time frames for processing the paperwork. Leaving this job to the pros who already have relationships established with states' offices is definitely worth the extra fee.

If you're short on cash and want to do everything yourself, then you'll want to check out the CD that accompanies this book. On it I include the dissolution form(s) for many states.

Generally, articles of dissolution consist of

- ✔ The name of the company
- ✔ A list of the members of the company
- ✔ The reason the company is dissolving
- ✔ The date that you wish the dissolution to become effective
- ✔ Any information regarding unpaid taxes
- ✔ The members' signatures and the date the form was signed

You may also need to include a statement, signed by the managers (or members, if member-managed), that states that the LLC has handled all its liabilities, has made its distributions to the members, has no lawsuits pending, and has made payment arrangements for all judgments (if any).

Some states have it backward and require you to file your dissolution papers before paying your creditors and winding up your affairs. You need to check your state's laws to see whether this is the case. To help you out, I collected all the state laws (current at the time of publication) on the issue. You can view them at www.docrun.com/wiki/llc_dissolution.

Dealing with the tax consequences

The tax consequences can be good and bad for the members when dissolving an LLC. Your accountant can go over the pros and cons with you when you run your dissolution plan by her before dissolving. Remember that if your

LLC isn't profitable, the losses can also be passed on to the members (assuming you elected partnership taxation), which can offset other income and save you and the other members a nice chunk of change come tax time!

If your LLC is canceling debt that the members were personally responsible for (for example, paying off bank loans), then the IRS treats these transactions as income to the members, which can cause some unexpected tax burdens. This is often referred to as *phantom income,* which I discuss in further detail in Chapter 12. You can also read more about this rule under Section 108 of the Internal Revenue Code, which I include at www.myllc.com/dummies.

You have many other tax considerations if your LLC has employees. You must make sure that you're caught up on your federal and state payroll taxes and unemployment insurance. Again, your accountant is the best person to help you.

Following the dissolution checklist

For help with the dissolution process and to make sure that no stone is left unturned, follow this checklist:

❑ Hold a meeting of the members and vote to terminate the LLC. Make sure this decision is reflected in the operating agreement or in a resolution signed by all members.

❑ Liquidate (sell off) all LLC assets for cash.

❑ Make any final federal tax deposits that are due (IRS Form 8109B).

❑ File final quarterly or annual employment tax forms (IRS Form 940).

❑ Issue final wage and withholding info to employees (IRS Form W-2).

❑ Report W-2 information to the IRS (IRS Form W-3).

❑ If necessary, file the final IRS Form 8027: Employer's Annual Information Return of Tip Income and Allocated Tips.

❑ File federal tax returns.

❑ Issue payment information to subcontractors (IRS Form 1099-MISC).

❑ Report information from 1099s issued (IRS Form 1096).

❑ Report business asset sales (IRS Form 8594).

❑ Report sale or exchange of property used in the LLC (IRS Form 4797).

❑ File final employee pension/benefit plan (IRS Form 5500).

❑ If necessary, report the exchange of like-kind property (1031 exchange).

❑ Cancel all state and local business permits.

❑ Cancel all fictitious firm name filings.

❑ Transfer all intellectual property (domain names, patents, state and federal trademarks, and so on).

❑ File the last state tax return.

❑ Pay all current and past due franchise and corporate tax fees.

❑ If necessary, obtain a certificate of good standing with your state tax bureau.

❑ Send notification of dissolution to vendors/creditors.

❑ Publish a notice of dissolution in the local newspaper in each jurisdiction where you have transacted business.

❑ Pay or reject all creditor claims.

❑ Pay all debts that are owed to members, including distributions that were never made.

❑ Distribute any remaining profit to the members according to their ownership percentage.

❑ Pay any back fees that are owed to the secretary of state in each jurisdiction where you transact business.

❑ Withdraw from all states in which you are foreign-filed.

❑ File articles of dissolution with the secretary of state.

❑ If necessary, notify your customers of the dissolution.

Part V

LLCs on Steroids: Advanced Strategies

The 5th Wave   By Rich Tennant

ORICHTENNANT

Art's AUTO PARTS

GIFT BASKETS

Gasket Greetings | Valentine Tune-Up | Spark-Plug Sampler

SALE
1/3 OFF
1/2 OFF

"I don't know, Art. I think you're just ahead of your time."

In this part . . .

What's the point of reading a book on LLCs if the book doesn't address the quality that LLCs are most known and admired for — liability protection? Limited liability companies are commonly used for protecting your business and personal assets. In Chapter 16, I cover the basics, as well as advanced strategies, that pertain to using an LLC for asset protection.

I devote Chapter 17 to LLCs and real estate — one of the most common purposes of LLCs. LLCs and real-estate investments were made for each other, and in this chapter, you find out why. You also get some pretty nifty strategies on how to better protect your investment properties by using multiple entities.

Lastly, in Chapter 18, I go over estate-planning techniques that you can use in conjunction with LLCs. For anyone looking to plan their estate, this chapter is a must-read.

Chapter 16

Using LLCs to Cover Your Assets

- -

In This Chapter

▶ Knowing who's eying your assets

▶ Understanding how LLCs protect your assets

▶ Looking at some easy strategies

- -

*T*his chapter very well may be the most important one you read. After all, why would you want to work so hard to build your future only to have someone else take away all the assets you've accumulated? If you think that because you observe good business practices this chapter doesn't apply to you, think again. Lawsuits are getting out of hand in this society, and no one is exempt. Simply owning something of value puts you at a much higher risk than even the most shady businessman. After all, there's a reason for the term *frivolous lawsuits* — lawsuits don't need to be soundly based or even well intentioned.

A lot of people out there are looking to get something for nothing. Unfortunately, that means that hardworking folks like yourself who have built up sizeable nest eggs are targets. Aside from expensive insurance policies that, when it comes down to it, may or may not have your back, the only thing that you can really do to protect yourself is to plan ahead and structure your assets so they're safe. It's important to do this now because when you're in a lawsuit, it's too late. From here on out, you must take steps to protect your assets every time you save money, start a new venture, register intellectual property, make any big purchases, get married, plan your estate, and so on.

Because LLCs have *dual liability protection,* they have been revolutionary for asset protection, especially personal asset protection. LLCs are such a big piece of the puzzle that often when an attorney sees you're protecting your assets in an LLC, she'll advise her client not to sue you in the first place. No insurance company can match that sort of protection!

In this chapter, I show you how you can protect your assets for the rest of your life by forming an LLC, and you find out how you can safely own high-risk assets (assets that are very likely to be sued) while protecting everything else you have worked for.

Knowing the Dangers: What Can Happen without LLC Protection

More than 50,000 lawsuits are filed in the United States every day, and the numbers keep growing. Litigation has become a way of life for Americans, and we are suffering because of it. Our collective mindset is shifting to that of "get somethin' for nothin'," and our small businesses — the lifeblood of the American dream — can pay a heavy price. Although large corporations have relatively little trouble covering the costs of an everyday lawsuit, the legal fees may be debilitating to a small business.

You may think you're exempt, but chances are, if you haven't been sued yet, it won't be long. Although businesses tend to get sued most often, you're also likely to be sued personally. Actually, statistics say that within your lifetime you'll be sued twice. And that's at today's numbers — can you imagine tomorrow's? As hard as a small business finds paying the $75,000 legal bill on a frivolous lawsuit, individuals usually have more trouble. Even if you win, you may have nothing left! Which is why using LLCs to protect assets and deter lawsuits is just as important for individuals as for businesses.

The birth of the frivolous lawsuit

Back in the old days, business was done on a word and a handshake. If a person didn't live up to his agreement, he would face the shame and disappointment of the people around him. That disgrace was enough to keep people in their place. Money was only associated with hard work, not simple accidents. If you slipped in the supermarket, you would just be embarrassed. That's all. You wouldn't be thinking about all the free cash you could get from the local family business.

Nowadays, things have changed. Lawyers patrol hospitals, and commercials run on TV for class-action lawsuits. If you've ever been in a car accident, however minor, you have most likely received a flood of letters from personal-injury attorneys looking to make a buck.

If you back out of a parking spot too fast and get into a fender bender, there's a good chance that an attorney will be looking to sue you. If you

don't have deep enough pockets, or they can't get to your assets, he will sue the insurance company, the car maker, your Aunt Margaret who purchased the car and loaned it to you to drive — basically, anyone and everyone who has money. Often, it doesn't matter whether you injured someone — all that matters is whether someone with deep pockets can be targeted. Lawyers play on jurors' emotions by making them sympathize with the plaintiff, who may work a dead-end job and can barely support her kids, and chastising you for being one of the lucky few who has struck it rich. The game is called Robin Hood, and it's one you needn't play.

According to the *Wall Street Journal,* frivolous lawsuits cost the average family approximately $3,520 per year. Don't be a statistic. Using LLCs to protect your investments and your assets is normally enough of a deterrent to keep you out of the courtroom in the first place!

Often, attorneys tie in asset protection with estate planning. Although protecting your estate is imperative — making sure that it actually makes it to your kids and not into the hands of some Joe Schmo who tripped over a sprinkler in your front lawn — estate planning doesn't really have much bearing on protecting your assets from litigators. In other words, just because you have an estate plan does *not* mean that your assets are protected while you're alive. See Chapter 18 for more on using an LLC with your estate planning.

Lawyers and creditors come calling

The saddest thing about lawsuits is that even if you win, you lose. A lot of these lawyers who take on frivolous cases work on a *contingency basis.* This means that they don't charge the client unless they win the case. So ultimately you may be the victor, but you are the only one paying legal fees. Legal fees for defending a frivolous case can easily amount to hundreds of thousands of dollars, which can be debilitating for a small business. The only way to protect against having to pay outrageous sums of money for seemingly petty arguments is to stay out of court in the first place. I'm not saying that you should settle a lawsuit brought against you. I'm saying that you should make your assets either unapparent or unattractive to the wolves who are scoping them out. LLCs can do just that.

The people and businesses who loan you money — your creditors — also have their eyes on your hard-earned assets. Had a bad month and didn't keep up with your debt? Your creditors will no doubt be looking at how they can capitalize on their loss — and rightfully so. They lent you the money, and they need to get it back. If you let an angry creditor have his way with your assets, you'll be in a huge hole with no way to climb out. To prevent this, make sure that you have an LLC in place that protects your assets. When you are in control of your assets, attractive settlements are pretty easy to come by.

The IRS stakes a claim

If you aren't at enough risk from lawsuits and creditors, remember that you still have to worry about the IRS. When given the right authority, the IRS can annihilate your financial life more than any individual creditor can. They get free reign. They can show up at your house and load your belongings on a truck, heading for an auction. They can seize your bank accounts and/or even withdraw the funds without any forewarning. Imagine waking up one morning to find that your accounts have been cleaned out, with no hope of getting the money back.

Now, although the IRS is part of the all-powerful government — especially where individuals are concerned — they are subject to a few rules, all of which you can use to your advantage. When the IRS deals with an LLC, they are subject to the same laws and restrictions as most creditors; except with a little bit more knowledge and disclosure. For instance, if the IRS goes after you personally, they can't seize your interests in the LLC and liquidate your company. They can only lay claim to your *economic interest* and must wait for you to pay out. This is unique to the limited liability company and is due to the *charging order protection* I mention throughout this chapter.

In order for charging order protection to be effective, you must have certain provisions in your LLC's operating agreement that provide for it. Don't leave it up to your state's laws to be in your favor when it comes to this. I show you how to draw up an ironclad operating agreement in Chapter 10.

Hiding your assets from the IRS can be difficult because you are most likely reporting them and/or depreciating them on your tax returns. You don't want to hide from the IRS (that's tax evasion), and you shouldn't have to. Your asset protection plan should be so solid that the IRS doesn't have the ability or, better yet, the justification to go after your assets to settle an IRS debt.

Liens can kill your business

Some lawyers are really good, and the worst thing that can happen is to get sued by one of them without having any sort of asset protection plan in place. Imagine you get taken to court over a contract dispute and the attorney talks the judge into placing a *prejudgment lien* on your assets — this means that you can't move, touch, or transfer your assets or even conduct business with them until the lawsuit has been decided.

Say the amount of the lien covers the entire amount due on a ten-year contract, and it's a pretty hefty amount. Your assets don't quite cover it, so your home and your bank account are attached to the lien, and you aren't even able to write checks. If this happens, you may have a hard time buying necessities, such as gas and food, but the worst thing of all is that you most likely won't be able to pay your attorney to defend the case. Eek! You're trapped! If this happens, unless you have some good friends to keep you going in the meantime, you may have to settle immediately and for unfavorable terms.

What about when this happens to your business? What if you're unable to move money, write checks, pay bills, pay your rent, pay on your business loans, or make payroll for two months or longer? Where will your business be then? The damage may be so great that you lose everything you've worked so long to build. Unless you have significant personal savings, a lien can be debilitating. I've never known a business to be able to survive this kind of situation.

Even if you get through the lawsuit without a prejudgment lien, you aren't necessarily in the clear. If you win the lawsuit, you're okay, but what if you lose? Say someone gets a judgment on you for more than you can afford to pay at the moment? Unless you can immediately write a check for a big chunk of change, the judgment creditor can request to have a *judgment lien* placed on your assets. This means that your bank account is completely frozen. Your home, rental property, savings account, mutual funds, CDs, kid's college fund, *everything* is frozen and can be liquidated to pay the lien. Have equity in your house that you want to use to pay for the lawsuit? You can't refinance or sell! Instead, your home will be put on the auction block, right before your eyes. You can't even collect income from your investment properties or invoice your clients in your business. Liens are the worst thing that can happen to you in business. Unless you have an LLC, that is.

You don't have to lose a lawsuit to have a judge impose a lien. Anyone can request a lien on your assets, including creditors or the IRS.

Getting the Best Asset Protection with LLCs

Some asset protection plans just try to hide your assets from prying creditors and potential plaintiffs. Although that should be the first line of defense, it isn't nearly enough. You see, if you do get dragged into court, you probably will be subpoenaed for the information or asked about it while on the stand. In either case, you shouldn't lie. If you do, you'll have a lot more to lose than your assets — you can lose your freedom.

If predators see that you have hordes of cash and real estate sitting in an LLC, there's a good chance they won't go after the assets in the first place. Why? Because LLCs are very tough nuts to crack, and they know this. They also know that if you are smart enough, you can trap them in a situation where they are paying out money for *you!* And because most credit agencies work on commission and attorneys work on a contingency basis, they don't want to waste their time on you if they know they aren't going to get paid.

Fort Knox for your personal assets

As the old adage goes, "You aren't in business until you've been sued." Nowadays, as litigious as this society is, you don't even need to be one of the bad guys to be dragged into court. By simply transacting business with the general public, you open yourself up for myriad potential lawsuits, and no matter how arbitrary the complaint is, the destruction it leaves in its wake can be crippling.

The states know that if every time entrepreneurs started new ventures they were forced to put their livelihoods at stake, many fewer businesses would be started. Therefore, certain entity types are afforded *limited liability,* which protects the owners and managers of the business from being held personally responsible for the debts, obligations, and misdeeds of the business. Out of all the entities, LLCs offer the most comprehensive form of this protection (hence the name *limited liability* company).

An LLC protects you from the liabilities that you inevitably come across during the normal, everyday course of business. Should your business get sued or go bankrupt, your *personal assets* (home, car, investments, and so on) and other businesses (if they are in different LLCs) *cannot* be taken away. Only the assets included in the LLC that got sued are at risk.

Using an LLC to protect your personal assets must be done in advance, not after you've already been sued. Too many victims of frivolous lawsuits have shown up at my office wondering what they can do to get out of them — asking how they can save their home and bank accounts that are about to be taken away. Unfortunately, at that point, it's always too late. If only they had spent some time planning, such as reading this book or working with an advisor, they could have saved everything.

The one exception to the normal protection of LLCs is professional limited liability companies (PLLCs), because personal responsibility is essential to being a licensed professional. I discuss this unique entity type at length in Chapter 2.

By establishing your new business or placing your existing business in an LLC, you sign your company up for the most cost-effective, ironclad insurance policy around. A business insurance policy may still have a role in keeping the business itself from having to pay for its own misdeeds. However, insurance policies are only effective in lawsuits arising from product or service liability and usually don't pay out to unsatisfied creditors if the company can't meet its debt obligations. Also, whereas insurance companies can be wishy-washy about paying out, the LLC is pretty fail-safe.

Here's the clincher: LLCs are so foolproof that most attorneys often avoid the time and cost of suing them in the first place and instead opt to negotiate a settlement. Now, that's protection!

An LLC's veil of liability protection is not infallible. If you don't take certain measures to establish and maintain that your LLC is not simply an extension of yourself (your *alter ego*), then a court can disregard the LLC and allow the plaintiff or creditor access to your personal assets. This is referred to as *piercing the veil* of liability protection. In Chapter 20, I show you ten important steps you can take to protect your veil of limited liability.

Although an LLC shields you from being held personally responsible for minor negligent acts, it will do nothing for egregious criminal acts or willful misconduct. Also, the LLC does offer some protection against certain government creditors, such as the IRS, with one main exception: As a member or manager of an LLC, you can be held *personally* responsible for the failure to pay payroll taxes. Therefore, if you're withholding taxes from your employees' checks and for some reason fail to submit that money to the tax man, you are putting your personal assets at risk.

Taking charge of charging order protection

Many moons ago, when a creditor obtained a judgment against a partner of a partnership, in order to get paid, the creditor could simply take the partner's interest in the business (and, proportionally, all related assets) and liquidate them, often leaving a ravaged business in his wake. Clearly, this wasn't fair to the other, innocent, partner(s) in the partnership who was just going about his business when suddenly everything he had worked for was destroyed!

To remedy these unfair acts, the courts amended the laws so that partners in an LLC, unlike owners of corporations, have another layer of liability protection called *charging order protection.* A member can have two different rights in an LLC: *economic rights,* the right to receive profit allocations and distributions from the company, and *other rights,* which include the right to vote on important matters or be involved in the management of the day-to-day business. Charging order protection grants *only* economic rights to the assignee, unless the operating agreement specifies otherwise. In other words, the creditor has no other choice but to shut his trap and sit back and receive whatever distributions you decide to grant him. You could stop profit distributions altogether and the creditor will have no say in the matter. Read on to find out how this arrangement works.

Seeing how corporations leave you vulnerable

To understand how a lack of charging order protection can leave you vulnerable, consider the example of Josh, who started a business, J.R. Marine Inc., when he was only 23. To get started, he borrowed some money from his grandfather by selling him a 5 percent share in the business. He was smart and good with numbers, and the business grew steadily over the years. Ten years in, J.R. Marine had taken over the market. It was good timing too, because Josh had just met the love of his life and was eager to start a family.

One day, he was in the parking lot of the local supermarket and accidentally backed into a woman's car. The woman was friendly; they traded insurance information, and he helped her on her way. Two months later, Josh was served with a lawsuit. The woman claimed that she was severely injured in the accident and was unable to work and support her four kids (she was a single mom). She was suing Josh for wages and emotional trauma.

Josh found a decent litigation attorney and was forced to slap down $20,000 as a retainer to defend the case. Four months later, the case went to trial. They were counting on a settlement, but the woman wouldn't budge. Josh had to fork over another $40,000 for attorney fees. At trial, Josh couldn't believe how the woman's attorney made him seem like the big, wealthy, bad guy who thinks he can "drive all over" a struggling cocktail waitress/single mother, who can't afford to feed her kids and now will never get ahead in life. The woman, wearing a neck brace, cried on the stand. Her attorney asked the jury to "do the right thing." Of course, their idea of the "right thing" was to award the woman more than $2 million of Josh's money.

At first Josh thought he was okay — after all, he didn't have too much money in his bank account. However, what he did have was his stock of J.R. Marine, Inc., a corporation, which is considered a personal asset. Before long, the business was seized. They liquidated the inventory, the building, everything — just to pay off his judgment. Josh's livelihood and all his assets were destroyed.

Taking the sting out of lawsuits with charging order protection

If J.R. Marine Inc. had been J.R. Marine LLC, Josh may not have been sued in the first place. When the personal-injury lawyer did an asset search to determine whether Josh had any seizable assets, he would have seen that Josh's business (or his share of the business) was held in an LLC. Attorneys know that LLCs are notoriously hard to get to, and the smart ones will avoid them at any cost.

But if the plaintiff's attorney was a rookie and had never been bitten by an LLC before, he may have tried to seize the LLC interests anyway. In that case, he would have hit a brick wall called a charging order. After the attorney obtained the charging order, his client would have received only the distributions that the LLC's manager decided to give to her. The manager — being the smart guy that he is — would have decided that instead of distributing the profits, he would just keep them in the company.

This situation is bad for Josh's judgment-creditor-to-be (the waitress), because while profit distributions are being withheld from her, she's still required to pay taxes on whatever share of the profits are allocated to her. This is called *phantom income,* which I dive into in Chapter 14, and usually isn't a good thing. In this case, however, it works in Josh's favor, allowing him to easily run a trap, forcing the whiny actress (ahem, waitress) to end up with nothing 'cept the pleasure of paying down his tax bill! It's funny how this arrangement can make even the most bull-headed creditors call up, ready to negotiate an extremely favorable settlement! Josh's business would be safe.

Setting up the booby trap

Imagine it — a naïve creditor, instead of receiving his check in the mail, gets a notice that he has to pay thousands of dollars in taxes. (If the other members complain about having to pay taxes and not receiving any income for a while, they can just borrow money from the LLC and sort it out at a later date.)

To ensure the creditor (also known as the unwelcome member) knows what's going on, here's what you do:

1. **Send a letter to the creditor making her aware of the tax debt that she owes and is obligated to pay.**

2. **Send a letter to the IRS letting it know how much the creditor owes.**

   Include in the letter a point stating that you want to keep your LLC current on its tax debt, and you suggest that, should the IRS not receive payment, an audit on the creditor may be required.

3. **Make sure to send a copy of the IRS letter to the creditor.**

I guarantee you that it won't be long before the creditor approaches you with a settlement amount that is definitely in your favor.

Even charging order protection comes with caveats . . .

Charging order protection is pretty straightforward and comprehensive. The laws do vary substantially from state to state, so be sure to review your state's laws on the issue before forming an LLC for asset protection purposes. If you don't like what you see, you can always form your LLC in a state with more favorable laws and then register to transact business in your home state. I have collected a list of state laws addressing charging order protection on a public wiki at www.docrun.com/wiki/charging_order_statutes.

Though making sure you guard your LLC's charging order protection may seem overwhelming or troublesome, it's worth it. By taking a few days to educate yourself and/or by hiring a qualified attorney to draft your LLC's operating agreement, you can establish an LLC that will provide an indomitable safe harbor for your business for years to come. No other entity offers dual-layer liability protection, protecting both your personal assets from the business liabilities and protecting your business from your personal liabilities. No wonder the LLC is by far the most popular entity formed today!

You must be a true partnership

If you are a single-member LLC (that is, an LLC with only one owner), you face a drawback: Substantiating case law from a Colorado bankruptcy case some years back established that single-member LLCs are not afforded charging order protection. The logic is that because there isn't another partner in the partnership who needs protection, charging orders shouldn't be applicable for single-member LLCs. This precedent should make you wary of forming an LLC for any sort of business or asset protection purposes with only one member. In community property states, adding your spouse as a second member doesn't count, so I recommend issuing a small percentage of your LLC to a close friend or relative as a safeguard.

What happens if your charging order protection fails you?

Lawsuits are still open to interpretation; thus, a judge can decide your case however she wants, depending on how she sees the evidence. Although uncommon, if a judge finds good cause, she can circumvent the charging order protections that LLCs offer and instead allow a creditor to foreclose on a member's interest. In this case, you and your partners can do a couple things to minimize the damage:

✔ **You can draft a provision in the operating agreement that requires a debtor member to sell his membership shares back to the LLC or to the other members.** You will have to give a formula that determines the value of those shares, or the buy-back can be done for the exact amount of the member's original investment in the LLC. This way, you and your partners are assured that you won't have to deal with any unscrupulous, transplanted members who don't have your company's best interests in mind.

✔ **If a member is already in the process of having his membership shares seized, creating a huge problem for the other members, the remaining members can vote to dissolve the LLC and purchase all the assets upon liquidation.** They can also choose to form a new LLC without the indebted member and transfer the assets to the new entity. Any monies that would be given to the indebted member instead go to the creditor who holds those membership shares.

Membership cannot be freely transferrable

Charging order protection relies heavily on restricting membership from easy access to the *other rights* — the management and control in the business. Each state has a default statute that dictates how membership interests are to be transferred and which rights are afforded to the new member (which is, on average, pretty restrictive). However, all states also give you some leeway, allowing you to lay out your own set of rules in your LLC's operating agreement. Just be careful that you aren't using this extra rope to hang yourself by allowing the free transference of membership shares and, in the process, inadvertently destroying your own charging order protection. When drafting your operating agreement, keep an eye out for this potential problem. In Chapter 10, I give you some suggestions for special rules and provisions you can add to the operating agreement to doubly uphold charging order protection for your LLC.

Your LLC must be manager-managed

Using charging order protections is a really powerful strategy for LLCs; however, a common mistake is for member-managed LLCs to rely on this strategy. The manager determines the profit and loss allocations, so if the LLC is member-managed, then a creditor stepping in as a member may be able to actually determine these allocations on his own (depending on the operating agreement and the judge's decision). To avoid this risk entirely, do not make your LLC member-managed. Even if all the current members are managing, you should still designate your LLC as manager-managed; then name all the current members as individual managers.

The charging-order trap only works if your LLC has elected some form of pass-through taxation. So, though corporate taxation may appeal to you for other reasons (see Chapter 8), you may want to think twice before electing corporate taxation for your LLC because it doesn't allow taxes to be passed through.

Like standard liability protection, which I go over in the previous section, charging order protection depends on you maintaining a proper separation of your LLC from yourself and keeping your records in an orderly manner. Chapter 11 is devoted to recordkeeping.

Exploring Strategies for Increased Security

Protecting your assets is so simple that I challenge you to come up with one good reason why you shouldn't do it — not later in the year, not in a couple of months, but *now.* Asset protection strategies only work if you do them *before* you ever get into trouble. After you are sued by a creditor (or if the IRS is after you), you can't transfer your assets into an LLC to protect them. Otherwise, you can be found guilty of *fraudulent conveyance of assets,* which means you set up your asset protection plan to defraud your creditors and prevent a specific claim. In this case, not only will you hand over your assets to the creditor on a silver platter, but you also may face some pretty steep fines and maybe even some jail time.

So you need to set up your asset protection plan when you don't have any lawsuits pending or creditors looming. After all, you never know what tomorrow may bring. Set up your defenses early and make sure that as you accumulate more and more in life, no one can take it away.

In the following sections, I go over a few simple strategies that you can use:

- Using a nominee to make it harder for others to find your assets
- Using multiple LLCs to segregate your assets from one another so that if one asset, such as a piece of property, is engaged in a lawsuit, the others are safe from seizure
- Forming two companies in different states to separate your business's assets from the actual operations of the company
- Transferring all your personal assets into a family LLC that keeps financial instruments, such as stocks, bonds, cash, and mutual funds, safe

Electing a nominee to protect yourself with privacy

Privacy is the first line of defense when it comes to asset protection. If people don't think you have anything, then they won't bother suing you in the first place. The saying goes, "Own nothing, control everything," but that doesn't mean that just because people will try to take your things, you shouldn't own and enjoy the finer things in life. You work hard, and you deserve to enjoy the fruits of your labor. And even if the world can see that you have money, you can keep them from knowing where it is. That's where privacy comes in handy.

Some states, like Nevada, protect the privacy of the LLC's members, which means that the members don't need to be publicly listed in the articles of organization or the annual reports your company files with the secretary of state; only the managers have to be listed. If the members don't need to be listed in your state, then you can just hire a nominee to serve as your LLC's manager. A *nominee* is a person who can truthfully state on the stand that she is unrelated and unknown to you. Having a nominee ensures that your name, as owner of the LLC, remains private and off public record. You can hire a nominee from a nominee company, usually for under $500 per year. Keep in mind, though, that this strategy only works if your LLC is manager-managed.

If you're in a state that doesn't allow privacy protection for members, consider forming your LLC in another state, such as Nevada, that does allow it.

After you have a nominee manager in place, unless you broadcast to the world that you own the LLC, people won't even think to look into the issue further. Your name won't be on public record, and unless they ask you directly, creditors will have no way of knowing that you are even associated with the LLC.

If your LLC is currently member-managed, then you need to amend your articles of organization to make it manager-managed. Otherwise, you have to list your members (namely, you) on your annual report — which is public record.

Privacy won't fully protect you. It's not a strategy in and of itself, per se, but more like an add-on. If you solely use a manager-nominee and think that you are completely protected, you'll get the shock of your life when you get dragged into court. The lawyers will ask you about your assets, and at that point, you have two choices: Give up the goods or perjure yourself. Considering that perjury is a pretty serious criminal offense, I would take door No. 1 — and that leads to you revealing the location of your assets so they can be taken.

Setting up multiple LLCs: The more, the merrier!

With an LLC, your business is protected from you, and you are protected from your business — but what protects your business from itself? When your business is sued, the creditors may not be able to go after your personal assets, but they can still go after the business's assets! You can fix that.

Any business or property that operates directly with the public is at risk of being sued. If you have all your business assets in your operating company and you get sued, all your business assets can be seized. The same goes for personal assets. If you own ten properties and put them all in the same LLC, then someone slips and falls on your first property and sues you, everything in that LLC is up for grabs — all ten properties.

The best and easiest way to protect what's yours is by insulating each of your major assets in its own LLC. Creating numerous LLCs can be somewhat costly, but on large assets, it's a small price to pay. For instance, New York taxi cab companies often place each taxi in a separate LLC. That way, if one driver gets into an accident and the cab company gets sued, only that one cab can be seized and liquidated to pay off the claim. That LLC can then be dissolved, and the taxi company is still standing. You don't have to worry about million-dollar judgments now!

Make sure you aren't already facing a lawsuit when setting up a structure like this. If you have been sued and start transferring entities to different LLCs to protect them from the creditor, then you are engaging in *fraudulent conveyance*. Not only will it not hold up in court, but it's also illegal.

A new version of the LLC that's popping up in some states and gaining popularity is called a *series LLC*. A series LLC is like having lots of smaller entities under one umbrella LLC; I go into more detail on this arrangement in Chapter 2. They are great entities and may save you some dough in state fees; however, they are newer entities and don't have much case law to back them up. Therefore, I recommend speaking with your corporate consultant at length before setting one up.

Following the dual-entity strategy

An easy way to protect your business's assets is to simply not keep them in the LLC that operates with the public. You can do this by creating a separate LLC that holds your primary LLC's assets (making this a *dual-entity* strategy). This protection strategy is my favorite by far, and in addition to keeping your assets safe, you also save on some of your state and local taxes. You can set up your LLC this way no matter the tax or management structure.

How dual entities work

Say you decide to start a local pizza delivery company. You live in a high-tax state such as California. In this case, you form your LLC in the state of California (not much you can do about this — if you're located there, you have to register and pay taxes there, no matter what), but you then place all your assets, such as your pizza ovens, cash registers, and so on, into a Nevada LLC that has elected corporate taxation (see Chapter 8 to find out how to make tax elections). For extra protection, make this Nevada LLC a completely private entity by hiring a nominee (see the "Electing a nominee to protect yourself with privacy" section earlier in the chapter).

Your Nevada LLC that owns the assets then leases them to your California LLC (your *operating company* — the one that deals with the customers, vendors, and so on). This way, your company's assets are 100 percent protected. Why? Because they are in a completely separate entity. Your California LLC controls the assets, but doesn't own them, which is the most powerful position to be in. If your company gets into a legal predicament, for example if a customer gets injured, the inquiring attorney will see that your company is completely devoid of assets. Even if he finds out that you own the Nevada LLC, he can't do anything.

If you choose to use this strategy, make sure the lease between the California LLC and the Nevada LLC is legitimate. You need to write up a contract and pay a reasonable leasing fee to the Nevada LLC every month or every quarter. This may seem like a pain in the butt, but believe me, this step ensures that your strategy is legitimate if you ever go to court.

The tax advantages

One of the main reasons you should form your LLC in Nevada is because Nevada has absolutely zero taxes. Zero business taxes, zero franchise taxes, zero personal income taxes — zilch. And you have to elect corporate taxation on that Nevada LLC because if you were to try this plan with an LLC with pass-through taxation, although your assets would still be protected, the profits would flow through to you personally, and you would be required to pay taxes in whatever state you live in.

So, here's how the tax reduction goes. If you have $100,000 in profit at the end of the year that you want to keep in the company, instead of having the profit flow through to you and your partners and paying state and federal taxes on it, you can have it go to your Nevada LLC as a lease payment for the use of the assets. This $100,000 payment is a legitimate tax deduction, so it eliminates the profit in your LLC. After the money is in your Nevada LLC, it's only taxed at the federal corporate tax rate (which is usually just above 15 percent), as opposed to the personal income tax rate (which can be 35 percent or more!). This strategy is great if you want to save money for assets or other business-related items.

Nevada isn't the only state with a favorable tax climate. In Chapter 5 I list other pro-business states and show you how to select the one that works best for you.

Protecting your family with the family LLC

Although a family LLC sounds official, it's really just an LLC like any other — you don't have to do anything different when you file your articles of organization. It just serves a different purpose. The family LLC protects the assets you and your family will need in the future. If you are like the majority of folks, you have a savings or money-market account that is coupled with your checking account. Maybe you have some mutual funds. Regardless, everything is in your name. That's not good. **Remember:** *Own nothing, control everything.* Let your assets grow under the protection of an LLC.

The usual arrangement for a family LLC is that you and your spouse both own 50 percent of the membership. If you can throw a couple of shares to a non–family member for good measure, that helps ensure that you'll get the benefit of charging order protection if you or your spouse are ever personally sued. After the LLC is set up, all savings accounts, insurance policies, brokerage accounts, mutual funds, CDs, bonds, and so on are transferred into the LLC in a nontaxable event.

Do not place your home in your family LLC. Your home can be the source of many lawsuits. For example, if a neighborhood kid sneaks onto your property and accidentally drowns in the pool (God forbid!), all the assets in the LLC can be taken. Instead, form a separate LLC for your home or get a homestead exemption.

Now, if you or your spouse is sued, the assets will be safe in the entity, and the creditor can only obtain a charging order. In this case, you use the booby-trap method that I outlined in the "Taking charge of charging order protection" section earlier in the chapter to resolve the situation.

Also, if your LLC acquires any debts or obligations, you (and your spouse) aren't liable for them. For instance, say you are extended a margin on your brokerage account and you make a few bad trades; unless you personally guaranteed the loan, you aren't responsible for it — although all your other assets in the LLC may be at risk of being liquidated to repay the debt.

What's the deal with trusts?

A couple years ago, trusts were the hot thing for asset protection, especially *spendthrift trusts* where your assets couldn't be touched by creditors. You just named yourself as the beneficiary and you were good to go! Unfortunately, thanks to a *New York Times* article that blasted these trusts for allowing the wealthy to avoid creditors, and Jim Talent, a Missouri senator, spendthrift trusts aren't what they used to be.

Here's the deal: Senator Talent slipped an act into a bankruptcy bill, right before it was about to pass, that allows creditors to get to any assets that were put into trusts within the ten years previous to the claim. Therefore, you can still create a spendthrift trust, but it doesn't do much good if anything happens within the next ten years. Not a good idea!

Unless you're looking to add a trust to your arsenal for estate-planning purposes, I'd just stick with an LLC.

The more that your family LLC is legally separated from you, the safer it is. You can use nominees and find a way to make your personal assets seem like a normal course of business. Create a paper trail that separates you from the assets in the LLC. For instance, if your vehicles are in the LLC, make sure to lease them to your family. This is also a good way to have a legitimate purpose for transferring savings into the LLC on a regular basis. Make sure to document everything — have legitimate contracts and keep your records in order as if it were a real business. The less obvious it is that the LLC only serves to protect your assets, the more certain you can be that the LLC will be rock solid in the courtroom.

Chapter 17

Protecting Real Estate with LLCs

In This Chapter

▶ Using an LLC to protect your real estate holdings

▶ Transferring the title and dealing with mortgage companies

*R*eal estate offers the easiest path to success . . . and the easiest path to lawsuits. If someone is living in a rental property that you own and is injured, he will most likely sue, especially because he doesn't even have to do an asset search to know that you have at least one valuable asset — the property he's living in.

Even if you just own vacant land, you're still open to multitudes of liabilities. No matter how clear the signs are, trespassers will always end up on your property, and if an accident happens, you will most likely be held responsible. Not to mention all the environmental liabilities that can occur with vacant land. Although real estate gives you good cause to be wary, all these potential liabilities aren't the end of the world. With some good advice (starting with this chapter!) and an LLC or two, you'll be fine!

Comparing LLCs to Other Possible Real Estate Entities

LLCs are the best entities for holding real estate, no doubt about it. They offer the most liability protection of any entity type out there (Chapter 2 goes into detail about the other entities), and when you're looking to protect valuable assets, this peace of mind is priceless.

Different people need different strategies. I'm writing in generalities, so keep in mind that you may be one of the few cases where a corporation or S corporation is your best bet. For instance, if you're flipping properties so often that it's considered an operating business, a corporation (more specifically, an S corporation) may not be such a bad thing. I go into more detail on that later in the chapter.

Before you create your plan for protecting your real estate investments, make sure to speak with a qualified professional. You need to get everything right in the beginning because you probably won't find out if you have made a mistake until it's too late to fix it.

In the following sections, I go over some of the alternatives to using LLCs for holding your real estate (or land trusts) and explain why I don't think they're good options. Before you proceed, though, here are some other perks to keep in mind about the benefits of an LLC:

- ✔ LLCs are the most flexible entities around. You decide how the property is managed — you make your own rules. You can put whatever you want in your operating agreement, including what rights, powers, and limitations the company's manager is subject to.

- ✔ LLCs don't require the same intensive formalities that corporations require. For LLCs, minutes, resolutions, and so on are optional (but recommended!). For instance, if you don't do your annual meeting minutes, you won't have to worry about such dire consequences as your entity being disregarded in court and your personal assets seized.

- ✔ Everyone involved in the LLC — all members, managers, and employees — is protected from liability for the actions of the company itself. This is a stark contrast to the limited partnership, in which only the limited partners, and not the general partners, are protected.

- ✔ LLCs offer a second level of liability protection (called *charging order protection*) that protects the business from the creditors of the owners. For instance, if your partner gets sued personally, you don't have to worry that the person suing will be able to seize your partner's interests and liquidate the company in order to get paid.

- ✔ With an LLC, you don't have to distribute profits or losses in proportion to ownership percentages. With a corporation, if you own 10 percent of the company, you are allowed 10 percent of the profits — no less or no more. Not so with an LLC! This freedom can be really beneficial when structuring a real estate investment that's attractive to financiers.

Holding real estate in corporations: The worst choice

When it comes to real estate, corporations are by far an inferior choice. Don't get me wrong — I don't dislike corporations at all. Actually, I recommend them to a lot of clients who are starting up small businesses. But when it comes to real estate, corporations are the worst! Corporations are to real estate what kryptonite is to Superman: They're poisonous. Don't do it.

Regardless of what I say, there's always a skeptic out there who needs more information, so here are some concrete, important things to keep in mind:

✔ Corporations don't offer the same level of liability protection that LLCs do. They only offer one layer instead of two. Your personal assets are protected in the event that the corporation gets sued; but if you get sued personally, your corporation is toast — it's liquidated to pay off your judgment. Considering that real estate is normally pretty expensive and not something you want to lose, this may sway you to use an LLC instead.

✔ Double taxation — the term alone should make you want to run far, far away — is the main reason why you should never use a corporation to hold your real estate assets, especially if they're rental properties. All income that the property receives is first taxed at the corporate tax level and then taxed at the high capital gains tax rate after you take the cash out of the company.

✔ If you think double-taxation of profits isn't bad enough, try to get the property *out* of the corporation after you sell it! Unlike LLCs, you can't move assets into and out of a corporation without triggering a taxable event. And don't think you can avoid it by simply selling the corporation along with the real estate it contains — any knowledgeable buyer will run far away from that deal! After all, who would want to be locked into the same high-tax situation you're currently facing?

Say you purchase an investment property *in an LLC* at $500,000. You're in for a real estate boom (at this point, real estate doesn't have anywhere else to go but up!), and, after holding it for four years, it appreciates to $1 million. At that point, you want to sell it. After all, if you learned anything from this last market cycle, you know that the market can turn on a dime. You sell, which means that you realize a $500,000 profit that passes directly to you, to be reported on your personal tax return. This profit is taxed at a long-term capital gains rate, which currently stands at only 15 percent — a pretty good deal!

Now here's an example of how double taxation can hurt you: Say, instead of the preceding scenario, you choose to hold that same investment property in a corporation. First, the profit from the sale of the property is taxed at the corporate rate, which means your corporation pays about $170,000 in taxes (15 percent on the first $50,000, then 34 to 37 percent on the remaining). Then, after you take the remaining $330,000 personally, you'll need to pay *personal* tax on the dividend income. That means you'll be paying an additional $129,030 in federal taxes (assuming you are in the 39.1 percent tax bracket) for a grand total of $299,030 in taxes. Yikes — and you haven't even figured in state taxes yet!

At this point, clients often bring up the value of the S corporation (a corporation that has elect S corporation tax status with the IRS). After all, S corporations have similar pass-through taxation as the LLC and therefore aren't subject to double taxation, so there is very little difference, right? Although the differences appear slight on the surface, you'll actually still dish out more cash for taxes with an S corporation than an LLC. Say you want to transfer the property out of the S corporation without selling it (maybe to convert it to a personal residence for the added tax benefits, for instance); you'll be taxed. LLCs, on the other hand, allow you to transfer property into and out of the entity without being taxed.

If you decide that S corporation taxation is your best option, you can always form your real estate company as an LLC and elect S corporation taxation. That way, you can switch back to partnership taxation if necessary. I go over electing your LLC's taxation in Chapter 8.

If your business is operating as a corporation and wants to purchase some property for its operations, you should put the property into a separate LLC. Not only will holding the property in an LLC insulate it from any lawsuits filed against the business, but it can also save you from the whole double taxation debacle. The corporation can be a member of that LLC and contribute the money for the purchase (which is a tax-free event). The corporation can then lease the office space, which is a deductible cost. As far as the LLC goes, the rental income it receives from the business is offset by the operating expenses of the property and its depreciation. You only pay taxes on what's left over.

Falling short with land trusts

If you are currently in real estate or have been heavily researching it, then you've probably heard of *land trusts,* which are arrangements in which one person, the *trustee,* agrees to hold the title of the property for the benefit of another person, the *beneficiary.*

Although they seem like a newer thing and are gaining popularity, land trusts have been around for a while — a long while. They go back as far as the Roman Empire. They were heavily used during the Tudor period in England, when owning land came with many more burdens than just kooky tenants, such as serving in the military. Because land trusts offer such a thick veil of privacy, citizens of England hid their land ownership to get out of fighting the war of the week.

Today, land trusts are used to avoid a different type of war — that which exists in the courtroom. Land trusts not only allow you to keep your real estate out of your name, but they also let you avoid probate and have the property immediately pass on to your heirs upon death. Because of a trust's privacy protection, large corporations often use them to secretly buy up large plots of land in little chunks without anyone being the wiser.

However, land trusts don't offer more than superficial protection. Although they can serve at the front lines of your privacy, without the added assurances of an LLC, you and your assets are still vulnerable.

Understanding land trust protection

Like all trusts, land trusts have a trustee and a beneficiary. The *trustee* is the name on public record and can be a person, LLC, corporation, or other type of entity. The *beneficiary* is the land owner and indirectly owns and ultimately controls the trust; however, the beneficiary's name is kept private and can't be accessed by the roving eye of a litigation attorney looking to sue.

Sounds great, right? Well, the downside is that although land trusts sound really official, the reality is that they're no more separate from you than a sole proprietorship. They aren't separate entities with separate identities. What does this mean for you? *Zero* liability protection. If one of your tenants burns himself while messing around with the water heater and decides to sue, you can kiss your house, your car, and the property in your land trust goodbye. Also, if your neighbor sues you personally for running over her cat (accidentally, of course!), your land trust is considered personal property and it and everything in it, including your real estate holdings, can be taken away. Your attorney may have you place your assets in a land trust for estate planning purposes, but considering the lawsuit statistics nowadays, your assets may not even make it past your retirement without being taken away by some snarling personal injury attorney.

Clients often ask me how an attorney can take away the land trust if he doesn't know they own it. Well, that's easy. He gets you on the stand and asks you point blank if you own any real estate properties. You can't lie. After all, you are the land trust's beneficiary, also known as a beneficial *owner*. You have to tell the court that you own the real estate and also disclose any other assets you have, whether in land trusts or not. So as soon as you get dragged into court, the little protection that your land trust offered you disintegrates.

Assessing the pluses and minuses of land trusts

Land trusts do have their benefits. Privacy is a huge issue for some people nowadays, and if you don't want to use a *nominee* (a person who allows you to maintain your privacy as the LLC's owner; see Chapter 16) for your LLC but do want to protect your privacy, then a land trust is perfect for you — as long as it's paired with a good ol' LLC that can deliver on its shortcomings. Put an LLC and land trust together and they make double trouble for anyone who wants to steal your hard-earned assets. The LLC has liability protection, and the land trust offers privacy and estate-planning advantages.

The best way to maximize the benefits of both the land trust and the LLC is to make the LLC the beneficiary of the land trust. That way, if you need to take the stand, you can honestly say that you don't own the land trust, your LLC does. If the plaintiff wants to continue to sue you, great! Then you can just snag him in the awesome LLC booby trap that I outline in Chapter 16. But that will rarely come to pass. The attorney probably won't want to mess with you any further, and he'll most likely drop the case or offer a reasonable settlement.

Holding your real estate in a land trust with an LLC as the beneficiary has some other pluses and minuses. Because it would take pages and pages to go over them all, I just give you a brief overview.

Here are some advantages:

- The property's sales price can be kept off public record. This can help keep property taxes lower than they would be at the property's fair-market value.

- When you sell or gift the property, it can be done quickly and efficiently. You don't have to record a new deed; you just name a new beneficiary.

- You can easily continue the project in the event that a partner dies.

Here are the disadvantages:

- Some states don't allow you to do a tax-free, like-kind (IRS Section 1031) exchange (which I describe at the end of this chapter) with property in a land trust. You must transfer the land out of the trust for the like-kind exchange to be possible. This may involve sizeable fees and taxes and also remove the veil of privacy during the transfer.

- Trustees are often unwilling to take certain necessary actions on your behalf, such as signing mortgage documents. The mortgage may need to be placed in your name, eliminating all privacy protection.

- Land trusts are often created by attorneys who are very specialized in their field. Although that specialization means you'll be in great shape should the viability of your trust ever be questioned, the (often sky-high) attorney fees can also make it cost prohibitive to form one in the first place.

Looking at LLC Property Logistics

Like many things, putting property into a newly formed LLC sounds easier than it actually is. Instead of just figuring it out as you go, you need some real-world advice to guide you. The reality is that mortgage companies are skittish about loaning money to newly formed LLCs. Wouldn't you be? The LLC has no financial history, no assets, no credit score to go by . . . the bank would probably be better off lending money to a 4-year-old. Transferring the title on property you already own can also quickly become a sticky situation. You need to prepare for these situations, among others, when setting up your asset protection plan.

Protecting your home

I know that with all the benefits of LLCs that I lay out in this book, you're going to be tempted to put your personal residence into an LLC. After all, you know that LLCs can protect your assets from creditors and lawsuits — and what more important asset do you have than the home you have built your life in? Well, as tempting as it may be, don't do it.

Owning a home comes with a lot of amazing tax benefits that you lose if you transfer it out of your name. (To better understand all the benefits of home ownership, I recommend you read *Home Buying For Dummies,* by Ray Brown and Eric Tyson.) For instance, when you sell the property, you won't get the tax-free benefit that you currently have. You also won't be able to take advantage of the Universal Exclusion that allows you and your spouse to exclude up to $500,000 in gain.

Most states have laws that automatically protect your home in the event of a lawsuit or lien, so you don't need the protection of an LLC. This kind of law is called a homestead exemption and only applies to your personal residence — investment properties don't count. Check your state laws to see whether this exemption is automatic or whether you have to file a claim to acquire it. With the exception of a possible small filing fee, homestead exemptions are free.

Depending on your state, your homestead exemption may cover all or part of the equity you have in your home. Some states, like Florida, Texas, and Oklahoma, cover 100 percent of your home, but other states only cover it up to a certain dollar amount.

Deciding which state to form in

Unfortunately, in the case of rental properties, you don't gain too many tax benefits by forming the LLC that holds the property in a tax haven, such as Nevada or Wyoming (unless, of course, the property is actually located in Nevada or Wyoming — in that case, good thinking!). Renting a property to someone may be considered "doing business," and therefore you are required to register in that state and also pay *franchise fees* (a common term for state business taxes or fees). For your convenience, I collected on a public wiki all state laws that address what exactly constitutes doing business. You can find them at www.docrun.com/wiki/definition_transacting_business.

Also, for the most part, the lawsuits against your property will be handled in the state where the property is and where the incident occurred. So even if your LLC is domiciled in another state with better laws, you may not be able to take advantage of them.

You may be able to avoid registering to transact business in a particular state if all you're doing is holding vacant land. Holding onto land is not considered conducting business as long as you haven't started the development process and aren't receiving any rent payments. In this case, you can probably form your LLC in Nevada or Wyoming and not have to worry about foreign filing or paying taxes in the state where the property is actually located.

If your rental property is going to make a lot of profit and your state imposes some pretty hefty taxes, then I suggest using the dual-company strategy that I outline in Chapter 12 to reduce the amount of state taxes you pay. In this case, you follow a few steps:

1. **Form an LLC in the state where your property is located, and then transfer the property to that LLC.**

2. **Form a Nevada or Wyoming corporation and set it up as a management company that you pay to manage the property.**

3. **Pay a reasonable percentage of the LLC's profits to the management company.** These profits are now safe and secure in a tax-free entity and are away from the potential creditors and lawsuits of the property.

Getting lenders to loan to an LLC

If you just formed your LLC yesterday, you may have a hard time getting your banker to loan it money. After all, when banks loan money, they have certain criteria that they use to evaluate credit-worthiness. For instance, with businesses, they look at cash flow and assets. With individuals, they look at income and credit scores. Your LLC has none of these. From the bank's perspective, your LLC has no credit history, no track record, and no assets. Therefore, you'll most likely be required to personally guarantee the loan.

You also have to try to persuade the bank to allow the LLC to hold the property's title, the legal document that shows the ownership of the property. Banks obviously don't like this. They want the person guaranteeing the loan to hold the title. However, the bank usually relents in certain instances.

I guarantee you that the worst way to get the bank to let the LLC hold the title is to tell your banker you want to transfer the property into the LLC for "asset protection purposes." Banks hate that phrase. After all, they are some of the biggest creditors around. However, bankers do understand (and respect!) estate planning issues. Let your banker know that you want to transfer the property into the newly formed LLC for estate planning purposes. If your banker isn't savvy enough to understand what you're doing, then shop around. I'm sure you can find a bank that is willing to accommodate you.

After you get a banker on board, you get the loan personally. Then, when the title is in your name, you can transfer it into the LLC's name. The whole process shouldn't take more than a few days to complete. You're still personally guaranteeing the loan; however, the title is in the name of your LLC and protected from creditors.

If you are currently financed and want to transfer the title into your LLC, check with your mortgage company first. Transferring the title may trigger a due-on-sale clause in your contract, which means that you'll have to pay your mortgage back in full. That will force you to refinance. Mortgage companies often enforce this when you have locked in a really low fixed rate and they want you to refinance at a higher rate.

If your mortgage company won't allow you to transfer your property into an LLC, you may want to see if it will allow you to transfer the property into a living trust for estate planning purposes. Most mortgage companies have policies that accommodate this sort of thing. If so, have an attorney form a *living trust* (a trust that a grantor creates while he is still alive), and then make your LLC the trust's beneficiary. With this arrangement you still get the protection that an LLC offers and you won't trigger a due-on-sale clause when you transfer your property.

Transferring the title

After the LLC has been formed and you are in the clear to transfer the title of the property to the LLC, you are ready to prepare a *deed,* a document that transfers the ownership of a property. You can choose from a lot of different types of deeds. Some make the original owner responsible for all current defects or liabilities of the property, whereas others waive the previous owner from all responsibility — the property is just transferred as is. If you're transferring the property from your own name to an LLC that you control, I recommend you use the latter, which is called a *quit-claim deed.* After all, it is a much easier deed to draft. You can download a copy of a sample quit-claim deed at www.myllc.com/dummies.

The deed needs to be in the LLC's name and be signed by you and anyone else who will be authorizing the transfer of the property, and it will most likely have to be notarized. Then you're ready to file! The deed must be filed in the county that the property is located in. As to exactly where you file it, the exact office differs from county to county, so you need to do a little bit of research to get the office's name and address. Start with the county recorder's office or the county clerk's office and go from there. Keep the following advice in mind when considering a title transfer:

- ✔ Your property should be held in the name of your LLC. For instance, your county recorder should show that your parcel number is titled to your LLC. If this isn't recorded properly, your assets may be in jeopardy.

- ✔ Make sure to check with your title insurance company before transferring the title. Some insurance companies cancel coverage if the title has been transferred to a new entity.

✔ Although contributions to an LLC are tax free, some states impose a separate transfer tax. It often depends on why the property is being transferred, and in some circumstances, the tax burden can be pretty hefty. To find out the details in your case, I recommend you do a quick phone consultation with a real estate attorney or tax advisor who specializes in the county that the property is located in.

Setting yourself up for future real estate success

If you've ever played Monopoly as a kid, you know that the best strategy for real estate success is to always trade up. You work on buying four small properties until you have enough to trade up to a hotel. Well, real life isn't much different, and the IRS has helped pave the way for your success by creating what's often referred to as a *1031 exchange* (or *like-kind exchange*). This nifty little tax law allows you to exchange the property you own for a bigger property *tax free*. Doing so allows you to defer any capital gains taxes you may owe on the appreciation of your current property.

In order to qualify for a 1031 exchange, certain rules need to be followed. The total purchase price of the new property must be of equal or greater value than the property you're selling. And all money received from the sold property must be put toward the purchase of the new property.

A 1031 exchange is a common tool that real estate investors use to build their property portfolio over the long term; however, 1031 exchanges *don't apply* to partnerships or corporations. Bummer, right? Well, not so fast. There is a little work-around. If you remember from Chapter 8, single-member LLCs are considered "disregarded entities" by the IRS, which means that the IRS disregards them, as if they were never there to begin with. Therefore, if you wish to leave yourself open to do a 1031 exchange in the future, yet still want to hold your property in an LLC, then consider making it a single-member LLC. Granted, you won't get the guaranteed charging order protection (see Chapter 16) that a regular LLC will provide you, but you can still rest assured that your own personal assets will be safe should one of your tenants slip and fall and decide to take action against your property.

Chapter 18

Estate Planning: Avoiding Death Taxes

Clients often ask me how much they need to be worth to make estate planning necessary. My answer is simple: If you have *anything* of value that you wish to pass on to your children or other heirs (other than your spouse), then you should have an estate plan. And by estate plan, I do not mean simply a *last will and testament* (a will). I mean a structure that avoids the need for *probate,* the costly and time-consuming process in which the courts supervise the distribution of your assets. Even if you don't leave enough behind to be concerned with heavy estate taxes, what little you have will quickly be eaten up by legal fees and court costs. A simple will does not avoid probate, but a simple limited liability company does. I show you how this strategy is enacted later in the chapter.

If you are worth more than $1 million, then you have additional considerations. *Estate taxes* were meant to be taxes on the super-rich, but under recent tax law, it has been proved that individuals with estates from $1 million to $5 million end up paying the most tax. I think this happens because the super-rich are generally more prudent about structuring their estates to take advantage of as many tax breaks as possible. After all, they can afford the best advisors!

In this chapter, I attempt to level the playing field by showing you some tax-saving tricks. I introduce you to estate planning and gift taxes, and then show you how LLCs give you better control over what happens to your assets and taxes after you pass away. I also give you a couple of pointers on using gifts and trusts in your estate-planning strategy.

I can't cover all the facets of estate planning in a single chapter, so here I only cover the federal estate tax structure and the role of LLCs in estate planning. For a more in-depth analysis of the topic, I highly recommend the book *JK Lasser's New Rules for Estate and Tax Planning* (Wiley) by Steward H. Welch

III, Harold Apolinsky, and Craig M. Stephens. I also encourage you to work with a qualified attorney who specializes in estate planning and family law.

Getting Acquainted with Estate Taxes

With the baby-boomer generation getting older, the largest transfer of wealth in the history of mankind is set to occur. Over the next 30 years, trillions of dollars — yes, *trillions* — are expected to be passed on to future generations, and the government is hankering for its share.

In 2001, President Bush passed the largest tax cuts in history, the Tax Reconciliation Relief Act, which lowered the federal estate tax on a year-by-year basis. The tax cuts were only set to last nine years, and boy, did they go out with a bang. In 2010, the federal estate tax rate was set to *zero*. Yup, for an entire year the U.S. got a much-needed breather. Unfortunately, if one were to save his last breath for 2011, his heirs would be faced with a much different picture.

The Tax Act expires on December 31, 2010, about the time this edition goes to print. If Congress doesn't decide on a new prevailing tax rate before that time, then the federal estate tax will revert back to its previous levels — the highest it's ever been. Estates passed on after December 31, 2010, could face upwards of 55 percent or more in taxation! Because this rate hike looks to be the eventuality (and it's the only information I can go on at this point), this is the tax structure I cover in this section. Never before have I more hoped to be wrong.

Understanding the basics

Estate taxes, often called *death taxes* or *inheritance taxes,* can be an astronomical burden to your children or grandchildren if you aren't careful. Upon your death, everything you own is added up — business interests, real estate, securities, insurance, cash, annuities, and so on — and this amounts to what the IRS calls your *gross estate*. Normally, these assets are calculated based on their current fair market value, not what you originally paid for them. After your gross estate is calculated, the IRS allows certain deductions, such as mortgages, certain charitable expenses, and any costs associated with administering the estate. Factoring in these deductions determines your *taxable estate*.

From here, all your *lifetime taxable gifts* (the amount of money you gift in your lifetime that goes over your $13,000 per year tax exclusion, which I discuss in more detail in a bit) are added, and the estate tax is computed. Uncle Sam allows a $1 million allowance to be subtracted from your taxable estate and your children are taxed on the remaining amount. So if your taxable estate is $1,250,000, then your children will owe estate tax on approximately $250,000. The tax rate ranges from 18 percent to 56 percent, depending on how large your estate is. The kids generally have to pay the estate taxes within nine months of the date of their parent's death.

This $1 million allowance — called a *unified exemption* — is the government's way of not imposing tax on the middle class. The problem, however, is that we're talking about a lifetime of assets here, most of which consist of property. Therefore, the total amount of a middle-class individual's estate often exceeds the exemption. A million dollars just ain't what it used to be!

When the exemption amount is exceeded and a sizeable taxable estate remains, the kids can face astronomical tax burdens. Unless the heirs are independently wealthy and have a lot of liquid cash to pay the tax outright, they'll need to sell the property or qualify for a loan to use the equity to cover the tax debt. Therefore, having an estate plan is even more important if you intend to pass on assets that aren't liquid.

Table 18-1 shows what you can expect your heirs to pay, depending on the value of your taxable estate.

Table 18-1	Estate Tax Levels According to Taxable Estate	
Value of Taxable Estate (After $1 Million Exclusion)	**Approximate Federal Estate Tax**	**Approximate Rate of Taxation of Excess**
$0–$10,000	—	18%
$10,001–$20,000	$1,800	20%
$20,001–$40,000	$3,800	22%
$40,001–$60,000	$8,200	24%
$60,001–$80,000	$13,000	26%
$80,001–$100,000	$18,200	28%
$100,001–$150,000	$23,800	30%
$150,001–$250,000	$38,800	32%
$250,001–$500,000	$70,800	34%
$500,001–$750,000	$155,800	37%
$750,001–$1,000,000	$248,300	39%
$1,000,001–$1,250,000	$345,800	41%
$1,250,001–$1,500,000	$448,300	43%
$1,500,001–$2,000,000	$555,800	45%
$2,000,001–$2,500,000	$780,800	49%
$2,500,001–$3,000,000	$1,025,800	53%
$3,000,001+	$1,290,800	55%

If you have just inherited an estate that contains simple assets such as cash, securities, and so on, that when totaled is valued under the $1 million exemption amount, then you don't have to file an estate tax return.

Under the 2001 Tax Relief Act, the exemption amount rose as high as $3.5 million before "sunsetting" and reverting to the pre-Act level of $1 million. Since then, Congress has tossed around the idea of keeping the $3.5 million exemption, but so far this hasn't happened. Before acting on any knowledge in this book, check my Web site at www.myllc.com/dummies to find out if any changes to the estate tax rates and/or exemption amount have been enacted.

Staying married to save some cash: An argument against divorce

If you pass away while you're still married, then the assets you leave to your spouse aren't subject to federal gift or estate taxes, no matter the amount. The U.S. has what is called an *unlimited marital deduction*. This means that whatever you pass on to your spouse is tax free and doesn't eat up any of your $1 million gift tax exemption or your estate tax exemption (which I discuss in further detail in the next section). Then when your spouse subsequently passes away, the estate you left behind will be taxed at that time (unless he or she remarried). So if you leave everything to your spouse, your children will have to pay taxes on (what's left of) your estate after your spouse passes away.

If your estate is valued at over $1 million, don't waste your $1 million exemption, giving your kids a future tax burden by leaving everything to your spouse. Instead, leave the $1 million exempted amount to your children and the remainder to your spouse. If you don't have children, then you may want to place the $1 million in an LLC or a trust with your spouse named as the beneficiary. I show you how to do this later in the chapter. *Note:* This strategy is also a good way to lock up your estate money if, for some unfortunate reason, you don't trust your spouse to not spend away your estate like Paris Hilton in a Gucci store.

Whatever amount you decide to pass on to your spouse must be included in the gross taxable estate, which determines your tax rate. In other words, if you have a $500,000 taxable estate (after the exemption), and you decide to leave your child $250,000 and your spouse $250,000, then your child will still be in the $500,000 tax bracket and pay a 37 percent tax (rather than 34 percent at the $250,000 tax bracket).

The unlimited marital deduction only applies to spouses who are U.S. citizens. If your spouse is not a U.S. citizen, then you should contact an experienced estate planning attorney about forming a *qualified domestic trust* (a QTOD) in order to take advantage of the unlimited marital deduction.

Skipping a generation can kill your estate

Way back in the day, the wealthiest families in America avoided paying estate taxes by using a loophole that allowed them to use repetitive life estates to freely pass assets on to their grandchildren. In 1976, Congress decided to close this loophole once and for all and created what we now know as the *generation-skipping transfer tax,* or GST tax for short.

This means that if you decide to transfer assets directly to your grandchildren, they'll be taxed as though your assets had gone to your child and then to your grandchildren. In short, the estate will be taxed twice. And unless you passed away in 2010 when this tax was temporarily suspended, your grandchildren most likely won't receive much more than the $1 million exclusion amount.

Starting January 1, 2011, the GST tax rate is set to be 55 percent. So, if your estate is worth $10 million, putting it in one of the higher tax brackets with an estate tax rate also at 55 percent, then your grandchildren will owe approximately $7.2 million in taxes. Here's how the math breaks down:

Total estate	$10,000,000
Minus exclusion	−$1,000,000
Subtotal	$9,000,000
55% estate tax	−$4,950,000
Subtotal	$4,050,000
55% GST tax	−$2,227,500
Subtotal	$1,822,500
Plus exclusion	+$1,000,000
Total amount inherited	$2,822,500

The GST tax only applies when you pass money to your grandchildren while their parents (your children) are still alive, thereby skipping a generation. It also applies if you pass money to someone (other than your own child) who is more than 37.5 years younger than you.

The GST tax applies to gifts also, so if you're planning on giving pieces of your estate to your grandchildren or to someone who is significantly younger than you while you are still alive, then you need to sit down with a qualified estate planning attorney to discuss your specific needs.

How LLCs Help with Estate Planning

You need to take control of your estate and not leave everything up to the fickle whims of the U.S. government. LLCs are the perfect tool for this. With LLCs, you maintain control of your assets as the ownership passes on to your heirs, all the while avoiding probate. You can also rest assured that your estate is protected from the roving eye of creditors and lawyers who want to take it away.

LLCs avoid probate

One of the greatest benefits of using LLCs in your estate planning is that your heirs can avoid *probate,* a lengthy and expensive process in which the court settles your estate for you. The court resolves all creditors' claims and distributes your assets according to law or your will (if you recorded one). Probate is managed by someone whom you designate in your will, called an *executor.*

When you set up your estate in an LLC, the LLC just transfers to your heirs, and all is said and done. This way, you can rest assured that your loved ones won't be hit with any huge legal fees that eat up your estate before it's ever delivered into their hands.

If you are married and live in one of the ten community property states (Alaska, Arizona, California, Idaho, Louisiana, Nevada, New Mexico, Texas, Washington, and Wisconsin), all your assets will be transferred to your spouse upon your death. In this case, no probate is necessary. If your spouse is no longer alive, then your estate will enter into probate. ***Note:*** If you don't live in one of these community property states, then your estate will enter probate whether your spouse is alive or not. The best way to avoid probate is to create an LLC.

LLCs provide asset protection

The biggest problem with most estate planning techniques is that as you collect assets to pass on to your heirs, the assets aren't protected from creditors and lawsuits. As long as you're alive, without this protection you are a walking target. Although most trusts help ease the transfer of your assets upon your death, they don't protect your assets from lawsuits or creditors like an LLC does.

When you work with your attorney on an asset protection plan, he will probably suggest using a trust. (A *trust* is a legal situation where someone gives financial control over certain assets to a person or institution for the benefit of another person, the *beneficiary*.) In my opinion, LLCs, when structured properly, offer the same benefits as trusts when it comes to avoiding probate and reallocating income, but many attorneys prefer trusts because they're the standard, age-old way of estate planning and LLCs are newer entities. If you find this to be the case with your attorney, I recommend that you have an open and frank discussion with him to find out why he doesn't wish to incorporate an LLC into your estate plan. If he doesn't have a concrete reason — such as the value of your estate is so small that it wouldn't warrant the extra fees — then I suggest getting a second opinion.

When you meet with your attorney to draw up an estate plan, make sure that he incorporates asset protection strategies into the plan. Preventing your assets from being taxed after your death is pointless if your assets get seized by a creditor before your heirs can even get to them. An LLC, if used by itself, should do the trick because it offers many layers of asset protection. You can read Chapter 16 for more information on how to protect your assets using an LLC.

If you want to use a special trust in your estate planning endeavors, then I recommend that you use an LLC (or two or three) to hold the assets, thereby protecting them from creditors. The trust will be the majority owner of the LLC to help avoid probate and reduce estate taxes. This way, if you get sued personally, the creditor can break the trust, but the assets (which are inside the LLC) are saved by the LLC's *charging order protection,* which I describe in detail in Chapter 16.

LLCs give you control

An LLC is *incredibly* flexible. You can structure the ownership, the management, and the profit allocations pretty much however you want by specifying these things in the company's *operating agreement.* Your LLC can be either member-managed, where all partners share equal control of the day-to-day affairs, or manager-managed, where one or a few people (who don't make up 100 percent of the partners) make managerial decisions. LLCs for estate planning are commonly manager-managed LLCs, with the parents taking the role of managing partners and the kids as nonmanaging *(silent)* partners. This way, as the LLC is transferred to the children, the parents can still manage the assets even if they no longer own the LLC.

Basically anything goes, as long as you set up the LLC's operating agreement accordingly. You can have different types *(classes)* of membership, where some partners have more voting rights than the others. You can restrict the transfer of ownership so your kids can't sell their shares in the family estate. You can describe in detail how you want the succession to go after you pass away, and you can name the successor managers. You can even distribute the profits and losses however you want, meaning they don't have to be distributed according to the membership percentages.

Giving Away Your Estate (Not to the IRS)

You can plan your estate in so many ways. You can't possibly discover them all in a book, so sitting down and working with a qualified attorney is really important. But before you do, you should understand some important concepts that will no doubt be brought up in the meeting.

Deciphering the gift tax

You can minimize estate taxes for your heirs by gifting assets to them while you are still alive. The IRS allows you to gift up to $13,000 per year per recipient, tax free (this amount is adjusted each year for inflation). If you have a spouse, you and your spouse can collectively gift $26,000 per year to each person, tax free (this is known as a *joint gift*).

If your estate is valued at more than the $1 million exclusion limit, this gift allowance lets you give away a portion of your assets over time without any tax liability. If you gift more than $13,000 in any one year to a particular recipient, then any overage amount will be added to your taxable estate upon your death.

Unfortunately, if you're gifting assets and/or cash to your heirs, this does not equate to a year-end tax deduction for you. Gifts to heirs aren't deductible expenses — unless your heirs are 501(c)(3) charities, that is.

As long as you're alive, you can gift as much as you want to educational institutions (such as for your grandchild's college education) or to pay for medical services. This money doesn't count toward your $13,000 allowance. However, the money must go directly to the educational institution or the medical service provider, not to the person using those services. Keep in mind that if you're paying for college expenses, the money for room, board, books, entertainment, and so on doesn't count — only tuition. The money you spend on these ancillary items goes toward the $13,000 tax-free allowance.

Giving away small pieces of big assets

For larger estates, gifting away your assets while you're alive is a common strategy. LLCs are especially good for this because only a limited amount of your assets can be gifted each year (see the preceding section). When it comes to large noncash assets, such as real estate, gifting shares of an LLC is the best way to slowly transfer ownership to your heirs. You simply place the property in an LLC and each year transfer some of the underlying shares. Unless you own a house worth less than $13,000, you should consider this strategy for most large gifts.

This scenario also applies to stock ownership. Say that you have a family business that's set up as a corporation. Being the smart cookie that you are, you place the stock (the ownership) of that corporation into a manager-managed LLC (that you and your spouse both own). You then follow the same strategy as outlined above: You slowly gift membership shares of that LLC to your heirs over time. As a bonus, this arrangement also offers you a bulletproof layer of asset protection!

Devaluing an LLC for more free gifts

After your assets are successfully placed in an LLC, you can take the gifting strategy described in the previous sections a step further by devaluing the membership shares of an LLC to allow you to gift more than $13,000 in assets each year, tax free. The IRS allows you to lower the fair-market value of the membership shares by making them less appealing; namely by not allowing the members to engage in the management of the business.

To devalue membership shares in an LLC, your LLC must be manager managed, with the managers being different than the owners (you and your spouse). If you don't have a family member who can serve as manager of the LLC, then you and your spouse can form a corporation to take over the job.

Here's how this strategy works: Say your business was worth $4 million at the time it was transferred into the LLC. At that point, 100 percent of the membership shares of that LLC equaled $4 million. However, if you restrict the control of those membership shares, the IRS allows you to knock 30 percent off that valuation, which makes those membership shares only worth $2.8 million.

If you have 100,000 shares, that means each share is worth $28. If you have five kids who will equally own and manage the family business after your death, then you and your spouse can transfer approximately 928 shares ($26,000 ÷ $28 = 928) to each of your children every year, tax free. This means that every year, you can lower the value of your estate by $130,000 ($26,000 × 5 = $130,000) by slowly gifting it away under the radar.

Without factoring in inflation or appreciation (which is where a really good accountant will be needed!), after 14 years, your estate will be under the $1 million exclusion amount, and after your death, your heirs won't be required to pay any estate taxes. If you simply gifted shares without devaluing them, it would take you over 23 years to reach the same result!

Your entire goal here is to continually reduce the value of your taxable estates. And no, that doesn't mean you want the real estate market to tank and your properties to go down in value! It means you want to slowly "leak" the assets to your children in such a way that it doesn't raise any red flags with the IRS. Currently, the best way to do this is to make sure that you and your spouse give a maximum combined amount of $26,000 to each recipient every year.

You have to be careful when you transfer noncash assets that have appreciated a lot. When your heirs decide to sell the assets after you pass away, they will have to pay long-term capital gains tax on the appreciation from the date you purchased the asset. If you have ever gone through a real estate boom, you can understand what sort of money I'm talking about here. LLCs have the unique ability to force a step-up in the tax basis by having certain provisions in their buy-sell agreements. If you have a lot of heavily appreciated assets, then you should definitely work with an accountant to assist you in minimizing your heirs' capital gains tax burdens.

Part VI
The Part of Tens

The 5th Wave — By Rich Tennant

"Cooked books? Let me just say you could serve this profit and loss statement with a fruity Zinfandel and not be out of place."

In this part . . .

Now for the easy stuff. The Part of Tens was made for readers who want to cram worlds of information into a few paragraphs. Here, you get need-to-know information on such topics as keeping your LLC intact and impenetrable from outside forces and avoiding common mistakes that some LLC owners make.

Chapter 19

Ten Good Reasons to Form an LLC

In This Chapter

▶ Protecting your real estate, intellectual property, and personal assets with an LLC

▶ Raising capital with your LLC

▶ Running your business as an LLC

*B*y now, you've probably figured out that I think LLCs are the best entity structure around. And for good reason! LLCs are flexible — you can use them for practically any purpose — and they offer more benefits than any other entity type. They have a favorable pass-through tax status, and with the dual liability protection that LLCs offer, corporations and limited partnerships can't compare.

What I love most about LLCs is that they are completely customizable. You can draft pretty much whatever rules you want in the operating agreement, even overriding many state laws with a simple paragraph. You can also choose whatever tax structure you want; LLCs can elect to be taxed like corporations or even S corporations.

Customizing Your Small Business

LLCs are great for small businesses because they're adaptable to all situations. No matter if you have 100 silent investors or are a 2-person small-business operation, the LLC is so flexible that you can pretty much write the operating agreement to suit your needs; you can make your own rules and tailor your entity to suit the intricacies of your business. With corporations, you're limited to the stiff corporate formalities and weighty, unbending infrastructure of shareholders, directors, and officers.

If you're operating as a sole proprietorship (which is how most small businesses are structured) or general partnership, I have no doubt that reading this book will convince you to form an LLC today, because a sole proprietorship or general partnership is the most dangerous form of doing business. It offers zero protection against creditors and lawsuits, and therefore leaves your personal assets on the table for pretty much anyone to grab. Not to mention that you can't raise capital as either of these entities (and you won't go very far when it comes to impressing people).

By combining a lot of the advantages of corporations and S corporations with their own special attributes, LLCs have become exceptionally attractive to small-business owners. They take the liability protection that corporations offer and build on it, adding an extra layer of protection by way of the charging order (see Chapter 16). They also offer a pass-through tax structure similar to S corporation tax status, but with *zero restrictions* — any person or entity can be an owner, and your LLC can have an unlimited number of members.

Protecting Real Estate Assets

LLCs are a perfect entity for real estate holdings — you just can't beat 'em! One advantage is that LLCs have dual liability protection that shields your investments from the frivolous lawsuits filed against people like you every day. So if you rear-end someone in a parking lot and he sues you personally, he can't seize and liquidate your investment properties to settle the claim if they're held by an LLC. If that's not reason enough to convince you to form an LLC, turn to Chapter 17, where I dig deep to show you all the powerful ways a limited liability company can protect your real estate holdings.

Another huge benefit of the LLC over other entity types is its taxation. With an LLC, you can easily transfer your property in and out of the entity because taxes aren't imposed on contributions or withdrawals of the assets as long as no money changes hands. Individual members can also take a deduction for recourse loans that they've guaranteed for the company, so members of LLCs that contain real estate can deduct mortgages that they personally guarantee. Of course, before taking any big steps, speak with your accountant about any hidden tax issues that could crop up. After all, with over 2,500 pages of federal tax code, you never know what you could be walking into.

LLCs are so great at holding real estate that I advise my clients to form one LLC per property that they own. This way, each property is isolated from the others, so if one property is sued, the others are safe from being seized. With the ease of operation and the limited recordkeeping requirements, having multiple LLCs isn't as difficult as you may think.

Shielding Intellectual Property

I am a firm believer in keeping your intellectual property as far away from your operating business as possible. After all, what's more valuable than your brand, which you have worked so hard to build? Or the patents that you centered your business around? You need to protect those things with your life. Or with an LLC. Your choice.

Unless you have a bunch of important patents, placing all your intellectual property in separate LLCs is overkill. You don't want your intellectual property to operate with the public; that's your operating company's job. So how do you link your intellectual property in your LLC to your operating company? Have the LLC that holds your intellectual property *lease* the patents, trademarks, or copyrights to the operating company for its use. You need to sign paperwork and transfer money to make the arrangement official. After all, if it doesn't look legit, then there's no point in doing it in the first place.

Because of charging order protection (see Chapter 16), it doesn't really matter too much who owns the LLC with the intellectual property. But investors generally like to have the intellectual property of the business owned by the business; therefore, the best setup is for the operating company to own the LLC. To be on the safe side, a common holding company can be the owner of both the operating company *and* the LLC with the intellectual property. The investors invest in the holding company, and voilà! They're happy, and the property is safe from lawsuits and angry creditors.

Only LLCs, not corporations, should be used for holding intellectual property. If that corporation is owned by the operating business and the business is sued, then the corporation that owns the intellectual property is considered an asset of the business and subject to liquidation. Corporations don't have the same charging order protections that LLCs have. Therefore, if the intellectual property is in a corporation and the owner (in this case, the business) gets sued, then the intellectual property is toast. If the intellectual property is held in an LLC owned by the operating company, then this wouldn't be a concern.

Raising Seed Capital for Your Business

LLCs are quickly becoming the entity of choice for raising *seed* or *angel capital* — early-stage investments under $500,000 or so. Whereas venture capital firms — I'm talking the big, big guys here — generally prefer to invest in corporations because they're most familiar with them, smaller investors *love* limited liability companies. The partnership pass-through taxation allows investors to deduct their contributions, and if your little start-up doesn't turn a profit, they can use the losses to offset other income they may have. That is a *huge* benefit to investors. If the business fails, they may not get their investment back, but they'll still get a nice little deduction.

S corporations also offer pass-through taxation; however, the result and implications aren't even close to being the same thing. Investors can only deduct their contributions if the business fails, not immediately, and S corporations restrict who can and can't be an investor. Why limit yourself like that? LLCs can have as many investors as you choose — even hundreds of thousands! — and anyone can invest. One investor can be a small business in Wichita, and another can be a newly formed hedge fund based out of London.

According to the laws of most states, the entire membership interests in an LLC cannot be transferred freely; only the economic interests can. This rule is the foundation for the second layer of liability protection — charging order protection — that LLCs offer. And although this restriction is a good thing, it can be a bit intimidating to old-school investors who are comfortable with the ownership structure of the corporation.

If you're dealing with a wary investor, you can simply remind her that an LLC is incredibly flexible. Assuming the laws of your state allow it (most do!), you can structure your membership shares to be freely transferable like a corporation. Granted, if you're ever sued personally and are relying on the charging order protection, you may face some problems in the court of law. In the worst case scenario, you are treated as a corporation. In the best case, you get the best of both worlds: freely transferrable ownership interests, favorable pass-through partnership taxation, and dual-liability protection.

With an LLC, you can have different *classes* of membership. For instance, you can give members with Class A membership full voting rights and members with Class B membership absolutely no voting rights. Or, you can allow one class of membership shares to be transferable, whereas the other class of membership shares can't be transferred without the approval of all members.

Planning Your Estate

Don't overlook the value of LLCs when you plan your estate. Although it's a simple entity in comparison to some of the über-complex trusts that your attorney may recommend, LLCs provide powerful asset protection. They protect you not only from creditors, but also from probate lawyers and court costs. LLCs allow you to avoid probate altogether, which means that your estate isn't subject to the nickel-and-diming (I wish they were just nickels and dimes!) that probate attorneys siphon from estates as the courts divvy up assets.

With LLCs, you can structure the management however you like, which is useful if you're minimizing your estate (to reduce or eliminate estate taxes) while you're alive by gifting a little bit of your assets to your heirs each year. An LLC is especially convenient for gifting property; you can just gift some membership interests. It beats having to retitle the property each year! You can be the LLC's sole manager as the membership interests are transferred so that you control the property but your heirs get to own it. Set it up so that when you die, your heirs become managers, or name someone else a temporary manager until they reach a certain age.

Additionally, you can structure your LLC in such a way that the membership interests are at a reduced value than the underlying assets you are gifting. This ability means that you can squeeze more into the $13,000 that the IRS will let you gift tax-free each year: You put all your assets into an LLC and then devalue the membership of that LLC (usually by taking away voting and management rights) before slowly gifting it away to your children. If estate planning is your goal and you want more information, turn to Chapter 18, which is devoted to the topic.

LLCs are commonly used with different types of trusts. Trusts are great and definitely have their place in most estate plans, but don't make the mistake of only looking at your estate from a tax-saving perspective. Trusts don't offer anything in the way of liability protection, and if you don't use an LLC to cover your assets, you may not have anything to leave your heirs. Those assets may go to the dogs (er . . . I mean creditors)!

Doing a Short-Term Project

LLCs were made for short-term projects. When these entities were first introduced, they were never supposed to live forever like corporations do. That's why when you create your articles of organization, you state a specific dissolution date or *term,* the number of years that the LLC is to be in existence. Although most states allow you to extend the LLC beyond this term with a simple vote of the members, this scheduled termination of the company is convenient for short-term projects such as real-estate development and film financing.

Because of their pass-through taxation for investors, LLCs are especially great for flash-in-the-pan projects that you have to raise money for. Investors can come together, pool their money, do the project, make the profit, and then dissolve the company. Upon dissolution, all assets are liquidated, the creditors are paid off, and the remaining profit gets split among the members according to their ownership percentages. All profits flow through to the investors' personal tax returns, so they don't have to worry about double taxation. (Chapter 15 covers the dissolution process in more detail.)

In the meantime, you and the other members can allocate the company's profits and losses however you like. This makes investors happy, because you can get more creative with the structure of the investment. For instance, a common agreement for LLCs raising financing for a film is that, upon making revenue, the investor gets her money back plus 10 percent. Afterward, all members share profits according to their percentage of interests in the company. Limited liability companies are the only entities that offer this sort of flexibility.

When you're doing a short-term project, all members must be on the same page from the get-go. When bringing on members, make sure that you give plenty of information about the project, be sure to specify that the LLC will be liquidated and dissolved, and tell them when the dissolution is expected to take place. Remember that you need a vote of the members to dissolve on a date other than the dissolution date specified in the articles of organization. If all members aren't in agreement, you'll have trouble moving forward with your plans.

Segregating Assets

Segregating assets is vital in business. By segregating your business assets into individual LLCs, you put them out of the reach of your company's creditors or people who may want to sue you.

A lot of people incorrectly think that if they're operating as a corporation or LLC, then their assets are safe, but that's not necessarily true. If you're like most entrepreneurs, your business is your biggest asset. If you lose the ability to operate, you're doomed. Your business may be protected from your personal creditors, and you may be protected from your business's creditors; however, what protects your business from its own creditors? If your LLC gets sued, everything inside of it can be seized and liquidated. Even worse, the courts can put a lien on your company and then do an *asset freeze*. This means that you have zero access to your operating capital — you can't write checks or receive funds from clients. How stable will your business be after three months or more of an asset freeze?

The best way to fully protect your assets (and your access to them) is to make sure that you keep no assets in the operating company. Instead, the company uses leased assets. Now, this doesn't mean that you have to start looking for furniture- and equipment-leasing companies. In this case, *you* own the leasing companies (or your business does). Each asset is put into a different LLC, and each LLC then leases these assets back to the operating company. When the operating company is sued, it has no assets with which to settle the claim. So, in the worst-case scenario, you dissolve the operating company and form a new one. You again set up the lease agreements with the various LLCs, and you're back in business!

The leasing aspect of this strategy is essential. Not only does it create an official transaction record, which will be of vital importance if the strategy is ever questioned in court, but it also serves to pull extra profit out of your operating LLC; don't forget that cash is also an asset that may be seized in the event of a lawsuit! In Chapter 16, I go into all the many ways an LLC can be used to protect your assets.

Minimizing Your Tax Burden

When you first go into business, chances are your company won't be profitable right away. It takes time for businesses to build up, and in the first year or two, you probably will incur thousands of dollars in losses. A lot of entrepreneurs, eager to soften the financial blow of the start-up phase, decide to form an LLC. With an LLC, the losses of the business flow through to the members so they can use them as deductions for other income.

Say, for instance, your business incurs $40,000 in losses in the first year of operation. If you and your partner each own 50 percent of the company, then you each get a $20,000 business deduction on your personal tax returns. That could save each of you as much as $6,000 in federal income taxes alone! When starting up your company, every dollar counts, and an extra 6,000 of them can really help get things off the ground!

Changing the Profit Distributions

An LLC's profits can be paid out disproportionately to the actual ownership percentages, so you and your partners can set up the company so that you receive all the profits and losses — even if you only own 10 percent of the company. Why would you want to do that? Well, a common reason for changing the distribution is to provide an extra incentive for investors. For instance, if an investor invests all the capital, he gets 50 percent of the company. However, the profit distributions can be varied so that he receives 100 percent of the profits until his investment has been paid back (plus 10 percent in some cases). Then the profit distributions return to normal, and the profit is split equitably among members.

The only contingency that the IRS places on altering the distributions is that it delivers *substantial economic effect*. This term is just a fancy way of saying that you need to have a decent reason for changing up the distributions. For instance, in the preceding example, you have proven substantial economic effect; that is, you aren't just varying the distributions for no other reason than to egregiously avoid taxes.

You may get yourself into some serious tax trouble if you act without taking the whole picture into account, so if you want to vary your profit distributions, work with an accountant who knows all the applicable IRS rules. Tax law is complicated, so save yourself a major headache and hire someone who spends all day learning and understanding it instead of trying to grasp it all yourself.

Protecting Your Personal Assets

Although I don't recommend putting your home into an LLC (you may lose some of the great tax breaks that you get as an individual), I do recommend putting all your other personal assets into one. When you spend your entire life saving for retirement, your children's education, or even that second home you've long dreamed about, nothing can be more crippling than losing it all in a lawsuit.

Rockefeller once advised people to own nothing and control everything. You don't have to be a billionaire to walk in his footsteps. If you're like most people, you currently hold all your personal assets in your own name. Your savings account is in your name; your cars are in your name; your mutual funds, stocks, and bonds are probably in your name. This means that the reverse of Rockefeller's advice is true — you own everything, yet control nothing, and it can all be taken away from you.

If you really want to follow in the footsteps of financial giants, start by forming an LLC. Better yet, form a series of LLCs. Then contribute all your personal assets to LLCs and make sure that they're isolated from each other. That way, if a creditor arises with one of your assets — for instance, you get a margin call that you can't quite pay for — then all your other assets are safe. LLCs are cheap; I form them for clients every day for under $200. You don't have to be a millionaire to take advantage of strategies of the rich. After all, whatever your net worth is at the moment, you worked hard for it and deserve to keep it safe.

Chapter 20

Ten Ways to Keep Your Liability Protection Intact

....

In This Chapter

▶ Avoiding the single-member LLC

▶ Creating an ironclad operating agreement

▶ Watching where the money goes (and comes from)

....

*N*ow, really — what is the point of a limited liability company without the *limited liability* part? Without limited liability, it's no better than an expensive sole proprietorship — no special protections, no special tax treatment, no ability to issue shares of ownership. If you don't take the simple steps necessary to keep your limited liability intact, you may as well save yourself the filing fee for creating your LLC and kiss all your hard-earned personal assets goodbye.

Before you even think about taking extra steps to protect your limited liability, I ask you to do one thing: Be on your best behavior. No, I don't mean keep your elbows off of the dinner table and say "please" and "thank you." I mean don't lie, cheat, or steal in the name of your LLC. Wrongful misconduct on the part of a member is the easiest way for your LLC's veil of limited liability to be pierced. Don't think that your company will protect you from purposeful fraud that you initiated.

File the LLC Properly

The first step to obtaining liability protection is filing the LLC. I know this may sound elementary, and I don't want to insult your intelligence, but plenty of extremely intelligent and accomplished individuals have failed at this first step and ended up being taken to the cleaners. Often, entrepreneurs get too busy and distracted — after all, they're running a business! They start their LLC paperwork and then leave it to sit on their desk, collecting dust, until they find the time to get around to filing it.

If this description makes you think I've been spying on you (I haven't), you should hire a formation company to file the documents for you. You don't even have to sign anything (except maybe the check to pay the company!). In most states, your formation company can list itself as the *organizer* — a temporary position that only lasts until the paperwork is filed — and handle the entire process for you. The fee is normally small, and it can get this incredibly important task off your plate.

Regardless of the situation, just file the paperwork. Use the forms I provide on the accompanying CD, do some research at your secretary of state's office or Web site, fill out the forms, and then drop them in the mailbox. You still have to take care of other filings and the creation of your LLC's operating agreement, but at least the company is formally created — your first step to protecting your assets.

Situations often come up when you want to file quickly and don't have any time for preparation. Keep in mind that when you rush to file, you run the risk of getting your articles of organization rejected because you didn't do the requisite research and preparation. Also, you need to take time to attach to your articles certain provisions, such as the limited liability provision and the charging order provision, that are never included on the state's generic articles of organization.

Find a Partner

Because LLCs were initially created as partnerships, some states don't even allow you to form an LLC with only one member (called a *single-member LLC*). Even if your state does allow the formation of a single-member LLC, don't blur the line between what is *allowed* and what is *advised.* You may be able to form and operate a single-member LLC without a problem; however, when a business lawsuit comes up, the court will probably treat you differently than a standard, multimember LLC — including, but not limited to, not giving you the benefit of charging order protection.

Charging order protection is a form of liability protection unique to LLCs that keeps your business safe in the event you get sued personally. If you're like most entrepreneurs, your business *is* your biggest personal asset, so this may be more important to you than the standard form of liability protection!

Charging order protection has a caveat — it exists to protect partners in the business from each other, not just to protect you. After all, if you get sued and your portion of the business is seized, it wouldn't be fair for your business partner to suddenly be in business with some stranger, would it? Charging order protection was created to remedy this injustice, and as you can see, it only applies to true *partnerships*. And the one thing you need to be a partnership is a partner!

If you are totally intent on having a single-member LLC, then you must do what you can to look like a legitimate LLC by following all the tips in this chapter — especially the ones about having meeting minutes and a good, solid operating agreement. Also, because single-member LLCs are considered *disregarded* entities by the IRS (as the name implies, this isn't really a good thing for liability protection purposes), I also recommend that you elect corporation or S corporation tax treatment (I show you how to do this in Chapter 8) and altogether treat your LLC as if it were a corporation. You may have to jump through more hoops, but the peace of mind will be worth it.

If you aren't dead set on having a single-member LLC and are willing to fight for your liability protection, then I recommend that you do one of two things:

- ✔ Find a friend or family member (not a spouse, for IRS purposes) whom you can trust, and issue them a small membership percentage. Make sure that you have a contract or that your operating agreement states that they can't sell or transfer the shares without your approval. Because they aren't contributing anything to the business, you can also state in your operating agreement that they get a very small percentage of the distributions or none at all.

- ✔ Form a corporation that you can control — preferably in a tax-free state — and make the corporation your second partner in the business. Remember — LLCs can have anyone as a member, and they don't even need to live in the same country.

 If you want a surefire way to completely protect your LLC, you should have more than ten members. Historically, any organization that has more than ten members has never had its veil of liability pierced or its second layer of liability protection, charging order protection, tossed aside by the courts. If you have more than ten members, you should be in the clear, no matter what.

Create an Operating Agreement

If you have read any part of this book, you may have a pretty good idea of how absolutely necessary I feel an operating agreement is. Your operating agreement is the backbone of your company. It creates the infrastructure and acts as an operations manual that you and your partners will fall back on time and time again to sort out the gray areas and disputes that occur during the normal course of business.

Until your operating agreement has been created, your LLC isn't complete. Creating a comprehensive, foolproof operating agreement for your LLC should be at the top of your list. LLCs are very flexible entities, and in your operating agreement you can tailor your LLC to whatever your needs are. Whether you are raising capital, building a business, or flipping a real estate property, you'll want different people in your organization to have different authority, and you can create a system for keeping everyone on the same page.

State law gives LLCs an incredible amount of leeway for how they want to be structured and operated, but without an operating agreement in place that includes all specifications, your LLC must abide by the states' default laws. These laws are often strict, unfavorable, and offer very little liability protection, so you *must* create an operating agreement for your LLC before engaging in any sort of business. You can create a customized agreement in less than a day, so don't put it off because you think it will be difficult! In Chapter 10, I give you specific instructions on how to put it together.

Capitalize the Company

The phrase *capitalizing the company* means investing money into your business. A business without even a little bit of money is not really a business at all. Although I don't like to trot out the old adage that it takes money to make money, usually you need to invest *some* capital to get your business going. I'm not the only one who thinks this — the courts agree.

The easiest way for a court to determine whether your company is a separate operating business or an *alter ego* (a company put into place to protect its owners) is to see whether you've invested in the business. After all, most small businesses aren't profitable when they're starting out, so the courts can't base their decision on profitability. They must go on capitalization.

What if you're starting small and didn't invest any money into your LLC? In this case, if you can show substantial cash flow and prove that your business is operational and deals regularly with the public, then you have a good chance of being in the clear. Make sure that you have a reason for your shares being issued to you, though — whether for services rendered, assets given, or money invested. You must put this information in your meeting minutes.

File Your Annual Reports

You must file your annual reports on time each year. If you fail to file your reports, you will go out of good standing with the secretary of state. If you remain out of good standing for a certain amount of time (usually a year), then your LLC will automatically be revoked, and you'll have no limited liability protection at all. Not good!

The filings are often one page and require minimal information, such as the names and addresses of the LLC's members and/or managers, the name and address of the LLC's registered agent, and the corporate office address (Chapter 11 has more details about annual reports). You either file your annual report with the same state office where you filed your articles of organization — in most states, the secretary of state's office — or you file it with the state tax board. Your registered agent should be able to provide you with the exact information regarding what's required to maintain your LLC in a particular state.

Hold Member Meetings Regularly

Although annual meetings are only required for corporations and not LLCs, you must hold them anyway. If a creditor of your LLC wants to attach your personal assets to a lawsuit, he will attempt to prove one of two things:

- ✔ Your LLC is an alter ego.
- ✔ Your LLC appears to be a sole proprietorship or general partnership and should be treated as one.

The best defense against these attacks is to choose to go through the same formalities that corporations are required to go through. I know what you're thinking: You're a busy entrepreneur! How on earth can you find the time to draft meeting minutes and issue financial reports? Rest assured, though, that it won't take as much time as you think. Not only does all this documentation help designate the LLC as a separate entity (so as to disprove it's an alter ego), but it helps prevent your LLC from being classified as a sole proprietorship or general partnership, which have no meeting minutes at all.

You must have annual meetings, but you also must hold a meeting whenever a major action affecting the company is to take place. When you have meetings, you must keep a record of the minutes and resolutions that take place. Meeting *minutes* are a record that shows that important business decisions, the *resolutions,* were made after a successful vote of the members. These records prove that an action of the company wasn't done by some rogue member deciding things himself (in which case, there is a good chance he would be personally liable), but instead by the company as a whole, with all in agreement as to the course of action.

The IRS also will look to your meeting minutes to show that certain loans and financial transactions were approved. In other words, if you issue yourself a loan from the company, the IRS may not allow it if they don't see it properly documented in the company's minutes or some other form of agreement. Minutes are also good to have when requesting a ruling from the IRS, such as a 1031 exchange (for all you real estate investors out there), or defending a position to the IRS or Department of Revenue during an audit of the company or an LLC member. The minutes must also authorize any major salaries and pension contributions, contractual relationships, and the election of managers.

In addition to all these things, minutes also can be used to explain any mistakes or company oversights that may have occurred. You can state what actions the company has taken to remedy the situation. Minutes are also good for justifying why the company took a certain questionable action. A good example of this is changing the income distributions to be disproportionate to the ownership percentages. (For more information about meetings, minutes, and resolutions, see Chapter 11.)

Obtain Your Licenses and Permits

Before opening your doors and taking orders from customers, you need to make sure that you are squared away in the eyes of the law. Many state governments, in an effort to control various industries and obtain tax revenue, require businesses to have licenses and permits. Most companies only need to file a state and city (or county) business license. However, if you're in a heavily regulated industry, such as gambling, alcohol, or land development, you need to inquire as to which licenses and permits you must obtain. (Chapter 11 covers licenses and permits in more detail.)

When you aren't in good standing with the state and its departments, you won't be held in high favor with the judge when he is determining whether to disqualify your LLC. If you find the ordeal of determining which business licenses you must file a bit overwhelming, contact your registered agent — he can either file the business licenses for you or point you in the right direction.

While you are applying for your state licenses and permits, don't forget the ever important federal *employer identification number* (also called an EIN or a tax ID number). Think of it as a Social Security number for your LLC. Until you obtain an EIN, you can't do much business. Applying for a number online at the IRS's Web site (www.irs.gov) is incredibly easy.

Avoid Commingling Funds and Assets

Commingling, treating your business's funds and assets as your own, is the easiest, surest way to kill your LLC's liability protection. If you're treating your company account as your personal piggy bank, stop. Not only do you run the risk of being heavily penalized by the IRS, but you also risk losing your personal assets and your livelihood, should you ever get dragged into court.

If the courts decide you're treating your money and the company's money as one in the same, they can easily disregard your entity as not being separate from you — hence the term *alter ego.*

Here are a few examples of commingling:

- ✔ You use the funds from your business for obvious personal expenses without documentation. For example, unless you're a model or newscaster, getting your teeth bleached is *not* a business expense. Good try!

- ✔ Your personal bank account and your business bank account are one and the same.

- ✔ You endorse checks to yourself that are made payable to your business.

- ✔ You often move money between your business and personal accounts without keeping proper records.

The best way to stay on the safe side and avoid mixing your personal and business funds is by taking the following advice:

- ✔ Make sure your LLC has its own bank account.

- ✔ Do not use the business money to pay for personal items. (If you absolutely must, then carefully document it on the company's books.)

- ✔ Do not pay yourself indiscriminately. The money you receive from the company should be in the form of a loan, salary, or distributions.

Sign Your Documents Correctly

In the course of business, you'll have to sign stuff. Lots of stuff. When you are doing business under your company name, you must sign as a representative of the company. What this means is that under your signature, you must include your title and the company name, or you must write "on behalf of" and your company name. Also, always use "LLC" or "Limited Liability Company" after your company name.

Your signature should look something like this:

Your signature

Your name

Your title (Manager or Member)

Your LLC Name, LLC

The *Wurzburg Bros. Inc versus James Coleman* case shows how important it is for you to sign documents correctly. In this case, James Coleman was the president of Coleman American Moving Services, Inc. When the company was behind on its payments to Wurzburg Bros. Inc., one of its vendors, Mr. Coleman decided to send over a promissory note to ease the tensions. When

Mr. Coleman signed the promissory note, he failed to put his title and the company name under his signature. Wurzburg Bros. successfully sued James Coleman, the person, and succeeded in taking his personal assets to cover the judgment.

Give Up Some Control

To avoid having the courts determine that your company is an alter ego, you need to limit your control somewhat. If you have 100 percent control over all the company's decisions and finances, and your company does something wrong, the courts could easily hold you personally liable. This is one of the most common ways to lose your liability protection. It happens most often in civil cases; however, the IRS has been known to force members to pay for their company's debts on this basis.

If you're a very small company, you often won't have too many people making decisions on a day-to-day basis, because you're likely controlled by a small handful of people. In this case, just make sure that you don't have any nonfunctioning managers — that is, anyone who can be viewed as your puppet — and that you observe all formalities.

Part VII
Appendixes

The 5th Wave   By Rich Tennant

STRENGTHS/WEAKNESSES

✓ NEVER CONVICTED
✓ INVESTIGATION STALLED
✓ AUDITS INCONCLUSIVE

"Okay, let's hear some weaknesses."

In this part . . .

Appendix A provides helpful state-by-state LLC information. The laws do vary from state to state, and you need to know who to contact for help. Appendix B explains how to use the book's accompanying CD.

Appendix A

LLC Formation Information by State

· ·

*H*ere I provide you with the contact information for the secretary of state's office (or equivalent), LLC statutes, and filing information for all 50 states (plus the District of Columbia). Use this information as a starting point for organizing your LLC and then seek competent advice from a corporate consultant or an attorney. I also suggest that you do your own research so you're aware of any changes that your state may have made after this book was published.

Alabama

Business formation department: Alabama Secretary of State Corporations Division	Physical location: RSA Union Building, Suite 770 100 North Union Street Montgomery, AL 36103	Mailing address: P.O. Box 5616 Montgomery, AL 36103
Phone: 334-242-5324	Fax: 334-240-3138	Web site: www.sos.state.al.us
Report due: Annually	When? 15th day of the fourth month after fiscal year end; online filing only	

Filing your articles: Articles must be filed with the probate judge in the county where the LLC's registered office is located. The filing fee is $40 (made payable to the secretary of state) plus any additional local fees that the county or probate judge may impose (normally $40). Single-member LLCs are allowed.

State franchise tax/annual report fee: LLCs operating in Alabama are subject to a privilege tax, which ranges from 0.25 to 1.75 percent, with a maximum of $15,000.

Alaska

Business formation department: Alaska Department of Community and Economic Development Corporations Section	Physical location: 333 W. Willoughby Avenue, Ninth floor Juneau, AK 99801	Mailing address: P.O. Box 110806 Juneau, AK 99811
Phone: 907-465-2550		**Fax:** 907-465-2974
Web site: www.commerce.state.ak.us/occ/home.htm		**E-mail:** corporations@commerce.state.ak.us
Report due: Biennially		**When?** Initial: 6 months from filing; January 2 thereafter

Filing your articles: Articles must contain a statement that says the LLC is being filed under the provisions of the Alaska Limited Liability Company Act. The filing fee is $250 — a $150 filing fee plus the $100 biennial license fee. Single-member LLCs are allowed.

State franchise tax/annual report fee: The only tax imposed is the biennial fee of $100.

Arizona

Business formation department: Arizona Corporation Commission Corporations Division	Phoenix office: 1300 W. Washington, First floor Phoenix, AZ 85007	Tucson office: 400 W. Congress, Suite 221 Tucson, AZ 85701
Phone: Phoenix: 602-542-3026 or 800-345-5819; Tucson: 520-628-6560		**Fax:** Phoenix: 602-542-4100; Tucson: 520-628-6614
Web site: www.cc.state.az.us		**E-mail:** filings.corp@azcc.gov
Report due: None due		

Filing your articles: Articles must be filed with the Arizona Corporation Commission with a filing fee of $50. Within 60 days after the filing date, the LLC must publish a public notice with the company's address and resident agent information in a publication of general circulation in the county that the LLC is headquartered. After the publication, the LLC must file an affidavit of publication with the Arizona Corporation Commission. Single-member LLCs are allowed.

State franchise tax/annual report fee: LLCs are not required to file periodic reports. LLCs with pass-through taxation are not taxed.

Arkansas

Business formation department: Corporations Division Arkansas Secretary of State	Address: 1401 West Capitol, Suite 250 Little Rock, AR 72201

Phone: 888-233-0325 or 501-682-1010

Web site: www.sos.arkansas.gov/corp_ ucc_business.html	E-mail: corporations @sos.arkansas.gov

Report due: Annually	When? May 1

Filing your articles: The filing fee is $50, and you can file online. When filing your articles, you must also file a Franchise Tax Registration Form. Single-member LLCs are allowed.

State franchise tax/annual report fee: You must file an LLC Franchise Tax Report with the secretary of state by June 1 of each year.

California

Business formation department: LLC Unit California Secretary of State	Physical location: 1500 11th Street, Third floor Sacramento, CA 95814	Mailing address: P.O. Box 944228 Sacramento, CA 94244

Phone: 916-657-5448	Web site: www.ss.ca.gov

Report due: Biennially	When? Last day of anniversary month

Filing your articles: File an original plus two copies of the articles with a $70 filing fee. Single-member LLCs are allowed.

State franchise tax/annual report fee: California imposes an $800 franchise tax on all newly formed LLCs. This tax is due the 15th day of the fourth month after your LLC is formed (all California entities have to pay this tax, foreign and domestic).

Colorado

Business formation department: Business Division Colorado Secretary of State	Address: 1700 Broadway, Suite 200 Denver, CO 80290

Phone: 303-894-2200, extension 2	Fax: 303-869-4864

(continued)

Colorado *(continued)*

Web site: www.sos.state.co.us/ pubs/business

E-mail: sos.business@ sos.state.co.us

Report due: Annually

When? Last day of second month following anniversary month

Filing your articles: The filing fee for the articles of organization is $50. The statutory life span of an LLC is 30 years, unless specified otherwise. Single-member LLCs are allowed.

State franchise tax/annual report fee: The fee is $25, unless you file online, in which case the fee is $10.

Connecticut

Business formation department: Commercial Recording Division Secretary of State	**Physical location:** 30 Trinity Street Hartford, CT 06106	**Mailing address:** P.O. Box 150470 Hartford, CT 06115
Phone: 860-509-6001		**Fax:** 860-509-6068
Web site: www.ct.gov/sots		**E-mail:** crd@po. state.ct.us

Report due: Annually   **When?** Last day of anniversary month

Filing your articles: The filing fee is $120. Single-member LLCs are allowed.

State franchise tax/annual report fee: The fee for the annual report is $10.

Delaware

Business formation department: Division of Corporations Delaware Secretary of State	**Physical location:** John G. Townsend Building 401 Federal Street, Suite 4 Dover, DE 19901	**Mailing address:** PO Box 898 Dover, DE 19903
Phone: 302-739-3073, extension 2		**Fax:** 302-739-3812 or 302-739-3813
Web site: www.corp.delaware.gov		**E-mail:** DOSDOC_WEB@state. de.us

Report due: None due

Filing your articles: The filing fee is $90, with a $50 additional fee for each certified copy of the certificate of formation. Single-member LLCs are allowed.

State franchise tax/annual report fee: All Delaware LLCs are required to pay a minimum franchise tax of $250, which is due June 1 of each year.

District of Columbia

Business formation department:	Physical location:	Mailing address:
Department of Consumer and Regulatory Affairs	1100 4th Street SW Washington, DC 20024	P.O. Box 92300 Washington, DC 20090

Phone: 202-442-4400	Web site: brc.dc.gov

Report due: Biennially	When? June 16 starting in second year

Filing your articles: The filing fee is $150. You must submit a Written Consent to Act as Registered Agent Form that is signed by your registered agent with your articles. You must also file a Form F500, a Combined Business Tax Registration Application, along with the articles.

State franchise tax/annual report fee: If your franchise tax liability potentially exceeds $1,000, then you must file a Declaration of Estimated Franchise Tax Voucher. If your company's gross receipts exceed $12,000 for the year, then you must file an Unincorporated Business Franchise Tax Return.

Florida

Business formation department:	Physical location:	Mailing address:
Division of Corporations Florida Department of State	Clifton Building 2661 Executive Center Circle Tallahassee, FL 32301	Corporate Filings P.O. Box 6327 Tallahassee, FL 32314

Phone: 850-245-6051	Web site: www.sunbiz.org/corp_dir.html	E-mail: corphelp@dos.state.fl.us

Report due: Annually	When? May 1

Filing your articles: The filing fee is $125, plus a $30 fee for a certified copy. A Designation of Resident Agent Form must accompany the articles of organization with an additional fee of $25. Single-member LLCs are allowed.

State franchise tax/annual report fee: A Uniform Business Report (UBR) must be filed before May 1 of each year. The fee for this annual filing is $50. If your LLC is classified as a partnership for tax purposes, then it must also file Form F-1065, an information statement, with the Florida tax board.

Georgia

Business formation department: Corporations Division Secretary of State	Address: 315 West Tower 2 Martin Luther King Jr. Drive Atlanta, GA 30334	
Phone: 404-656-2817	**Fax:** 404-657-2248	**Web site:** `sos.georgia.gov/corporations`
Report due: Annually	**When?** Initial: within 30 days of formation; April 1 thereafter	
Filing your articles: The filing fee is $100. Single-member LLCs are allowed.		
State franchise tax/annual report fee: All LLCs that are taxed as partnerships and are operating in Georgia must file Form 700, a Georgia Partnership Income Tax Return.		

Hawaii

Business formation department: Business Registration Division Department of Commerce and Consumer Affairs	Physical location: King Kalakaua Building 335 Merchant Street, Room 201 Honolulu, HI 96813	Mailing address: P.O. Box 40 Honolulu, HI 96810
Phone: 808-586-2744	**Fax:** 808-586-2733	
Web site: `www.hawaii.gov/dcca/areas/breg`	**E-mail:** `breg@dcca.hawaii.gov`	
Report due: Annually	**When?** Last day of anniversary quarter	
Filing your articles: The filing fee is $50. Single-member LLCs are allowed.		
State franchise tax/annual report fee: LLCs must pay Hawaii's general excise tax at a 0.4 to 0.5 percent tax rate.		

Idaho

Business formation department: Business Entities Idaho Secretary of State	Physical location: 700 E. Jefferson, Room E205 Boise, ID 83720	Mailing address: P.O. Box 83720 Boise, ID 83720
Phone: 208-334-2301	**Fax:** 208-334-2080	

Web site: www.sos.idaho.gov/corp/corindex.htm

E-mail: sosinfo@sos.idaho.gov

Report due: Annually   **When?** Last day of anniversary month

Filing your articles: The filing fee is $100. Single-member LLCs are allowed.

State franchise tax/annual report fee: The fee for the annual report is $30. The state tax rate on LLCs is 7.6 percent (the minimum payment is $20). If you have elected partnership taxation, you must also file Form 65, an Idaho Partnership Return of Income.

Illinois

Business formation department: Business Services Secretary of State	**Springfield office:** Michael J. Howlett Building 501 S. Second Street, Room 328 Springfield, IL 62756	**Chicago office:** 69 W. Washington, Suite 1240 Chicago, IL 60602

Phone: Springfield: 217-782-6961; Chicago 312-793-3380

Web site: www.cyberdriveillinois.com

Report due: Annually   **When?** Last day of month previous to anniversary month

Filing your articles: The filing fee is $500. Single-member LLCs are allowed.

State franchise tax/annual report fee: The filing fee for the annual report is $200. LLCs are imposed a replacement tax of 1.5 percent of your company's net income. You must file a Form IL-1065, an Illinois Partnership Replacement Return.

Indiana

Business formation department: Business Services Division Indiana Secretary of State	**Address:** 302 W. Washington Street, Room E018 Indianapolis, IN 46204

Phone: 317-232-6576   **Web site:** www.in.gov/sos/business   **E-mail:** INbiz@sos.IN.gov

Report due: Annually   **When?** Last day of anniversary month

Filing your articles: The filing fee is $90. Single-member LLCs are allowed.

State business/franchise tax: The annual filing fee for the Indiana Business Entity Report is $30. You must also file Form IT-65 if you have elected partnership taxation. This is an information return, and no fee is due.

Iowa

Business formation department: Business Services Division Iowa Secretary of State	Address: First Floor, Lucas Building 321 E. 12th Street Des Moines, IA 50319
Phone: 515-281-5204	**Fax:** 515-242-5953
Web site: www.sos.state.ia.us/ business/index.html	**E-mail:** sos@sos.state. ia.us
Report due: Annually	**When?** March 31
Filing your articles: The filing fee is $50. Single-member LLCs are allowed.	
State franchise tax/annual report fee: LLCs that have elected partnership taxation must file Form IA-1065, an Iowa Partnership Return. This is a purely informational return, and no tax is due.	

Kansas

Business formation department: Business Services Department Secretary of State	Address: Memorial Hall, First Floor 120 SW 10th Avenue Topeka, KS 66612	
Phone: 785-296-4564	**Web site:** www.kssos.org/ business/business.html	**E-mail:** corp@ kssos.org
Report due: Annually	**When?** 15th day of the fourth month after fiscal year end	
Filing your articles: The filing fee is $165. Single-member LLCs are allowed.		
State franchise tax/annual report fee: With your annual report, you must submit your franchise tax, which is $1 for every $1,000 of net capital accounts that are located in Kansas (with the minimum being $20).		

Kentucky

Business formation department: Business Services Kentucky Secretary of State	Physical location: 700 Capital Avenue, Suite 154 Frankfort, KY 40601	Mailing address: P.O. Box 718 Frankfort, KY 40602
Phone: 502-564-3490	**Web site:** www.sos.ky.gov/ business	

Report due: Annually   **When?** June 30 starting in second year

Filing your articles: The filing fee is $40. Single-member LLCs are allowed.

State franchise tax/annual report fee: The filing fee for the annual report is $15.

Louisiana

Business formation department:	Physical location:	Mailing address:
Corporations Section	Twelve United Plaza	P.O. Box 94125
Secretary of State	8585 Archives Avenue	Baton Rouge, LA 70804
	Baton Rouge, LA 70809	

Phone: 225-925-4704   **Fax:** 225-925-4726

Web site: www.sos.louisiana.gov/tabid/813/Default.aspx   **E-mail:** commercial@sos.louisiana.gov

Report due: Annually   **When?** Anniversary date

Filing your articles: The filing fee is $75. Single-member LLCs are allowed.

State franchise tax/annual report fee: The filing fee for the annual report is $10. If your LLC has elected partnership taxation, then you must file Form IT-565, a Partnership Return of Income. No tax will be assessed; this is for informational purposes only.

Maine

Business formation department:	Address:
Julie Flynn, Deputy Secretary of State	148 State House Station
Bureau of Corporations, Elections	Augusta, ME 04333
& Commissions	

Phone: 207-626-8400   **Fax:** 207-287-8598

Web site: www.maine.gov/sos/cec/corp/index.html   **E-mail:** cec.corporations@maine.gov

Report due: Annually   **When?** June 1; online filing only

Filing your articles: The filing fee is $175. Single-member LLCs are allowed.

State franchise tax/annual report fee: A $60 filing fee is due with each annual report. If you have elected partnership taxation, you must file Form 1065ME. No tax will be assessed; this is for informational purposes only.

Maryland

Business formation department: Corporate Charter Division Department of Assessments and Taxation	**Address:** 301 W. Preston Street, 8th floor Baltimore, MD 21201
Phone: 888-246-5941	**Fax:** 410-333-7097
Web site: www.dat.state.md.us/ sdatweb/charter.html	**E-mail:** charterhelp@ dat.state.md.us
Report due: Annually **When?** April 15	

Filing your articles: The filing fee is $100. Single-member LLCs are allowed.

State franchise tax/annual report fee: You must file an annual Form 1, Personal Property Report, by April 15 of each year, along with the filing fee of $300. If you have elected partnership taxation, you must file Form 510, Pass-Through Entity Income Tax Return. This is an informational return, and no tax is due unless you have members who don't live in Maryland. In this case, the LLC must pay a 4.8 percent personal income tax.

Massachusetts

Business formation department: Corporations Division Secretary of the Commonwealth	**Address:** State House, Room 116 Boston, MA 02133
Phone: 617-727-9640	**Fax:** 617-742-4538
Web site: www.sec.state.ma.us/cor/ coridx.htm	**E-mail:** corpinfo@sec. state.ma.us
Report due: Annually **When?** Anniversary date	

Filing your articles: The filing fee is $500. Single-member LLCs are *not* allowed.

State franchise tax/annual report fee: The filing fee for the annual report is $500. If you have elected partnership taxation, you are required to file Form 3, a partnership return, each year. This form is for informational purposes only; no tax is required.

Michigan

Business formation department: Corporation Division Department of Labor and Economic Growth	**Physical location:** 2501 Woodlake Circle, First floor Okemos, MI 48864	**Mailing address:** P.O. Box 30054 Lansing, MI 48909
Phone: 517-241-6470		**Fax:** 517-241-0538
Web site: www.michigan.gov/cis		**E-mail:** corpsmail@ michigan.gov
Report due: Annually	**When?** February 15	

Filing your articles: The filing fee is $50. Single-member LLCs are allowed.

State franchise tax/annual report fee: You must file an annual statement by February 15 each year. If you were formed after September 30, then you can skip a year. Unless you have elected corporate taxation and your gross receipts are more than $250,000 each year, then you are not required to pay business tax.

Minnesota

Business formation department: Business Services Secretary of State	**Address:** Retirement Systems of Minnesota Building 60 Empire Drive, Suite 100 Saint Paul, MN 55103	
Phone: 877-551-6767 or 651-296-2803	**Web site:** www.sos. state.mn.us	**E-mail:** business. services@state.mn.us
Report due: Annually	**When?** December 31 starting in year after filing	

Filing your articles: The filing fee is $160. Single-member LLCs are allowed.

State franchise tax/annual report fee: If you have elected partnership taxation, then you must file Form M3, a partnership return. You may be imposed franchise fees up to $5,000.

Mississippi

Business formation department: Business Services Secretary of State	**Physical location:** 700 North Street Jackson, MS 39202	**Mailing address:** P.O. Box 136 Jackson, MS 39205

Phone: 601-359-1350   **Fax:** 601-359-1499   **Web site:** www.sos.ms.gov/

Report due: None due

Filing your articles: The filing fee is $250, plus $25 for the Application for Appointment of Registered Agent. Single-member LLCs are allowed.

State franchise tax/annual report fee: Each year by April 15, you must file Form 86-105, a partnership tax return. This is purely an information statement; no tax is imposed.

Missouri

Business formation department: Business Services Secretary of State	**Physical location:** 600 W. Main Street Missouri State Info Center, Room 322 Jefferson City, MO 65101	**Mailing address:** James C. Kirkpatrick State Info Center P.O. Box 778 Jefferson City, MO 65102

Phone: 866-223-6535   **Web site:** www.sos.mo.gov/business   **E-mail:** corporations@sos.mo.gov

Report due: None due

Filing your articles: The filing fee is $105. Single-member LLCs are allowed.

State franchise tax/annual report fee: You must file Form MO-1065, Partnership Return of Income, each year. This is for informational purposes only; no tax is imposed.

Montana

Business formation department: Business and Licensing Division Secretary of State	**Physical location:** State Capitol, Room 260 Helena, MT 59620	**Mailing Address:** P.O. Box 202801 Helena, MT 59620

Phone: 406-444-3665   **Fax:** 406-444-3976

Web site: sos.mt.gov/Business/index.asp   **E-mail:** sosbusiness@mt.gov

Report due: Annually   **When?** April 15

Filing your articles: The filing fee is $70. Single-member LLCs are allowed.

State franchise tax/annual report fee: The fee for the annual report is $10. You must also file Form PR-1, a Partnership Return of Income, for each year. No taxes are due; this is an informational return only.

Nebraska

Business formation department: Business and Licensing Division Secretary of State	**Physical location:** State Capitol P.O. Box 94608 Lincoln, NE 68509	**Mailing address:** State Capitol, Suite 1301 Lincoln, NE 68509

Phone: 402-471-4079   **Fax:** 402-471-3666

Web site: www.sos.state.ne.us/business/corp_serv   **E-mail:** Corporate_Inquiries@sos.ne.gov

Report due: Biennially   **When?** April 1 on odd-numbered years

Filing your articles: The filing fee is $100, plus an additional $10 fee for the certificate of organization that you receive from the state after your articles have been filed and $5 per page of your articles. Single-member LLCs are allowed.

State franchise tax/annual report fee: If you have only Nebraska residents as members and your income is only derived from Nebraska, then you must file a Partnership Return of Income with the tax board by the 15th day of the fourth month of your company's fiscal year. If your company operates on a calendar year, this means that the return is due by April 15.

Nevada

Business formation department: Commercial Recordings Division Secretary of State	**Address:** 202 N. Carson Street Carson City, NV 89701

Phone: 775-684-5708   **Fax:** 775-684-5725

Web site: sos.state.nv.us/business   **E-mail:** sosmail@sos.nv.gov

(continued)

Nevada *(continued)*

Report due: Annually	**When?** Initial: last day of month following filing; last day of each anniversary month thereafter

Filing your articles: The filing fee is $75. Also, before the second month of your formation date, you must file an Initial List of Managers or Members and Resident Agent Form with a fee of $165. Single-member LLCs are allowed.

State franchise tax/annual report fee: The filing fee for the annual report is $125. There are no business or franchise taxes in Nevada, and no tax returns need to be filed; however, a business license fee of $200 (for both foreign and domestic LLCs) is set to expire at the end of the year 2010.

New Hampshire

Business formation department: Corporation Division Department of State	**Physical location:** State House Annex, Room 341 25 Capitol Street, Third floor Concord, NH 03301	**Mailing address:** 107 N. Main Street Concord, NH 03301
Phone: 603-271-3246	**Web site:** www.sos.nh.gov/ corporate/index.html	**E-mail:** corporate@ sos.state.nh.us
Report due: Annually	**When?** April 1	

Filing your articles: The filing fee is $100. This is comprised of $50.00 for the LLC-1 plus $50.00 for the SRA form. Single-member LLCs are allowed.

State franchise tax/annual report fee: The filing fee for the annual report is $100. If you gross more than $50,000 in one year, then you must also file a Business Profits Tax Return and pay an 8.5 percent tax. If you gross more than $150,000 in one year, then you must file a Business Enterprise Tax Return and pay the tax rate of 0.75 percent of the total value of your company. All gross amounts only count income that is derived within the state of New Hampshire.

New Jersey

Business formation department: Business Services Division of Revenue	**Address:** P.O. Box 308 Trenton, NJ 08625	
Phone: 866-534-7789	**Fax:** 609-984-6851	**Web site:** www.nj.gov/ njbusiness
Report due: Annually	**When?** Last day of anniversary month; online filing only	

Filing your articles: The filing fee is $125. Single-member LLCs are allowed.

State franchise tax/annual report fee: The filing fee for the annual report is $50. If you have elected partnership taxation, you must also file Form NJ-1065, which is an information return only and requires no accompanying tax payment.

New Mexico

Business formation department:	Physical location:	Mailing address:
Public Regulation Commission Corporations Bureau	1120 Paseo de Peralta PERA Building Santa Fe, NM 87501	P.O. Box 1269 Santa Fe, NM 87504
Phone: 505-827-4508	**Fax:** 505-827-4387	**Web site:** www.nmprc. state.nm.us/cb.htm

Report due: None due

Filing your articles: The filing fee is $50. Single-member LLCs are allowed.

State franchise tax/annual report fee: If your LLC has elected partnership taxation, it must file Form PTE, a New Mexico Income and Information Return for Pass-Through Entities. As long as you have pass-through taxation, no tax is due. If you have elected corporate taxation, then you are required to pay a $50 annual franchise tax.

New York

Business formation department:	Address:
Division of Corporations New York Department of State	41 State Street Albany, NY 12231
Phone: 518-473-2492	**Fax:** 518-473-0730
Web site: www.dos.state. ny.us	**E-mail:** corporations@dos.state. ny.us
Report due: Biennially	**When?** Last day of anniversary month

Filing your articles: The filing fee is $200 plus $10 for a certified copy. Single-member LLCs are allowed.

State franchise tax/annual report fee: The filing fee for the biennial statement is $9. You must also pay an annual filing fee to the Department of Revenue. This fee ranges from $325 to $10,000, depending on the number of members your LLC has. New York law requires all LLCs to publish a Notice of Publication eight to ten weeks after formation in two authorized newspapers in the county of formation.

North Carolina

Business formation department: Department of the Secretary of State	**Physical location:** 2 S. Salisbury Street Raleigh, NC 27601	**Mailing address:** P.O. Box 29622 Raleigh, NC 27626

Phone: 919-807-2225	**Fax:** 919-807-2039	**Web site:** www.secretary. state.nc.us/corporations

Report due: Annually	**When?** April 15

Filing your articles: The filing fee is $125. Single-member LLCs are allowed.

State franchise tax/annual report fee: The filing fee for the annual report is $200. No other franchise fees or taxes are imposed.

North Dakota

Business formation department: Business Services Secretary of State	**Address:** 600 E. Boulevard Avenue, Department 108, First floor Bismarck, ND 58505

Phone: 800-366-6888, extension 8-4284, or 701-328-4284	**Fax:** 701-328-2992

Web site: www.nd.gov/sos/ businessserv	**E-mail:** sosbir@nd.gov

Report due: Annually	**When?** November 15

Filing your articles: The filing fee is $135. Single-member LLCs are *not* allowed.

State franchise tax/annual report fee: The fee for the annual report is $50. You must also file Form 1065, North Dakota Return of Income, which, like the IRS version, is an informational return only.

Ohio

Business formation department: Office of Business Services Ohio Secretary of State	**Physical location:** 180 E. Broad Street, Suite 103 Columbus, OH 43215	**Mailing address:** P.O. Box 670 Columbus, OH 43216

Phone: 877-767-3453 or 614-466-3910   **Fax:** 614-466-3899   **Web site:** www.state.oh.us/sos

Report due: None due

Filing your articles: The filing fee is $125. Single-member LLCs are allowed.

State franchise tax/annual report fee: Ohio doesn't subject LLCs to any periodic reports or franchise tax reports, which means no fees. Pretty cool!

Oklahoma

Business formation department:
Business Filing Department
Secretary of State

Address:
2300 N. Lincoln Boulevard,
Room 101
Oklahoma City, OK 73105

Phone: 405-521-3912   **Fax:** 405-521-3771   **Web site:** www.sos.ok.gov/business/default.aspx

Report due: Annually   **When?** July 1

Filing your articles: The filing fee is $100. Single-member LLCs are allowed.

State franchise tax/annual report fee: The filing fee for the annual report is $25. Oklahoma doesn't impose any tax or franchise fees on LLCs, and you don't need to file any returns.

Oregon

Business formation department:
Corporation Division
Secretary of State

Address:
255 Capitol Street, NE,
Suite 151
Salem, OR 97310

Phone: 503-986-2200   **Fax:** 503-378-4381

Web site: www.filinginoregon.com   **E-mail:** BusinessRegistry.sos@state.or.us

Report due: Annually   **When?** July 1

Filing your articles: The filing fee is $55, including a $5 confirmation copy fee. Single-member LLCs are allowed.

State franchise tax/annual report fee: Your first annual report must be accompanied by a $20 fee. The filing for the subsequent years after the first is called a *renewal coupon,* not an annual report. If you have elected partnership taxation, you are required to file Form 65, Partnership Return, each year. This form is for informational purposes only, and no tax is imposed.

Pennsylvania

Business formation department: Corporations Bureau Department of State	Address: 206 North Street, Room 206 Harrisburg, PA 17120

Phone: 888-659-9962 or 717-787-1057

Web site: www.dos.state.pa.us/ corps/site/default.asp	E-mail: RA-CORPS@state. pa.us

Report due: Decennially	When? Last day of anniversary month

Filing your articles: The filing fee is $120. You must also file a docketing statement along with the articles, which you can obtain from the Department of State's Web site. Single-member LLCs are allowed.

State franchise tax/annual report fee: If you have elected pass-through taxation, you must file Form PA-20s/PA-65, PA S Corporation/Partnership Information Return, each year. This is an informational return only, and no tax is imposed.

Rhode Island

Business formation department: Corporations Division Secretary of State	Address: 148 W. River Street Providence, RI 02904

Phone: 401-222-3040	Fax: 401-222-3879

Web site: www.sec.state. ri.us/corps	E-mail: corporations@sec. state.ri.us

Report due: Annually	When? November 1

Filing your articles: The filing fee is $150. Single-member LLCs are allowed.

State franchise tax/annual report fee: The filing fee for your annual report is $50. You must also pay a franchise tax of $250 each year.

South Carolina

Business formation department: Secretary of State	Physical location: 1205 Pendleton Street, Suite 525 Columbia, SC 29201	Mailing address: P.O. Box 11350 Columbia, SC 29211

Phone: 803-734-2158	**Web site:** www.scsos.com/ Business_Filings

Report due: Annually   **When?** Last day of the month following anniversary date

Filing your articles: The filing fee is $110. Single-member LLCs are allowed.

State franchise tax/annual report fee: Annually, you must file Form SC-1065, which is an informational return only and doesn't require any accompanying tax payment.

South Dakota

Business formation department: Secretary of State	**Address:** Capitol Building 500 E. Capitol Avenue, Suite 204 Pierre, SD 57501
Phone: 605-773-4845	**Fax:** 605-773-4550
Web site: www.sdsos.gov/ busineservices/ corporations.shtm	**E-mail:** corporations@state. sd.us

Report due: Annually   **When?** Last day of the month following anniversary date

Filing your articles: The fee for organizing a South Dakota LLC is $150. With your articles, you must file your first annual report. Single-member LLCs are *not* allowed.

State franchise tax/annual report fee: No franchise or business taxes are imposed on South Dakota LLCs.

Tennessee

Business formation department: Business Services Department of State	**Address:** 312 Rosa L Parks Avenue, Sixth Floor, Snodgrass Tower Nashville, TN 37243
Phone: 615-741-2286	
Web site: state.tn.us/sos/ bus_svc/index.htm	**E-mail:** business.services@ state.tn.us

(continued)

Tennessee (continued)

Report due: Annually   **When?** First day of fourth month after fiscal year end

Filing your articles: The filing fee for your articles of organization is $300. There is also a $20 fee for the certificate of formation, which is issued by the Department of State. Single-member LLCs are allowed.

State franchise tax/annual report fee: If you operate on a calendar year, then your annual report is due by April 1. The filing fees are $50 per active member, with the minimum fee being $300 and the maximum being $3,000. You must also file Form FAE 170, Franchise and Excise Tax Return, along with a tax payment of 0.25 percent of the LLC's entire value, with a minimum payment of $100. Additionally, LLCs must pay an excise tax of 6 percent on all income derived from business transactions in Tennessee.

Texas

Business Formation Department: Corporations Section Secretary of State	**Physical location:** 1019 Brazos Austin, TX 78701	**Mailing address:** P.O. Box 13697 Austin, TX 78711
Phone: 512-463-5555	**Fax:** 562-463-5709	**Web site:** www.sos. state.tx.us

Report due: None due

Filing your articles: The filing fee is $300. Single-member LLCs are allowed.

State franchise tax/annual report fee: You must file Form 05-143 and pay a franchise tax of 0.25 percent of the LLC's net taxable capital.

Utah

Business formation department: Division of Corporations and Commercial Code Utah Department of Commerce	**Physical location:** 324 S. State Street, Suite 500 Salt Lake City, UT 84111	**Mailing address:** P.O. Box 146705 Salt Lake City, UT 84114
Phone: 801-538-8700	**Fax:** 801-538-8888	**Web site:** business.utah. gov/business/#
Report due: Annually	**When?** Anniversary date	

Filing your articles: The filing fee is $70. Single-member LLCs are allowed.

State franchise tax/annual report fee: If you have elected partnership taxation, you must file Form TC-65, Partnership Limited Liability Company Return of Income. This is an informational return only; you aren't subject to taxation.

Vermont

Business formation department: Secretary of State Corporations	Address: 26 Terrace Street Montpelier, VT 05609	
Phone: 802-828-2386	Fax: 802-828-2853	Web site: www.sec.state.vt.us/corps/corpindex.htm
Report due: Annually	When? 15th day of third month after fiscal year end	

Filing your articles: The filing fee is $100. Single-member LLCs are allowed.

State franchise tax/annual report fee: The filing fee for the annual report is $20. You must also file a Business Income Tax Return, even if you are a pass-through entity. LLCs with pass-through taxation must pay only the minimum tax of $250.

Virginia

Business formation department: Department of Business Assistance	Physical location: 707 E. Main Street, Suite 300 Richmond, VA 23219	Mailing address: P.O. Box 446 Richmond, VA 23218
Phone: 804-371-9733	Web site: www.dba.virginia.gov	Email: vbic@vdba.virginia.gov
Report due: Annually	When? July 1	

Filing your articles: The filing fee is $100, plus $4 for a 2-page certified copy. Single-member LLCs are allowed.

State franchise tax/annual report fee: You must pay a $50 annual registration fee by September 1 of each year to the State Corporation Commission. You aren't required to file any tax returns with the Department of Taxation, however.

Washington

Business formation department: Secretary of State	Physical location: Dolliver Building 801 Capitol Way South Olympia, WA 98501	Mailing address: P.O. Box 40234 Olympia, WA 98504
Phone: 360-725-0377	Web site: www.secstate.wa.gov/corps/	E-mail: corps@secstate.wa.gov
Report due: Annually	When? Last day of anniversary month	

Filing your articles: The filing fee is $180. You must also file your first annual report within 120 days of your formation date. Single-member LLCs are allowed.

State franchise tax/annual report fee: You must also pay the business and occupation tax each year. The amount of this tax depends on a variety of things, such as your gross income or the total value of your products.

West Virginia

Business formation department: Secretary of State	Address: Building 1, Suite 157-K 1900 Kanawha Boulevard, E. Charleston, WV 25305
Phone: 304-558-8000	Fax: 304-558-0900
Web site: www.business4wv.com	E-mail: business@wvsos.com
Report due: Annually	When? April 1

Filing your articles: The filing fee is $145. Single-member LLCs are allowed.

State franchise tax/annual report fee: The fee for your annual report is $10. You must also file a Business Franchise Tax Return each year at a tax rate of 0.75 percent of your LLC's taxable income, with the minimum tax payment being $50.

Wisconsin

Business formation department: Department of Financial Institutions Division of Corporation and Consumer Services	Physical location: 345 W. Washington Avenue Madison, WI 53703	Mailing address: Corporations Bureau, Third Floor P.O. Box 7846 Madison, WI 53707

Phone: 608-261-7577   **Fax:** 608-267-6813   **Web site:** www.wdfi.org

Report due: Annually   **When?** Last day of anniversary quarter

Filing your articles: The fee for filing your articles is $170; however, you can reduce that fee to $130 by filing online using the Department's QuickStart program. Single-member LLCs are allowed.

State franchise tax/annual report fee: The fee for the annual report is $25. The filing date of the report varies depending on which quarter of the year your formation date falls in. If you have elected pass-through taxation, you must also file Form 3, Partnership Return of Income. This is an informational return only, and no tax will be due.

Wyoming

Business formation department:	**Address:**
Secretary of State	The Capitol Building, Room 110
	200 W. 24th Street
	Cheyenne, WY 82002

Phone: 307-777-7311   **Fax:** 307-777-5339

Web site: soswy.state.wy.us/ Business/Business.aspx   **E-mail:** business@ state.wy.us

Report due: Annually   **When?** First day of anniversary month

Filing your articles: The filing fee is $100. Single-member LLCs are allowed.

State franchise tax/annual report fee: If you are transacting business in Wyoming, you must pay an Annual Report License Tax, which is 0.02 percent of all assets located and employed in Wyoming, with the minimum fee being $50.

Appendix B

About the CD

*U*sing the CD that accompanies this book couldn't be easier. You can pop it into pretty much any Mac or Windows computer made in the last ten years as long as that computer has an optical drive capable of playing good, old-fashioned CDs. If you're the hesitant type, check out the following system requirements.

System Requirements

Make sure that your computer meets the minimum system requirements shown in the following list. If your computer doesn't match up to most of these requirements, you may have problems using the software and files on the CD. You need

- A PC with a Pentium or faster processor; or a Mac OS computer with a 68040 or faster processor

- Microsoft Windows 98 or later; or Mac OS system software 7.6.1 or later

- At least 32MB of total RAM installed on your computer; for best performance, we recommend at least 64MB

- A CD-ROM drive

- A monitor capable of displaying at least 256 colors or grayscale

If you need more information on the basics, check out these books published by Wiley: *PCs For Dummies,* 10th Edition, by Dan Gookin; *Macs For Dummies,* 8th Edition, by David Pogue; *iMac For Dummies,* 4th Edition, by Mark L. Chambers; *Mac OS X Tiger For Dummies,* by Bob LeVitus; *Windows 98*

For Dummies, by Andy Rathbone; *Windows 2000 Professional For Dummies,* by Andy Rathbone and Sharon Crawford; or *Windows XP For Dummies,* 2nd Edition, by Andy Rathbone.

Using the CD

To install the items from the CD to your hard drive, follow these steps:

1. **Insert the CD into your computer's CD-ROM drive.** The license agreement appears.

   Note to Windows users: The interface won't launch if you have autorun disabled. In that case, choose Start⇨Run. In the dialog box that appears, type **D:\start.exe**. (Replace D with the proper letter if your CD-ROM drive uses a different letter. If you don't know the letter, see how your CD-ROM drive is listed under My Computer.) Click OK.

   Note to Mac users: The CD icon will appear on your desktop. Double-click the icon to open the CD and double-click the Start icon.

2. **Read through the license agreement, and then click the Accept button if you want to use the CD.** After you click Accept, the license agreement window won't appear again.

   The CD interface appears. The interface allows you to install the programs and run the demos with just a click of a button (or two).

What You'll Find on the CD

The following sections are arranged by category and provide a summary of the software and documents you'll find on the CD. If you need help installing the items provided on the CD, refer to the installation instructions in the preceding section.

Software

You'll find **Adobe Reader** on the CD. Adobe Reader is a freeware program that allows you to view, but not edit, Adobe Portable Document Files (PDFs).

Freeware programs are free, copyrighted games, applications, and utilities. You can copy them to as many computers as you like — for free — but they offer no technical support.

PDF files

The CD contains state-specific forms, in the PDF file format, organized by state. The forms vary from state to state and include applications, general LLC information, articles of organization and dissolution, and more. Some states provide more forms than others, so you won't see the same amount of forms for every state.

Most states now have an online system that can provide you with up-to-date forms and information. Check Appendix A for more state-specific information.

Troubleshooting

We tried our best to compile programs that work on most computers with the minimum system requirements. Alas, your computer may differ, and some programs may not work properly for some reason.

The two likeliest problems are that you don't have enough memory (RAM) for the programs you want to use or you have other programs running that are affecting installation or the running of a program. If you get an error message such as *Not enough memory* or *Setup cannot continue,* try one or more of the following suggestions and then try using the software again:

- ✔ **Turn off any antivirus software running on your computer.** Installation programs sometimes mimic virus activity and may make your computer incorrectly believe that it's being infected by a virus.

- ✔ **Close all running programs.** The more programs you have running, the less memory is available to other programs. Installation programs typically update files and programs, so if you keep other programs running, installation may not work properly.

- ✔ **Have your local computer store add more RAM to your computer.** This is, admittedly, a drastic and somewhat expensive step. However, adding more memory can really help the speed of your computer and allow more programs to run at the same time.

If you have trouble with the CD-ROM, please call the Wiley Product Technical Support phone number at 877-762-2974. Outside the United States, call 1-317-572-3994. You can also contact Wiley Product Technical Support at http://support.wiley.com. Wiley Publishing, Inc., will provide technical support only for installation and other general quality control items. For technical support on the applications themselves, consult the program's vendor or author.

To place additional orders or to request information about other Wiley products, please call 877-762-2974.

Index

• N •

• O •

• Z •

Apple & Macs

iPad For Dummies
978-0-470-58027-1

iPhone For Dummies,
4th Edition
978-0-470-87870-5

MacBook For Dummies, 3rd
Edition
978-0-470-76918-8

Mac OS X Snow Leopard For
Dummies
978-0-470-43543-4

Business

Bookkeeping For Dummies
978-0-7645-9848-7

Job Interviews
For Dummies,
3rd Edition
978-0-470-17748-8

Resumes For Dummies,
5th Edition
978-0-470-08037-5

Starting an
Online Business
For Dummies,
6th Edition
978-0-470-60210-2

Stock Investing
For Dummies,
3rd Edition
978-0-470-40114-9

Successful
Time Management
For Dummies
978-0-470-29034-7

Computer Hardware

BlackBerry
For Dummies,
4th Edition
978-0-470-60700-8

Computers For Seniors
For Dummies,
2nd Edition
978-0-470-53483-0

PCs For Dummies,
Windows
7 Edition
978-0-470-46542-4

Laptops For Dummies,
4th Edition
978-0-470-57829-2

Cooking & Entertaining

Cooking Basics
For Dummies,
3rd Edition
978-0-7645-7206-7

Wine For Dummies,
4th Edition
978-0-470-04579-4

Diet & Nutrition

Dieting For Dummies,
2nd Edition
978-0-7645-4149-0

Nutrition For Dummies,
4th Edition
978-0-471-79868-2

Weight Training
For Dummies,
3rd Edition
978-0-471-76845-6

Digital Photography

Digital SLR Cameras &
Photography For Dummies,
3rd Edition
978-0-470-46606-3

Photoshop Elements 8
For Dummies
978-0-470-52967-6

Gardening

Gardening Basics
For Dummies
978-0-470-03749-2

Organic Gardening
For Dummies,
2nd Edition
978-0-470-43067-5

Green/Sustainable

Raising Chickens
For Dummies
978-0-470-46544-8

Green Cleaning
For Dummies
978-0-470-39106-8

Health

Diabetes For Dummies,
3rd Edition
978-0-470-27086-8

Food Allergies
For Dummies
978-0-470-09584-3

Living Gluten-Free
For Dummies,
2nd Edition
978-0-470-58589-4

Hobbies/General

Chess For Dummies,
2nd Edition
978-0-7645-8404-6

Drawing
Cartoons & Comics
For Dummies
978-0-470-42683-8

Knitting For Dummies,
2nd Edition
978-0-470-28747-7

Organizing
For Dummies
978-0-7645-5300-4

Su Doku For Dummies
978-0-470-01892-7

Home Improvement

Home Maintenance
For Dummies,
2nd Edition
978-0-470-43063-7

Home Theater
For Dummies,
3rd Edition
978-0-470-41189-6

Living the
Country Lifestyle
All-in-One
For Dummies
978-0-470-43061-3

Solar Power Your Home
For Dummies,
2nd Edition
978-0-470-59678-4

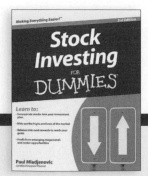

Internet

Blogging For Dummies,
3rd Edition
978-0-470-61996-4

eBay For Dummies,
6th Edition
978-0-470-49741-8

Facebook For Dummies,
3rd Edition
978-0-470-87804-0

Web Marketing
For Dummies,
2nd Edition
978-0-470-37181-7

WordPress
For Dummies,
3rd Edition
978-0-470-59274-8

Language & Foreign Language

French For Dummies
978-0-7645-5193-2

Italian Phrases
For Dummies
978-0-7645-7203-6

Spanish For Dummies,
2nd Edition
978-0-470-87855-2

Spanish
For Dummies,
Audio Set
978-0-470-09585-0

Math & Science

Algebra I
For Dummies,
2nd Edition
978-0-470-55964-2

Biology For Dummies,
2nd Edition
978-0-470-59875-7

Calculus For Dummies
978-0-7645-2498-1

Chemistry For Dummies
978-0-7645-5430-8

Microsoft Office

Excel 2010 For Dummies
978-0-470-48953-6

Office 2010 All-in-One
For Dummies
978-0-470-49748-7

Office 2010 For Dummies,
Book + DVD Bundle
978-0-470-62698-6

Word 2010 For Dummies
978-0-470-48772-3

Music

Guitar For Dummies,
2nd Edition
978-0-7645-9904-0

iPod & iTunes For
Dummies, 8th Edition
978-0-470-87871-2

Piano Exercises
For Dummies
978-0-470-38765-8

Parenting & Education

Parenting For Dummies,
2nd Edition
978-0-7645-5418-6

Type 1 Diabetes
For Dummies
978-0-470-17811-9

Pets

Cats For Dummies,
2nd Edition
978-0-7645-5275-5

Dog Training For Dummies,
3rd Edition
978-0-470-60029-0

Puppies For Dummies,
2nd Edition
978-0-470-03717-1

Religion & Inspiration

The Bible For Dummies
978-0-7645-5296-0

Catholicism For Dummies
978-0-7645-5391-2

Women in the Bible
For Dummies
978-0-7645-8475-6

Self-Help & Relationship

Anger Management
For Dummies
978-0-470-03715-7

Overcoming Anxiety
For Dummies,
2nd Edition
978-0-470-57441-6

Sports

Baseball
For Dummies,
3rd Edition
978-0-7645-7537-2

Basketball
For Dummies,
2nd Edition
978-0-7645-5248-9

Golf For Dummies,
3rd Edition
978-0-471-76871-5

Web Development

Web Design
All-in-One
For Dummies
978-0-470-41796-6

Web Sites
Do-It-Yourself
For Dummies,
2nd Edition
978-0-470-56520-9

Windows 7

Windows 7
For Dummies
978-0-470-49743-2

Windows 7
For Dummies,
Book + DVD Bundle
978-0-470-52398-8

Windows 7 All-in-One
For Dummies
978-0-470-48763-1

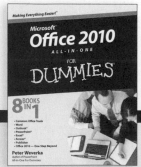

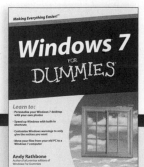

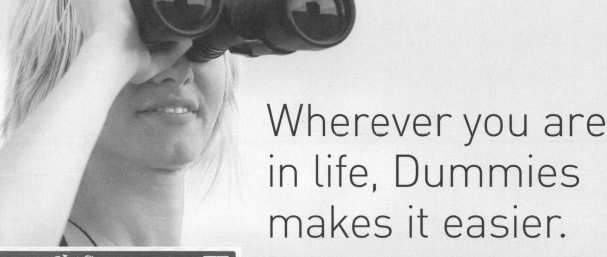

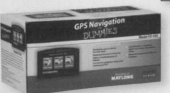

Wiley Publishing, Inc.
End-User License Agreement

READ THIS. You should carefully read these terms and conditions before opening the software packet(s) included with this book "Book". This is a license agreement "Agreement" between you and Wiley Publishing, Inc. "WPI". By opening the accompanying software packet(s), you acknowledge that you have read and accept the following terms and conditions. If you do not agree and do not want to be bound by such terms and conditions, promptly return the Book and the unopened software packet(s) to the place you obtained them for a full refund.

1. **License Grant.** WPI grants to you (either an individual or entity) a non-exclusive license to use one copy of the enclosed software program(s) (collectively, the "Software") solely for your own personal or business purposes on a single computer (whether a standard computer or a work-station component of a multi-user network). The Software is in use on a computer when it is loaded into temporary memory (RAM) or installed into permanent memory (hard disk, CD-ROM, or other storage device). WPI reserves all rights not expressly granted herein.

2. **Ownership.** WPI is the owner of all right, title, and interest, including copyright, in and to the compilation of the Software recorded on the physical packet included with this Book "Software Media". Copyright to the individual programs recorded on the Software Media is owned by the author or other authorized copyright owner of each program. Ownership of the Software and all proprietary rights relating thereto remain with WPI and its licensers.

3. **Restrictions on Use and Transfer.**

   (a) You may only (i) make one copy of the Software for backup or archival purposes, or (ii) transfer the Software to a single hard disk, provided that you keep the original for backup or archival purposes. You may not (i) rent or lease the Software, (ii) copy or reproduce the Software through a LAN or other network system or through any computer subscriber system or bulletin-board system, or (iii) modify, adapt, or create derivative works based on the Software.

   (b) You may not reverse engineer, decompile, or disassemble the Software. You may transfer the Software and user documentation on a permanent basis, provided that the transferee agrees to accept the terms and conditions of this Agreement and you retain no copies. If the Software is an update or has been updated, any transfer must include the most recent update and all prior versions.

4. **Restrictions on Use of Individual Programs.** You must follow the individual requirements and restrictions detailed for each individual program in the "About the CD" appendix of this Book or on the Software Media. These limitations are also contained in the individual license agreements recorded on the Software Media. These limitations may include a requirement that after using the program for a specified period of time, the user must pay a registration fee or discontinue use. By opening the Software packet(s), you agree to abide by the licenses and restrictions for these individual programs that are detailed in the "About the CD" appendix and/or on the Software Media. None of the material on this Software Media or listed in this Book may ever be redistributed, in original or modified form, for commercial purposes.

5. **Limited Warranty.**

    (a) WPI warrants that the Software and Software Media are free from defects in materials and workmanship under normal use for a period of sixty (60) days from the date of purchase of this Book. If WPI receives notification within the warranty period of defects in materials or workmanship, WPI will replace the defective Software Media.

    (b) WPI AND THE AUTHOR OF THE BOOK DISCLAIM ALL OTHER WARRANTIES, EXPRESS OR IMPLIED, INCLUDING WITHOUT LIMITATION IMPLIED WARRANTIES OF MERCHANTABILITY AND FITNESS FOR A PARTICULAR PURPOSE, WITH RESPECT TO THE SOFTWARE, THE PROGRAMS, THE SOURCE CODE CONTAINED THEREIN, AND/OR THE TECHNIQUES DESCRIBED IN THIS BOOK. WPI DOES NOT WARRANT THAT THE FUNCTIONS CONTAINED IN THE SOFTWARE WILL MEET YOUR REQUIREMENTS OR THAT THE OPERATION OF THE SOFTWARE WILL BE ERROR FREE.

    (c) This limited warranty gives you specific legal rights, and you may have other rights that vary from jurisdiction to jurisdiction.

6. **Remedies.**

    (a) WPI's entire liability and your exclusive remedy for defects in materials and workmanship shall be limited to replacement of the Software Media, which may be returned to WPI with a copy of your receipt at the following address: Software Media Fulfillment Department, Attn.: *Limited Liability Companies For Dummies,* 2nd Edition, Wiley Publishing, Inc., 10475 Crosspoint Blvd., Indianapolis, IN 46256, or call 1-800-762-2974. Please allow four to six weeks for delivery. This Limited Warranty is void if failure of the Software Media has resulted from accident, abuse, or misapplication. Any replacement Software Media will be warranted for the remainder of the original warranty period or thirty (30) days, whichever is longer.

(b) In no event shall WPI or the author be liable for any damages whatsoever (including without limitation damages for loss of business profits, business interruption, loss of business information, or any other pecuniary loss) arising from the use of or inability to use the Book or the Software, even if WPI has been advised of the possibility of such damages.

(c) Because some jurisdictions do not allow the exclusion or limitation of liability for consequential or incidental damages, the above limitation or exclusion may not apply to you.

7. **U.S. Government Restricted Rights.** Use, duplication, or disclosure of the Software for or on behalf of the United States of America, its agencies and/or instrumentalities "U.S. Government" is subject to restrictions as stated in paragraph (c)(1)(ii) of the Rights in Technical Data and Computer Software clause of DFARS 252.227-7013, or subparagraphs (c) (1) and (2) of the Commercial Computer Software - Restricted Rights clause at FAR 52.227-19, and in similar clauses in the NASA FAR supplement, as applicable.

8. **General.** This Agreement constitutes the entire understanding of the parties and revokes and supersedes all prior agreements, oral or written, between them and may not be modified or amended except in a writing signed by both parties hereto that specifically refers to this Agreement. This Agreement shall take precedence over any other documents that may be in conflict herewith. If any one or more provisions contained in this Agreement are held by any court or tribunal to be invalid, illegal, or otherwise unenforceable, each and every other provision shall remain in full force and effect.